Philosophy of Mathematics and Economics

T0330691

With the failure of economics to predict the recent economic crisis, the image of economics as a rigorous mathematical science has been subjected to increasing interrogation. One explanation for this failure is that the subject took a wrong turn in its historical trajectory, becoming too mathematical. Using the philosophy of mathematics, this unique book re-examines this trajectory.

Philosophy of Mathematics and Economics re-analyses the divergent rationales for mathematical economics by some of its principal architects. Yet, it is not limited to simply enhancing our understanding of how economics became an applied mathematical science. The authors also critically evaluate developments in the philosophy of mathematics to expose the inadequacy of aspects of mainstream mathematical economics, as well as exploiting the same philosophy to suggest alternative ways of rigorously formulating economic theory for our digital age. This book represents an innovative attempt to more fully understand the complexity of the interaction between developments in the philosophy of mathematics and the process of formalisation in economics.

Assuming no expert knowledge in the philosophy of mathematics, this work is relevant to historians of economic thought and professional philosophers of economics. In addition, it will be of great interest to those who wish to deepen their appreciation of the economic contours of contemporary society. It is also hoped that mathematical economists will find this work informative and engaging.

Thomas A. Boylan is Professor Emeritus of Economics of the National University of Ireland, Galway. His main research and teaching interests have been in Economic Growth and Development Theory; Applied Econometrics; Philosophy/Methodology of Economics; Post-Keynesian Economics; and the History of Irish Economic Thought.

Paschal F. O'Gorman is Professor Emeritus of Philosophy of the National University of Ireland, Galway. His main research and teaching areas have been in the Philosophy of Science; Logic; Philosophy of Mind; and, since the 1980s, the Philosophy and Methodology of Economics.

Routledge INEM Advances in Economic Methodology

Series Edited by Esther-Mirjam Sent, the University of Nijmegen, the Netherlands.

The field of economic methodology has expanded rapidly during the last few decades. This expansion has occurred in part because of changes within the discipline of economics, in part because of changes in the prevailing philosophical conception of scientific knowledge, and also because of various transformations within the wider society. Research in economic methodology now reflects not only developments in contemporary economic theory, the history of economic thought, and the philosophy of science; but it also reflects developments in science studies, historical epistemology, and social theorizing more generally. The field of economic methodology still includes the search for rules for the proper conduct of economic science, but it also covers a vast array of other subjects and accommodates a variety of different approaches to those subjects.

The objective of this series is to provide a forum for the publication of significant works in the growing field of economic methodology. Since the series defines methodology quite broadly, it will publish books on a wide range of different methodological subjects. The series is also open to a variety of different types of works: original research monographs, edited collections, as well as republication of significant earlier contributions to the methodological literature. The International Network for Economic Methodology (INEM) is proud to sponsor this important series of contributions to the methodological literature.

For a list of titles please visit: www.routledge.com/Routledge-INEM-Advances-in Economic-Methodology/book-series/SE0630

Philosophy of Mathematics and Economics

Image, Context and Perspective

Thomas A. Boylan and
Paschal F. O'Gorman

Routledge
Taylor & Francis Group
LONDON AND NEW YORK

First published 2018 by Routledge

2 Park Square, Milton Park, Abingdon, Oxfordshire OX14 4RN
52 Vanderbilt Avenue, New York, NY 10017

Routledge is an imprint of the Taylor & Francis Group, an informa business

First issued in paperback 2020

British Library Cataloguing-in-Publication Data
A catalogue record for this book is available from the British Library

Library of Congress Cataloging-in-Publication Data
Names: Boylan, Thomas A., author. | O'Gorman, Paschal F.
(Paschal Francis), 1943- author.
Title: Philosophy of mathematics and economics : image, context and
perspective / Thomas A. Boylan and Paschal F. O'Gorman.
Description: 1 Edition. | New York : Routledge, 2018. | Series: Routledge
INEM advances in economic methodology | Includes bibliographical
references and index.
Identifiers: LCCN 2017051813 (print) | LCCN 2017054526 (ebook) |
ISBN 9781351124584 (Ebook) | ISBN 9780415161886 (hardback :
alk. paper) | ISBN 9781351124584 (ebk)
Subjects: LCSH: Economics, Mathematical.
Classification: LCC HB135 (ebook) | LCC HB135 .B69 2018 (print) |
DDC 330.01/51--dc23
LC record available at https://lccn.loc.gov/2017051813

ISBN: 978-0-415-16188-6 (hbk)
ISBN: 978-0-367-59243-1 (pbk)

Typeset in Bembo
by Taylor & Francis Books

We would like to dedicate this book to our respective grand-children, Aifric Donald, Lara Boylan, Alison O'Sullivan and Symone O'Gorman.

Contents

Preface

This book has had arguably a uniquely long gestation period. The original proposal was first drafted while we attended the 10th International Congress of Logic, Methodology and Philosophy of Science in the magnificent setting of the Palazzo dei Congressi in Florence in 1995. In its initial formulation the central figure was Henri Poincaré and his philosophy of science, and more particularly what would have been the consequences for economics, as a discipline, if it had followed the path contained in Poincaré's philosophy of science as we interpreted it at that time, based on Paschal O'Gorman's earlier work on Poincaré's conventionalism. A central informing thesis for us at that time was what we regarded as the high epistemic cost that economics had inflicted on itself arising from the application of a particular philosophy of mathematics from the late nineteenth century, which was further intensified in the formalistic philosophy of mathematics that dominated for most of the twentieth century in economics. In contrast to the formalism reflected in the neo-Walrasian programme and in particular in the work of Debreu for instance, our initial proposal was informed and heavily influenced by our attraction to the intuitionism of Brouwer, Heyting and later in the twentieth century in the work of Michael Dummett, which we felt provided a more adequate and epistemically satisfying philosophy for our discipline. On reflection our work in economic methodology over the last quarter of a century has been, in a variety of ways, influenced by the broad philosophical framework of Brouwerian intuitionism.

Since 1995 and the intrusions of new and varied work demands at university and national levels, along with the completion of a number of book projects and edited collections, conspired to delay sustained engagement with this book project. As a result the current book proposal was persistently relegated to the 'for completion' file! But we were determined to honour this project, which could only have been achieved with the extraordinary patience and forbearance of all at Routledge, for which we are deeply grateful. But in this extended intervening period our thinking also underwent change which generated a considerable amount of reconfiguration with respect to the dimensions and topics to be addressed in the central domain of interest to us, namely the relation and influence of major developments in the philosophy of mathematics and their influence on economics. It became clear to us arising from our teaching at both undergraduate and postgraduate levels, that the need for an extended reflection on the major developments within the philosophy of mathematics and their impact on economics was an emergent and pressing intellectual challenge which required inclusion as an integral component in the philosophical and methodological pedagogy of economics, particularly at the postgraduate level. While this book is not a textbook in any conventional understanding of the term, it does explore in some considerable depth a range of topics that we deem paramount in any extended intellectual understanding of the complex interaction between economics and mathematics (incorporating the processes of quantification, measurement and formalisation). We can concur with Lawson that in 'the history of the modern mainstream, the rise to dominance of formalistic modelling practices and the manner of their "survival" in this role, constitutes a central chapter in the history of academic economics that remains largely unwritten' (Lawson 2003: 256). It awaits the comprehensive scholarly treatment exemplified for instance in Ingrao and Israel's (1990) outstanding work on the emergence and development of general equilibrium theory. In the remainder of this Preface we provide, albeit briefly, an outline of the rationale that motivated our initial formulation, but more particularly as we extended our consideration to embrace a more extended array of topics related to the focus of our central concern, namely the relation between the major developments in the philosophy of mathematics and their influence on economic theorising and modelling.

This book is motivated by the conviction that both philosophers of economics/ economic methodologists and theoretical economists have much to gain by addressing the philosophy of mathematics. The indispensable skill set of mainstream theoretical economists includes a competent, preferably expert command of particular areas of advanced mathematics to facilitate the construction of sophisticated economic models required for the rigorous analytical exploration of complex economic systems. The challenges theoretical economists face pre-suppose the acquisition of increasing competence. Consequently our recourse to the philosophy of mathematics is predicated on two objectives. Firstly, it is used to critically interrogate the intricate and complex process of what is called the formalisation/mathematisation of economics. Secondly, the philosophy of mathematics opens up ranges of novel logico-mathematical techniques for the theoretical modelling of rationality on the one hand and economic systems on the other, which result in outcomes at variance with orthodox/mainstream economic theorising.

Vis-à-vis the philosophy of economics/economic methodology this work may be read as a contribution to the research agenda identified by Weintraub namely 'to study how economics has been shaped by economists' ideas about the nature and purpose and function and meaning of mathematics' (Weintraub 2002: 2). In this connection we distinguish the philosophy of pure mathematics from the philosophy of applied mathematics and analyse how these evolved over the course of the twentieth century (with particular reference to the twentieth century). Thus we examine how major figures, including Walras and

Debreu among others exploited divergent philosophical perspectives on applied mathematics along with their relationship to pure mathematics in their methodological defences of their mathematical economics.

This book, however, is not limited to enhancing our understanding of the intriguing, often divergent, defences of the formalisation of economics by some of its major architects. It is also engaged in the critical evaluation of these defences, thereby complementing challenging critiques by, among others, Bridel and Mornati (2009), Mirowski and Cook (1990), Ingrao and Israel (1990), Lawson (1997, 2003a) and his critical realist colleagues. Our critique is distinct in its extensive exploitation of both the philosophy of pure mathematics and the philosophy of applied mathematics. For instance, in connection with the neo-Walrasian programme, our critique is based on Brouwer's novel philosophy of pure mathematics and his alternative mathematics which is fundamentally grounded in that philosophy. This Brouwerian mathematics is *not* another chapter in the vast book of advanced mathematics exploited by mainstream mathematical economists: it is a different mathematics grounded in a different logic. A central contention of this book is that this Brouwerian mathematics is crucially significant for the epistemic critique of the neo-Walrasian programme. If a Brouwerian analysis of a rigorous mathematical proof stands up to critical scrutiny the very core of the neo-Walrasian programme, i.e. the existence proof of general equilibrium is *mathematically undermined*.

This book is not, however, limited solely to the enrichment of our understanding of the dynamics of some of the major critical junctures in the long and intricate process of the formalisation of economics and to the epistemic critique of the often intriguing views of some of its major contributors. It is also concerned with the current state of academic economics. Vis-à-vis mainstream mathematical economics some commentators such as Dow (2002) perceive a process of increasing fragmentation. Others, for instance Lawson (1997, 2003a) maintain that current academic economics is experiencing a deep malaise. The extent of either increasing fragmentation or malaise within academic economics is a question of empirical research which is not a central focus of this book. Rather, assuming an increasing fragmentation whether slow or fast, we pose the question: what is the relevance of the philosophy of mathematics in the contemporary economic climate? We argue that the relevance of the philosophy of mathematics is both positive and negative. Firstly, developments in twentieth-century logic expose the logical limitations of the advanced mathematics exploited in academic economics even when fragmented. Simultaneously, these developments offer theoretical economists a novel range of rigorous logical tools to be used in their mathematical modelling of rationality – a range not exploited in mainstream academic economics. Secondly, we explore the thesis that Brouwerian mathematics – used in our critique of the neo-Walrasian programme – is a more appropriate mathematics than the mathematics exploited in mainstream economics. By recourse to the philosophy of mathematics we expose the descriptive inadequacy of various results of orthodox theorising. In particular we show how these results exploit non-algorithmetic theorems of advanced mathematics and argue that non-algorithmetic models of economic decision making hold only for God-like beings whose decisions are not in any way constrained by temporal considerations. Non-algorithmetic models cannot be applied to actual economic decision makers who, even with the aid of the most sophisticated computers, take real time to make decisions. On the other hand if economic modelling was limited to computable mathematics then its models of rational decision making, by virtue of the algorithmetic nature of the mathematics used, would in principle be compatible with the time constraints of actual economic decision making. In this vein our sympathies totally lie with those economists, such as Velupillai (2000), who argues for the limitation of mathematical modelling to a judicious synthesis of computable mathematics with developments in Brouwerian mathematics.

A few caveats are in order. We are not claiming that the philosophy of mathematics should colonise the philosophy of economics/economic methodology. Rather the philosophy of mathematics makes an intriguing and unique contribution to our reflections on how economics became a mathematical science and on the contemporary status of mathematical economics. Neither is there any suggestion that mathematical economics exploiting the resources of Brouwerian-computable mathematics should colonise the discipline of economics. In so far as mathematical economics influences the construction of specific economic models, these models must be empirically interrogated. While theoretical economics cannot emulate the experimental sophistication of theoretical physics, economics is an empirical endeavour and thus its models must come before the bar of experience. Whether or not its models will or will not successfully pass this indispensable constraint, is a question for sophisticated economic testing which cannot be answered by any philosophy of economics.

As with the production of any book there are many debts incurred, of which we would like to mention a small number. We would like to convey our thanks to our colleagues in the Departments of Economics and Philosophy respectively at the National University of Ireland Galway (NUIG) for their support and co-operation during the writing of this book. In particular we would like to thank Professors John McHale and Alan Ahearne and Dr Aidan Kane for their support, encouragement and assistance during their respective terms as Head of the Department of Economics at NUIG. We also recall with fond memory the friendship, generosity and intellectual insights of Professor Vela Velupillai during his sojourn as the J.E. Cairnes Professor of Economics at NUIG. Vela's work in computable or algorithmic economics stands, in our estimation, as one of the truly pioneering contributions of the late twentieth century in the area of mathematical economics which is informed by a sophisticated philosophy of mathematics. We are also very grateful to Professor Gerhard Heinzmann and his colleagues at the Poincaré Archives (ACERHP) at the University of Nancy 2 in France for their help and hospitality to Paschal O'Gorman on the occasion of his visits there.

As always we would like to thank a number of people at Routledge, who as publishers have been exceptionally facilitating, patient and encouraging to us over the last twenty-five years. To Terry Clague we are deeply grateful for welcoming us back so warmly when contacted after a long period of absence on our part with this particular project. While Terry has moved on to other areas in Routledge, he directed us to Andy Humphries the current Publisher for Economics at Routledge and to Anna Cuthbert the current Editorial Assistant for Economics. It has been a particular pleasure to work with both of them and we would like to thank them for their advice, help and assistance in bringing this project to fruition. Finally, a very special thanks must go to Claire Noone of the Department of Economics, who with her usual extraordinary cheerfulness, expertise and efficiency managed to convert various unruly drafts of a difficult manuscript, that changed both direction and content at various junctures over its extended period of production, into a final presentable version, while overseeing the various requirements for the electronic versions for transfer to Routledge. For all of this we are deeply indebted and sincerely grateful to Claire not only for this particular project but for all our previous publications with Routledge.

Introduction

Formalism – the extensive exploitation of mathematics in economic theorising – has been a distinguishing characteristic of economics since the Marginalist Revolution of the 1870s, a process that has intensified through the course of the twentieth century. The application of mathematics to economics has been particularly reflected in the domain of general equilibrium which represented the most fundamental attempt to unify the foundations of the discipline from Walras's contribution through to its current variant of the Dynamic Stochastic General Equilibrium (DSGE) model, which is at the centre of so much of current orthodox macroeconomics. Meanwhile critics of orthodox economics have stridently criticised what they perceive as the excessive use of mathematics in general in economics, while at the frontiers of research in the discipline, new mathematical approaches have been suggested by a number of pioneering figures who are not opposed to the mathematisation of economics per se, but are opposed to the type of mathematics – classical mathematics in the main – that has been used and continues to be applied in economic theorising. From a methodological point of view, there is an urgent need for economic methodologists and economic theorists in general to direct their attention to a cognate domain of study, namely the philosophy of mathematics particularly its influence on the development of the mathematisation of economics. This is a fundamental informing rationale for this book if our understanding of the genesis, evolution and current developments at the foundational frontier of our discipline are to be methodologically engaged, analysed and understood.

Arising from the unwavering formalisation of economics throughout the twentieth century, and in our view the influence of developments in the philosophy of mathematics on this formalisation process, it is surprising that developments in the philosophy of mathematics have not played a more central role in the discourse of economic methodology. This book will address this critical relationship thereby redressing an existing gap in the methodological literature by posing the question: what can the philosophy of mathematics contribute to our methodological understanding of the trajectory of the formalisation of economics from Walras's initial attempts to the current situation in the foundations of the discipline? One considered answer is that the philosophy of mathematics is indispensable for both the enrichment of our methodological understanding of the complex process of the mathematisation of economics and the critical evaluation of that process.

Methodologically, this work is woven about five central methodological themes. These are the implications of the philosophy of mathematics for (i) mathematical modelling in economics, (ii) the mathematical modelling of equilibrium, (iii) the mathematical modelling of rationality, (iv) the manner in which theoretical economics is conceived as an applied mathematical science, (v) the axiomatisation of economic theory. In terms of the history of economic thought, the focus is on Walras, Keynes, Debreu and Simon. In this connection we are engaged in three complementary tasks. Firstly we use the philosophy of mathematics to enrich our understanding of the divergent philosophies of economic theorising adopted by Walras and Debreu. We attempt to be as objective as possible in presenting their sophisticated and creative methodological positions. Secondly, having identified these methodological positions, we use the philosophy of mathematics to critically evaluate their respective mathematisations of economics. Finally, we use the philosophy of mathematics to suggest how creative ideas, like Keynesian conventions and Simon's bounded rationality, may be methodologically reconstructed by recourse to the philosophy of mathematics. We assume the reader is not familiar with the philosophy of mathematics. Both within the text itself, including footnotes, and the appendix, we introduce key developments in the philosophy of mathematics which impinge on the methodological interrogation of the mathematisation of economics.

Broadly speaking we divide the philosophy of mathematics into two groups. The first group takes classical mathematics – the mathematics used by Debreu and other general equilibrium theorists – as being unproblematical and sets about defending it on logico-philosophical grounds. By the second decade of the twentieth century Hilbert and his formalist school at Göttingen were acknowledged as the principal exponents of this heterogeneous group. Hilbertian formalists defend classical mathematics by reconstructing it as an axiomatic system which is shown to be consistent, complete and decidable. The elaboration of this definitive defence of classical mathematics is known as the Hilbertian formalist programme.

In the other group we find mathematicians like Poincaré in France, Brouwer in Holland and philosophers like Dummett in England who do *not* take classical mathematics as it stands: some of the methods and theorems of classical mathematics are illegitimate! Thus Brouwer in the opening decades of the twentieth century developed an alternative mathematics to classical mathematics, called intuitionism. According to intuitionists the very core of classical mathematics is logically flawed and consequently classical mathematics must be replaced by intuitionistic mathematics. According to intuitionists, pure mathematics is created by the time-bound human mind and consequently is constrained by constructive, algorithmetic methods. In this way intuitionistic mathematics rejects what it sees as the infinitist extravagances of classical mathematics.

This fundamental conflict between Hilbert formalists and Brouwerian intuitionists raises a central question for the methodological analysis of the mathematisation of economics. It is frequently assumed that the mathematisation of economics is in principle not problematical: there is one and only one way to mathematise economics or indeed any other discipline, namely recourse to classical mathematics. The upshot of the foundational conflict between Hilbertian formalists and Brouwerian intuitionists is that theoretical economists have a genuine choice. Should they use intuitionistic rather than classical mathematics in their economic modelling? Is there a better fit between the subject matter of economics and intuitionistic mathematics than between the subject matter of economics and classical mathematics? In this connection we argue that intuitionists, not classical, mathematics is the more appropriate mathematics for economic theorising. Indeed we go much further. We contend that the neo-Walrasian programme of the mathematisation of economics is utterly undermined at its logico-mathematical core by intuitionistic mathematics.

For various reasons Brouwer's attempted intuitionistic revolution in mathematics failed: the majority of mathematicians continued to adhere to the framework of classical mathematics. However, within this framework of classical mathematics, events in the foundations of mathematics in the 1930s undermined the received view of classical mathematics as an axiomatic system which is consistent, complete and decidable. These events gave birth to what we call computable mathematics, a specialised branch of classical mathematics. We argue that these events, combined with computable mathematics, have major implications for the project of mathematisation of economics in general and for the neo-Walrasian project in particular.

Prior to the astounding results of Gödel, Church and Turing – the progenitors of computable mathematics – it was widely assumed that classical mathematics is an axiomatised system which is consistent, complete and decidable. Given that assumption, there is, in principle, no problem in exploiting the full resources of classical mathematics in theoretical economics. In the 1930s, Gödel, Church and Turing, by rigorous logico-mathematical analysis, undermined that assumption: the received view of classical mathematics as an axiomatic system which is consistent, complete and decidable must be rejected. Gödel's theorems established that there are, as it were, trade-offs between consistency and completeness in the axiomatisation of classical mathematics while Church and Turing proved that classical mathematics contains algorithmatically undecidable propositions. Contrary to the received view, classical mathematics contains both algorithmatically decidable and algorithmatically undecidable theorems.

Our methodological concern is with the implications of this post Gödel-Church-Turing view of classical mathematics for the mathematisation of economics. As we already indicated, given the received view of classical mathematics, theoretical economists can in principle exploit the full resources of classical mathematics in their theorising. Does the post-Gödel-Church-Turing view of classical mathematics undermine this thesis? That is, can economists continue to exploit the full resources of classical mathematics without any adverse economic consequences? What effect has recourse to an algorithmetical undecidable theorem on the project of the mathematisation of economics? In this connection we address three issues: (i) the implications of Gödel's theorems for economic methodology, (ii) the implication of the use of undecidables for economic theorising; (iii) should economic theoreticians confine their mathematical modelling to computable mathematics, the algorithmetically decidable part of classical economics? Vis-à-vis (i), we argue that Gödel's theorems undermine Debreu's own unique 'philosophy of economic analysis' (Debreu 1992: 114) but that these theorems as such do not undermine Debreu's mathematical model of a private ownership economy. In connection with our second issue, viz. the implications of recourse to undecidables in economic theorising, we argue that both Debreu's mathematical model of an economy and his methodological defence of that model are undermined. The neo-Walrasian explanation of prices is rendered economically vacuous by recourse to undecidables. Vis à vis our third issue we address the feasibility of the programme of the mathematisation of economics when economic modelling is confined to computable mathematics, i.e. the algorithmetically decidable theorems of classical mathematics. Our thesis is that prima facie, the computable mathematical resources furnished by the Church-Turing thesis have the potential to open up an interesting research programme for theoretical economists. Whether or not this research programme will evolve into an algorithmetic revolution in economic theorising will depend on future economic research.

Vis à vis the mathematical modelling of rationality we address three issues. The first issue concerns the mathematical model of rationality used at the birth of the Marginalist Revolution, particularly that advocated by Walras. When Walras wrote and re-edited his *Elements*, the intellectual climate was hostile to the project of the mathematisation of economics. Walras wrote to Poincaré – the leading European mathematician at the turn of the twentieth century – for the support for his project of the mathematisation of economics. In his brief correspondence with Walras, Poincaré, while sympathetic to Walras' project, raised a hierarchy of reservations and objections to Walras' specific defence of his mathematical modelling of rationality. In this connection we re-examine Poincaré's reservations and objections in light of Poincaré's own philosophy of mathematics, particularly his suggestion that Walras' model of rationality violates some methodological limits.

The second issue concerns the implications of computable mathematics for the orthodox modelling of rationality. In this connection we take up the theme of Simon's bounded rationality. In particular we engage a Hahn-type defence of the orthodox model of rationality, namely Simon's bounded rationality is no match for the orthodox theory because the potential for mathematical elaboration and sophistication is poor in Simon's approach. We engage the thesis that computable mathematics, as is evident in Velupillai's computable economics, is a fruitful source for a mathematical model of bounded rationality matching the mathematical sophistication of orthodoxy. Prima facie this novel research programme offers theoretical economists with new challenges and a rich reservoir of algorithmetic techniques by which these challenges can be met. Indeed we concur with Simon that Velupillai's algorithmetic model of rationality shows how the orthodox model of rationality transcends the outer bound of what is humanly rational. Of course, as one moves from thin to thick descriptions of economic decision-making, whether or not such a computable model of rationality will be vindicated is a matter for economic research, it is not a matter for economic methodology.

The third issue we address is the re-examination of the rationality of the Keynesian notion of convention in the context of radical uncertainty. When Keynes employed the concept of convention, he introduced a complex set of ideas that continues to present challenges of both interpretation and application. In the literature to date two pivotal figures have emerged, separated in time by two hundred years, namely David Hume and David Lewis. Hume's analysis of convention has remained a remarkable fruitful source of formative ideas on the creation, development and application of conventions in the social domain. In his seminal work *Convention*, first published in 1969, Lewis developed a framework broadly Humean in character but articulated within the analytic framework of game theory and centred on the notion of co-ordination. Central to the co-ordination problem is the idea that there exists a number of alternatives to choose from by which social agents can co-ordinate their actions to achieve mutual benefit. This idea informs a large portion of contemporary conventionalist theory. In this work we argue that post-Keynesian scholars should add another key figure to the line from Hume to Lewis, namely Henri Poincaré, the same mathematician to whom Walras wrote in connection with the mathematisation of economics. Within the philosophy of mathematics both pure and applied, Poincaré is known as the father of conventionalism. As Carnap remarked, 'Poincaré was a philosopher who emphasised more than previous philosophers the great role of convention' (Carnap 1966: 59). In this work we identify some of the principal tenets of Poincaré's analysis of convention and we relate this analysis of convention to the post-Keynesian methodological agenda. In particular we show how Poincaré places conventions at the core of pure mathematical reasoning, thereby rejecting the received view of mathematics as being nothing but a deductive system. We argue that this Poincaré analysis of convention liberates post-Keynesians from the influential legacy of Humean sceptical philosophy on the one hand and from the intimate association of Lewis' convention with the salient solution to co-ordination games with multiple equilibria on the other. Post-Keynesian conventional decision-making is thereby shown to be fundamentally rational.

Intimately related to the theme of which mathematics is most appropriate for economic theorising is the issue of the conceptualisation of theoretical economics as an applied mathematical science. With respect to the birth of formalism in the Marginalist Revolution we focus on Walras' philosophy of applied mathematics. Like the majority of his contemporaries, Walras took mechanics/mathematical physics as the exemplar of an applied mathematical science. In this connection we argue that Walras developed a scientific realist philosophy of mechanics: the principles of mechanics, mathematically represented by differential equations, convey the fundamental mechanisms operating in the physical universe. Given the analogy between mechanics and his mathematical economics shown by the existence of differential equations in both, Walras maintains that theoretical economics, like mechanics, reveals the fundamental principles of the economic world. Thus, while Mirowski in his analysis of the Marginalist Revolution emphasises the energy transfer from mechanics to economics, in the case of Walras we emphasise a different transfer, viz. the transfer of his scientific realist philosophy of mechanics to theoretical economics: just as the principles of mechanics reveal the fundamental mechanisms of the physical university, the principles of mathematical economics reveal the fundamental principles of the economic world. By way of critique we examine Walras' recourse to Poincaré in his final defence of his scientific realist reading of Walrasian economics contained in his 'Mechanics and Economics.' Despite Walras' total silence on the matter, Poincaré never espoused a scientific realist reading of mechanics. Indeed we show how Poincaré's reading of the principles of mechanics undermines Walras' scientific realist reading.

In connection with the neo-Walrasian programme, we focus on Debreu's *Theory of Value* – the paradigm of economic theorising for a generation of orthodox economists – to show how Debreu's philosophy of applied mathematics is very specific and quite unlike that of Walras. The analogy to mechanics exploited by Walras plays no role in Debreu's philosophy of economic theorising. Thus Debreu, unlike Walras, does not transfer a scientific realist philosophy of mechanics to theoretical economics. Rather Debreu emphasises a crucial difference between theoretical economics and mathematical physics, viz. mathematical physics, by processes of very sophisticated experimentation exemplified in research at CERN, is experimentally testable, whereas theoretical economics is not similarly testable. Debreu's philosophy of economic theorising as an applied mathematical science has a different source to that of Walras. Its source is, we argue, the philosophy of applied mathematics developed by Hilbert and his formalist school in the 1920s. By analysing Debreu's *Theory of Value* we show how he uses the Hilbertian formalist template for an applied mathematical science in his celebrated proof of the existence of general equilibrium, thereby enhancing our methodological understanding of Debreu's economic theorising.

The theme of the philosophy of applied mathematics used in economic methodology is intimately related to the theme of axiomatisation. Various orthodox economists insist that theoretical economics is or can be reconstructed as an axiomatic system. This reference to axiomatisation is frequently seen as being methodologically unproblematical. It is assumed that there is one and only one way of axiomatising economics. This traditional approach to the axiomatisation of a scientific domain we call the Euclidean model of axiomatisation of an empirical science. In this Euclidean model one first identifies the fundamental economic axioms and, secondly, the theoretical economist uses logic cum mathematics in association with economic assumptions to derive the implications of these economic axioms. In this Euclidean model of the axiomatisation of economics the axioms are generated from the economic domain and are frequently taken to be the fundamentals of the economic domain. Our thesis is that, while Walras did use this Euclidean model, Debreu, despite his commitment to axiomatisation, did not exploit this Euclidean model in his economic theorising. Rather, in line with his explicit commitment to the Hilbertian formalist school, Debreu used a different model of axiomatisation to the Euclidean one in his neo-Walrasian research. In the 1920s Hilbertian formalists developed a novel, non-Euclidean model for the rigorous axiomatisation of any empirical science.

In this Hilbertian formalist conception of the axiomatisation of any empirical science, the axioms are *not* generated in the scientific domain. Thus in the case of economics, its axioms are not generated from the economic domain. In this formalist approach to axiomatisation of any empirical domain, the only axioms are those of pure mathematics! Rigorously axioms reside only in the pure mathematics side of the divide between pure and applied mathematics. The formalist canons of axiomatisation hold only in pure mathematics which is the consistent, complete and decidable servant of applied mathematics. Given this consistent, complete and decidable axiomatic system, the applied mathematician identifies an appropriate sub-domain and finds an empirico theoretical interpretation of that sub-domain of axiomatised pure mathematics. We contend that it is this formalist Hilbertian model of axiomatisation of any empirical science, and not the traditional Euclidean model, which informs Debreu's commitment to axiomatisation in his *Theory of Value*. Moreover in this Hilbertian formalist model of axiomatisation of economic theory, the tacit assumption frequently associated with the Euclidean model, viz. the axioms convey the fundamental mechanisms operating in a real economy, does not hold. The umbilical cord between axiomatised economic theory and the fundamental mechanisms of an economy is severed. Rather in Debreu's Hilbertian formalist approach, axiomatisation is the vehicle for the rigorous presentation and expansion of economic theory. For Debreu theoretical economists, like other applied mathematical scientists, wish to attain the highest standards of rigour. This issue is not to be confused with the totally different issue of the empirical adequacy of axiomatised economic theory. Successful axiomatisation throws no light on empirical adequacy, nor is it intended to do so. Axiomatisation is the handmaiden of rigour, not empirical adequacy.

Overall, a central thesis of this work is that the philosophy of mathematics is a gale of creative destruction through the programme of the mathematisation of economics. While exposing the limitations of mathematical modelling in orthodox economics it offers alternative ways of formalising economics. Thereby it enables economic methodologists to address in novel and more precise terms the long-standing debate as to whether or not formalism in economics has gone too far. However, while emphasising the indispensable role of philosophy of mathematics in economic methodology, there is no suggestion that the philosophy of mathematics should colonise the philosophy of economics. The philosophy of economics has many mansions, one of which is constructed on the site of the philosophy of mathematics. Finally, we assume that readers are not familiar with the philosophies of mathematics exploited in the various chapters. With that assumption in mind we have attempted to balance the demands of communication with our potential readers and the demands of the accurate presentation of the complexity and sophistication of the logico-philosophical analyses in the various philosophies addressed in this work.

1 Economics and mathematics
Image, context and development

Introduction

In a recently published anthology, entitled *Mathematics and Modern Economics*, the editor, Geoffrey Hodgson, provides what would arguably be a widely accepted overview of many, but not all, practising economists of the relationship between mathematics and economics:[1]

> Today it is widely believed that economics is a mathematical science and the extensive use of mathematics is vital to make economics 'scientific.' Even if this is questioned, it must be conceded that anyone trying to grapple with economic concepts, their development and their applications must have at least some rudimentary knowledge of mathematics and statistics. It is also undeniable that some mathematical formalizations have played a key role in the development of economic ideas, from the link between marginal utility and calculus to the analysis of strategic interaction in game theory. Few would deny that such formalizations have enhanced our understanding. Economics stands way above the other social sciences in its degree of utilisation of mathematics, and consequently in terms of claims of its purported rigour.
>
> (Hodgson 2012: xiii)

Following this account, Hodgson immediately notes that for 'many practising economists, this will be the end of the story'. For those who subscribe to the above account, economics 'is essentially and unavoidably mathematical' which confers on it a number of salient characteristics, including the following: 'Mathematics means precision. Mathematics means rigour. Mathematics means science' (ibid.: xiii). Faced with the prospect of the conceptual enhancements to be gleaned from the importation of mathematics of this trinity of precision, rigour and science into the domain of social and economic theorising, those opposed to this expanding colonisation of economics by mathematics are deemed to be either a species of 'pre-scientific Neanderthals', who clearly lack an adequate understanding of the role of mathematics in the development of human knowledge in general and of science in particular, or serious doubts 'may also be cast on their mathematical capability'. As Hodgson summarises his condensed account of the presiding account for many practising economists, 'Doing economic theory is doing mathematics. Hence calls for less mathematics are misguided calls for "less theory"' (ibid.: xiii).

But Hodgson, a leading scholar in institutional and evolutionary economics and a prolific writer on economic methodology including the issue of formalism in economics, is quick to point out the inadequacies of the above account of the relation of mathematics and economics, as captured in his cryptic comment, 'if only things were so simple.' The 'many practising economists' that he refers to as subscribing to the above account would find Hodgson's Introduction to this valuable and extensive Anthology very informative, not to mention the substantive contents of many of the excellent readings he has selected for inclusion. These readings provide an excellent starting point for the variegated agenda that has emerged around the relation of mathematics and economics. The readings and the issues contained in this Anthology are confined to the post–1945 period and extend to the financial crisis of 2008. This was of course a pivotal period in the consolidation of the formalisation of economics through the use of mathematics. Taking a longer view, the post–1945 period appears parochial in time given the extended historical relationship between mathematics broadly interpreted and economics. A less restricted time-horizon would greatly extend the period of coverage if the complex interaction of the mathematical mode of reasoning within the socio-economic domain is to be adequately portrayed. If we relax our conception of mathematics as we currently deploy it in the twentieth-first century, complete with it all its associated resonances of 'precision', 'rigour' and 'science', then a more appropriate historical starting point would be the seventeenth century. This extended historical horizon would provide the framework for a more satisfactory and adequate understanding of the complex network of issues involved in the intellectual, institutional and philosophical interactions at play in the relationship between mathematics and economics.

Even a cursory examination of this complex relationship between mathematics and economics over this extended period makes clear that the relationship between the two domains has followed an erratic and contentious path of mutual reinforcement and even constructive development. But to claim this interpretation over a four-hundred-year period is not to downplay, much less to deny, that the relationship has neither been smooth nor straightforward. On the contrary, the relationship has been punctuated by periods of opposition and hostility to the increasing encroachment of mathematics into economics. Nevertheless, it would perhaps appear strange to a disinterested observer that the issue of the use of mathematics in economics has remained a source of contention and to many an issue of fundamental contention in the twenty-first century. The question can be posed as to what constitutes the possible sources of this tension, or methodological fault-line, between the proponents of the use of mathematics in economics and their critics. While there is a large array of possible sources, we identify three domains that would, in our view, be germane to the pursuit of insight into this complex dynamic between mathematics and economics. There is firstly, the general philosophical question which has, over the last four hundred years, been a presiding presence at the centre of European social thought, namely whether there exists discoverable social laws of development, akin to those in the physical sphere. If there are such discoverable social laws, what role would or could mathematical thinking contribute to their elucidation? Depending on one's disposition to this question could greatly influence how one might treat the employment of mathematics in socio-economic inquiry. In his book, *The Nature of Social Laws* (1984), Robert Brown poses an interesting set of ancillary questions relative to this question. The question Brown poses is 'why the efforts by so many people during the last four-hundred years, to discover laws of society have not been better rewarded?' (ibid.: 6). He poses the following intriguing set of issues:

> Is it because their character has been misconceived? Or is it simply that they have been sought in the wrong area of social life? Do they exist unrecognized, or is the long search for social laws the unhappy outcome of a gross misunderstanding? Are these laws of society with which we are all familiar and which are not difficult to state? Or are there reasons of logic, or fact, or both, which ensure that social laws do not – perhaps cannot – exist?
> (Brown 1984: 6).

These questions or variations of them, no doubt, will continue to present a very challenging array of issues to both social theorists and philosophers of society. Secondly, there are issues with respect to what we may call the specificity of economics as a social science that may militate against a dominant role for the application of the mathematical mode of analysis to the economic domain, or at least to key parts of that domain. In other words can economics lay claim to some form of exceptionalism, arising from either a range of ontological considerations or epistemic issues, or are there generic conditions that apply to all the social sciences? In recent years some attention has been paid to this issue of the unique or distinctive features of economics as a discipline, but this hasn't been explicitly related to the issue of the application of mathematics and its implications (Hausman 1992). Thirdly, we identify what is the main concern of our book, namely the influence on and the implications for economic theorising arising from the major developments in the philosophy of mathematics from the late nineteenth century. These developments in the philosophy of mathematics arose from the 'foundations of mathematics' debate which occurred at this time and continued into the twentieth century. Our motivation in engaging this topic is predicated on the assumption that if insight into the current state of economics, particularly the relationship between mathematics and economics, is to be achieved, then an extended and more adequate appreciation and understanding of the outcomes of developments in the philosophy of mathematics, along with their implications for economics, must become an integral part of the self-referential methodological understanding of economics as a discipline.

Against the background of these fundamental methodological questions, the relationship of changes in the philosophy of mathematics on economic methodology is the central focus of this book. There is little disputing of the trend in the intensification of the use of mathematics in economics particularly during the course of the twentieth century. This is particularly reflected in two areas where considerable empirical examination has been undertaken. One concerns the increasing volume of articles in the leading journals in the discipline which deploy mathematics as their principal mode of analysis while the second area concerns the reconfiguration of the curricula, at both undergraduate and postgraduate levels, to accommodate the increasing demands for courses with a mathematical orientation. In a number of studies that sought to quantify the extent of mathematics in economics, including Stigler (1965), Anderson, Goff and Tollison (1986), Grubel and Boland (1986) and Debreu (1986), the trend in the dramatic extension of mathematics was clearly evident. Mirowski (1991) reports on an extensive survey and review of the journal literature for the period 1887–1955. This exercise included four major journals, described as 'representative general journals of the fledging economics profession in the three countries of France, Great Britain and the United States'. The four journals included were the *Revue D'Economie Politique*, the *Economic Journal*, the *Quarterly Journal of Economics* and the *Journal of Political Economy*. The survey was not based on a sample but included an examination of every volume within the period in question. Mirowski finds that over the period 1887 to 1924 'most economics journals look very much alike when it comes to mathematical discourse' (ibid.: 150), with the journals devoting in general no more than 5 per cent of their pages to mathematical discourse. However, between 1925–1935 a very noticeable change occurred with regard to the intensification of mathematical discourse within the discipline. In fact Mirowski characterises this decade 1925–1935 as the second major 'rupture' which marked a critical inflection point in the rise of mathematics in economics, which took place as he notes 'in the decade of the Depression' (ibid.: 151). This trend was to be hugely consolidated and extended in the post-War period (Mirowski 2002).

When Stigler and his collaborators revisited this topic in the 1990s and analysed the application of mathematical techniques in a number of major economic journals, they found a decrease from 95 per cent in 1892 to 5.3 per cent in 1990 in articles that did not deploy either geometrical representation or mathematical notation in their analytical expositions (Stigler et al. 1995). This pronounced trend in the expanding use of mathematics in economics during the course of the twentieth century and in particular in the post-World War II period is characterised as the 'formalist revolution', which according to numerous studies was essentially consolidated by the late 1950s (Backhouse 1998; Blaug 1999; and Weintraub 2002). The publication of the lengthy report of Bowen (1953) on graduate education in economics for the American Economic Association, which advocated substantial extension of mathematical training, lent very considerable support to the reconfiguration of the graduate curriculum, as did the views of individual influential economists, such as Samuelson, who in

1952 provided a pragmatic but nuanced assessment of the desired relationship between economic theory and mathematics (Samuelson 1952).[2]

A related area where the influence of the increasing incorporation of mathematics into economics is clearly evident is in the domain of curriculum structure and design. This for some contemporary commentators has led to an unbalancing of the economics curriculum in favour of mathematics at the expense of other areas of economic studies. This is particularly pronounced in the areas of the more historical, discursive and qualitative areas of discourse within the discipline. The dramatic contraction, if not the complete demise, of economic history along with courses in the history of economic thought clearly illustrates this development in recent years. In passing, mention could be made in this context of the increasing retreat from the provision of cognate courses in politics, sociology and geography (urban and spatial analysis) that previously enhanced the intellectual contextualisation for the study of economics. While the issues of curriculum structure, design and development are not central to the aims of this book, they nevertheless represent an interesting locus of the tensions underlying the contents and design of what constitutes an adequate or, even more pejoratively, a proper curriculum for students of economics. The concern is that the teaching of economics has become disproportionately dominated by inclusion of an expanding volume of mathematics, mathematical statistics and econometrics leading to the exclusion of valuable material when viewed from a broader intellectual perspective. Given the finite number of hours available for the development and delivery of economic courses within the prescribed curriculum structure, the relation between the mathematical and the 'non-mathematical' contents has the property of a zero-sum configuration. The inclusion of more historical and qualitative material in the curriculum is not in principle incompatible with the position that mathematics has a pivotal role and that its influence will become more pronounced in the future. The issue is one of seeking balance and some may argue that the central concern is maintaining the intellectual integrity of the discipline.

Closely related to this issue of overall curriculum development and the search for a better balance between different dimensions of the discipline, in particular as between the desirability of 'more' or 'less' mathematics, is the very recent emerging debate concerning the crucial question as to what kind of mathematics should be taught (Velupillai 2000, 2005a, 2005b; Potts 2000; Colander et al. 2008). This agenda raises altogether more fundamental issues, both philosophical and methodological, and will be examined in later chapters of this book. A great deal of the future course of the role of mathematics in economics, or more precisely what kind of mathematics will or should play a pivotal role in the future, will hang on the outcome of developments currently underway in developing a different kind of mathematics that is both philosophically and methodologically better suited to the domain of economics.

To return to the longer view. In this chapter we will provide a short account of what is both historically and methodologically a very complex, challenging and extensive set of issues. The aim is to do no more than provide a context, which emphasises the historical dimension of the connection between the quest for initially the quantification of socio-economic phenomena and the ensuing search for 'social laws' which sought to be articulated in a mathematical mode in an attempt to capture the essential features of the pivotal socio-economic relationships and underlying mechanisms. The search for such relationships goes back, we would argue, to the seventeenth century and has gone through a number of critical phases, each with its own emphasis as to what they perceived to be the desired aim of their central endeavours.

The structure of this chapter will reflect our attempt to provide an overview of these phases of the interactive development of the relations between the construction of political economy as a discipline and its quest for a format of presentation which would establish its greater coherence, intellectual rigour, scientific status and relevance to socio-economic policy. The phases involved could be gathered broadly around the following periodisation: from the middle of the seventeenth century the articulation of 'political arithmetic' by William Petty and his followers launched the process of quantification and measurement of socio-economic phenomena informed by a combination of pragmatic policy concerns on the one hand, and the influence of Newtonian empirical data-gathering on the other. During the course of the eighteenth century and under the influence of the French Enlightenment, the emphasis shifts to the search for 'laws' in the socio-economic domain and the desire to formulate these laws in mathematical terms if possible. But it is during what we will call the 'long nineteenth century' that the momentum for the mathematisation of economics gathered pace and continued relentlessly into the twentieth century under the influence of the Walrasian and later the Neo-Walrasian programmes centred on general equilibrium theorising. The final phase represents developments in the post-World War II period, which arising from crucial developments in the philosophy of mathematics from the 1930s has thrown up fundamental problems for the methodology of economics in the domain of mathematical economics. In attempting to address this extensive historical span of time and the complex array of themes and issues associated with each specific period within the context of a chapter, we must of necessity be highly selective with respect to both topics and the role of individual contributors. This reflects our limited aim, in the context of a single chapter, of providing no more than an overarching overview of both the longevity and complexity of the critical relationship of economics and mathematics in the course of their extended historical interaction.[3]

Political arithmetic: the emergence of quantification of socio–economic phenomena

In his insightful study of the history of economics, Stark (1944) posed three interesting questions with respect to the problems of the historical development of economics, which in principle could be applied arguably to every discipline. Stark's delineation of the issues was as follows:

The historical interpretation and explanation of theories put forward in the past is the first and foremost task which the historian of political economy has to fulfil. But besides the great problem, which might be called his material problem, he is confronted with several others more or less formal in character. Three of them are of outstanding importance. They are indicated by the following questions: When did political economy arise? What were the phases in its evolution? How can it be defined and divided from other fields of thought? ... The first problem – the problem of origin – naturally and necessarily arises with regards to any science, but it is especially intricate in political economy.

(Stark 1944: 59).

If we replace 'political economy' with the 'mathematicisation of economics' in the above quotation, the issues identified by Stark apply with equal force and relevance. While there is widespread agreement that political economy was 'a creation of the European Enlightenment – more specifically, at first, of the French and Scottish Enlightenments' (Tribe 2003: 154), the genesis of the quantification of economic phenomena preceded the Enlightenment and was a product of the seventeenth century.

Schumpeter (1954) was quite clear that in the course of the eighteenth century 'economics settled down into what we have decided to call a Classical Situation' which gave rise to economics acquiring 'the status of a recognized field of tooled knowledge' (Schumpeter 1954: 143). But as he observed 'the sifting and co-ordinating works of that period' not only deepened and broadened the 'rivulet that flowed from the schoolmen and the philosophers of natural law' from an earlier period, they 'also absorbed the waters of another and more boisterous stream that sprung from the forum where men of affairs, pamphleteers, and, later on teachers debated the policies of their day' (ibid.: 143). This 'more boisterous stream' of material was produced by what Schumpeter called Consultant Administrators, whose primary preoccupation was the production of factual investigations to serve the purposes of the emergent nation states. They were connected by a common informing principle, notwithstanding their different backgrounds, namely 'the spirit of numerical analysis' (ibid.: 209).[4]

This commitment to 'the spirit of numerical analysis' was greatly enabled in the course of the seventeenth and eighteenth centuries by the development of specialised courses, particularly at the German universities, which focused on the presentation of purely descriptive data pertinent to the needs of public administration and policy.[5] But notwithstanding these developments in Europe, particularly in Germany, the decisive momentum to pursue the art of statecraft through the schematic collection and presentation of data was provided by a pioneering group in England, the pivotal figure of which was unquestionably William Petty (1623–1687). His work and that of his like-minded colleagues represented the crucial impulse for the quantification of economic, social and demographic phenomena. This quest for quantification, under the rubric of 'political arithmetic', represented a critical phase in the search for the schematisation and later progressive formalisation of the newly emerging discipline of political economy. We would argue that Petty deserves a distinguished place in the intellectual origins of the quest for the systematic quantification of socio-economic phenomena which provided the platform that facilitated, at least in part, the later mathematisation of our discipline. Consequently we outline in some detail Petty's career and his seminal contribution in the form of his 'political arithmetic' as he chose to designate it.

Petty's career was both mercurial and meteoric and displayed a promiscuous disregard for disciplinary boundaries, a salient characteristic of the seventeenth century. A prodigious talent, whose occupations and activities included, amongst others, that of 'anatomist, physician, professor of music, inventor, statistician, Member of Parliament, demographer, cartographer, founding member of the Royal Society, industrialist and author' (Murphy 2009: 22). He was born into a humble family in Romsey, Hampshire, who were involved in the clothing trade, a pursuit in which Petty himself saw little future. Abandoning this environment he went to sea as a cabin-boy at the age of thirteen. Sustaining an injury at sea he was put ashore in Normandy, an event that would have major consequences for his future career. He applied for admission to the Jesuit-run University of Caen, where he received an excellent education in Latin, Greek, French, Mathematics and Astronomy. He would later attest to his early academic achievements: 'At the full age of fifteen years I had obtained the Latin, Greek and French tongues, the whole body of common arithmetick, the practical geometry and astronomy, conducing to navigation dialling, with the knowledge of several mathematical trades' (Petty 1769: iv).

Clearly Petty, whom Karl Marx claimed as 'the founder of political economy', perceived himself even at this early age as a precocious linguist, navigator and an accomplished mathematician. For our purposes the 'founder' of the emerging discipline of political economy was indeed imbued with the 'spirit' of mathematics, which would find expression for Petty's later work in the form of quantification rather than formal mathematics as we currently understand it.

Nor was Petty's education in mathematics at Caen the end of his exposure to mathematics and mathematicians. When he left Caen in 1640 he 'seems to have spent some three years in the Royal Navy' (Hutchison 1988: 27). By 1643 he returned to the Continent and pursued the study of medicine in Holland where he became friendly with John Pell, Professor of Mathematics at Amsterdam (Malcolm and Stedall 2005). Petty moved to Paris to continue his study of anatomy, and through the good offices of Pell he was introduced to Thomas Hobbes. For over a year in 1645–1646, Petty became Hobbes's secretary and research assistant, whose intellectual influence on the young Petty was to prove very significant. Through Hobbes, Petty became acquainted with some of the leading scientists, mathematicians and philosophers in Europe. He participated in the Paris-based circle of Father Marin Marsenne, which included, among others, Fermat, Gassendi, Pascal and Descartes. From this experience Petty combined not only the Baconian inspired methodology of Hobbes, but presumably also the insights gleaned from exposure to this distinguished circle as to the potential of mathematical analysis.[6]

Following his sojourn in Paris, Petty returned to England in 1646 to continue his medical studies at Oxford. Pioneering the study of anatomy, Petty's medical academic career progressed rapidly, being appointed to the Professorship of Anatomy in Oxford in 1650 and later to the Vice-Principalship of Brasenose College in Oxford. In 1651 he was appointed Professor of Music at Gresham College in London, though there appears some ambiguity as to the precise remit of this particular professorship.[7] Gresham College was a new institution dedicated to the mechanical and experimental arts, and it has been suggested that Petty 'may have taught music in its mathematical rather than aesthetic aspect' (Letwin 1963: 188 fn. 2). While at Oxford Petty forged a close friendship with Samuel Hartlib, who would exert considerable influence on Petty's Baconian methodology, and through Hartlib he became acquainted with Robert Boyle. The extended circle of Petty's friends and acquaintances formed a very influential circle, or 'Invisible College' as it became known, many of whom would later contribute to the establishment of the Royal Society of London for the Improving of Natural Knowledge in 1662.[8] The Royal Society was dedicated to the Baconian programme of empirical observation and experiment as the basis of scientific knowledge initially in the natural world and later by extension in the social domain.

Having scaled the heights of the academic world by 1651, at the age of 28, a long and potentially outstanding academic career seemed assured for Petty. However in the same year he secured a leave of absence from Oxford which was to last for two years. In the event Petty was never to return to academic life and his career took a very different direction which would have important consequences for the development of his method of political arithmetic and his claim as the founder of that particular approach to the broader discipline of political economy. The circumstances surrounding his change of career direction were embedded in a mixture of domestic politics, colonial policy in Ireland and a deep personal ambition to amass a personal fortune if the opportunity presented itself.

The opportunity did arise following the end of the English Civil War in the midst of Cromwell's brutal conquest and decimation of Ireland. Jonathan Goddard, one of the members of the 'Oxford Club' and a physician by training, was appointed as chief physician of Cromwell's army in Ireland. After two years in Ireland Goddard returned to England as Warden of Merton College, Oxford in 1851. Petty replaced Goddard in 1652 as chief physician and would spend the next seven years in Ireland. In fact Ireland would preoccupy Petty for the remainder of his life, one way or another. Ireland would also be the site of one of Petty's major achievements in the application of his method of political arithmetic, as it would also be the source of his acquiring the personal fortune he desired. The circumstances which facilitated this were hardly auspicious. By the end of Cromwell's campaign of 'appeasement' of Ireland, great tracts of land were 'lying unoccupied, or depopulated by the butcheries of Cromwell's army, and was thus "up for grabs,'" which as Hutchison sardonically notes 'the slang is not inappropriate' (Hutchison 1988: 28). Cromwell's campaign in Ireland was financially constrained and as a consequence his principal means of payment at the end of the campaign to his financial creditors, mainly the soldiers and officers of his army and sundry supporters, was by allocating to them various portions of the conquered and confiscated Irish land. But in order to implement these allocations an extensive survey was deemed necessary. This job was conducted by Dr Benjamin Worsley, the surveyor-general. However, Petty seizing the opportunity launched an insidious campaign against Worsley's tardiness in completing the survey, and offered his services to complete the survey in a mere thirteen months. Petty replaced Worsley and with stunning efficiency, in what were very difficult circumstances which included a difficult physical terrain, frequent attacks by an alienated and hostile native population, and Worsley's continued interference, the survey was nevertheless completed within Petty's agreed time-frame by March 1656. It became known as the Down Survey and stands as one of the most outstanding exercises in quantitative surveying of its time, setting a benchmark for the methodology, precision and logistical implementation for later exercises of its type. As one of Petty's biographers' described it:

> The organisation of the Down Survey was on any account a remarkable feat of foresight, administrative ability and penetrating common sense … Only a man of boundless self-confidence would have undertaken such a project, only a man of infinite resource could have designed the bold plan of campaign and improvised the great organisation which it required, and only an administrator of genius could have ensured the practical execution within the stipulated period.
>
> (Strauss 1954: 65)[9]

Petty invested his earnings from the Down Survey project in the purchase of debentures or land claims from soldiers who mismanaged their newly acquired land allocations. Other Irish lands he acquired as payment-in-kind and still other land he purchased outright. By 1660 he owned estates amounting to 100,000 acres, which at the time made him one of the largest landowners in Ireland. A great deal of his property was, however, seriously encumbered. In addition he was continuously accused of having acquired much of his Irish land by fraudulent means. As a result, Petty, having returned to London in the late 1650s, spent a great deal of the remainder of his life 'chained to his possessions and his lawsuits, unwilling to buy ease at the cost of surrendering an inch of land' (Letwin 1963: 120).[10]

Notwithstanding the problems Petty endured as a result of his investment ventures in Ireland, fraudulent or otherwise, it did not deter him from pursuing an extremely active life on his return to London in the late 1650s and producing an extensive and influential volume of writings.[11] Following Hull (1900), Petty's main economic writings can be arranged chronologically into three groups.

Firstly, there were the two major works of the early 1660s, *A Treatise of Taxes and Contributions* (1662) and the much shorter work *Verbum Sapienti*, written in 1665 and published posthumously in 1691. The *Treatise*, ostensibly a work on public finance, engaged fundamental questions of economic theory, including value, price and money. The *Treatise* remains perhaps his most important work and had Petty written little else, he would arguably be assured of a secure place in the history of economic analysis. Secondly, there were the two major works of the 1670s, which for our purposes highlight Petty's innovative quantitative approach to socio-economic phenomena. Those were *The Political Anatomy of Ireland*, written in 1671–1672 and published in 1691, and his *Political Arithmetic*, written in 1672–1676 and published in 1690. The latter was primarily concerned with a comparative assessment of the economic strengths and weaknesses of England relative to that of her principal rivals at the time, France and Holland. Thirdly, there were a number of works on population estimation, which were to complement and extend the work of his friend John Graunt, whose path-breaking work *Natural and Political Observations mentioned in a following Index, and made upon the Bills of Mortality* was published in 1662. Other works in this third group included *Another Essay in Political Arithmetic* (1683) and his pamphlet *Sir William Petty's Quantulumcunque concerning Money, 1682* (1695) and *An Essay Concerning the Multiplication of Mankind* (1686). Authoritative accounts of Petty's writings, particularly his economic writing have been provided in the work of Hutchison (1988), Roncaglia (1985, 2005), Aspromourgos (1986, 1988, 1996, 1998, 1999, 2000, 2001a, 2001b, 2005), Amati and Aspromourgos (1985) and Ullmer (2004). Petty's economic writings, while covering a wide range of issues, can be grouped around a number of major topics. These include national income accounting; the theory of the velocity of money, the theory of the rate of interest; and the theory of value and distribution. We do not propose to address these or Petty's other economic writing as these are covered extensively in the writings cited above.

Our interest is with Petty's methodological commitments and the extent to which these are reflected in his practice in the applied domain. More particularly we are interested in establishing to what extent Petty may be credited with being a major figure in the genesis of the quantitative and mathematical approach in economics at a crucial period in the emergence of the European scientific revolution. The debate on Petty's method has focused on the respective influences of Francis Bacon on the one hand and on the other that of Thomas Hobbes. Advocates of the influence of Bacon on Petty's approach to political economy will identify Bacon's method as being characterised by the over-arching framework of induction, for which textual evidence, albeit limited, can be found in Petty. Certainly Bacon himself appeared quite clear about his inductive approach to knowledge. In a letter to King James I of England in 1620 with reference to his *Novum Organum*, Bacon writes that 'The work ... is no more than a new logic, teaching to judge and invent by induction, (as finding syllogism incompetent for sciences of nature)' (Bacon 1963: 119–120). Petty's scientific method, according to Ullmer, at least in Petty's own estimation, 'was the unvarnished scientific approach developed and promoted by Sir Francis Bacon in the late 16th and 17th centuries' (Ullmer 2011: 2). In contrast the influence of Hobbes on Petty, which represented an approach based on deduction from a priori premises, was identified by Quentin Skinner in his discussion of Hobbes's influence on an array of scholars, including Petty, in mid-seventeenth-century France and England (Skinner 1966). In the economic domain Aspromourgos is a leading advocate of the dominant influence of Hobbes rather than Bacon on Petty's methodological approach to economics. Mary Poovey's depiction of Petty's methodological approach is characterised as a 'complex theoretical amalgam', which is arrived at by 'mixing Baconian induction with Hobbesian deduction' (Poovey 1998: xviii). Ullmer proffers the view that 'there has been confusion and disagreement among historians of economic thought on how to characterize Petty's scientific method' (Ullmer 2011: 2).[12]

But with respect to Petty's claim as a progenitor of the quantitative and mathematical approach to economics, three components of Petty's life and work can be pointed to in order to indicate a substantive and deep commitment to the use and application of mathematics and quantification in economics. There was firstly, already noted in this section, Petty's exposure to mathematics at the Jesuit University at Caen in the 1630s. Secondly, there was his acquaintance with the Mersenne Group in Paris in the 1640s and his interaction with some of the most distinguished mathematicians, scientists and philosophers of the day. Thirdly, there was the influence of Hobbes for whom Petty worked as secretary during these years. Ullmer's assessment is surely correct when he indicates 'that the deductive aspect of Petty's scientific model owes much to his experience on the continent' (Ullmer 2011: 11).

This unique exposure during the 1630s and 1640s was not lost on Petty. He developed a clear and deep appreciation of the potential power of mathematics, not only in the natural sciences but also in the socio-economic domain, as providing the presiding framework for reliable systematic analysis. Aspromourgos, quoting from a contemporary of Petty's, suggests that Petty's methodological approach to economics could be summed up as follows: 'that Mathematical Reasoning is not only applicable to Lines and Numbers, but affords the best means of judging in all the concerns of humane Life' (originally quoted in Hull 1899: vol. II, 513n). But Aspromourgos correctly points out that Petty 'was sophisticated enough to recognise that even the most precise methods of inquiry would be as vacuous in execution as the concepts to which they were applied' (Aspromourgos 1996: 57). This assessment perceptively highlights two of Petty's central methodological tenets which underlay his method of approach to economics, namely the power and precision of mathematics on the one hand and on the other the fragility of the empirical objects to which mathematics would be applied. Petty was quite clear as to the potency and rigour of mathematics, by which he primarily meant 'arithmetick and geometry', as being 'the best grounded parts of speculative knowledge' in addition to being 'sure guides and helps to reason, and especial remedies for a volatile and unsteady mind' (Petty 1648: 144–145).

But if mathematics is the framing model that provides the most reliable methods for reasoned inquiry, the second presiding principle that pervades Petty's writings is the status of the empirical objects and their quantification without which the use, or misuse, of mathematics will only be to 'unprofitably apply without resolving needless questions, and making of new difficulties' (Petty 1648: 13–14). At the level of his methodological commitments, Petty maintained a clear distinction between the benefits of mathematics as the basis of reasoned argument but at the same time the necessity of empirical data was paramount. In the depiction of the scientific method he wishes to apply in the socio-economic domain, under the rubric of his 'political arithmetic', he is quite clear as to the requirements and necessity for its empirical foundations. In the following oft-quoted passage he stated:

> The Method I take to do this, is not very usual; for instead of using only comparative and superlative Words, and in intellectual Arguments, I have taken the course ... to express myself in Terms of *Number, Weight* or *Measure*; to use only Arguments of Sense, and to consider only such Causes, as have visible Foundations in Nature; leaving those that depend upon the mutable Minds, Opinions, Appetites, and Passions of particular Men, to the Considerations of others.
>
> (Petty 1690, repr. 1899: 244; italics in original)

Notwithstanding the seductiveness of the relative clarity of the above quotation in depicting Petty's 'not very usual' method of approach, it does convey the full richness or complexity of his methodological commitments. It is not possible to elaborate at length within the confines of a short chapter the full extent of his approach to political economy, including his innovative contribution of political arithmetic, nevertheless a brief sketch of his novel approach must suffice to convey his status as a precursor of the quantitative approach to socio-economic phenomena. Casting Petty as either an uncritical advocate of Baconian induction on the one hand or a Hobbesian deductivist on the other is not, we believe, the most fruitful path to pursue. Rather we would argue that based on a careful examination of Petty's writings on his methodological approach, albeit scattered across a wide array of his writings and over an extended period of time, a more useful way of approaching Petty is to posit his methodological approach as a quest for an objectivist basis for the quantification and analysis of socio-economic phenomena, thereby undermining the unconstrained intrusion of the subjectivist musings of 'the mutable Minds, Opinions, Appetites, and Passions of particular Men.' There is a consistency of continuity in his thinking from his *Treatise of Taxes and Contributions* (1662), and the three discernible models of production contained in this work which he argued should be analysed in physical terms rather than in nominal monetary terms given his mistrust of the vagaries of changing nominal values of monetary measurements as a secure basis for socio-economic measurement in the first instance. In the *Treatise of Taxes* he provided ground-breaking analysis of a theory of surplus, the social division of labour and his insightful analysis of the division of labour among other topics. This analysis found favour with Marx, who would confer on Petty the accolade of 'the founder of political economy' and with considerable justification in contrast to the 'vulgar' political economists as Marx would designate his successors.

It is clear that Petty saw mathematics as the most compelling, robust and reliable method of rational inquiry, arising as noted earlier from his own solid education in mathematics in Caen conjoined with his interaction with some of the leading mathematicians in Europe during his sojourn in Paris as Hobbes's assistant. But Petty is clear that the application of 'those most excellent sciences' of mathematics must be related to 'empirical objects', for without such 'empirical objects' the use or misuse of mathematics will only be to 'unprofitably apply without resolving needless questions, and making of new difficulties' (Petty 1648: 13–14). Petty is here advocating the constructive use of mathematics which will deliver concepts with clarified precision which when combined with reliable knowledge of the empirical world would lead to the emergence and development of new empirical sciences or what Petty termed 'mixt mathematical arts.' As far back as 1648 Petty had written that mathematics, by which he meant arithmetic and geometry, was 'the best grounded parts of speculative knowledge and of … vast use in all practical art' (Petty 1648: 146). Later he went on to elaborate that with respect to the method to be applied in analysing well-defined concepts, he favoured what he termed the 'algorithme of Algebra', which he explained was 'a kind of Logick' with the aid of which 'not only numbers but the several species of things' could be manipulated and analysed. This 'kind of Logick' which facilitated the application of algebra was made possible by designating the array of different 'species' by letters or similar type characters or more generically by an agreed set of symbols. We concur with Aspromourgos's broad conclusion that this 'is the particular mathematical method which in Petty's opinion is paradigmatic for politico-economic analysis: a calculus of symbolic forms which finds concrete expression in arithmetic' (Aspromourgos 1996: 59). Petty's aim appears to be informed and framed within the framework of the 'Algorithme of Algebra', which was to be applied not only to purely mathematical matters, but in his economic work the principal domain of application was to be the realm of policy. This was to be achieved by the translation of as many terms as possible in this domain into number, weight and measure, which provided the more secure empirical grounding of these terms and then to be analysed mathematically. This was the kernel of what Petty termed his 'political arithmetic'.

Was there then an underlying set of informing ideas that provided a coherent methodological basis for Petty's political arithmetic? We would argue that there was and it included an approach that would justify the identification of Petty as a significant precursor, perhaps the earliest, in the genealogical line in the quest for the mathematisation of socio-economic phenomena. The principal components of his methodological approach could be summarised as follows. Firstly, his overall approach to the systematic inquiry of economy and society was implicitly and explicitly based on mathematics, which as we have indicated earlier is hardly surprising given his early education and later his acquaintance with leading mathematicians. Secondly, as he makes clear in the Preface to his *Political Arithmetic* (1690), there is the emergence of a clear commitment to an objectivist approach which sought to undermine the damaging effect of exaggeration, hyperbole and the influence of unconstrained subjectivism in the domain of the socio-economic. This is patently clear from his desire to deploy his newly articulated method, a method 'not yet very usual', which through the primacy of 'Number, Weight, or Measure' would undermine and replace 'comparative and superlative words', through the discipline and constraints of treating matters in terms of 'Number, Weight, or Measure.' Thirdly, this primacy of 'Number, Weight, or Measure' as advocated by Petty reflected his position as an empiricist which is a more accurate and correct designation of Petty rather than his depiction as an unreconstructed Baconian inductivist. Petty was acutely aware of the need to ground, where possible, the concepts to be encountered in the domain of socio-economic policy in a solid empirical base. But these empirically established concepts and ideas were to be negotiated and analysed through the medium of already constructed theoretical concepts whose function was to provide a coherent explanatory framework where possible.

Petty's political arithmetic was an innovative, challenging and subtle methodological framework, which was motivated by pragmatic considerations with a view to enhancing the 'art of statecraft.' But as a methodological pioneer Petty constructed a conceptual framework which in its economic content sought firstly to furnish as precise as possible empirical estimates which in principle, if not always in practice, reflected the theoretical concepts used to provide a coherent explanatory framework informed by the methodological principles identified above, and to be used in the interest of policy-making and implementation. Petty was also alert to the value of comparative studies of the historical economic circumstances and performance in actual economic case studies, as reflected in his detailed analysis of Holland and Ireland in his *Political Anatomy of Ireland* (1691). In the absence of the framework contained in his political arithmetic he saw governments pursuing policy which in his view was metaphorically equivalent to throwing dice, a metaphor he invoked on numerous occasions in his writings. For him this was surely not the basis for conducting policy exercises on experimentation in the socio-economic domain. In his own words Petty provided a succinct and insightful summary of his methodological objectives: 'God send me the use of things, and notions, whose foundation are sense and the superstructures mathematical reasoning; for want of which props so many Governments does reel and stagger, and crush the honest subjects that live under them' (Lansdowne 1927: vol. 1, iii).

In this brief statement we see the three principal pillars of Petty's political arithmetic as a guiding methodological framework for the emerging discipline of political economy: the imperative of the empirical foundations; the application of 'mathematical reasoning'; and all with a view to informing and guiding public policy. Had Petty's political arithmetic been nurtured and developed in the ensuing decades political economy may have been spared some wrong turnings at critical junctures in its troublesome methodological trajectory. Be that as it may, it can be argued that Petty deserves to be acknowledged as a pioneering and significant figure in any extended contextualisation of the complex process of the mathematisation of economics. Following his death, his political arithmetic was not to enjoy the attention or development that might have been expected or deserved.[13] In any event by the beginning of the eighteenth century the centre of activity was moving to France and the emergence of major developments in that country. France was to play a pivotal role in the process of the mathematisation of economics in one way or another during the course of the eighteenth century within the context of the Enlightenment, a role that extended into the nineteenth century culminating in the contribution of Leon Walras, whose work represents for many the agreed starting point in the conventional narrative of the mathematisation of economics. In the next section, however, we will provide an account of the French intellectual and technical contribution to the project to 'mathematise' economics, which was initiated long before Walras.

From political arithmetic to political economy: the Enlightenment and beyond

Hutchison (1988), in his seminal study of the period 1662–1776, distinguishes between two distinct phases which witnessed the production of important publications in the domain of 'trade' and 'commerce' which eventually transmogrified into the term 'political economy.' The first phase, for Hutchison, was that of the 1690s and was dominated by English contributions, which as he argues was 'given such a decisive initial impetus by Petty' and which 'culminated in a remarkable concentration of important writings.' However, by the turn of the century and for the first forty years of the eighteenth-century the 'English advance rather suddenly and markedly slowed down' and 'Paris, to a significant extent, replaced London as the place of publication of major works' (Hutchison 1988: 185). However, from the late 1740s a remarkable number of pivotal works were produced which had a distinctly international character, mainly European, which were marked by the 'convergence upon … certain fundamental ideas and theories and … by the emergence of a new kind of systematization' (ibid.: 185). Here Hutchison makes an interesting distinction between two phases in the eighteenth-century: the first he terms the 'international mid-century efflorescence' (1747–1755), which was followed by the second phase, 'the French pre-eminence' (1756–1770).

The international dimension of the first phase is justified with even a cursory perusal of the works produced in this phase. In 1747 Francis Hutcheson, who was a teacher of Adam Smith, published his *Introduction to Moral Philosophy*. The following year Montesquieu's pivotal book, *L'Esprit des Lois* was published, and while not a contribution to political economy *per se*, it provided an influential philosophical framework with which to approach political and social analysis and represented a major intellectual contribution from the culture of the

Enlightenment.[14] Between 1749 and 1752 major contributions came from different parts of Europe, which included from Italy Galiani *Della Moneta* (1751), from Scotland Hume's *Political Discourses* (1752) and from England Josiah Tucker's early economic writings. But it was in 1755 that saw additional major contributions that shaped the intellectual, conceptual configuration and content of the emerging discipline of political economy. These included Tucker's most important work, *The Elements of Commerce*, along with Johann von Justi's *Staatwissenschaft*, considered one of the most engaging contributions from the German cameralist tradition.[15] But what has come to be regarded as one of the most important and innovative works in the history of economic thought made its appearance in French in 1755, written by the enigmatic but extraordinary accomplished Irishman Richard Cantillon, whose *Essai sur la Nature du Commerce en Géneral*, holds a distinguished place in the pantheon of canonical works in the history of economics.[16] But these developments, as Hutchison acknowledges, owe a great deal to the writers of the later seventeenth-century with Petty as a central figure. As he noted:

> it should be emphasized and re-emphasized, that neither the mid-century efflorescence, nor the great phase of French pre-eminence which followed directly after, could have happened without the intellectual platform provided by the work of Petty and writers, mostly English, of the latter part of the seventeenth-century.
>
> (Hutchison 1988: 187).

Developments in eighteenth-century France and in particular from the mid-century period of French pre-eminence in Hutchison's terminology were increasingly embedded, informed and shaped by the Enlightenment. The momentum to pursue a radical intellectual programme of the systemic analysis of a reconfigured society and economy was central to this endeavour. Integral to this programme was the commitment to the application of mathematics to the social and economic domains. Ingrao and Israel (1990) in their outstanding and authoritative study of general equilibrium theory succinctly capture the situation at this time when they noted that the: 'Historiography of philosophical thought has long identified the "mathematization" of the social sciences as one of the major themes of contemporary culture generated and molded in the rich melting pot of the Enlightenment' (Ingrao and Israel 1990: 34).

The use of the term 'melting-pot' to describe the Enlightenment is indeed resonant of the vibrancy, intellectual ferment and the contention of ideas that constituted the Enlightenment, an altogether too vast a spectrum to be engaged here.[17] However for our purposes in this chapter in attempting to trace a 'lineage' in the complex trajectory of the 'mathematization' of political economy, a number of key strands of developments within the 'melting pot' are central to our endeavour.

Critical to the contextualisation of developments in France at this time is the role and influence of Newton's contribution, or more specifically the dissemination of Newton's ideas within the scientific and intellectual communities of eighteenth-century France and Europe in general.[18] As is well documented the conflict between Newtonianism and the Cartesian heritage in France included the use of Newtonianism as a weapon to gain intellectual primacy among the elite academic, philosophical and political communities. Voltaire in his *Elements de la Philosophie de Newton* (1838) deployed Newtonian physics as the intellectual counterpoint against the metaphysical components of Cartesianism (Rattansi 1982). The 'Newton Wars' as they came to be called were launched early on in the Enlightenment and they remain a vibrant area of current research (Israel 2006; Shank 2008). Of crucial interest here was the divergent reception of Newtonianism in France and England. For Ingrao and Israel, Newtonianism 'was to assume totally original features in France.' But interestingly they argue this arose in no small part from the interaction of Newtonianism with Cartesian deductivism which they argue led to a 'moderate rehabilitation' of 'metaphysics', a process which tempered the 'empiricism of Newtonian natural science', particularly in the work of D'Alembert. The outcome of this process of interaction between the contending approaches in France resulted in their adoption of a physico-mathematical approach which prioritised the development of the mathematical mode of presenting Newton's body of work, which imparted a powerful impetus within the French intellectual and scientific communities to pursue this model of approach to most, if not all, realms of knowledge. Ingrao and Israel capture very perceptively the far-reaching consequences of the success of Newton's physico-mathematical approach as developed in France and the benchmark status conferred on it with the philosophy of the Enlightenment when they write:

> It is therefore hardly surprising that for a scientist like D'Alembert – but also for so many other thinkers of the Enlightenment or cultured men inspired by its philosophical ideas – the scientific intellectual became the model intellectual and the scientific community the model for scholarly communities. In the reformist view of the values and decrepit institutions of absolutism, Newton's scientific philosophy and the model of the scientific intellectual established in France became points of reference for an ideal renewal of the whole of society. In its new Newtonian garb, science puts itself forward as the *center* of society and *driving force* of reform, promising new horizons in all fields of knowledge to which the new methods of scientific thought could be applied. This scientistic (in the full and broad sense) vision was thus projected beyond the confines of traditional science and under the urgent promptings of institutional, economic and social problems – first under the *Ancien Regime* and then during the Revolution – the question of the *scientific* government of society and the economy achieved full status also in theoretical terms.
>
> (Ingrao and Israel 1990: 35–36, italics in original).

Meanwhile in England the version of Newtonianism that was pursued was dominated by small-scale empirical studies, which 'led them into repetitive and fragmentary studies' (ibid.: 35).[19] These developments were reflected in the status of the prestigious institutions in both countries, with the Royal Society going into decline at this time, while the French Académie des Sciences went on to become the leading learned society in Europe.

Newtonianism clearly represented a presiding and major source of intellectual influence in France during the course of the eighteenth century. Mainly due to the influence of Voltaire, arising in particular from his *Eléments de la Philosophie de Newton* (1738), Newtonian philosophy of science dominated the larger cultural and social milieu of French intellectual life, becoming in effect the recognised method for scientific reasoning, particularly in its physico-mathematical guise. This was cogently articulated by Ernst Cassirer in his classic study of the Enlightenment:

> The philosophy of the eighteenth century takes up this particular case, the methodological pattern of Newton's physics, though it immediately begins to generalize. It is not content to look upon analysis as the great intellectual tool of mathematico-physical knowledge; eighteenth century thought sees analysis rather as the necessary and indispensable instrument of all thinking in general. This view triumphs in the middle of the century. However much individual thinkers and schools differ in their results, they agree on this epistemological premise.
>
> (Cassirer 1951: 12).

The 'universal twist' imparted by Newtonian science arose from its success in articulating and representing the universe as perceived by Newton through the medium of mathematical analysis. The impetus thus imparted by Newton's approach and methods of analysis stimulated hopes that similar types of results could be achieved across all areas of knowledge including the human and social branches (Cohen 1994). But the difficulties of an uncritical generalised application of 'rational mechanics' to all branches of knowledge were identified from early on. As was the emergence of an 'unresolved tension' in Enlightenment thinking between the promise of Newtonian science to provide scientific criteria of verification as alternatives to metaphysical or 'revealed truth' thinking. Similarly the difficulties encountered in its application to fields of knowledge outside those of natural phenomena were evident to many writers, including some who were major advocates of Newtonianism (Ingrao and Israel 1990).

But the influence of Newtonianism in France was greatly buttressed and enhanced by writers of immense influence within the broader culture of the Enlightenment. Montesquieu was certainly influenced by the overall approach of Newtonian physics, an influence that can be detected in his influential *Esprit de Lois* of 1748, whose central focus was on the analysis of the relative merits of alternative types of institutions of governance such as monarchy, republicanism, and despotism. But he also grappled with the more fundamental processes of social harmony and the achievement of equilibrium among the contending forces and clash of interest with the body politic and the broader society. These concepts and issues paralleled the analysis in 'rational mechanics', and would feature as pivotal in the development and content of mathematical economics later in the nineteenth and twentieth centuries. Montesquieu is often credited with being the father of sociology as it later came to be termed, but more fundamentally the *Esprit des Lois* could be viewed as an early attempt to identify the processes and mechanisms that operated within society and how they contributed to the achievement of an 'equilibrium', albeit imperfect, which would provide the conditions for enhanced political freedom in a progressive society. Montesquieu can also be attributed with the early search for the existence of laws in the social domain, reflecting again the influence of Newton's work in physics. But Montesquieu's writing on this topic is a complex story which involved the inherited influence of the natural law theorists of the seventeenth century, such as Pufendorf (1632–1694), and a more empiricist approach to social laws, which would later dominate Comte's positivism in the nineteenth century. While neither the earlier natural law theorists nor later Montesquieu and his followers forged any attempt to represent social laws in mathematical terms, they imparted to the general culture of the Enlightenment the desirability of pursuing the quest for establishing social laws which held out the prospect, if not the promise, of articulating laws parallel or analogous to those provided by Newton in the physical domain.

While Montesquieu's *Esprit des Lois*, was not in any way a contribution to political economy, it set critical parameters for a new philosophical approach to social theorising and the search for 'laws' in the social domain. However, the explicit articulation of a more scientific approach to the analysis of socio-economic phenomena emerged with the Physiocratic School of Political Economy in France. Its leader was Francois Quesnay (1694–1774) who along with Turgot (1727–1781) represent the pivotal figures in the development of political economy at this time. We do not propose to address their pioneering contributions in the many areas of political economy to which they contributed, since these are comprehensively treated in the extensive literature on the history of economic thought.[20] It must be noted however that Quesnay was imbued with the Enlightenment philosophical commitment to the progress of humanity in all respects, central to which was the provision of the goods and services necessary for material well-being, and this was to be achieved by enlightened reason based on a science of natural order informed by the contribution of natural law. Quesnay came to view economic science, with its central focus on the production and distribution of goods and services, as 'a great science, and the very science upon which the government of society rests' (Ingrao and Israel 1990: 44).

Quesnay's methodological approach to this 'great science' was not going to be based on the outcome of history as a primary source of insight: 'We seek no lessons from the history of nations or of mankind's blundering, which represent for us only an abyss of disorder' (ibid.: 43). Nor was he attracted to the use of algebra as a mode of representing his economic ideas, and like many of his contemporaries his view of mathematics primarily embraced arithmetic and geometry as the central components of that discipline. He did however assign great importance to extensive and rigorous calculation, which emanated in the construction of his celebrated 'Tableau Économique', first published in 1760. This was an elaborate arithmetical scheme representing production and distribution within an economy using hypothetical data. It was also to facilitate the investigation of taxation measures on the part of the central authority with a view to evaluating the impact on the national well-being of the nation. Similarly the impact of external events on the economy could be investigated and evaluated. While the *Tableau* is viewed as the seminal contribution of Quesnay and the Physiocratic movement, Quesnay's elaborate calculations were related to a systematic conceptual structure, which represented an innovative model of economic growth in which Quesnay demonstrated how surplus emerged in the production system and how the allocation of this surplus could contribute to future economic growth. The unique feature of the Physiocratic model of economic growth was that it referred exclusively to land as the exclusive source of surplus. Quesnay in fact argued that surplus could not be produced in the manufacturing sector. Within his conceptual framework, albeit limited to the agricultural sector, Quesnay also provided original insights into the role of the entrepreneur and the crucial role of the provision of 'advances' to producers as part of his explanation of the economic growth process.

Quesnay's contribution to the formalisation of economics, narrowly interpreted, may be deemed to be modest but his contribution to the quantitative schematisation is altogether more significant; Ingrao and Israel point out that:

> On more than one occasion Walras, though little given to generosity in acknowledging his 'forerunners,' evinced a predilection for the Economistes, who he indicated as the school that had laid the most correct foundations for the subsequent mathematical theory of general equilibrium
>
> (Ingrao and Israel 1990: 45)

The *Tableau* was a major source of inspiration in the twentieth century to Leontief's input-output analysis of the United States economy in 1941 (Leontief 1941: 9), which generated the extensive input-output analysis that featured as a major strand of quantitative economic research in the post-World War II period. The Physiocratic contribution, and in particular that of Quesnay, laid the foundations for the intensification of the schematic quantification and increasingly formal analysis of the economy and society that would follow in the latter part of the eighteenth and into the nineteenth centuries.[21]

Closely associated with Quesnay was his contemporary Turgot (1717–1781), who contributed many original insights to the emerging discipline of economics. Though never the creator of a large-scale framework of analysis compared to Quesnay, he shared the commitment to the systematic measurement of socio-economic phenomena as the necessary basis for the pursuit of informed and rational policy decisions. Turgot's major work, the *Réflexions sur la formation et la distribution des richesses* (1769–1770), which was translated in 1793 as

Reflections on the Production and Distribution of Wealth, developed his theory of capital and its role in the economic growth process. As a result of Turgot's work, capital was now perceived as a crucial input along with land in the structure of production and economic growth. He also developed a model of interest rate determination based on the supply and demand of loanable funds, and traced the role of low interest rates in facilitating economic growth. Turgot did not contribute any formalisation of his many original contributions, but perhaps his more indirect influence on the process of formalisation may have come from his close friendship with Condorcet who was to contribute an explicit momentum to the Enlightenment project of the analytic schematisation of the socio-economic domain.[22]

In the process of the 'mathematisation' of economics within the broader culture of social reform and progress of the Enlightenment, Condorcet (1743–1794) occupies an interesting and significant position (Baker 1975; Rothschild 2001). A mathematician of outstanding ability and a committed adherent of the Enlightenment values, he was well placed to engage the potential application of the physico-mathematical approach to provide insight into the framing of a more rational order in the socio-economic domain. His originality and innovative contribution at a technical level was the central position he gave to the application of the probability calculus to socio-economic analysis, rather than the choice of the infinitesimal calculus of Newtonian analysis. If the probability calculus was Condorcet's technical technique of choice, this was informed and embedded within his larger conceptual framework which attempted to reconcile a science of society which would combine a rigorous objective status, similar to that of the physico-mathematical sciences. As in the physical domain, scientific laws would be articulated and would elaborate the empirical regularities, systematically observed. However, at the same time, it was to be recognised that the 'material' to be analysed was the outcome of the subjective choice of free social agents based on their autonomous capacity to choose. In this latter 'subjectivist' component of his conceptual framework Condorcet was greatly influenced by Turgot. Condorcet's choice of the interesting term 'social mathematics' was perceptive in conveying what was central to his conception of the new sciences of society, the conjoining of the rigour of mathematics to the complex domains of the socio-economic world.

From 1780 he devoted his efforts primarily to the articulation of the social sciences, which he argued needed to pursue a path of development that would lead to the achievement of a new intellectual standing. But this would have to combine both a well-established empirical basis conjoined with the rigour of the physico-mathematical sciences, a theme that was resonant of Petty's earlier efforts and which was now a presiding and integral part of the Enlightenment culture. In a telling speech delivered in his *Discours de Réception* delivered at the *Académie des Sciences* in 1782 and quoted in Ingrao and Israel (1990), Condorcet's provides a potent statement of his position and ambitions for the future of social sciences and the approach to be pursued:

These sciences, whose object is man himself and whose direct end is man's happiness, are now almost established and their developments will be as certain as that of the physical sciences. The cherished idea that our grandchildren will surpass us in wisdom is no longer an illusion. Whoever reflects upon the nature of the moral sciences cannot, in fact, but see that, supported by factual observation like the physical sciences, they must follow the same method, acquire an equally precise and exact language, and attain the same degree of certainty.

(Ingrao and Israel 1990: 50)

During the course of the 1780s and into the 1790s, before his premature death in unfortunate circumstances in 1794, Condorcet produced a number of important works which elaborated his project of 'social mathematics', which was inclusive of all the problems of the socio-economic realm that needed to be addressed, including the political and moral sciences along with political economy which he viewed as a particular discipline within the larger domain of the social sciences. Condorcet's project maintained the stream of thought that distinguished between the normative and descriptive dimension of Enlightenment thinking. But for a variety of complex reasons Condorcet's attempts to mathematise the 'social sciences' in line with his innovative conceptual and mathematically probabilistic approach did not emerge victorious, due in part to the tensions and weaknesses within his conceptual framework but also in part to the major political and cultural changes that emerged with the decline of the hegemony of the revolutionary period and the arrival of the Napoleonic era.

In the period following this political and cultural shift the development of 'social science' took two different paths of development. The lineage based on the foundations of 'political arithmetic', or later 'economic arithmetic', along with Condorcet's social mathematics continued to enjoy support and further development at least for a comparatively short period, particularly in the class of Moral and Political Sciences of the *Institut de France*, which was established following the suppression of the *Académie des Sciences*, where it still found a hospitable environment. However, by the end of the eighteenth century critical voices were raised against the suitability of the Newton-inspired mechanical model and its corollary of the physico-mathematical methods of analysis to provide an adequate explanatory framework for a 'science of man.' These criticisms began to emerge also in certain areas of the natural science community such as the biological study of natural-life processes. But the more serious, some might even term it the fatal, blow to the programmatic framework of the mathematisation of the socio-economic domain informed by the Enlightenment values and in particular Condorcet's social mathematics came with the increasing demise of leading mathematicians of the day such as the towering figures of Lagrange and Laplace who had shown genuine interest and support for Condorcet's social mathematics. However, on Lagrange's death Laplace assumed the leading role within the scientific community and in particular with the very prestigious Class of Geometry in the *Institut de France*. Whatever the basis for his earlier support for Cordorcet's social mathematics, his opposition and intensifying hostility became quickly apparent which found expression in his 'purging' of the remnants of the project and people associated with it.

The intellectual consequences of these developments when conjoined with the instalment of the new Napoleonic political order was to reorientate the trajectory of the development of the social sciences. The idealism, intellectual innovativeness and the inclusiveness of the social sciences were undermined. The focus of Newtonian philosophy was to be retrieved as it were as the exclusive focus on natural phenomena and based on the methods of the physico-mathematical sciences. If the social sciences were to pursue their development, then it was to be under the shadow of the correct application of the canonical methods of the physico-mathematical sciences and methods, as reflected for instance in the infinitesimal calculus predicated on the deterministic framework of analysis. The courageous attempts by Condorcet to provide a 'probabilistic' foundation of analysis in response to the reality of the socio-economic world which he perceived was effectively to be discarded. In the domain of analysis the new presiding ethos was conformity to the dominant mode of a deterministic methodology dictated by the Newtonian-inspired analytical framework and its arsenal of approved methods and techniques. In the specific domain of political economy, the prestige accorded to Adam Smith's *Wealth of Nations*, with its mixture of historical examples, components of inductive reasoning and the use of pragmatic case-studies and well-marshalled empirical supporting data was perceived as the paradigmatic way forward. This was in contrast to the search for schematic search for the rational ordering of society based on the articulation of 'social laws', both explanatorily descriptive laws along with normative rules to guide a rational and progressive society, the framework for which had been provided in large part in the work of Montesquieu, the Physiocratic contribution and that of Condorcet.

Apart from the later strident hostility of Laplace to the project of the 'mathematisation' of areas outside the natural domain, a major source of opposition within political economy in France came from the emergent French Liberal School of political economy and in particular from J B Say (1767–1832), its effective intellectual leader.[23] This school of thought was the dominant influence on French economic thought for most of the nineteenth century, and adherents to its central doctrines could be found in the United States and Italy and among prominent British and German economists. For our purposes of attempting to outline the continuity of linkages, or lack thereof, that sustained the intellectual mind-set and the pursuit of the mathematisation/formalisation of economics, the emergence of the French Liberal (or Classical) School represented a major intellectual resistance to this project. Say was personally opposed to the importation of mathematics into the shifting view of 'social science', including political economy, and spear-headed the opposition to the project. The contributing factors to account for his opposition and ensuing influence are varied and complex. He was arguably picking up on the shift in the conception of the proper approach to the study of the social realm and the need to liberate this domain from the dominance of the physico-mathematical approach to all realms of knowledge. In this the opposition of Laplace, referred to above, may have been an important contributing factor. By the end of the eighteenth century the pathways of the future development of the social sciences were diverging in France. Say and his colleagues, collectively known as the 'Idéologues', including Destutt de Tracy, Garnier and later such notables as Bastiat, Rosso, Courcelle-Seneuil and many others who aligned themselves with the French Liberal School, criticised the Physiocratic legacy along with that part of the Enlightenment inheritance that pursued the schematisation of political economy informed by the aims and methods of Newtonianism and the use of physico-mathematical sciences. Their critique of the Physiocrats and associated endeavours included the overly abstract conceptual schemes of analysis, the inadequacy of extensive observational studies and their propensity for excessive speculative analytical thinking. Ingrao and Israel (1990), quoting the work of Moravia (1974) who provides an intriguing and insightful account of Say's conception of what should inform the construction of political economy:

> Neither mathematical calculation nor the abstract disciplines in general are able to provide a really valid explanatory heuristic model. Rational mechanics, algebra, and logic achieve certain results only insofar as they are based on ideal data divorced from living reality. Now, political economy proceeds, and can only proceed, on the terrain of real facts. It must take into account all the concrete data, even when imponderable or variable, to which the exact sciences (statistics and political arithmetic among them) pay no heed. The sciences Say regards as analogous to political economy are of another type. As the science of the living *corps social*, he regards it as qualitatively no different from physiology, the science of the individual body.
> (Moravia 1974: 782–783, quoted in Ingrao and Israel 1990: 59)

Say's opposition to the mathematisation of economics was in the opinion of Ingrao and Israel pushed, in their estimation, to an extreme position of rejection by Say 'to the point of the idiosyncratic rejection of mathematics *tout courts*' (Ingrao and Israel 1990: 60). But 'idiosyncratic' may not quite convey what was in effect a committed and fundamental philosophical and methodological position on the part of Say and the French Liberal School.

Say's own pronouncements convey on the one hand what appears as a more modest aim on his part with respect to the advancement of political economy, namely the promotion and advocacy of Adam Smith's *Wealth of Nations*. Smith's work was viewed as providing a more convivial intellectual approach to the grounding of political economy in a philosophy of inter-personal relations which generated outcomes that reflected pathways to social harmony and the achievement of something approximating to overall equilibrium. Within the *Wealth of Nations*, Smith extolled the acceptability and virtues of laissez-faire, free trade, competition and specialisation in production, as the economic and social means of achieving the larger goals of social harmony, individual liberty and political stability, characteristics of an ordered and civilised society for the new 'commercial society' which was emerging with the Industrial Revolution.

The *Wealth of Nations* synthesised brilliantly a great deal that had gone before, not only in Britain but more significantly in France with which he was acquainted. It also contained many original insights and attempts to articulate particular topics. But notwithstanding these achievements, it was hardly a paragon of organisation and clarity and was in many respects an inconsistent and understandably an incomplete work. This was how it was viewed by contemporaries following its publication and these included Say among others. The need to address its weaknesses and to provide modifications, extensions and corrections to Smith's *magnus opus* became a major programme of activity among leading figures in political economy, and in the struggle for apostolic succession as to who would succeed Smith by virtue of their contributions to a more clarified articulation of his theories redounded arguably to three principal contenders, namely Say in France, and Malthus and Ricardo in Britain. All three were informed by different perspectives on the future of political economy. We do not propose to pursue here the specific differences of approach of the three figures with respect to the content of their economic theories.[24] Of interest to us is the differences that quickly emerged at the methodological level, particularly between Say and Ricardo. Say opposed Ricardo's adoption of a deductivist methodology, which became the latter's presiding approach to economic theorising, an approach which exerted very considerable influence during the course of the first third of the nineteenth century. While Ricardo did not himself use mathematics in his economic writing, his committed and consistent use of a powerful deductivist structure of argumentation facilitated the translation of his work into a mathematised mode of presentation, which was undertaken later within mathematical economics (Pasinetti 1974).

In Say's own words he indicts not only Ricardo and the Ricardians but the legacy of Quesnay and the Physiocrats:

> Without referring to algebraic formulas that would obviously not apply to the political world, a couple of writers from the eighteenth century and from Quesnay's dogmatic school on the one hand, and some English economists from David Ricardo's school on the other hand, wanted to introduce a kind of argumentation which I believe, as a general argument to be inapplicable to political economy as to all sciences that acknowledge only experience as a foundation.

Continuing his specific critique of Ricardo, he accuses him of setting truth

> in a hypothesis that cannot be attacked because, based on observations that cannot be questioned, he imposes his reasoning until he draws the last consequences from it, but he does not compare its results with experience. Reasoning never waivers, but an often unnoticed and always unpredictable vital force diverts the facts from our calculation. Ricardo's followers ...

considered real cases as exceptions and did not take them into account. Freed from the control of experience, they rushed into metaphysics deprived of applications; they have transformed political economy into a verbal and argumentative science. Trying to broaden it they have led only to its downfall.

(Say 1971: 15)

Ricardo would later be accused of perpetrating the 'Ricardian vice' through the deployment of assumptions that lacked empirical adequacy and the derivation of conclusions that purported to accurately depict the future empirical course of events. In the above depiction of Ricardo and his followers, Say is accusing them of a Ricardian reductionism decoupled from experience that misdirected them into the realm of metaphysics. Say and the emergent French Liberal School along with its doctrines, theories and overall vision of political economy prevailed in France, and as the nineteenth century progressed its dominance became firmly established. Its influence was pervasive, particularly within other higher educational domains, including within scientific and learned societies, and in the direction followed by the leading economics journals of the day (Arena 2000). The intellectual, academic and educational environment became less and less hospitable to the project of the mathematisation of the social sciences, and in particular the economic domain. Notwithstanding the complex factors that led to the tectonic intellectual shift in the nineteenth century, particularly in France, by the 1870s what was to emerge was in the form of Walras's contribution, which is generally accepted within the conventional interpretative narrative as the pivotal development that launched the resuscitation of the mathematisation of economics that would eventually lead to its intellectual dominance within the economic academy in the course of the twentieth century. In the next section we will provide a brief overview of what is now a well-documented narrative over the course of the twentieth century even as the explanation for the dominance of mathematics remains an understudied topic as both a historical process and even more significantly the study of the methodological implications of the importation of mathematics into economics particularly given the changing character of mathematics itself.

The triumph of formalism: from Walras to Debreu and beyond

Notwithstanding the formidable cultural, sociological and technical forces that had emerged by the late eighteenth century in France against the endeavours to 'mathematise' the social domain, which had congealed into a very influential position during the course of the nineteenth century, the commitment to continue the efforts to mathematise the social sciences continued. The efforts to sustain this were now represented by individual contributions and lacked the approval or support of the official establishment or academic community. However, the source and strength of the opposition to this commitment grew stronger and more influential. The almost total withdrawal of intellectual and academic support of the scientific community for the project of furthering the mathematisation of the social sciences, conjoined with Laplace's insistence on the prescriptive correctness of the paradigm of mechanics as the correct conceptual approach, with its corollary of a deterministic methodology based on the use of infinitesimal calculus, provided the presiding mathematical framework for scientific analysis. More specifically within political economy the emergence of the French Liberal School and the influence of J.B. Say during the course of the nineteenth century and the explicit philosophical opposition to the methodological pursuit of the formalisation of political economy made for an extremely hostile and inhospitable environment within which to pursue the mathematisation of political economy or the social sciences in general.

Against this background the accepted interpretive narrative of the period identifies a small number of individuals in France who at this time made original contributions that have earned them a place of some distinction in maintaining the link with the efforts to further the mathematisation of the social sciences. This was something of a solidary track for these writers who are generally designated as being 'precursors' of Walras, whose seminal work emerged in the 1870s and represented a watershed in the evolution of mathematical economics. These 'precursors' need not detain us beyond some very brief comments to acknowledge their place in sustaining the lineage of mathematical economics in difficult circumstances. A number of them belonged to what is referred to as 'engineer economists', which were not uncommon in nineteenth-century France, arising from a certain pre-eminence conferred on engineering within the French academic tradition from the eighteenth century and into the nineteenth century. Their mathematical training as engineers along with their technical contributions to the development of the physical dimensions of the French economy and its implication for investment, public finance and in particular taxation, all provided the conditions that led to their involvement in the intersection of engineering and economics.

Achylle-Nicolas Isnard (1749–1803) was such an engineer-economist whose main contribution was contained in his *Traité des Richesses* of 1781.[25] In this he dissented from the central Physiocratic doctrine, which maintained the primacy of the agricultural sector as being the only source of economic activity that could produce a net surplus for the economy. Isnard, in contrast, argued that industrial activity was also capable of producing a surplus, which had significant implications for distribution within the economy in that this surplus accrued not only to landowners, as argued by the Physiocrats, but to all the owners of the productive resources that had contributed to the production of the surplus, with their remuneration being determined by the scarcity of their resources. Walras would later acknowledge Isnard's contribution to his own thinking in the formulation of general equilibrium theory.

Jules Dupuit (1804–1866), like Isnard, was also a good example of the engineer-economist tradition in nineteenth-century France (Ekelund and Hébert 2000). While civil engineering was his central occupation, rising to become the chief municipal engineer in Paris in 1850, his interest in political economy arose from his interest in industrial development and issues arising from this wide-ranging topic. Dupuit's central claim to fame is based on his contribution to the concept of utility, more particularly its measurement which Dupuit regarded as pivotal for political economy (Stigler 1965). Dupuit differed from Say and the English classical economists on this topic and provided a number of original insights which essentially combined the idea that utility was to be thought of as being fundamentally linked to the quality of a good or service that satisfied some desire while at the same time acknowledging as an integral part of his analysis that utility varied from individual to individual along with the quantities of the good or service consumed by the economic agent. The implications of these insights and their formalisation by Dupuit would provide the foundations of the neoclassical paradigm of economics that would emerge in the last third of the nineteenth century, including that of Walras's general equilibrium theory. Dupuit represents in his work, mathematically articulated, 'an important link between the ideas of the first generation of expounders of economic arithmetic and social mathematics and the generation of those scholars who were to contribute most directly to the founding of general economic equilibrium theory' (Ingrao and Israel 1990: 77). His methodological approach was informed by the Newtonian framework and his desire to provide a formal foundation for political economy based on the physico-mathematical sciences, an ambition that was shared by Walras. Dupuit's work greatly facilitated the 'mathematisation' of the new mainstream paradigm that was to emerge later in the nineteenth century, including that of Walras.

Two other names that have earned their place in the designated 'gallery' of precursors to Walras in nineteenth-century France include Nicholas-Francois Canard (1750–1833) and Augustin Cournot (1801–1877). Canard was trained in science and was recognised as a mathematician of some standing. His interest in socio-economic issues arose from his interest in particular issues which involved social mathematics, i.e. his attempt to provide a mathematical solution to the problem of the outcomes of the legal judgments of the court system in France and a number of issues of political economy (Baumol and Goldfeld 1968). Unlike the Physiocrats, Canard subscribed to the doctrine that labour was the source of all wealth. Canard distinguished between three categories of income: landed income; industrial income; and income on movable property. From the dynamics of the circulation of income and money and heavily influenced by the laws of liquid dynamics and the theory of the circulation of blood, Canard contributed original and influential insights on the achievement of equilibrium. He also addressed the topic of price determination and is credited with the first application of marginal analysis, all of which were informed by his ambition and optimism in applying the methods of physico-mathematical methods to political economy, sustaining the commitment to the 'mathematization of political economy' (Larson 1989). Canard experienced in his lifetime sustained opposition from a variety of sources, not least from Cournot, arguably the most celebrated of Walras's precursors.

Augustin Cournot (1801–1877) would, within the historiography of political economy, be regarded as the premier mathematician-economist within the French tradition who made major analytical contributions to the emerging framework that would later feature prominently in the neoclassical paradigm.[26] In the domain of mathematical economics, he was the first to formulate the method of applying functional analysis to problems in the socio-economic realm. The use of functional analysis was attractive to Cournot by virtue of the fact that it required, in his analysis, the specification of no more than the most generalised properties of the functional forms which were to describe the underlying law reflected in the articulated functional equations. He also recognised that functional analysis facilitated the relationship between magnitudes that were incapable, for a variety of reasons, of being expressed numerically or the relationship between functions where the underlying law was not capable of being expressed mathematically. While committed to rational mechanics as the paradigmatic framework for use in the economic domain, Cournot was clear in his distinction between the capacity of the generalised mathematically articulated framework such as rational mechanics to provide mechanics with general theorems. However, when it came to their applications they required considerable insight and experience to generate plausible numerical estimates. By analogy, Cournot held that in the application of mathematics to economic problems the same requirements would hold and in the economic domain to an even greater degree. Consequently, he was cognisant of the need for successive applications and approximations arising from the variation in numerical results (Touffut 2007). In the exercise of the application and the pursuit of numerical approximations, Cournot saw a very useful role for the use of statistics, though in general he was not particularly partial to the use of statistics or the application of probabilities in the socio-economic domain.

Cournot differed from the Physiocratic writers and others imbued with the reformist ethos of the Enlightenment in that he eschewed 'normative ambition' from his work, and that, according to Ingrao and Israel, for two explicit reasons. One was 'the limits he himself saw to the application of formal methods to the study of economics.' For Cournot and those who shared his view, only 'certain types of problems are susceptible of formalisation, one of these being the theory of wealth.' The second reason was the problem of deriving normative prescriptions from abstracted theoretical analysis or in his own words the 'immense step in passing from theory to governmental applications' (Ingrao and Israel 1990: 81). Both reservations on Cournot's part provide, in the light of hindsight, salutary reservations that later contributors to the 'mathematisation' of economics should perhaps have been more attentive. Apart from his engaging methodological nuances and indeed his reservations about even the possibility of pursuing a general equilibrium approach in economics, his contributions to economic theorising as later incorporated into the neoclassical paradigm included his contributions to the theory of demand, relating the quantity demanded of a good or service to its monetary price in a single market, and his celebrated theory of market forms, all of which were incorporated into the canon of economic analysis and are well known to students of economics. In addition he articulated such seminal concepts as the elasticity of demand, marginal revenue, marginal cost, monopoly, duopoly, perfect competition and many others. Notwithstanding his theoretical creativity he remained an isolated figure, whose economic work during his own lifetime encountered the various hostile forces, identified earlier, to the project of the 'mathematisation' of economics. It was only later, with the extensive incorporation of mathematics into the economic academy in the twentieth century and to the fact that Cournot was arguably the writer that exerted the most profound influence on Walras, that his contribution to the mathematisation of economics was duly acknowledged.

The 'precursors' as represented by Isnard, Dupuit, Canard and Cournot within the accepted historiographic narrative were critical to maintaining the commitment to the values of Newtonian rational mechanics and the larger cultural ethos of the Enlightenment during the course of the nineteenth century even in the face of the formidable opposition which emerged against the project of mathematising the socio-economic realm. The French contribution, which we have concentrated on here for justified reasons of its centrality and sub-stantive contributions, could be said to have culminated in the work of Léon Walras (1834–1910) and his formulation of a mathematical theory of general equilibrium and its subsequent influence in the twentieth century. In this Walras was 'standing on the shoulders of giants', from his absorption and commitment to Newtonian rational mechanics as the normative paradigm for the analysis of the socio-economic system to the various insights provided by his 'precursors', in particular Cournot. Mention must also be made of Walras's successor at the University of Lausanne, Vilfredo Pareto (1848–1923), a Frenchman by birth but raised in Italy. Pareto, like Walras, was also imbued with the commitment to the mechanical framework as the correct framework to further the analysis of the socio-economic domain and in particular to ground it in a theory of equilibrium using methods and techniques of the physico-mathematical sciences. For Pareto, his aim was to anchor economics in the analytical framework of rational mechanics and to buttress it with empirical data consistent with the framework (Tarascio 1968; Crillo 1978; Cunningham Wood and McLure 1999; McLure 2001).

But Walras is unquestionably the central figure who emerges from this complex trajectory in the evolution of economics and in particular the development of the mathematisation of the discipline. Not that the reception of his work in his own life-time would reflect his pivotal position as now enshrined in the cano-nical narrative. Recognition of his contribution and the conferring of status, which Walras so desired in his own lifetime, would only come later. Since then and particularly during the course of the twentieth century, a voluminous corpus of work on Walras has emerged largely related to his contribution to general equilibrium theory.[27] But something of the flavour of the indifference and active hostility that Walras encountered is vividly conveyed when he first presented his efforts at providing a mathematical interpretation of the economic system at the Institut de France's Académie des Sciences Morales et Politiques.

Pierre Émile Levasseur (1828–1911), French economist and historian, displayed the more vitriolic end of the spectrum of critique and dismissal of attempts to apply mathematics to socio-economic phenomena, which he viewed as methodologically futile. He argued against Walras of the danger:

> that lies in the desire to bring together, as a unit, at any cost, things that are complex by their nature, as in wishing to apply to political economy a method that is excellent for the physical sciences but could not be applied indiscriminately to an order of phenomena whose courses are so variable and complex and that above all involve one eminently variable cause that can absolutely not be reduced to algebraic formulae: human freedom.
>
> (Levasseur in Walras 1874: 119)

The reaction to Walras's endeavours to formulate a mathematical economics based on the equations of exchange within an interdependent system met with similar criticism, even if less dismissive in tone than that of Levasseur, from many of his contemporaries. This forced Walras to secure the support of leading mathematicians and scientists of his day. The most celebrated interchange, albeit brief in content, was unquestionably with the leading French mathematician of his time, Henri Poincaré. Given that in this book we commence our analysis of the relationship between developments in the philosophy of mathematics and economic theorising with Walras, and more specifically with the Walras-Poincaré correspondence, which is the subject of the next chapter where we provide a philosophical analysis of the implications of this correspondence, we will not pursue this topic here.

Walras's campaign to win over the mathematicians, philosophers and scientists of his day following the publication of his *Élements d'economie politique pure* in 1874–1877 was less than successful and even into the early part of the twentieth century the prospects for the project of mathematising the social sciences, with economics being the front-runner, was widely believed to be unworthy of support, if not impossible to achieve. Notwithstanding these setbacks, the mathematisation project was in the course of the 1920s and 1930s to receive major stimulus from contributions which now came from a number of other countries including Britain, Germany, Sweden and in the post-World War II period were to be centred in the United States, to where many of the leading European contributors emigrated during the course of the 1930s under the threat of Nazism. During the nineteenth century individual contributors from a number of countries other than France contributed to the use of mathematics in economics. These included from Germany, Johann Heinrich von Thünen (1783–1850) and Hermann Heinrich Gossen (1810–1858); from Britain, William Stanley Jevon (1835–1882), Francis Ysidro Edgeworth (1845–1926), an Irishman, and Alfred Marshall (1842–1924); from Sweden Knut Wicksell (1851–1926) and from the United States Irving Fisher (1867–1947).[28]

In a rather idiosyncratic account of the march of the 'mathematisation' project in economics, Gerard Debreu, himself a major contributor to twentieth-century mathematical economics and whose philosophy of mathematics will be examined in a later chapter of our book, provides what we may call the 'scientific accidents' theory of the growth of mathematical economics (Debreu 2008). He argues, without elaboration, that the 'steady course on which mathematical economics has held for the past four decades sharply contrasts with its progress during the preceding century, which was marked by several major scientific accidents' (ibid.: 454). He cites three such 'scientific accidents.' The first was the publication of Cournot's *Recherches sur les principes mathématiques de la théorie des richesses* in 1838, which by both 'its mathematical form and economic content ... stands in splendid isolation in time.' The second 'scientific accident' he considers to be the risk that the University of Lausanne took in appointing Walras to a professorial position in 1870, who as Debreu notes 'had held no previous academic appointment, he had published a novel and a short story ... and had not contributed to economic theory before 1870, and he was exactly 36' (ibid.: 454). Hardly a ringing endorsement as far as Debreu was concerned, particularly given what was to follow. Similarly he includes the appointment of Pareto as Walras's successor as part of the risk that Lausanne continued to take, but one that paid off when Pareto published his *Cours d'economie politique* (1896–97), followed by his *Manuel d'economie politique* (1909) and his article 'Economie mathématique' (1911). The third 'accident' for Debreu refers to 'the contemporary period of development of mathematical economics' which was 'profoundly influenced' by John von Neumann and in particular his article of 1928 on games and his 1937 paper on economic growth.

The seminal papers by Wald (1935, 1936a, 1936b) provided further stimulus to the intensification of the mathematisation of economics, as did the introduction of algebraic topology into economic theory when von Neumann generalised Brouwer's fixed point theorem as part of a proof of the existence of an optimal growth path in his growth model. The mainstay of mathematical economics was differential calculus and linear algebra, which had been incorporated into the classic works of John Hicks's *Value and Capital* (1939), Maurice Allais' *A la recherche d'une discipline économique* (1943) and Paul Samuelson's *Foundation of Economic Analysis* (1947). But with the publication of von Neumann and Oskar Morgenstern's *Theory of Games and Economic Behaviour* (1944), new innovations in mathematical forms were introduced into mathematical economics in the form of convex analysis, which was to become central, initially in activity analysis and linear programming and later in mainstream economic theorising. By 1954 proofs of the existence of general equilibrium based on fixed point theorems, albeit under very stringent assumptions, had been delivered. The trajectory and development of the neo-Walrasian programme, as it came to be termed with respect to the development of general equilibrium theory, is comprehensively analysed in Weintraub (1983, 1985).[29] Rehearsing the details of the changing mathematical techniques and methods that came to dominate mainstream economics during the course of the twentieth century is beyond the scope of this section and will not be pursued further here. The remainder of our book will address what we consider to be the major shifts within the philosophy of mathematics in the twentieth century, with the primary focus being on a philosophical analysis of these shifts and their implications for how economic theorising was influenced by these shifts.

The rise of mathematical economics and its influence on the perception, curricular content and internal status of individuals within the discipline has been both dramatic and profound during the course of the twentieth century. Even as this dominance is now being challenged from a variety of sources ranging from those who are opposed to the overuse or misuse of mathematics in economics to a more fundamental dimension by those who argue that the problem is the use of the wrong type of mathematics which has dominated in economics with disastrous results. This latter critique has two dimensions: one methodological as reflected in the extensive corpus of work produced by Tony Lawson of Cambridge University (Lawson 1997, 2003a, 2003b, 2015);[30] in this context mention must also be made of the work of Philip Mirowski, a strident critic of mainstream neoclassical economics, who in recent years had advocated an alternative to the mainstream paradigm in the form of a theory of markets viewed as automata, a view inspired by the work of John von Neumann (Mirowski 2002, 2007, 2012). A second line of critique is the mathematically based work of Vela Velupillai, which represents a rigorously articulated and challenging perspective to the mainstream framework of mathematical economics (Velupillai 2000, 2005b, 2010).[31] This latter contribution must be viewed within developments in twentieth-century philosophy of mathematics, including Brouwerian intuitionism and the work of Turing, Church and Bishop in the field of computation. In later chapters of our book we will examine aspects of these developments in the philosophy of mathematics in the course of the twentieth century.

With the spectacular rise to dominance of the mathematical formalisation of economics particularly during the twentieth century, this dominance is now coming under increasing critical scrutiny within the discipline.

Notwithstanding the variegated sources of critique and contra-voices being raised against the rapid rise to dominance of mathematical economics, more pertinently a particular type of mathematical economics, a pertinent question has emerged which is of considerable interest in the historiography of twentieth-century economics. This question is encapsulated in the title of Weintraub's book, *How Economics became a Mathematical Science* (2002). If this issue is to be adequately addressed, considerable work will need to be undertaken in at least three dimensions: historiographical examination of the evolution and lineage of quantification, formalisation and the importation of mathematics into economics; a rigorous analysis of the philosophical/methodological principles that underlie the mathematical frameworks advocated and deployed in socio-economic analysis along with a critical examination of their contribution to our understanding of the economic systems and their working; and finally the sociological/cultural background of larger external forces that have and will continue to exert very considerable influence on the shaping of socio–economic analysis as they have done in the past.

In this chapter we have attempted to provide no more than a skeletal outline of the historical evolution, from Petty's 'political arithmetic' in the seventeenth century to developments in the twentieth century. The modest aim of the chapter was to convey the central idea that concern with quantification/formalisation is not of recent origin and to portrait it otherwise would be to display an extremely parochial view in time and place. A second subsidiary aim was to provide a context against which to view the developments in the philosophy of mathematics during the course of the twentieth century and its implications for economics from a philosophical perspective. The remainder of the book will address these developments in the philosophy of mathematics during the twentieth century, so that serious students of economics will be motivated to explore further and reflect at some length on what kind of discipline economics has become under the influence of mathematics in order to establish both the benefits and the costs of that influence.

Notes

1 Hodgson has compiled and edited an excellent collection of papers dealing with the relationship of Mathematics and Economics organised around a number of thematic areas covering the post-1945 period.

2 In his 1952 paper, Samuelson at the outset stated that he came 'not to praise mathematics, but rather to slightly debunk its use in economics. I do so out of tenderness for the subject, since I firmly believe in the virtues of understatement and lack of pretension.' At the end of the paper Samuelson noted that 'one of my older friends' who complained to Samuelson that, 'These days one can hardly tell a mathematical economist from an ordinary economist', which reflected the perception of an older generation that by 1952 the take-over by mathematics was near to completion, if not complete!

3 Tracing this relationship and providing an adequate intellectual context would warrant a major study in its own right. All that can be provided in this chapter is a skeletal outline of some of the principal developments in this complex relationship.

4 Schumpeter in fact refers to them as 'Econometricians', which may strike present-day readers as somewhat odd. He further insists that 'their works illustrate to perfection what Econometrics is and what Econometricians are trying to do' (Schumpeter 1954: 209). He refers the reader in a footnote to the fact that 'The word Econometrics is, I think, Professor Frisch's', and Schumpeter directs the reader to the first number of *Econometrica*, published in January 1933, as the new journal of the Econometric Society which had been founded two years earlier. In a short Editorial to the first issue of *Econometrica*, Frisch provides a succinct and perceptive overview of his understanding of Econometrics. Schumpeter's insistence on the use of the word 'Econometricians' to describe the work of eighteenth-century contributors in the light of Frisch's Editorial appears somewhat off to say the least.

5 Hermann Conring (1608–1681) in the seventeenth century was a leading pioneer in the provision of such courses (Lindenfeld 1997). Schumpeter in fact claims that Contring 'is usually credited with having been the first to give lectures of this kind' (Schumpeter 1954: 209). Later in the eighteenth century Gottfried Achenwall (1719–1772), an economist and statistician, and professor of philosophy at Gottingen (1750–1772), gave similar courses. Ackenwall was claimed by German academics as the 'Father of Statistics', a claim disputed by British writers who would defend William Petty's right to that title. If Achenwall was not the originator of the science

of statistics, he was certainly one of the first; if not the actual first, to articulate and define its purpose.

6 Hobbes had served as secretary to Bacon, during the middle of the 1620s, and translated a number of the latter's essays into Latin (Martinich 2005).

7 Petty's appointment in Gresham College was largely due to his good friend John Graunt (1620–1674), who for many is regarded as the 'founder of statistics'. Whatever of this overarching claim he was certainly the pivotal figure in England or elsewhere in the development of population statistics or demography. In a tercentenary tribute, it was stated of Graunt that he 'was the first person to whom it occurred that numerical information on human populations could be of more than ephemeral interest' (Sutherland 1963: 554).

8 The 'Invisible College' was more specifically the 'Oxford Club' of experimentalists imbued with the Baconian approach to scientific knowledge which formed around John Wilkin (1614–1672), who was Warden of Wadham College in Oxford from 1648 to 1659. He attracted an extremely talented group of scientists, mathematicians, and philosophers and distinguished physicians among others to the so called 'Oxford Club'. These included, among others, Jonathan Goddard, John Wallis, Seth Ward, Ralph Bathurst, Robert Boyle, William Petty, Thomas Willis, Christopher Wren and Matthew Wren.

9 In addition to Strauss (1954), earlier profiles and biographies of Petty include John Aubrey, *Brief Lives*, edited and annotated in Bennett (2015) and Fitzmaurice (1895). It should be noted that Aubrey's *Brief Lives* has an interesting publication career in its own right since they were first compiled in the seventeenth century. The 2015 edition cited here represents the most complete and scholarly compendium in two volumes and is the first annotated critical edition of *Brief Lives* by the leading authority on Aubrey's work, Dr Kate Bennett of Magdalen College, Oxford, and are published by Oxford University Press.

10 For an extended historical treatment of the Cromwellian period and the following Restoration period see Barnard (2000), Dennehy (2008), Jordan (2007). For Petty's more elaborate and outlandish proposals for the colonisation of Ireland or what became known as the 'transmutation of the Irish', see McCormick (2008), and Fanning (2015). For a comprehensive and detailed scholarly account of Petty's career, particularly in Ireland, and the intellectual origins, commitment and use of political arithmetic by Petty, see McCormick's excellent study (McCormick 2009). See also Fox (2009) for an interesting account of Petty's involvement in Ireland.

11 While the legal defence of his Irish estates did indeed preoccupy an inordinate amount of time and effort on Petty's part, on his return to London in the late 1650s he delved back into a very active life mainly focused on politics, science and writing. He served briefly as a Member of Parliament, and having re-established his contacts with his scientific acquaintances he was centrally involved in the establishment of the Royal Society of London for the Improving of Natural Knowledge in 1662, and remained an active member for the remainder of his life. Four years before his death, Petty was one of the founding members of and first President of the Dublin Philosophical Society in 1683. This was the period, following his return to London and over the next three decades, that Petty would produce most of his major works, even though several of them were not published until after his death. For a bibliography of Petty's writings see Keynes (1972).

12 Pursuing the issue as to whether Petty's methodological approach was predominantly informed by either an inductive or deductive approach has not proved particularly fruitful or insightful. A careful reading of Petty's work would clearly indicate, in our estimation, that methodologically Petty was much more indebted to Hobbes than to Bacon.

13 For a brief account of Petty's 'political arithmetic' following his death see Aspromourgos (1996), but for a more extended examination see Hoppit (1996).

14 For some recent studies of the broader intellectual culture of the Enlightenment, see Dupré (2004), Pagden (2013), and Ferrone (2015).

15 On the Cameralist tradition, see the older study by Small (2001 [1909]) and Wakefield (2009).

16 On Cantillon's life and seminal contribution to economics, see Murphy (1986) and Brewer (1992).

17 For a more contested view of the Enlightenment, see the challenging work of Jonathan Israel in particular Israel (2001, 2006, 2010, 2011).

18 For interesting overviews on this topic, see Guerlac (1981), Dobbs and Jacob (1995).

19 There is an extensive literature on this period, or what is sometimes referred to as 'Newtonian Britain'. See Stewart (1992) for an informative overview of this topic and period in England.

20 See Schumpeter (1954), Pribam (1983), Hutchison (1988), Screpanti and Zamagni (1995), Robbins (1998), Roncaglia (2005) and Agnar (2011).

21 On Quesnay, see the classic work by Meek (1962), along with Kuczynski and Meek (1972), Eltis (1975a, 1975b), and Vaggi (1987).

22 Turgot's work is comprehensively covered in Groenewegen (1977, 2002), Meek (1973), Palmer (1976), and Brewer (1987). For a broader and insightful intellectual perspective on Physiocracy, see Hochstrasser (2006).

23 Over the last twenty years there has been a renewed interest in the work of Jean-Baptiste Say within French political economy more generally. See Palmer (1977), Faccarello (1998), Steiner (1998), Forget (1999), Whatmore (2000), Arena (2000), Kates (2003), Hollander (2005).

24 For an analysis of these differences see the references in Note 14 above. For an intellectual overview of political economy in the nineteenth century see Rothschild (2011).

25 For an analysis of Isnard's work and his contribution to Walras's general equilibrium theory, see Jaffé (1960), Theocharis (1983) and van der Berg (2005).

26 Cournot's work is examined in all the major works on the history of economic thought, for instance, those in Note 20 above.

27 Pre-eminent among the many writers who have contributed to Walrasian scholarship has been the work of William Jaffé and more recently Donald A. Walker. See among other works of these writers the following: Jaffé (1965, 1983), Walker (1996, 2006). See also Van Daal and Jolink (1993), Jolink (1996), Arrow and Hahn (1971), Morishima (1977), Mas-Collel (1985). For an interesting account of the history of the proof of the central theorem of general equilibrium, see Düppe and Weintraub (2014).

28 See Ekelund and Hébert (2014) for an overview of their contributions and the excellent individual entries for these economists in Durlauf and Blume (2008).

29 There is an extensive literature on general equilibrium theory. In addition to the outstanding study by Ingrao and Israel (1990), see Kirman (1998), Petri and Hahn (2003) and Bridel (2011). For a useful compendium of entries pertaining to general equilibrium see Eatwell, Milgate and Newman (1989).

30 Over the last thirty years Lawson has produced an extensive and impressive volume on work in which he has emerged as the leading advocate of critical realism and the centrality of social ontology as the most appropriate philosophy to underlie economics and the social sciences more generally. See more recently Lawson (2015) and for evaluations of his work see Boylan and O'Gorman (1995), Fleetwood (1999) and Fullbrook (2009).

31 Velupillai has produced an astonishing and challenging volume of work over the course of his career in his relentless search for an 'alternative' mathematics for the formalisation of economics based on a deep and reflective reading of the philosophy of mathematics. For tributes to and assessment of his contributions see Zambelli (2010) and the *Special Issue* of the journal *New Mathematics and Natural Computation*, 8 (1), 2012: 1–152.

2 Walras' programme

The Walras–Poincaré correspondence reassessed

Introduction

Over recent decades a diversified and stimulating scholarship on Walras' contribution to the history of economic thought has been developed. This scholarship is so extensive it would take more than one volume to critically engage it. In this chapter, in line with the overall theme of this work, we have a very limited focus, namely the philosophy of applied mathematics used by Walras in his unique defence of his theoretical economics. To this end we engage both his *Elements* and his famous, definitive defence of it in his 'Economique et Mechanique' through the lens of Poincaré's philosophy of applied mathematics. This novel approach was inspired by Walras' correspondence with Poincaré – the leading French and European mathematician of Walras' era.

When his programme for the mathematisation of economics received a hostile reception, even among some leading French mathematicians, Walras wrote to Poincaré for support and included with his first letter a copy of his *Elements*. By contextualising Poincaré's response in Poincaré's own philosophy of applied mathematics we offer the reader a more detailed understanding of the originality of Walras' own philosophy of economic theorising. On the level of critical evaluation, as opposed to the exposition of Walras' philosophy of economic theorising, we show how Poincaré developed a hierarchy of reservations about Walras' specific programme culminating in Poincaré's suggestion (politely expressed) that some of Walras' economic theses in his *Elements* went beyond the proper limits of a theoretical mathematical science.

Vis-à-vis Walras' central defence of his philosophy of economic theorising in his 'Economique et Mechanique' (translated by Mirowski and Cook and published in 1990), we focus on Walras' take on Poincaré's philosophy of mathematical physics. We show how Walras used Poincaré as a stepping-stone in developing his own (Walras') scientific realist philosophy of mathematical physics. In his scientific realist philosophy, the principles of mechanics, enunciated in differential equations, are the essential causal mechanisms governing motion in the universe. We show how Walras transfers this scientific realist philosophy to his principles of economics also articulated in differential equations: his principles of economics are the fundamental causal mechanisms governing the economic world.

We conclude by arguing that, while Walras was within his rights in using Poincaré's stature as the leading European mathematician to support the general programme of the mathematisation of economics, he fails to draw the reader's attention to the fact that Poincaré explicitly rejected the same scientific realist reading of the principles of mechanics adumbrated by Walras in his methodological defence of his economic theorising.

This chapter is structured as follows. We open by contextualising Walras' novel agenda of the mathematisation of economics in the context of Walras' own time. Then we introduce what we call three phases in the Walras-Poincaré correspondence where Poincaré raises various reservations about the details of Walras' defence of his programme. We follow with an elaboration of Walras' scientific realist reading of theoretical economics in light of his scientific realist reading of the principles of mechanics. We conclude by comparing and contrasting Walras' scientific realist reading of his principles with Poincaré's alternative explanation of the robustness of such principles.

The Walrasian programme in the context of the moral sciences

As Jaffé pointed out, as early as 1873, in his address to the Académie des sciences morales et politiques in Paris, Walras justified his thesis of the measurability of utility by analogy to mechanics, especially the measurement of the mass of a body. Walras was attacked 'by the bigwigs of the Académie', on the grounds that 'it was "false and dangerous" to treat imponderables mathematically' (Jaffé 1977b: 301). Taken in the intellectual context of its time, this hostility to the mathematisation of theoretical economics, as correctly suggested by Mirowski and Cook for instance, should not be read 'as a tale of ignorance and backwardness' (Mirowski and Cook 1990: 194). We note two influential trends which buttress this suggestion.

Firstly, in so far as theoretical economics was seen as being contained within the ambit of the moral sciences, it would be seen by a considerable number of moral scientists as not being comparable to the physical sciences in general and mechanics in particular. In broad philosophical terms the domain of the moral sciences is *human action*. A human action has two distinct dimensions: an *external behavioural dimension* and an *internal, private, mental dimension*. The behavioural, external dimension is intersubjectively observable and thus in principle may be studied by the method of the physical sciences. However, the internal private mental world of any individual is not intersubjectively observable: each individual has privileged access to the contents of his/her own private mind or stream of consciousness. This private internal dimension, studied in philosophy, is not accessible to the methods of the physical sciences. In this context Walras' analogy to mechanics is not persuasive: the fundamentals of mechanics, such as distance, velocity and acceleration, are intersubjectively measurable but these, unlike the fundamentals of a private mind, have no internal dimension. For moral scientists with this kind of disposition, Walras' utility belongs to the private mental sphere and not the sphere of what is measurable à la physics/mechanics.

Of course not all French moral scientists were resolutely committed to this philosophical conception of the domain of the moral sciences. Some, under the influence of Auguste Comte, would be sceptical about a separate domain of philosophy, which smacked of metaphysics. However, while sharing Comte's suspicion of metaphysics, they retained a Comteian suspicion vis-á-vis the application of mathematics to the moral sciences. Comte viewed the sciences in a hierarchical order of abstractness and complexity, ranging from mathematics and astronomy to sociology. As Porter, for instance, points out, Comte 'firmly refused to privilege mathematics or measurement as motors of the progress of science' (Porter 2001: 5). This hostility was buttressed by various scandalous attempts at the application of probability theory – then in its infancy – to specific, concrete issues in the moral sciences.

One notorious scandal was the use of probability theory in the infamous Dreyfus affair which polarised French citizens and rocked the Third Republic. Captain Dreyfus was a Jewish army officer, convicted in the 1890s of spying for Germany and imprisoned in Devil's Island. The prosecution used probability theory to buttress its contention that the handwriting on the central piece of evidence was that of Dreyfus. Eventually a group of experts, led by Poincaré, who was correctly perceived as the leading French probability theorist of the time, evaluated the evidence.[1] After exposing various errors in the use of probability theory by the 'experts' for the prosecution, Poincaré, who authored the report, sums up as follows.

> However, a priori, probability *in questions such as the one in which we are engaged* is simply made up of moral elements which are totally excluded from calculation ... Thus Auguste Comte has quite rightly stated that the application of probability calculation to the moral sciences was the scandal of mathematics. Wishing to eliminate moral elements by substituting numbers is as dangerous as it is useless.
>
> Simply put, the calculus of probability is not, as one would appear to believe, a marvellous science which exempts the learned (savant) from having common sense.
>
> This is why one should never apply calculations to moral issues; if we do this it is us who are constrained by it.
>
> (Poincaré, Darboux and Appell 1908: 503 as quoted
> in Rollet 1997: 88, italics added)

While the Dreyfus affair exemplified the specific difficulties with the application of probability theory *when one attempts to infer from a given effect to its cause in the domain of the moral sciences*, it also clearly indicates the influences exerted by Comteian scepticism towards the mathematisation project for the moral sciences. Needless to say, Walras was not impressed by any such scepticism. He dismisses his hostile reception in the Académie in his preface to the fourth edition of his *Elements* as follows:

> I grieve for this learned body ... So far as I am concerned the cold reception I had from the Académie actually brought me good luck, for

since that time the doctrine I espoused twenty seven years ago has gained wide acceptance both in form and content.

Everyone competent in the field knows that the theory of exchange ... which was evolved almost simultaneously by Jevons, Menger and myself and which *constitutes the very foundation of the whole edifice of economics*, has become an integral part of the science in England, Austria, the United States, and wherever pure economics is developed and taught.

(Walras 2003: 44)

Vis-á-vis those opposed to his project on philosophical grounds Walras adopted the strategy of ignoring them. Thus in concluding his preface to the fourth edition of his *Elements* he says:

As for these economists who do not know any mathematics, who do not even know what is meant by mathematics and yet have taken the stand that mathematics cannot possibly serve to elucidate economic principles, let them go their way repeating that 'human liberty will *never* allow itself to be cast into equations' or that 'mathematics ignores frictions which are *everything* in social sciences' and other equally forceful and flowery phrases. They can never prevent the theory of the determination of prices under free competition from becoming a mathematical theory.

(Walras 2003: 47)

The Walras–Poincaré correspondence, Phase I: the mathematisation of economics

Twenty-seven years later, however, all was not well for Walras' programme of the mathematisation of 'the very foundation of the whole edifice of economics' among various French mathematicians, particularly those open to the use of mathematics in economics. The distinguished French mathematician Hermann Laurent had an extensive correspondence with Walras. In 1898 he described himself as one of Walras' 'most devout (plus fervent) followers' (Jaffé 1965, 3: letter 1383). Laurent, to what must have been the utter surprise and disappointment of Walras, at a meeting in June 1900 of the L'Institut des Actuaires Francais – which according to Laurent had extended its interests to the issue of furnishing a real scientific basis for political economy – attacked Walras' efforts to construct a theory of price determination by making utility measurable. While Laurent praised Walras for 'opening up new horizons' and, with Pareto, for 'supplying a corner stone in the edifice', he posed the rhetorical question 'how can one accept that satisfaction be measured? No mathematician will ever consent to that' (Jaffé 1965, 113, letter 1448, note 2). Not surprisingly, as Jaffé notes, Walras was cruelly shaken (Jaffé 1977b: 301). In September of the following year Walras wrote to Poincaré and included a copy of the fourth edition of his *Elements*. In this letter he points out that he has devoted thirty years improving it in four successive editions. It is clear from Walras' letter that he was fully aware of the mathematical genius of Poincaré: he states that his own (Walras') mathematical ability is modest, at least in comparison with his own economic competence. He identifies for Poincaré the key issue which is 'crucial for both scientific and social progress', namely 'the cause of the application of the mathematical method to political economy in a country as conservative and authoritarian as ours' (Jaffé 1965, 3: 158, letter 1492).

Poincaré is quick in responding. He informs Walras that he has read his work and immediately adds that he is 'not, a priori, hostile to the application of mathematics to the science of economics provided one does not go beyond *certain limits*'. He concludes by saying that Walras' efforts 'have led to interesting results' (Jaffé 1965, 3: 160–161, letter 1494). Certainly Poincaré's response is brief and to the point, namely a priori he has no objection to using mathematics in economic theorising, on condition that certain limits are not transgressed. This may appear surprising in view of how Poincaré used the Comteian thesis as noted in the previous section.[2] Poincaré, however, was there concerned with the difficulties in exploiting probability theory in applied areas of the moral sciences. Walras' *Elements* concerns theoretical, as distinct from applied, economics and thus Poincaré would not necessarily read it through Comteian eyes.

Moreover, we know that Poincaré supervised Louis Bachelier's thesis *Théorie de la Spéculation*, which exploits probability theory and which today is acknowledged by some as a 'pioneering analysis of the stock and options market' and 'the birthdate of mathematical finance' (Courtault et al. 2000: 341). As Bru points out Bachelier's thesis was out of the ordinary for its time: 'it was a mathematical physics thesis (Poincaré held the chair of mathematical physics and the calculus of probability) but since it was not physics, it was about the Stock Exchange, it was not a recognised subject' (Taqqu 2001: 6). In his report in March 1900, Poincaré alludes to this and points out that Bachelier's thesis 'focuses on the application of Probability Theory to the Stock Exchange'. Echoing Comteian reservations, Poincaré continues 'one might fear that the author has *exaggerated* the applicability of Probability Theory *as has often been done*. Fortunately this is *not* the case … he strives to *set limits* within which one can *legitimately apply* this type of calculation' (Courtault et al. 2000: 348. The authors have added Poincaré's report as an appendix to their research, italics added). Once again we see Poincaré's preoccupation with the issue of limits to the legitimate application of mathematics in the human sciences. This issue is a core theme of subsequent sections of this chapter. For the moment, we see that in writing to Poincaré, Walras was not only addressing an internationally recognised mathematical genius, he was also writing to an openminded academic who was willing to encourage theoretical innovation and to push out the boundaries of theoretical research. It is the same Poincaré who once remarked that 'thanks to the education it has received, our imagination, like the eagle's eye the sun does not dazzle, can look truth in the face' (Poincaré 1958: 88).

Vis-à-vis Walras' modest competence at mathematics,[3] this was not a problem for Poincaré. According to Poincaré there are 'two entirely different kinds of minds' in the mathematical sciences (Poincaré 1958: 15). The first is pre-occupied with logic and the quest for the highest standards of rigour possible. The second kind of mind is 'guided by intuition and at first stroke makes quick but sometimes precarious conquests, like bold cavalrymen of the advance guard' (Poincaré 1958: 15). Both kinds of minds are equally necessary. 'Each is indispensable. Logic, which alone can give certainty is the instrument of demonstration, intuition is the instrument of invention' (Poincaré 1958: 23).

According to Poincaré 'there are many kinds of intuition' in the mathematical sciences (Poincaré 1963: 20). In particular intuition is indispensable in applied mathematics: 'without intuition (young minds) would never become capable of applying mathematics' (Poincaré 1958: 21). Of course intuition is fallible: expert pure and applied mathematicians make mistakes, they 'are not infallible' (Poincaré 1952: 47). In Poincaré's eyes 'an imperfect solution may happen to lead us towards a better one' (Poincaré 1956: 38). Thus one may reasonably speculate that Poincaré viewed Walras' *Elements* as a piece of applied mathe-matics[4] in its infancy and which would require much more work before attaining anything comparable to the status of mathematical physics. Indeed Walras was fortunate in appealing to an intuitive mathematical mind like that of a Poincaré, rather than the strictly rigorous mathematical mind of a Hilbert, who would have no tolerance for lack of expertise in mathematics.

Be that as it may, we now turn to Poincaré's reservation: a priori he has no objection to the use of mathematics in economic theorising, on condition that one remains within certain limits. Unfortunately he gives no indication to Walras of what these limits might be. As we have already noted, we know from his report on Bachelier's thesis, written eighteen months prior to his response to Walras, he was concerned about 'exaggerations' which result from the abuse of probability theory in the moral sciences and he praises Bachelier for acknowledging '*the limits* within which one can legitimately apply this type of calculation' (Courtault et al. 2000: 348, italics added).

We also know from Poincaré's reflections on other mathematical disciplines that he was concerned about misconceptions/exaggerations about what is achievable in these disciplines. For instance, while acknowledging the con-tribution of Russell's logic,[5] Poincaré was concerned about the exaggeration in Russell's logicist programme which, in Poincaré's eyes, erroneously attempted to reduce pure mathematics to logic. Any such programme fails to do justice to mathematical practice and thereby ignores the intuitive-creative dimension of pure mathematics. Was Poincaré signalling to Walras that, while he had attained interesting results, his thesis that his *Elements* 'constitutes the very foundation of the whole edifice of economics' (Walras 2003: 44) was an unjustifiable exaggeration? We will return to this issue in a later section. What we do know is that Poincaré's qualification rang alarm bells for Walras, in particular, it flushed out Walras' more specific concern, i.e. the cardinal measurability of utility, raised by Laurent.

The Walrasian–Poincaré correspondence, Phase II: the measurement of utility

In his response to Poincaré, Walras gets directly to the point. Basically he tells Poincaré that Laurent – the Vice-President of l'Institut des Actuaires – accused Walras of transgressing proper limits in propounding the measurability of utility.

> I have supposed rareté (or intensity of the last want satisfied) to be 'a decreasing function of the *quantity consumed* of a commodity' and I added that while this rareté is not a measurable magnitude, it suffices to think of it as such in order to obtain the principal laws of political economy from the fact that rareté decreases.
>
> (Jaffé 1965, 3: 161–162, letter 1495)

This is what Laurent perceived as going beyond proper limits. Walras justifies his thesis by analogy to celestial mechanics, in particular, the indispensable role which the concept of the mass of a body plays in that mathematical science. He draws Poincaré's attention to Poinsot's *La Statique*, where the mass of a body is defined as 'the number of molecules of a body' or 'the amount of matter it contains' (Jaffé 1965, 3: 162, letter 1495).[6] Clearly the notion of the mass of a body is central to the success story of mathematical physics and the articulation of the laws of mechanics. According to Walras this central notion is treated as 'an appreciable magnitude' in mechanics, but it is *not* so, since 'no one has ever counted the number of molecules in any body' (Jaffé 1965, 3: 162, letter 1495).

Unfortunately Walras does not expand on this central point. We take him to mean something along the following lines. The concept of the mass of a body is unquestionably a central concept in mechanics/mathematical physics. However, when scientists come to define this notion they end up with something like Poinsot's definition: the amount of matter in a body – a rather metaphysical definition based on the metaphysical notion of matter – or the number of molecules in a body, a number which no one has counted! Whichever definition of mass one prefers, being 'an appreciable magnitude' is not explicitly contained in its definition. Yet the success of mechanics depends on the assumption that mass is an appreciable magnitude. Similarly with the concept of rareté: in theoretical economics it is taken to be an appreciable magnitude, even though that is not part of its conventional definition. In other words, just as the concept of mass, taken as an appreciable magnitude, is indispensable to the proper articulation of the laws of mechanics, the concept of rareté, as a measurable magnitude, is indispensable to the proper articulation of the fundamental laws of economics.

In his reply, which is much longer than his first letter, Poincaré raises a number of key issues, the first being Walras' defence of the cardinal measure of utility. Vis-à-vis Laurent's critique of Walras, Poincaré says 'You misunderstood my thoughts. I never wished to say that you have gone beyond proper limits' (Jaffé 1965, 3: 162, letter 1496). Laurent's accusation, in Poincaré's eyes, is not justified. Without reading any further, Walras must have been relieved.

Poincaré was not siding with Laurent on this crucial issue. Indeed Poincaré immediately adds that 'your definition of rareté seems to me to be legitimate' (Jaffé 1965, 3: 162, letter 1496) – again music to Walras' ears. Poincaré, however, proceeds to legitimate Walras' definition of rareté as the intensity of the last want satisfied, without any reference to the notion of the mass of a body in mechanics – a cornerstone of Walras' justification. Whatever difficulties one may encounter vis-à-vis the proper definition of the notion of the mass of a body – the notion of the mass of a body is what is frequently called a cardinal magnitude concept.

For any cardinal magnitude concept, e.g. weight, one has a unit, e.g. kilogram, which is used to determine *how much* greater/smaller or *how many times* greater/smaller the weight of one body is relative to another. If body A weighs 88 kilos and body B weighs 22 kilos the following inferences make *empirical* sense: (a) A is heavier than B, (b) A is four times heavier than B, (c) if any other body C weighs 88 kilos it is equal in weight to A. Moreover, if we change the unit of measurement to, say, a pound weight, the above relationships (a), (b) and (c) still hold. According to Poincaré, Walras' notion of utility/rareté is *not* a cardinal magnitude concept. If cardinality, thus understood, is taken as a defining characteristic of a measurable magnitude, then satisfaction, in Poincaré's terminology, is a 'non-measurable magnitude' (Jaffé 1965, 3: 162, letter 1496).

Poincaré, however, points out that there is another kind of magnitude in the physical sciences to which differential calculus (a distinguishing characteristic of Walras' approach) is also, in principle, applicable. We will call this non-cardinal, or ordinal magnitude. In non-cardinal or ordinal measurement questions about *how much* or *how many times* greater are meaningless. Poincaré uses *temperature* as a clear example of an ordinal magnitude. Here the scales used are limited to determining the *order* in a continuous increasing/decreasing way, but they do not enable one to say *how much or how many times* greater. There is nothing in the process of constructing a temperature scale which justifies making such a claim. For instance if the temperature of liquid A measures 122°F and the temperature of liquid B measures 61°F these transfer into 50°C and 16.1°C in the Celsius Scale. Whereas 122 is twice 61, clearly 50 is greater than twice times 16.1. In this case both scales are ordinal telling us that liquid A is hotter than liquid B but not that it is so many times hotter.[7]

Clearly, Poincaré is suggesting that Walras' analogy to the measurement of the mass of body is misleading: the measurement of mass is cardinal, whereas the measurement of satisfaction – where satisfaction is linked by Poincaré to an individual's preferences – is ordinal. Satisfaction, thus understood in terms of preferences, can be defined by any monotonically increasing function, which in principle opens the door to Walras' exploitation of differential calculus. As Jaffé perceptively notes, with Poincaré's very brief analysis 'we seem to be brought to the threshold of the modern ordered preference analysis of consumers' behaviour' (Jaffé 1977b: 304).

As we will see later, despite Poincaré's critique, Walras continued to use his analogy to the measurement of the mass of a body to justify his mathematical approach to utility. In his correspondence with other interested parties, Walras frequently quotes Poincaré as a supporter of his thesis of the measurability of satisfaction. In December 1906 he obtained permission from Poincaré to quote whole or part of Poincaré's correspondence. Walras eventually published the second letter in full in an appendix to his piece 'Economics and Mechanics' (1909).

The Walras–Poincaré correspondence, Phase III: Poincaré's hierarchy of reservations

To recap, Walras must have been rather pleased with Poincaré's response thus far. The leading French mathematician and one of the most prestigious European mathematicians at the time has no objection in principle to the use of mathematics in theoretical economics (subject to certain constraints). Moreover he legitimates the (ordinal) measurement of utility, thereby opening up theoretical economics to the rich repertoire of tools available in differential calculus. Poincaré now begins to change direction: reservations and possible pitfalls are signalled.

The first reservation concerns the use of what Poincaré calls 'arbitrary functions' in Walras' *Elements* (Jaffé 1965, 3: 163, letter 1496). Poincaré agrees that Walras has every right to draw out the consequences of these by the proper use of mathematics. The pitfall, according to Poincaré, lies in the status of the conclusions thus obtained: 'if the arbitrary functions still appear in the conclusions, the conclusions are not false, *but they are totally without interest*' (Jaffé 1965, 3: 163, letter 1496). Consequently one must do one's utmost to eliminate these arbitrary functions and '*that is what you are doing*' (ibid.). In his letter, Poincaré unfortunately does not define what he means by arbitrary functions and neither does he expand on how the conclusions are totally without interest. Vis-à-vis the latter, i.e. totally without interest, conclusions impregnated by Walras' arbitrary functions are presumably without interest to the theoretical economist: since they are correctly derived they would be of interest to the pure mathematician whose primary concerns are *consistency* and *logical validity*. Perhaps Poincaré is here suggesting an important research project for the Walrasian theoretical economist. This project would entail (a) identifying the arbitrary functions in Walras' theoretical economics, (b) ascertaining whether or not the arbitrary dimension is contained in the conclusion, (c) eliminate, if possible, this arbitrary element. If this programme is not successfully completed, i.e. if the arbitrary is not eliminated, the theory is economically speaking without interest. In this connection Jaffé argues that the cardinal measurability of utility is an arbitrary presence as demonstrated by Poincaré and that it remains present in Walras' 'proof of the fundamental proportionality of marginal utilities to parametric prices as a condition of equilibrium' (Jaffé 1977b: 304). Poincaré gives a different example.

I can tell whether the satisfaction experienced by the same individual is greater under one set of circumstances than under another set of circumstances; but I have no way of comparing the satisfactions experienced by two individuals. This increases the number of arbitrary functions to be eliminated.

(Jaffé 1965, 3: 163, letter 1496)

Thus Poincaré is challenging Walras to systematically and comprehensively engage the issue of the *interpersonal comparison of utility*. Poincaré is clearly cognisant of the individual and subjective characterisation of Walras' rareté and a priori he can't see how the raretés of different individuals can be either compared or aggregated. Until this issue is successfully addressed, Walras' theory is potentially arbitrary and thus possibly without interest to theoretical economists.

Vis-à-vis the issue of what Poincaré means by the expression 'arbitrary function/hypothesis', it is useful to consult his *Science and Hypothesis*. In that work he repeatedly contrasts the successful or fruitful hypotheses of the mathematical sciences with arbitrary hypotheses. All of the hypotheses of applied mathematics discussed go beyond what is given in experience or experimentally verified. These hypotheses have proved to be very fruitful, whereas an arbitrary hypothesis is 'not fertile' (Poincaré 1952: xxiii). Moreover, an arbitrary hypothesis 'is the child of our caprice' (Poincaré 1952: 136). Furthermore, hypotheses which go beyond the boundaries of experience would be arbitrary 'if we lost sight of the experiments which led the founders of the science to adopt them and which, imperfect as they were, were sufficient to justify their adoption' (Poincaré 1952: 110). In short a hypothesis is arbitrary if it is a capricious construct which lacks roots in experience or which fails to approximate to some observable situation. The pitfall of the failure to eliminate the arbitrary from the conclusions of an applied mathematical science has to be balanced with Poincaré's appreciation of what he calls 'daring hypotheses' (Poincaré 1952: 239). These are hypotheses which initially have no experimental support but after a number of years are experimentally vindicated.[8] Our suggestion in the previous section, viz. that Poincaré read Walras' *Elements* as a pioneering piece of research in its early phase of development was motivated by Poincaré's appreciation of the pitfall of *arbitrary* hypotheses on the one hand and his appreciation of *daring hypotheses* on the other. For instance his challenge to Walrasian theoreticians to systematically and comprehensively engage the issue of the intersubjective comparison of utility could possibly turn this prima facie arbitrary hypothesis into a daring one. Only future research can decide this issue: one has no crystal ball to foretell how this will pan out. However, if the arbitrary still persists, then Walrasian theory will lack interest to economic theoreticians.

Poincaré opens his final paragraph by pointing out that all of the above has nothing to do with his requirement of staying within proper limits stipulated in his first letter. This would suggest that the reservations outlined above do not imply that Walras' use of arbitrary hypotheses, like the hypothesis of the interpersonal comparison of utility, puts Walras' project outside the domain of what is legitimate theoretical research in applied mathematics. Future research will ultimately decide whether this range of hypotheses is devoid of theoretical interest. To explain what Poincaré had in mind by his requirement to stay within proper limits, he starts with the truism that all applied mathematical research at the theoretical level uses hypotheses. He immediately adds that if that theoretical research 'is to be fruitful, it is necessary (as in applications to physics) that one be aware of these hypotheses. If one forgets this condition one oversteps proper limits' (Jaffé 1965, 3: 163, letter 1496). Poincaré, rather politely, proceeds to provide clear examples of how Walras forgot this elementary truth and thereby overstepped the proper limits. His examples are Walras' hypotheses that agents are infinitely self-seeking and infinitely clairvoyant. These *arbitrary hypotheses,* especially the second one, prima facie at least, place Walras' theoretical work beyond the pale of applied mathematical science. Such arbitrary hypotheses, unlike the arbitrary hypothesis of the intersubjective comparison of utility, go beyond the acceptable limits for a scientific theory.

Why? The reason is to be found in Poincaré's thesis that 'isolated theory is empty and experience is blind; and both are useless and of no interest alone. To neglect one for the other would be folly' (Poincaré 1952: 275). Walras' hypothesis of *infinite clairvoyance* (what economists call perfect foresight) falls foul of Poincare's basic requirement that *theoretical hypotheses* cannot be taken in total isolation from experience: Walras' hypothesis falls foul of the vast repertoire of knowledge about humans and their actions accumulated by historians and other social scientists.[9] Thus it exceeds proper limits. It is so arbitrary it falls outside the pale of an empirical mathematical science.

Moreover, Poincaré insists that these Walrasian hypotheses cannot be read as approximations. Again he illustrates his point by means of an example. The abstraction from friction in mathematical physics – the principles of mechanics assume that there is no friction – is a good example of an acceptable approximation. The principles of mechanics hold approximately for various surfaces, even though they are based on the assumption of infinite smoothness. Thus one can use these principles to predict how far a train, with smooth wheels on a smooth track, will travel before it halts when a specific force is applied to the brakes. The prediction will be approximately correct. Poincaré's point is that the Walrasian hypotheses of infinite self-interest and infinite clairvoyance are not like the hypothesis of infinite smoothness in mechanics. These Walrasian hypotheses do not approximate to human reality the way the mechanical hypothesis approximates to imperfectly smooth surfaces. Here is how Poincaré, concisely and subtly, puts the above point.

> For example, in mechanics one often neglects friction and assumes that bodies are infinitely smooth. You on your side regard men as infinitely self-seeking (égoistes) and infinitely clairvoyant. The first hypothesis can be admitted as a first approximation, but the second hypothesis calls, perhaps, for some reservations.
>
> (Jaffé 1965, 3: 163, letter 1496)

In this connection, it is useful to recall that when Poincaré read Walras' *Elements,* he read it in a very short period of time. Nonetheless Poincaré was gifted with an exceptionally quick mind, capable of grasping the core of a case. One such core claim is stated in Lesson 3 of Walras' *Elements*. There he maintains

> Everyone who has studied any geometry at all knows perfectly well that only in an abstract ideal circumference are the radii all equal to each other and that only in an abstract, ideal triangle is the sum of the angles equal to the sum of two right angles. *Reality confirms these definitions and demonstrations only approximately* and yet reality admits of a very wide and fruitful application of these propositions.
>
> (Walras 2003: 71, italics added)

He continues by maintaining that this is also true of his theoretical economics.[10] In his letter Poincaré is signalling that he rejects this basic claim. For instance, Walras' hypothesis of infinite clairvoyance is not like the hypothesis of friction in mechanics.

To sum up, Poincaré's response to Walras is very concise, rather sophisticated and polite.[11] A priori, he is not opposed to the use of mathematics, including differential calculus, in theoretical economics, provided one remains within proper limits. Vis-à-vis Walras' own programme of the mathematisation of theoretical economics, Poincaré has a hierarchy of reservations, some concern hypotheses which arise within the sphere of proper limits for theoretical economics and other hypotheses which exceed proper limits to theoretical economics. Clearly the latter must be abandoned. Poincaré's first reservation concerns Walras' cardinal measure of utility. Poincaré, by linking Walrasian utility to individual preferences, justifies the measurement of utility on ordinal grounds: any reference to cardinal utility in Walras' conclusions must be eliminated. This reservation does not mean that Walras has exceeded the proper limits imposed on mathematico-theoretical research in economics. Rather Poincaré is outlining a challenge for future research. For instance one could argue that the subsequent development of ordinal utility goes some way in meeting Poincaré's challenge.

Poincaré's next reservation concerns another hypothetical assumption on the part of Walras, namely the *interpersonal comparison of utility*. Poincaré correctly notes Walras' emphasis on the subjective and individual nature of utility. In Poincaré's view human beings, the subject matter of social sciences and history, are shown to be '*too dissimilar, too variable, too capricious*' in comparison with the entities studied in physics and the biological sciences (Poincaré 1956: 19, italics added). Given this conception of human beings, it is not at all evident how one could compare or aggregate the individual, subjective utilities of millions of economic agents. Once again Poincaré is not dogmatic – future research may succeed. However any satisfactory completion of the Walrasian programme has to engage this challenge. The extent that these issues are not satisfactorily resolved, the theory lacks economic interest. Poincaré's reservation at the pinnacle of this hierarchy, however, is damning. Poincaré is implying that Walras at this stage has gone beyond acceptable limits in his theorising. This reservation concerns Walras' hypothesis, that *economic agents are infinitely clairvoyant*. This hypothesis is so far removed from what is shown to be the case by history and the other social sciences, its inclusion in any piece of mathematico-economic research means that that research does not merit consideration as a science.

Walras' 'Economics and Mechanics' in the context of his platonic-scientific realism

Walras published his short piece 'Economics and Mechanics' in 1909. This 'in his opinion provided an outline of the irrefutable basis of his theories' (Ingrao and Israel 1990: 90). Consistent with his attitude of ignoring non-mathematical economists, Walras' target audience was mathematicians. We know from his correspondence with Aupetit that his intention was 'to disseminate' his method among mathematicians (Jaffé 1965, 3: 339, letter 1666). His core thesis is that 'his procedure is rigorously identical to that of two of the most advanced and uncontested mathematical sciences, rational mechanics and *celestial mechanics*' (Mirowski and Cook, 1990: 208).[12] Clearly, this short piece is both rhetorical and methodological. Walras is engaged in Aristotelian rhetoric: he, being an expert on mathematical economics and, after serious reflection on his metier, takes his mathematical audience into account in presenting his core thesis. The piece is also methodological: his mathematico-economic methods and those of both rational and celestial mechanics are identical.[13]

Hence it is crucial to ascertain how Walras understood rational and celestial mechanics, which for short we call mathematical physics. Fundamentally mathematical physics 'is the most advanced and most uncontested' of the sciences (Mirowski and Cook 1990: 208). This view was shared by many of his contemporaries at the close of the nineteenth century, including Poincaré. If the principles of mathematical physics are nothing but contingent experimental laws then they are provisory or, in Walras' terminology, contestable. These principles, however, have proven to be, in our terminology, much more robust. This robustness is emphasised by those who view mathematical physics as a deductive, a priori science. As we will see Walras is sympathetic to this view and he gives his own unique justification for the robustness of the principles of mathematical physics. In this connection we argue there are four intertwining cords to Walras' philosophy of mathematical physics which he projects onto mathematical economics. These are (i) Platonic realism, (ii) essentialist scientific realism, (iii) a (Cartesian) deductive method, (iv) causal scientific realism. In short Walras reads mathematical physics, and ipso facto theoretical economics, in a metaphysical way, while Poincaré reads mathematical physics in an empirical-conventionalist way.[14] In this section we focus on Walras' Platonic realism and his essentialist scientific realism. We will discuss his deductivism and causal scientific realism in the next section.

In Lesson 2 of his *Elements*, Walras introduces his overall conceptions of Science, Arts and Ethics. He starts his brief, skeleton-like, sketch of his general philosophy of a mathematical science with Platonic Philosophy (Walras 2003: 61). In Platonic philosophy 'science does not study corporeal entities but universals of which these entities are manifestations' (Walras 2003: 61). This thesis is not a piece of speculative philosophy. On the contrary, according to Walras, this truth was 'demonstrated' a long time ago by Platonic philosophy (Walras 2003: 61). In line with this Platonic commitment, the subject matter of all scientific inquiry is 'universals, their relations and their laws' (Walras 2003: 61). There is no further elaboration of this very brief sketch. In our opinion it is crucial to appreciate how Walras has synergised Platonic realist metaphysics with modern, i.e. post-seventeenth-century, scientific revolutionary science, especially mathematical physics. More precisely Platonic realism is inextricably conjoined to an essentialist scientific realist reading of mathematical physics, i.e. the realist claim that mathematical physics reveals the essential characteristics realisable in the observable world.

In its conventional presentation in elementary textbooks, Platonic realism does prioritise what Walras calls universals, or what some historians of philosophy call Platonic Forms, over the entities in the observable world. The observable world is, in Plato's metaphor, but a shadow of the real world of Forms. In Walras' terminology 'corporeal entities come and go but universals remain for ever' (Walras 2003: 61). Moreover, according to Platonic realists, the universals express essential, as distinct from accidental, characteristics. To take Walras' own example, the universal 'circle' specifies the essential characteristics of the Form 'circle'. A circle drawn on paper is not a true circle. The drawn figure is circular only to the extent that it approximates to, or manifests, or exemplifies the essential characteristics of the Form 'circle'. Essentialist scientific realism is inextricably intertwined with this Platonic realism by Walras' additional thesis, namely the uncontested mathematical sciences such as geometry and mathematical physics reveal these essences. Once again Walras starts with geometry – for instance the essence of the universal circle is exposed in the science of geometry – and extends the claim to mathematical physics. In this Walrasian synthesis of Platonic realism and essentialist scientific realism of mathematical physics, scientific explanation is not, as for Popperians and many others, hypothetico-deductive. Explanation for Walras is certainly deductive – there is extensive consensus among scholars on that – but it is not hypothetical. For instance, take a geometrical figure drawn on paper. One asks what is it? One looks and sees it is a circle. The ultimate *explanation* of this fact is that the relevant empirical characteristics of the observed figure approximate to, or manifest, the essential characteristics of a circle, defined by geometry. Similarly the empirical natures of the entities studied in mathematical physics are ultimately explained by reference to their essential natures revealed by mathematical physics.

Walras puts a little flesh on this skeleton sketch in the concluding section of Lesson 3 'Social Wealth and Value and Exchange'. He briefly outlines how mathematical physics arrives at these universals/essences. Firstly, these sciences 'draw their type concepts from experience' (Walras 2003: 71). Next, 'from real-type concepts, these sciences *abstract* ideal-type concepts which they define and then on the basis of these definitions, they construct *a priori* the whole framework of their theorems and proofs' (Walras 2003: 71, italics added for 'abstract'). In taking these steps mathematical physics goes beyond experience. Poincaré would concur with this but would not accept that the concepts of mathematical physics are derived by abstraction.[15] Consider, for instance, the concept of the mathematical continuum which is basic to geometry. Poincaré's analysis of this mathematical continuum also starts with experience, namely 'the physical continuum drawn from the rough data of the senses' (Poincaré 1952: 27). The concept of the mathematical continuum goes beyond this. So far this is in agreement with Walras' overall position. The concept of the mathematical continuum, however, is not the result of abstracting from accidental characteristics of the physical continuum. Rather it is 'a creation of the mind' of the mathematician suggested by his/her experiences (Poincaré 1952: 28). The notion of abstraction fails to do justice to this creative power of the mathematical mind.[16] By emphasising mental creativity in the construction of the notion of the mathematical continuum – where, as it were, the physical continuum is simply the catalyst for the creative mathematical mind – Poincaré is signalling that the derivation of various concepts of mathematical physics is much more nuanced and complex than that outlined by Walras.

At the next phase, Walras' methodology is totally at variance with the methodology of straightforward empirically minded mathematical physicists. After constructing and developing a mathematical model, straightforward empirically minded scientists will *test* the model by recourse to the bar of experience. If its predictions correspond to the experimental/observable facts then the model is well confirmed. If not, then the model will be challenged. According to Walras this attitude is mistaken vis-à-vis mathematical physics: if this straightforward empirical attitude did apply to the principles of mathematical physics, these principles would be contestable but, as we have already seen, these principles are 'uncontested' (Mirowski and Cook 1990: 208). Walras was not unique in holding this position vis-à-vis the principles of mathematical physics. A similar thesis is advocated by Poincaré vis-à-vis the principles of mathematical physics. Indeed at times Poincaré puts the matter more forcefully than Walras.

> An experimental law is always subject to revision; we may always expect to see it replaced by some other more exact law. But no one seriously thinks that the law of which we speak (the principles of inertia) will ever be abandoned or amended.
>
> (Poincaré 1952: 95)

This robustness enjoyed by the principles of mathematical physics renders them apart from other experimental laws.

The crucial issue here is raised by Poincaré's next question, why? Why are the principles of mathematical physics so different from other experimental laws or hypotheses? Poincaré's explanation of the robustness of the principles of mechanics is very different to Walras' explanation. According to Walras the principles of mathematical physics are robust precisely because they reveal the Platonic essences. Having grasped the true essences, there is no need for any subsequent empirical testing. Thus for Walras, after the deductive development of mathematical physics, mathematical physicists '*go back to experience not to confirm but to apply their conclusions*'. (Walras 2003: 71, italics added). Having abstracted the real essences, the only avenue open is to see how to apply these to the observable world. The issue of further testing does not arise.

Poincaré refused to read mathematical physics in a metaphysical way. The mathematical physicist starts with 'a law (which) has received sufficient confirmation from experiment' (Poincaré 1958: 124). Mathematical physicists now have a choice: they 'may leave this law in the fray; it will then remain subjected to an incessant revision, which without any doubt will end up demonstrating that it is only approximate' (Poincaré 1958: 124). This is the normal fate of experimental laws: they remain in the fray of experimental testing. There is, however, an alternative. The mathematical physicist 'may elevate it (the law) into a principle by adopting conventions ...' (Poincaré 1958: 124).[17] By elevating the law into a conventional principle, the mathematical physicist is taking the conventional principle out of the fray of the normal testing of empirical laws. According to Poincaré 'great advantages have often been found in proceeding in that way' (Poincaré 1958: 125). Among these advantages are abbreviation and simplification in the enunciation of empirical laws. These conventional principles also supply scientists with additional linguistic resources, used in the articulation of scientific facts (Poincaré 1952: 91–92). For Poincaré this conventionalist approach is subject to two indispensable caveats. First 'it is clear that if *all* laws had been transformed into (conventional) principles *nothing* would be left of science' (Poincaré 1958: 125). The conventionalist strategy is to be justified by its fruitfulness. Secondly, while the purpose of the conventionalist strategy is to ensure that the principle is elevated above the fray of normal testing, 'if a principle ceases to be fecund, experiment without contradicting it directly will nevertheless have *condemned* it' (Poincaré 1958: 110, italics ours). In other words 'experiment without directly contradicting a new extension of the principle will nevertheless have condemned it' (Poincaré 1952: 167). Clearly for Poincaré the principles of mathematical physics are unique. They are much more robust than other experimental laws. Their robustness, however, is conventional. Moreover, this conventionalist strategy of taking its principles out of the fray of normal testing must be fruitful. If the strategy ceases to be fruitful, the mathematical physicists will reject the conventional principles. This possibility is excluded by Walras' Platonic realist reading of these principles.

According to Walras the methodology of theoretical economics is the same as that of mathematical physics. Theoretical economics obtains its type concepts such as those of exchange, supply, demand, capital and so on from experience. Next the theoretical economists 'abstracts and defines ideal-type concepts in terms of which it carries out its reasoning' (Walras 2003: 71). Finally 'the return to reality should not take place until the science is completed and then *only* with a view to practical applications' (Walras 2003: 71).[18] As Walras expressed it earlier 'corporeal entities come and go but universals *remain for ever*' (Walras 2003: 61). So too with the universals of theoretical economics. For Poincaré, the universals of mathematical physics, though more robust than empirical universals, do not remain forever. Their life span depends on how fruitful they will prove in the future developments of that science.

Mathematical physics as a deductive a priori science: Walras' response to the Poincaré critique

In the previous section we identified four themes central to Walras' understanding of mathematical physics. Thus far we have dwelled on two, viz. his Platonic realism and his essentialist scientific realism. We now turn to the other two, namely the deductive method and causal scientific realism. Jaffé (1977a) and others have extensively discussed Walras' deductive method and, in particular, the influence of Descartes. It is clear from the previous section that Walras wished to develop economic theory along the Cartesian lines of '*more geometrico*'. Time and again he cites geometry to legitimate his methodology. This deductive method is inextricably linked to his Platonic realist reading of the principles of mathematical physics. In a Cartesian fashion this Platonic realism, combined with essentialist scientific realism, provides Walras with a solid starting point for his deductive inferences, namely Platonic universal truths. Descartes' principle that clear and distinct ideas are true is replaced by the methodological principle that mathematical physics identifies true essences. Moreover, mathematics furnishes the theoretician with a logically impeccable deductive method. With these pillars, Walras' methodology of mathematical physics, and ipso facto of mathematical economics, is based on solid foundations. Walras, however, does not stop here. He buttresses this methodological edifice with another corner stone, namely causal scientific realism.

In his 'Economics and Mechanics' he used Poincaré to introduce his causal scientific realism. In *Science and Hypothesis*, Poincaré rejects the thesis that mathematical physics is a deductive, a priori science, with the emphasis on a priori. Walras sums up Poincaré's position as follows.

> After quoting and then criticising the attempts at definition of *mass* by Newton, Thompson and Tait and of *force* by Lagrange and Kirkhoff, one of the masters of modern science (Poincaré) concluded that: *masses are co-efficients which it is found convenient to introduce into calculations.*
> (Mirowski and Cook 1990: 213)

We have altered the translation by substituting 'attempts at' for 'essais on'. When stated so concisely Poincaré's position is, to say the least, enigmatic. Walras is clearly aware of this. After quoting Poincaré's position in italics (as it was in the original), Walras immediately remarks 'A la bonne heure!', which Mirowski and Cook correctly translate as 'Fine!' Collins French Dictionary draws our attention to the irony of this phrase in French and translates it as 'that's a fine idea!' (Collins Robert French Dictionary 2006: 479). If Poincaré's conclusion accurately sums up all that can be legitimately said about the notion of mass in the differential equations enunciating the fundamental principles of mathematical physics, then mathematical physics has nothing of significance to say to anybody interested in the real physical world. Thus, according to Walras, Poincaré's conclusion is not satisfactory. Indeed according to Poincaré himself it is '*a confession of failure*' of the a priori deductive interpretation of mathematical physics (Poincaré 1952: 103, italics ours). Thus according to both Walras and Poincaré an alternative explanation to that of the a priori deductive one is required. Unlike Poincaré, the alternative espoused by Walras is to combine the deductive character of mathematical physics with causal scientific realism. For the causal scientific realist 'forces would be the causes of the traverse of space, masses the causes of the elapsed time'.[19] Similarly 'utilities and raretés would be the causes of *supply* and demand …'.[20] In short, according to Walras' causal realism, the principles of mathematical physics, enunciated as differential equations, are causal, i.e. they correctly identify masses and forces as *ontologically* fundamental causal factors operating in the real physical world. Similarly the principles of mathematical economics are causal differential equations, which correctly identify utility and rareté as the fundamental causes of supply and demand and thus the fundamental source of (exchange) value.

Walras' starting point in deriving his causal realism, namely his brief summary of Poincaré's critique of the a priori deductive approach to mathematical physics, totally ignores the context of Poincaré's specific analysis. Poincaré begins his discussions of the principles of mathematical physics by noting two dominant views of mathematical physics. According to one view it is an experimental science. According to the other view mathematical physics is an a priori deductive science. In Poincaré's opinion neither view 'distinguishes between what is experiment, what is mathematical reasoning, what is convention and what is hypothesis' (Poincaré 1952: 89). The identification of the diverse contributions of these to mathematical physics is essential to the project of ascertaining the correct understanding of the principles of mathematical physics. Indeed the task of achieving the correct understanding of the fundamental principles of mathematical physics is more complicated than that. The principles of mathematical physics are not presuppositionless: to comprehensively understand these principles, one must unearth their presuppositions. Among these presuppositions Poincaré identifies (1) Newtonian absolute space, which does not exist, (2) absolute time which erroneously assumes that the notion of the simultaneity of two events occurring in two different places to be unproblematical and (3) Euclidean geometry, the choice of which in Newtonian absolute space is conventional.[21] Poincaré sums up his earlier chapters which explored in detail these presuppositions as follows. These 'no more existed before mechanics than the French language can be logically said to have existed before the truths which are expressed in French' (Poincaré 1952: 90). Poincaré is forewarning the reader that the correct understanding of the principles of mathematical physics is much more complex than that suggested by the direct ontological reading of causal realists. The causal realist ignores (a) the diverse presuppositions of the principles of mathematical physics, and (b) the divergent roles of experiment, mathematical reasoning, convention and hypothesis in that unique, distinctive science. Poincaré's empirical-conventional account of the principles of mathematical physics, outlined in the previous section, fulfil these conditions.

Clearly we need to examine this empirical-conventionalist view of the principles of mathematical physics to see why, in Poincaré's eyes, they cannot be read in the causal realist way suggested by Walras. Prima facie, Walras' causal realist interpretation is plausible. Numerous mathematical physicists, including Poincaré, maintain that *the laws* of mathematical physics are expressed by differential equations. Hence when these laws are combined with appropriate initial conditions they furnish causal explanations. *The principles* of mathematical physics are also expressed by differential equations. Hence according to realists these principles are also integral to causal explanation. Poincaré, however, rejects this latter causal realist claim. The fundamental principles of mathematical physics are not ontologically causal: they are not fundamental causal truths. To appreciate Poincaré's rejection of the causal explanatory role attributed by realists to the principles of mathematical physics we need to reflect on (a) what exactly is a scientific causal explanation: or, if one prefers, the domain of scientific causality; (b) the construction of the linguistic-conceptual scheme of science; (c) the relationship between an experimental law and a fundamental principle; (d) the implications of the history of science for scientific conceptual schemes.

Vis-à-vis the domain of *scientific* causality, Poincaré is not exceptional in limiting it to the domain of observation/experimentation. In physics 'experiment is the sole source of truth. It alone can teach us something new' (Poincaré 1952: 140). If an explanation, be it causal or otherwise, is not *open to experimental investigation* it is *not* a scientific explanation. In the physical sciences the only way of discovering and investigating causal relationships is by observation/experimentation. If, for some reason, one identifies something which is not open to empirical investigation as a true cause then one has stepped beyond the bounds of science. Some varieties of metaphysics engage in this non-scientific kind of explanation. For instance, Thomistic metaphysicians identify God as the first cause of the universe. This causal explanation is metaphysical because it is not open to empirical/experimental investigation. For Poincaré the domain of metaphysics and the domain of science do not overlap. Causes in science, unlike metaphysics, must be subject to empirical investigation.

Moreover experimental sciences are not reducible to crude untrained observation. As distinct from crude observation, scientific observation has two indispensable components: the human contribution, namely the language in which scientific facts and laws are articulated, and, secondly, the contribution of the world gained by trained observation and experimentation. Poincaré illustrates the importance of both by means of the following example. An untrained visitor is in the laboratory with Poincaré while he is conducting an experiment in electricity. Both observe the galvanometer and Poincaré asks is the current passing? The untrained visitor 'looks at the wire to try to see something pass; but if I put the same question to my assistant who *understands my language* he will know what I mean' (Poincaré 1958: 119, italics ours). The progress of science occurs on two distinct fronts: the construction of more and more sophisticated experimental equipment to gain further access to the world and the construction of a more sophisticated conceptual-linguistic scheme in which scientific facts and laws can as accurately as possible be articulated.

We now turn to Poincaré's crucial distinction between a principle of mathematical physics and a law. These principles are *not* scientific laws. A scientific law is open to experimental scrutiny and thus open to revision. Indeed quite often this empirical scrutiny ends up by demonstrating the law as an approximation. As we saw in the previous section a principle is much more robust or durable. In Poincaré's terminology they are 'elevated above the fray of experimental enquiry' (Poincaré 1958: 124). Crucially for Poincaré the robustness of a principle is not due to anything in the real world which can be discovered by observation or experimentation. Rather the robustness is due to scientists' conventional *decision* to place the principle, for a time, beyond the bar of experience. However, by so removing them, principles are denied scientific causality. As we have just seen in our summary of the domain of causality, anything not open to empirical investigation cannot be deemed to be scientific causes, and principles, by virtue of the decision of scientists, are explicitly excluded from empirical investigation.

This becomes clearer when we see how Poincaré analyses the relationship between a principle and a law. This relationship is a genetic one: a principle is not a law, but it originated from a law. When a law has received sufficient confirmation from experiment, theoreticians have a choice: they may leave the law in the fray of experimental enquiry or else they 'may elevate it into a principle' (Poincaré 1958: 124). Schematically the procedure of elevating a law into a principle is as follows. The experimental law expressed an approximately true relationship between terms A and B. The mathematical physicist now introduces an intermediary term C and 'C is by definition that which has with A *exactly* the relation expressed by the law' (Poincaré 1952: 139). Thus, the law is transmogrified into a principle, expressing an absolute, rigorous, robust, universal relation between A and C. But this is only one part of what the mathematical physicist is doing. In addition to decomposing the original, contingent law relating A to B into a rigorous robust, universal principle relating A to C, mathematical physicists complete the process by adding to that principle another revisable experimental law expressing the relation of C to B. Thus the original law is 'broken up' into a principle and another law, 'thereby it is very clear however far this partition be pushed, there will always remain laws' (Poincaré 1958: 125). If the new law expressing a relation between C and B were not added the whole of mathematical physics would become devoid of scientific interest. Poincaré offers us the following example of this genetic process. Take the claim the stars obey Newton's law. This may be broken up into (a) gravitation obeys Newton's Law and (b) gravitation is the only force acting on the stars. (a) is a principle which 'is no longer subject to the test of experiment' (Poincaré 1958: 124). It is neither true nor false. (b), however, is subject to experimental testing. If (b) were not added, the whole process would be devoid of scientific interest.

In short what is unique or distinctive about mathematical physics in comparison with other sciences is the creative way in which mathematical physicists can transmogrify a well-confirmed experimental law into a rigorous, conventional robust principle *and* a new experimental law. In the case where the original scientific law was correctly used in a causal explanation, this causal explanatory role is transferred to the new experimental law, but not to the principle. Since the principle is placed beyond the bar of experience it cannot be used referentially in a causal explanation.[22] As we have already seen, any explanation, if it is scientific, rather than metaphysical, must be open to experimental investigation.

Does this mean that for Poincaré the principles of mathematical physics are metaphysical truths? Not at all. The domains of science and of metaphysics are distinct and separate. They do not overlap. Principles, by virtue of the manner in which they are elevated above the bar of experience, are not located in metaphysics. Rather they are new additions to the evolving conceptual-linguistic scheme indispensable to scientific progress. In this sense they are fundamental. Contrary to Walras, being fundamental to the current scientific conceptual-linguistic scheme does not imply that the principles are causally fundamental. Because an experimental law and a principle share the mathematical structure of a differential equation, scientific causal realists like Walras incorrectly assume that both are ontologically indispensable to causal explanation in science. Also, because they are robust, realists incorrectly assume principles are causally more fundamental than laws. Science, however, unlike metaphysics, is limited to observation and experiment in exploring the causal structure of the observable world and thus, though principles are fundamental to its conceptual scheme, they are incapable of revealing fundamental causes. Hence after identifying the appropriate principle anyone claiming, as Walras does, that 'force is the cause of motion is talking metaphysics' which is 'absolutely fruitless' to the scientist (Poincaré 1952: 98).

We now turn to the implications of the history of science for the scientific conceptual-linguistic scheme. By reviewing in broad sweep the history of science, Poincaré sees no reason as to why one should ontologically or causally privilege the principles of mathematical physics fundamental to the highly fruitful conceptual scheme used in the 1890s. Poincaré sums up his position as follows. 'Descartes used to commiserate with the Ionians. Descartes in his turn makes us smile, and no doubt some day our children will laugh at us' (Poincaré 1952: 141). The scientific conceptual scheme used by Poincaré and his contemporaries, in which the principles of mathematical physics are indispensable, has served contemporary science very well. According to Poincaré, however, its continued success is not guaranteed. It all depends on its fruitfulness going into the future. Future research may force scientists to abandon it, including the presently robust principles of mathematical physics. We know from the history of science that successful scientific conceptual schemes of past eras have not lasted the test of time. The same fate awaits any dominant scientific conceptual scheme. Though no one can foretell how it will happen, the successful principles of mathematical physics will in the future be replaced when a more fruitful scientific conceptual-linguistic scheme is constructed to accommodate unforeseen empirical discoveries. Thus these principles have no ontological standing: they do not enunciate the fundamental causes operational in the observable world. Their standing is gauged by their pragmatic usefulness or fruitfulness in supplying the linguistic resources required for the articulation of new facts and new laws. Moreover, their future demise will not entail the demise of current empirical causal knowledge. That true empirical knowledge will be re-articulated and indeed added to in a better conceptual scheme. In short Walras' scientific realist analysis of the principles of mechanics fails to recognise the sophisticated and complex character of the mathematical science of mechanics and its non-causal, robust, conventional principles.

It is evident that Walras read Poincaré's *Science and Hypothesis*. Yet in his final defence given in 'Economics and Mechanics', where he quotes Poincaré and uses him as a launching pad for his causal scientific realism, Walras makes no reference to Poincaré's rejection of this causal scientific realism outlined above. In this connection one may be tempted to extend Jaffé's thesis concerning Walras' attitude to historical forerunners to his contemporaries. According to Jaffé, Walras'

> only interest was either to bolster his own theoretical contributions by invoking the posthumous support of respected forerunners, or else to berate as fatal flaws anything he found in the writings of others that did not accord with his own ideas.
>
> (Jaffé 1977a: 26–27)

We suggest that this explanation of Walras' failure to even mention Poincairé's alternative analysis of the principles of mathematical physics may be complemented by the following hypothesis. Walras was so deeply committed to his metaphysical reading of these principles that any reference to Poincaré's alternative would lead to a pointless polemic, distracting from his central claim that mathematical economics reveals rareté, not labour as claimed by classical economists, as the fundamental source of value. Be that as it may, Walras had a deep-seated commitment to a metaphysical interpretation of the principles of mathematical physics, whereas Poincaré had a different deep-seated commitment which unequivocally excluded any metaphysical essentialist or fundamental causal interpretation. It is this metaphysical interpretation which Walras transfers to his mathematical economics.[23] As we have already seen, Walras sees no need to test his principles of mathematical economics by recourse to the bar of experience. His principles are applied to but not tested by the economic world. The basic reason for this is his metaphysical reading of economic principles, by analogy to his metaphysical reading of the principles of mathematical physics. If one does not subscribe to this metaphysical reading, which Poincaré does not, then mathematical economics loses its ontological privilege. In short, even if Walras' principles of economics were analogous to the principles of mechanics which, as we have seen they are not, for Poincaré Walras' principles would be incapable of revealing the causal structure of economic systems.

Conclusion: Walras' ontological lock-in

It is evident from Walras' extensive correspondence that he was a passionate mathematical economist with a clear mission. This mission was to persuade open-minded, reasonable moral scientists and political economists, that, despite appearances to the contrary, theoretical economics is an applied mathematical science which, when pursued along the lines of his *Elements*, would attain the same success as that achieved in the unique and distinctive science of mathematical physics/rational mechanics. Thus the paradigm for theoretical economics is not experimental physics. Rather it is the distinctive science of mathematical physics. In particular, Walras' mission includes a number of central theses. Firstly, contrary to the received view, theoretical economics shares a specific deductive method with mathematical physics, namely the mathematical resources of differential calculus. Walras' mission was to convince open-minded moral scientists and political scientists of this unprecedented methodological discovery. To this end he frequently uses Poincaré's correspondence to argue from authority for this methodological innovation – the most famous French and perhaps European mathematician and mathematical physicist of that time supports his innovation. Moreover, there is little doubt that with this methodological innovation, theoretical economics would undergo a revolutionary change: by recourse to differential calculus, a novel research programme, undreamt of in classical economics, is opened up to theoretical economists.

Vis-à-vis mathematical physics, a small number of differential equations constitute the fundamental principles of that science. Moreover, as is evident in the writings of Poincaré, these principles were perceived by numerous scientists as privileged, being distinct from the experimental laws of the other sciences. This unique, distinctive feature is evident in the fact, acknowledged by Poincaré and others, that these principles are *not* tested in the manner in which the laws of experimental physics are tested. Walras' mission was to convince his readers that mathematical economics had the same kind of core principles. In this connection, Poincaré was not convinced. The principles of mathematical physics are path-dependent: they are the outcome of a long historical process of trial and error, grounded in experimentation. The principles of Walras' *Elements* lack this tried and tested historical trajectory. His *Elements*, at best, mark the birth of an innovative research programme which lacked the validation of extensive empirical research. Hence it is premature to identify its core hypotheses as principles, à la mathematical physics.

Thirdly, like Poincaré, Walras holds that the distinctive robustness of the principles of mathematical physics requires explanation. He proceeds to explain this robustness by recourse to the realist thesis that these principles reveal the essential, as opposed to the accidental, characteristics of their domain of application. Fundamentally, they reveal the basic causes of the motion of bodies in the universe. Similarly, the principles of mathematical economics reveal that rareté is the fundamental source of exchange value. Poincaré, however, offers an alternative, non-realist, explanation of the robustness of the principles of the exceptionally successful discipline of mathematical physics. One might say that he skilfully uses Ockham's razor to shave off the excessive explanatory beard of scientific realism. Poincaré starts with the methodological truism that in any scientific discipline, causality is explored by recourse to observation and experimentation. If any scientific hypothesis is not open to rigorous experimental investigation, it cannot be used as a causal explanation. Ipso facto this applies to the principles of mathematical physics: these principles cannot function as scientific causal explanations precisely because their privileged status within mathematical physics rules out any immediate effort at probing them by experimentation. Secondly, the privileged status of the principles of mathematical physics can be explained internally, i.e. within the boundaries of science understood historically, without recourse to essentialist scientific realism. According to Poincaré mathematical scientists operate under two indispensable constraints: on the one hand the extension of the boundaries of the observable by the invention of sophisticated experimental equipment, and on the other the extension of their conceptual-linguistic schema necessary for the precise articulation of scientific facts and laws. These two constraints give rise to a choice situation in mathematical physics when, after years of testing, a law-like generalisation continues to be well confirmed. The physicist may leave the law as it is, i.e. subject to more experimental testing, or transmogrify it into a principle, which is now privileged, and another experimental law, which is not privileged. By opting for the second alternative, the principle is integrated into the conceptual linguistic scheme while the new law is experimentally probed. Scientific realists, à la Walras, fail to appreciate (i) the two constraints noted above on mathematical scientists, (ii) the historical trajectory of a principle, (iii) the only route to causality in science is observation/experimentation, (iv) current conceptual schemes, like those of the past, may be shown to be inadequate by future experimental research. Thus Poincaré sums up as follows:

> the object of mathematical theories is not to reveal to us the real nature of things; that would be an unreasonable claim. Their only object is to co-ordinate the physical laws with which physical experiment makes us acquainted, the enunciation of which, without the aid of mathematics, we should be unable to effect.
>
> (Poincaré 1952: 211)

Contrary to Poincaré, according to Walras, both mathematical physics and mathematical economics reveal the real natures of things. The equations of mathematical physics reveal the essential, as opposed to the accidental, causes of motion, while the fundamental equations of mathematical economics reveal the essential cause of exchange value. For Poincaré this kind of claim is scientifically 'unreasonable' (Poincaré 1952: 211) whereas for Walras it is based on 'a truth long ago demonstrated by the Platonic philosophy' (Walras 2003: 61). In short, Poincaré's deep-seated commitment is to a non-realist reading of the principles of mathematical physics, whereas Walras' deep-seated commitment is to a realist reading of these principles. Clearly the philosophy of applied mathematics one adopts is crucial to the account one gives of the privileging of the principles of mathematical physics and to the methodological evaluation of Walras' equation of the principles of mathematical economics with those of mathematical physics.

Moreover, Walras' synthesis of essentialist realism with his causal realist reading of his principles of mathematical economics necessarily entails that mathematical economists are locked into these principles. This lock-in is not like the historical, path-dependent lock-in, highlighted by Brian Arthur and others in their economic analyses of technological innovation (Arthur 1994: 13–33). Rather it is an ontologically based, not a contingent path-dependent, lock-in. Like mathematical physicists, mathematical economists are blessed with being in possession of essential truths conveyed by their principles. Being essential truths, these principles are invariable. Future empirical research cannot upend them. Since mathematical economics has correctly identified essential causes, aside from discovering other essential causes, the only scope for further empirical research is in the domain of accidental characteristics. Thus there is no inconsistency in Walras' central thesis that economists do not test their fundamental equations, rather they merely apply them to the actual economic world. This ontologically based lock-in guarantees that future observational research will never succeed in showing these principles to be in need of radical restatement.

As we have already seen, Walras' case for this ontological privileging of his principles of theoretical economics rests on (a) his equation of these principles with the principles of mathematical physics and on (b) his essentialist causal realist reading of these principles. As we have outlined in the previous sections, Poincaré rejects both of these claims. Walras' mathematical economics is in its infancy whereas mathematical physics is a mature science. Furthermore some of Walras' principles, e.g. perfect foresight, are not analogous to the principles of mathematical physics which evolved out of well-confirmed laws. Others, e.g. interpersonal comparison of utility, require further investigation and thus the jury is out on their scientific status. Also Walras' essentialist causal realist reading of the principles of both sciences is open to question. In short, if one is sympathetic to a Poincaré-type empirical analysis of Walras' *Elements*, then at best one can say is that his *Elements* has achieved interesting results. Ironically, in a Poincaré-type empirical approach, the Achilles' heel of Walras' ontological lock-in to the fundamental equations of Walrasian economics lies in the manner in which he equated mathematical economics with mathematical physics. For any empirical minded economist, the ontological lock-in to the principles of neo-classical economics would require an altogether different legitimation to that supplied by Walras.

Notes

1 For a more detailed analysis of Poincaré's role in the Dreyfus affair, see Rollet (1997).

2 As noted by Bru, for instance, Poincaré was sceptical about the application of probability theory to concrete issues in the moral sciences (Taqqu (interview of Bru) 2001). Poincaré's reasons for this scepticism are not confined to a Comteian influence. Some of these reasons are outlined in his chapter 'Chance' in his *Science and Method*.

3 Ingrao and Israel (1990), among others, tell us that Antoine Paul Piccard, Professor of Mechanics at the Academy of Lausanne from 1869 to 1881, helped Walras with his mathematics.

4 A terminological confusion may arise here. Walras distinguishes theoretical economics from applied economics. But in so far as mathematical physics or Walras' economics exploit mathematics, though each is *theoretical*, each is also a branch of *applied mathematics*.

5 According to some philosophers 'Poincaré was categorically opposed to the naissant mathematical logic' of Russell in England and Frege in Germany (Schmid 1978: 9). In our view this utterly misrepresents Poincaré. For instance he concludes his chapter 'The New Logic' of *Science and Method* as follows: 'To sum up Mr. Russell and Mr. Hilbert have both made a great effort, and have both of them written a book full of views that *are original, profound and often true*. These two books furnish us with subject for much thought and *there is much that we can learn from them. Not a few of their results are substantial and destined to survive*' (Poincaré 1956: 176, italics ours).

6 As van Daal and Jolink point out, the origin of Walras' general equilibrium theory has often been attributed to Poinsot's *Élements de Statiques*. We are not concerned about the extent of this influence − a point disputed by van Daal and Jolink against Jaffé. Clearly it exerted some influence.

7 For a detailed account of the differences between what we called ordinal and cardinal measurement, the reader may usefully consult chapters six and seven of Carnap (1966).

8 Poincaré uses the phrase 'daring hypothesis' vis-à-vis Maxwell's theory where Maxwell's 'conception was only a daring hypothesis which could be supported by no experiment; but after twenty years Maxwell's ideas received the confirmation of experiment' (Poincaré 1952: 239). We are not suggesting that Maxwell's conception was, in Poincaré's eyes, arbitrary. Rather our suggestion is that there is no evidence to suggest that Poincaré would outlaw the use of a daring hypothesis at the conception/birth of a science.

9 Poincaré held history in very high esteem. Indeed theoretical scientists who forget the histories of their disciplines could easily misunderstand their disciplines.

10 In the next section we will examine in detail how Walras draws this analogy.

11 In order to expose its implications, we have taken the politeness out of Poincaré's response.

12 Unless otherwise stated we are using Mirowski's and Cook's translation.

13 In particular, he argues for a perfect similarity between (a) the formula of minimum satisfaction and the formula of the equilibrium of the Roman balance and (b) the equations of general equilibrium and the equations of universal gravity.

14 In this connection the Bridel and Mornati (2009) article, with the perceptive title 'De L'Équilibre Général comme "Branche de la Métaphysique"' is very interesting. While they largely focus on Pareto's critique of Walras, they do not make our four-fold distinction.

15 Walras does not elaborate on his understanding of abstraction. In philosophy the term, at times, connotes abstracting from accidental characteristics and thereby giving one immediate access to the essential characteristics. For instance, a mathematician sees a specific circular figure. Its circumference is coloured and it has a specific thickness. The mathematician, however, abstracts from those accidental characteristics and thus discovers the essential characteristics.

16 For instance, the mathematical continuum presupposes Dedekind cuts and Poincaré is clearly correct in claiming that the notion of a Dedekind cut is not derived from abstracting away the accidental features of the physical continuum.

17 As Carnap points out 'Poincaré has been accused of conventionalism in this radical sense (which says that all concepts and even the laws of science are a matter of convention)' (Carnap 1966: 59). Carnap correctly notes that this accusation is based on a misunderstanding of his writings. 'Poincaré can be called a conventionalist only if all that is meant is that he was a philosopher who emphasised, more than previous philosophers, the great role of convention. He was not a radical conventionalist' (Carnap 1966: 59).

18 Numerous commentators, e.g. Jaffé (1977a) note the influence of Natural Law on Walras. Perhaps it is worth noting that much the same kind of reasoning informs Natural law morality: the moral codes/rules/institutions found in different societies are truly moral only to the extent that they approximate to the essence of morality revealed by Natural Law. Thus one does not test Natural Law against the observed moral practices. Rather one applies Natural Law to these practices. In particular, in connection with the influence of Natural Law on Walras, Jaffé concludes that Walras' 'latent purpose in contriving his general equilibrium model was not to describe or analyse the working of the economic system as it existed, nor was it primarily to portray the purely economic relationships within a network of markets under the assumption of a theoretically perfect regime of free competition. It was rather to demonstrate the possibility of formulating axiomatically a rationally consistent economic system that would satisfy the demands of social justice without overstepping the bounds imposed by the natural exigencies of the real world' (Jaffé 1977a: 31). Walras' Platonist reading of the principles of mathematical economics may help us in appreciating how Walras reconciled his mathematical economics and Natural Law. Both are to be applied to their respective domains because both unearth what is essential in each. And, for a Platonist, the essence of goodness/justice cannot be incompatible with the essence of truth, discovered by mathematical economics.

19 Les forces seraient ainsi des causes *d'espace parcouru,* les masses des causes de temps employé au parcours desquelles résulterait la *vitesse* dans le *movement,* des causes physiques plus constants mais plus caches … (Walras 1909: 325).

20 Les *utilitès* et les *raretés* seraient des causes de *demande* et *d'offre*, desquelles resulterait la *valeur* dans *l'eschange*, des causes psychiques plus sensibles mais plus variables (Walras 1909: 325).

21 Poincaré is drawing our attention to the manner in which Newtonian mechanics and physics conceptualises space and time. Poincaré, like Lorentz, had done much work akin to Einstein's special theory of relativity. This is extensively discussed in Greffe, Heinzmann and Lorentz (1996).

22 Like facts, scientific laws have two dimensions: (1) a linguistic component and (2) an empirical component. The contribution of a principle to the enunciation of a fact or a law is limited to (1).

23 According to Mirowski, it is the energy metaphor which is transferred from mathematical physics to mathematical economics (Mirowski 1989). For us it is the Platonist-realist methodology which is transferred by Walras. It should be noted that we do not agree with Mirowski, or indeed anyone else's reading of scientific models as metaphors. For our position on this general methodological theme see Boylan and O'Gorman (1995). In this work, however, we have chosen to avoid this general methodological issue.

3 The formalisation of economics and Debreu's philosophy of mathematics

Introduction

In the previous chapter we interrogated Walras' 'programme' of the mathematisation of economics by recourse to a series of issues raised in the Walras–Poincaré correspondence. As we have already seen, the resistance, and even the hostility, to what economic methodologists call formalism in economics among French economists and mathematicians was a central concern to Walras – hence his appeal to Poincaré as an outstanding mathematician for support in his efforts. In addition to his central thesis that economics, as outlined in his *Elements*, is a legitimate applied mathematical science, Walras also had recourse to a number of other methodological claims. One such claim is that there is a significant analogy between mathematical physics/rational mechanics and theoretical economics. Like Poincaré and numerous other mathematicians at the turn of the twentieth century, mathematical physics was in Walras' eyes the paradigm of a successful applied mathematical science. In this context, by drawing attention to the common element of differential equations in economics and rational mechanics and by reading rational mechanics in a scientific realist way, Walras argued that his *Elements* revealed the fundamental principles of economics.

We are not claiming that Walras' economic methodology was shared by the other progenitors of what is called the marginalist revolution. As a key figure in the marginalist revolution, Walras made a unique methodological case for the adoption of a specific kind of formalism in economics. By recourse to Poincaré's reflections on rational mechanics, especially his non-realist, methodological reading of its principles,[1] we identified the unique manner in which Walras defended his formalism on methodological grounds.[2]

The central focus of this chapter is what is called the neo-Walrasian programme. Like the previous chapter, we concentrate on one of its principal architects, namely Debreu, especially his 1959 monumental *Theory of Value*. This short monograph is frequently read as a prime example of formalism in economic theory. For instance, according to Weintraub and Mirowski 'it still stands as the benchmark axiomatization of the Walrasian general equilibrium model' (Weintraub and Mirowski 1994: 257). Of course Debreu's monumental work is the outcome of a specific historical trajectory which has been the subject of excellent historical research.[3] This chapter complements this research in arguing that, among the neo-Walrasian theoreticians, Debreu was a committed formalist in the technical sense of formalism as this term is used in the philosophy of mathematics: his explicit aim is to treat the theory of value 'with the standards of rigor of the contemporary formalist school of mathematics' (Debreu 1959: x). Thus we take Debreu's admiration of the contemporary formalist school seriously. That school, largely shaped by Hilbert and his collaborators at Göttingen university in the first three decades of the twentieth century, revolutionised the received views of (a) pure mathematics, (b) applied mathematics, (c) the relationship between (a) and (b). In particular we contend that Debreu exploits this novel formalist view of applied mathematics in his *Theory of Value*. Moreover we show how Debreu's formalist conception of theoretical economics as an applied mathematical discipline has little in common with Walras' conception of applied mathematics.

In this and the following chapter, we respond to Weintraub's challenge to investigate 'how economics has been shaped by economists' ideas about the nature and purpose and function and meaning of mathematics' (Weintraub 2002: 2). We do this by focusing on Debreu's own philosophy of economic analysis. In order to gain a fuller appreciation of Debreu's formalist views on the nature, purpose, function and meaning of mathematics we compare and contrast these with other philosophical views. We then show how Debreu's formalist views shaped his *Theory of Value*. The chapter is structured as follows. In the following section we give a very preliminary account of some of the central methodological claims of this chapter. This is followed by an exposition of Debreu's contingency approach to the mathematisation of economics. The following three sections investigate Debreu's values of rigour, generality and simplicity which, for him, permeate mathematico-economic theorising. We then turn to how Debreu articulates the limitations of the contingency approach to economic theorising and analyse how he complements that contingency approach with what he calls a 'global view' of the mathematisation of economics where 'a perfect fit' between some mathematical and economic concepts is shown to exist. This is followed by what we call the Poincaré malaise vis-à-vis Debreu's mathematisation of economic theory. Finally we conclude by comparing and contrasting Debreu's proof of the existence of equilibrium with that of Walras.

Core theses: a preliminary account

Very schematically, our thesis is the following. During the course of the nineteenth century our contemporary demarcation between pure and applied mathematics was not explicitly formulated. When, for instance, Walras was re-editing his *Elements* the notion of pure mathematics was not clearly defined. Pure mathematics would be introduced by examples, such as non-Euclidean geometries or Cantorian set theory-mathematical innovations, which were perceived to be of little or no practical use. Applied mathematics was similarly demarcated.[4] A central example of applied mathematics was rational mechanics, which included Euclidean geometry. Largely because of its empirical success, exemplified in Newtonian physics, rational mechanics was, with some justification at that time, taken as the paradigm of applied mathematics.

However, due to the logico-philosophical quest for the foundations of mathematics by, among others, Frege in Germany and Russell in Britain, logicians, philosophers and mathematicians began to *systematically* reflect on the natures of pure and of applied mathematics. As we already mentioned, over the course of the first three decades of the twentieth century the formalist conceptions of (a) pure mathematics, (b) applied mathematics and (c) the relationship between (a) and (b) were articulated and defended by Hilbert and his colleagues at Göttingen. In this unique and controversial philosophy of mathematics the traditional relationship between pure and applied mathematics espoused by Walras and others is transmogrified. This transmogrified conception of applied mathematics is central to what Debreu calls his 'philosophy of economic analysis' (Debreu 1992: 114).

According to the formalist school, pure mathematics is an uninterpreted or purely formal axiomatic system. There appears to be nothing unusual here. We are all familiar with axiomatic systems – Euclid being the paradigm. However, what is novel here is the qualification uninterpreted or purely formal. This qualification means that any shred of meaning or content intuitively connected to an axiomatic system must be completely eliminated. For instance, there cannot be anything specifically spatial or geometrical in Euclid's axiomatic system. According to Weyl, Hilbert's remark that 'it must be possible to replace in all geometric statements the words, *point, line, plane* by *table, chair, mug* contains the axiomatic standpoint in a nutshell' (Weyl 1944: 635). Thus anyone who holds that pure geometry is about spatial relationships or that arithmetic is about numbers is, from the formalist point of view, *not* doing pure mathematics. This received conception of pure mathematics is, for the formalist, relocated into applied mathematics. Pure mathematics is a meaningless syntactical calculus consisting of empty signs or symbols which are manipulated according to clearly formulated rules of syntax and which are systematically organised into a formal axiomatic system which can be proven to be consistent, complete and decidable. This formalist conception of pure mathematics is counter-intuitive to some. Formalists, however, do not value intuition. Rather their concern is with what rigorously holds. We have to sacrifice our intuitions to the more fundamental requirements of rigour.

In the formalist school, applied mathematics is *any interpretation* or model of this meaningless, purely formal axiomatic system. According to this school, the scope of applied mathematics is much broader than what was traditionally assumed when Walras was re-editing his *Elements*. In redrawing the boundaries between pure and applied mathematics, the formalist school confines pure mathematics within the boundaries of syntax, i.e. rules for the purely mechanical manipulation of empty, uninterpreted symbols, and characterises applied mathematics as any semantical, i.e. meaningful, interpretation of that purely syntactical system. Thus, the scope of applied mathematics can range from purely fictitious worlds on the one hand to the empirical world on the other. A central thesis of this chapter is that Debreu explicitly exploits this formalist conception of applied mathematics in his *Theory of Value*. [5]

In short Debreu's 'philosophy of economic analysis' is very different to that of Walras. This difference is due to their different philosophies of applied mathematics. According to Debreu the best available, most rigorous, conception of applied mathematics to be used in economic theorising is spelled out by the formalist school where (a) the concept of applied mathematics is necessarily linked to the purely formalist conception of pure mathematics and thus (b) where the concept of applied mathematics is not paradigmatically linked to describing the empirical world. This formalist conception of applied mathematics was simply not available to Walras.

Vis-à-vis the methodological evaluation of Debreu's programme of the mathematisation of economics we interrogate his formalist way of understanding the mathematical values of rigour, generality and simplicity. While these values are universally accepted, the specific formalist understanding of these, adopted by Debreu, is not universally accepted. In this connection we introduce the Poincaré malaise. This malaise concerns the issue of whether or not Debreu, like Walras, transgresses the limitations imposed by the finite nature of real economies in his formalist mathematisation of economic theory.

Debreu on the contemporary period of economic formalism

When Debreu throws a quick eye over the mathematisation of economic theory, he views its historical process in two complementary ways, one which he calls 'local' and the other which he calls 'global' (Debreu 1986: 1260). In the local view the development of the mathematisation of economic theory is marked by 'several historical accidents' (Debreu 1986: 1260). Thus Weintraub, for instance, points out:

> the rise of mathematical formalism in economics is not a simple phenomenon of the imperative of the subject matter, as it is sometimes claimed; rather it is the product of contingencies of the intersection of diverse disciplines and, as Debreu is the first to acknowledge, numerous personal accidents and fortuitous encounters.
>
> (Weintraub 2002: 120)

The first historical accident noted by Debreu is Cournot's *Recherches sur les Principes Mathématiques de la Théorie des Richesse*, published in 1838, 'the symbolic birthdate of mathematical economics' (Debreu 1984: 267). Another significant historical accident was the University of Lausanne's appointment of Walras in 1870. Interestingly, Debreu notes that in appointing Walras the University of Lausanne took a risk which few universities today would take – Walras had no previous academic appointment and at the time of his appointment had no publications in theoretical economics. This risk, however, was vindicated by the publication of Walras' *Élements*, 'one of the greatest classics, if not the greatest of our science' (Debreu 1984: 268). The University of Lausanne was also the source of another historical accident in 1893 by appointing Pareto to succeed Walras. This second gamble also paid off with Pareto's *Cours d'Economie Politique* (1896–1897) and other publications.

Debreu's local account now moves on to what he calls the contemporary period which, relative to the nineteenth century, is marked by a 'steady course' (Debreu 1986: 1259).[6] Among the first key accidents in the contemporary period is von Neumann's 1928 article on game theory: 'Zur Theorie der Gesellschaftsspiele'. For Debreu this publication is notable in that it marks the first incursion into economic theory by 'one of the foremost mathematicians of his generation' (Debreu 1991: 2). Unlike Walras, von Neumann was recognised as an exceptionally talented mathematician by Hilbert and his 'school' at Göttingen and indeed throughout the wider mathematical world. In his Nobel Laureate lecture Debreu identifies 1944 as 'the symbolic birthdate' of the mathematisation of economics in the contemporary period – the year in which von Neumann and Morgenstern published their first edition of the *Theory of Games and Economic Behaviour*. Its publication was 'an event that announced a profound and extensive transformation of economic theory' (Debreu 1984: 267). It 'set a new level of logical rigor for economic reasoning and it introduced convex analysis into economic theory' (Debreu 1986: 1261). In particular Debreu notes that von Neumann in 1937 had already introduced algebraic topology into economic theory when he 'generalized Brouwer's fixed point theorem in a lemma devised to prove the existence of an optimal growth path in this model' (Debreu 1986: 1261).[7] In this local approach to economic formalism Debreu's own entry into economic theorising is another notable historical accident. Weintraub's interview with Debreu (Weintraub 2002) and Debreu's 'Random Walk and Life Philosophy' (Debreu 1992) fill in some of the details. One could say that, if 1944 is the symbolic birthdate of the contemporary period of economic formalism, 1959 – the year of the publication of Debreu's *Theory of Value* – dates its symbolic coming of age.

Debreu identifies two distinguishing characteristics of this contemporary period of economic formalism relative to its earlier period. Prior to the contemporary period 'theoretical physics had been an inaccessible ideal toward which economic theory sometimes strove. During that period this striving became a powerful stimulus in the mathematization of economic theory' (Debreu 1991: 2). In the previous chapter we discussed in detail a specific instance of this stimulus in the case of Walras. More generally, Debreu correctly points out 'the privileged relationship that developed over several centuries between physics and mathematics … (and) the benefits of that special relationship were large for both fields' (Debreu 1991: 2). However, theoretical physics is, according to Debreu, an 'inaccessible ideal' for economic theorising. Why? Theoretical physics has a 'secure experimental base' which is lacking in theoretical economics. As Debreu puts it, 'the experimental results and factual observations that are at the basis of physics, and which provide a constant check on its theoretical constructions occasionally led its bold reasonings to violate knowingly the canons of mathematical deduction' (Debreu 1991: 2). Debreu's point is, for instance, evident in the emergence of quantum mechanics which, grounded in experimental results, challenged classical mechanics. In short, according to Debreu, in the very special relationship between theoretical physics and mathematics, 'physics did not completely surrender to the embrace of mathematics and its inherent compulsion toward rigor' (Debreu 1991: 2). Theoretical economics, however, lacks the sophisticated experimental checks which occur in physics.

> In these directions economic theory could not follow the role model offered by physical theory. Next to the most sumptuous scientific tool of physics, the Superconducting Super Collider ... the experiments of economics look excessively frugal. Being denied a sufficiently secure experimental base, economic theory has to adhere to the rules of logical discourse ...
>
> (Debreu 1991: 2)

Debreu is thus maintaining that theoretical economics is a unique, applied mathematical science. In particular it is distinct from mathematical physics in that theoretical economics is not open to empirical testing by the sophisticated type of experimentation which occurs in theoretical physics. Theoretical physics has two indispensable cornerstones: sophisticated mathematics and sophisticated experimentation. Since theoretical economics lacks this kind of sophisticated experimentation, it must, methodologically speaking, adhere to the highest standards of logic in implementing the template of applied mathematics furnished by the formalist school.[8]

The second distinguishing characteristic of the contemporary period of economic formalism noted by Debreu is the exploitation of highly advanced, very sophisticated mathematics – what Weintraub aptly calls 'the substantial racheting upwards of the standards of mathematical sophistication within the profession' (Weintraub 2002: 101). As Debreu points out, 'fifty years ago basic undergraduate preparation in mathematics was almost always sufficient. Today graduate training in mathematics is necessary' (Debreu 1991: 2). This, as he points out, is evident in the increasing numbers of theoretical economists who have PhDs in pure mathematics. From the point of view of economic methodology, this racheting upwards of mathematical sophistication is quite significant. As Debreu perceptively points out, this training in mathematics is inextricably value-laden. 'Values (are) imprinted on an economist by his study of mathematics ... those values do not play a silent role; they may play a decisive role' (Debreu 1991: 5). In this connection three questions arise. First, what are these values? Secondly, how do they operate? Thirdly, what are the advantages and disadvantages of these values for economists? We address these issues in the following three sections.

Debreu and the achievement of rigour

Debreu sums up the mathematical values espoused by the economic theoretician as follows: 'As a formal model of an economy acquires a mathematical life of its own, it becomes the object of an inexorable process in which rigour, generality and simplicity are relentlessly pursued' (Debreu 1986: 1265). Five years later he expresses a similar point. 'Ceteris paribus, one cannot prefer less to more rigor, lesser to greater generality or complexity to simplicity' (Debreu 1991: 5). These values of rigour, generality and simplicity are subject to a crucial qualification: they are to be understood according to 'the contemporary formalist school of mathematics' (Debreu 1959: x). This formalist understanding of these values, however, was not universally accepted: it was challenged by mathematicians of the standing of Poincaré and logicians of the standing of Frege. In short, while mathematicians and logicians all share the values of rigour, generality and simplicity, they do not share the formalist understanding of these values.

Vis-à-vis rigour, the standards of rigour of the formalist school have both negative and positive dimensions. Negatively the formalist conception of rigour precludes recourse to intuition in pure mathematics. Here we are not using 'intuition' in its technical Kantian sense. Rather we are using the term intuition as a kind of a hold-all term ranging from situations where a very gifted mathematician uses the whole of his/her creativity and mathematical expertise sharpened by experience to overcome an unanticipated impasse in a proposed proof to the situation where an experienced teacher exploits the historical origins of a term to motivate the introduction of its abstract definition.[9] The formalist conception of mathematical rigour excludes any recourse to intuition within pure mathematics. In this formalist vein, Debreu in the opening chapter of his *Theory of Value* makes no concession to readers who find intuition useful in gaining an understanding of its mathematical concepts. Indeed in the very first paragraph of this chapter he insists 'its reading requires in principle *no* knowledge of mathematics' (Debreu 1959: 1). A few paragraphs later he concedes that the claim is true only in principle: the reader requires an ability to think abstractly and also the ability to assimilate 'new concepts the motivation for which may not be clear at first' (Debreu 1959: 2). Presumably one acquires these abilities by proper mathematical training, a training given in the contemporary formalist school of mathematics where intuition is marginalised.

Positively the formalist conception of mathematical rigour is inextricably linked to what Weyl calls the thesis of 'the methodological unity of mathematics' (Weyl 1944: 617). This is the name for the formalist programme of the rigorous axiomatic derivation of the extensive edifice of the whole of pure mathematics from its axiomatised foundational base in formal logic and the formal theory of arithmetic. In this formalist vein Debreu, in the preface to his *Theory of Value*, insists that 'allegiance to rigor dictates the axiomatic form of analysis' (Debreu 1959: viii) and in Chapter 1 he outlines how in principle one can logically derive the real number system, n-dimensional vector spaces, topology, especially Brouwer's fixed point theorem and so on from their axiomatic foundational base in set theory and arithmetic. These logically derived mathematical domains are exploited in subsequent chapters, thereby providing the highest standards of rigour for theoretical economics.

Since we devote the next chapter to Debreu's conception of an axiomatic system, in this section we focus on another dimension of rigour noted by Debreu, namely 'the terse language' which mathematics imposes on economics (Debreu 1992: 114). As Arrow perceptively notes this is 'so elementary we hardly notice it' (Arrow 1982: 6). This terse language is what logicians call an extensional language and Arrow draws our attention to the fact that experimental psychology shows that actual choices violate this extensionality.

> A fundamental element of rationality, so elementary that we hardly notice it, is, in logicians' language, its *extensionality*. The chosen element depends on the opportunity set from which the choice is made, independently of how the set is described. To take a familiar example, consider the consumer's budget set. It is defined by prices and income. Suppose income and all prices were doubled. Clearly the set of commodity bundles available for purchase are unchanged. Economists confidently use that fact to argue that the chosen bundle is unchanged, so that consumer demand functions are homogenous of degree zero in prices and income. But the description of the budget set, in terms of prices and income, has altered. It is an axiom that the change in description leaves the decision unaltered.
>   The cognitive psychologists deny that choice is in fact extensional ...
>   (Arrow 1982: 6–7)

Arrow's explicit aim in drawing our attention to these findings of experimental psychology is to make 'a case for the proposition that an important class of intertemporal markets shows systematic deviations from rational behaviour and that these deviations are consonant with evidence from different sources collected by psychologists' (Arrow 1982: 8). In this connection Arrow notes that:

> any argument seeking to establish the presence of irrational economic behaviour meets with a standard counter argument: if most agents are irrational then a rational individual can make a lot of money; eventually therefore, the rational individuals will take over all the wealth. Hence, rational behaviour will be the effective norm.
>   (Arrow 1982: 7)[10]

While Arrow emphasises the discovery on the part of cognitive psychologists that choice is not in fact extensional, we extend Arrow's analysis by radically interrogating the appropriateness of the orthodox definition of rationality in terms of extensonality. By recourse to the development of non-extensional, modal logic[11] in the course of the twentieth century one can challenge the orthodox definition of rationality in terms of extensionality. Our thesis is that there is no reason why orthodox economists should exclude modal logic from an accurate definition of economic rationality. Moreover, if theoretical economists were to include modal logic as an integral part of their definition of rationality, many of the so-called deviations noted by cognitive psychologists from rational behaviour would not be deviations at all. In this way the 'standard counter argument', noted by Arrow above, would not arise.

To defend our thesis we first explain the contemporary logician's concept of extensionality. Historically Aristotle is recognised as the founder of logic – the categorical syllogism being the centrepiece of his logical achievements. This Aristotelian logic, as the science of valid reasoning, was assumed to be more fundamental than mathematics. Any deductive reasoning, be it legal, mathematical, philosophical, political or whatever, was subject to logical scrutiny. Thus the scope of traditional logic is much broader than that of mathematics. Over the centuries, for a variety of reasons, including 'the privileged relationship that developed over the centuries between physics and mathematics' (Debreu 1991: 2), the paths of logic and of mathematics went their separate ways. In the nineteenth century, however, their paths began to converge. This convergence was dramatically accelerated in the new, emerging domain, called the foundations of mathematics.

The foundations of mathematics has its origins in Frege's fundamental question: what are numbers? [12] In our everyday calculations as well as in advanced mathematics the concept of number is extensively used without any reflection on the question what precisely is a number? Frege set about a rigorous answer to that question. The outline of his famous logicist answer is found in his classic *The Foundations of Arithmetic*. In achieving this answer, Frege revolutionised logic by rigorously constructing what today is called propositional or truth-functional logic and quantification theory. This Fregian logic replaced traditional Aristotelian logic.[13] As Anthony Kenny points out, propositional logic and quantification theory 'have a permanent place in the heart of modern logic' (Kenny 2000: 208). For our purposes what is crucial here is (a) that these new logical systems were explicitly constructed to elucidate the deductive nature of pure mathematical reasoning; (b) that these systems are an integral part of 'the terse language' which mathematics imposes on economic theorising; and (c) these logical systems are extensional.

In contemporary logic, extensionality applies to both terms and propositions. Vis-à-vis terms, the notion of extension is sometimes introduced as follows. The expression 'the meaning of a term' as used in ordinary language is not sufficiently precise. In its place the logician uses two distinct terms, namely 'extension' and 'intension'.[14] The properties an object must possess so that the term can be correctly applied to it is called the term's intension. The extension of a term is the class of objects to which the term correctly applies. In other words the intension of a term is its defining characteristics and its extension is the set of objects referred to by the defined term. The logical function of the intension of a term is to determine the extension. In short while the intension determines the extension, the extension does not determine a unique intension. Thus when intensions differ we cannot necessarily imply that the extensions are different. Frequently when intensions differ, extensions are different. However, sometimes the same extension is determined by different intensions. For instance the intension of the term 'equiangular triangle' is different from the intension of the term 'equilateral triangle'. These two terms with different intensions, however, have the same extension. Thus any place where a mathematician uses the term 'equilateral triangle' it can be replaced by the term 'equiangular triangle' and vice versa *without changing the truth value of what is asserted*. This is an example of the principle of extensionality as applied to terms. In general this principle of extensionality is summed up by Quine as follows: 'Any two predicates which agree extensionally (i.e. are true or false of the same objects) are interchangeable *salva veritate*' (Quine 1953: 30). In other words when the extension is fixed a change in its description does not alter the validity of inferences concerning that extension.

One twentieth-century logical challenge to extensionality arose from renewed interest in medieval, modal logic on the part of C.I. Lewis and others. According to modal logicians there is no good reason to confine the discipline of logic to extensional logic. When modal logicians compare traditional Aristotelian logic with contemporary extensional logic they, of course, fully acknowledge that extensional logic is a much more sophisticated and powerful tool than Aristotelian logic. Also they tend to acknowledge the adequacy of extensional logic for classical mathematics.[15] However, they concur with traditional logicians, that the full range of logical reasoning, *conveyed in natural languages*, is not captured by extensional logic. An additional *intentional* logic, called modal logic, is required for the logical analysis of the non-extensional dimension of human decision-making conveyed in natural languages. In particular, modal logic has been exploited to logically analyse the intentional world of beliefs and of inter-temporal discourse in ways inconceivable to those who limit the domain of logic to extensionality.

This twentieth century modal logic, at the hands of C.I. Lewis, arose out of his analysis of 'if-then-' propositions. Take, for example, the proposition 'if the shares fall by 10 per cent the company is ruined'. In extensional logic this proposition has the following meaning: the conjunction of the shares falling by ten per cent and the company not being ruined *is not the case*. According to Lewis, however, 'if-then-' propositions can have a much stronger sense. The proposition 'if the shares fall by 10 per cent the company is ruined' could also mean that one is *ruling out any possibility* of the shares falling by 10 per cent and the company not being ruined. In this vein modal logic rigorously analyses the concepts of possibility and of necessity in a manner which goes beyond the boundaries of extensionality. Moreover, and what is crucial for economic methodologists, is the fact that modal logic has been exploited to rigorously elucidate the intentional domain of beliefs and choices where real time plays a significant role. We introduce the following elementary example to illustrate the significance of modal logic for economic methodologists.

Peter has shares in the Bingo Meat Company. Peter *fears* that the euro *will* collapse *next year* and he *believes* that the Bingo Meat Company will not take *the necessary* steps to avoid the worst of the negative impact of that catastrophe, *were it to occur*. Peter decides to sell his shares. Modal logicians claim that extensional logic cannot give a logically adequate account of the concepts of possibility, necessity, belief and time used by Peter which we italicised above. In addition to the inability of extensional logic to give a logically adequate account of the modal concepts of possibility and of necessity used by Peter, modal logicians also maintain that extensional logic cannot furnish a logically adequate account of how *time* functions in Peter's rationale. To see this we turn to another fundamental characteristic of extensionality, in contemporary logic, namely that any and every proposition has two and only two truth values: the true and the false. By virtue of this fundamental characteristic, extensional logic abstracts from time in its attribution of truth-values. Contrary to this characteristic, for modal logicians the proposition 'the euro will collapse next year' is a *future, contingent, unrealised possibility*, the truth-value of which *at the present moment does not exist*. The standard extensional strategy for dealing with such temporal considerations is to date all events, past, present and future. According to modal logicians this strategy amounts to adopting a cosmic exile view of the world. Peter has not *now* got the advantage of such a cosmic exile position: this idealised cosmic exile approach to time fails to appreciate that Peter is now basing his decision on a future, contingent unrealised possibility. In short extensional logic fails to adequately analyse in a rigorous way the manner in which tensed propositions function in our inferences in natural languages. As one of the pioneers of the logical investigation of time by recourse to modal logics, A.N. Prior, suggests the following is the key question. 'Is there anything special about time?' (Prior 1957: 117), where special means logically special. Ancient and medieval logicians answered yes, extensionalists (i.e. logicians who hold that extensional logic is the only true logic) answer no, while a number of contemporary modal logicians agree with the ancient and medieval logicians.[16] These logicians have gone on to systematically explore temporal applications of modal logic. Clearly these applications push the boundary of logic beyond extensionality.

In addition to its use of the modal notions of possibility and of necessity and its temporal references, the Peter example also contains the propositional operator 'X believes that –'. 'X believes that – ' is a propositional operator in the sense that when the variable X is replaced by a person's name and the logical gap is filled in by a proposition, one obtains a new proposition. However, unlike the propositional operators of extensional logic – frequently, called logical constants – namely 'it is not the case that – ', '- and – ', '– or – ', 'if – then – ', the propositional operator 'X believes that – ', is *not* extensional. Take, for instance, the propositional operator 'it is not the case that – '. Schematically its extensionality is conveyed by Truth-table 3.1, where 'T' is short for 'true' and 'F' is short for 'false'.

The proposition operator 'it is not the case that – ', when applied to a true proposition results in a new proposition which is false and when it is applied to a false proposition it results in a new, true proposition. The *extensional* table

Truth-table 3.1

p	It is not the case that p
T	F
F	T

Truth-table 3.2

p	X believes that p
T	?
F	?

(Truth-table 3.1) defines the propositional operator 'it is not the case that −'. Similar extensional definitions can be given for the other extensional operators '− and −', '− or − ', and 'if − then −'. However, an extensional truth-table cannot be devised for the propositional operator 'X believes that −'.

A proposition of the form 'X believes that p' is either true or false (Truth-table 3.2). However, simply because p is actually true, unlike the extensional operators, we cannot assert that X believes p − we just don't know. Similarly simply because p is actually false we cannot assert that X believes p is false. For this reason beliefs are *not* extensional. Once again modal logicians have developed what is called doxastic logic to rigorously explore the logic of beliefs in a non-extensional way. This doxastic logic is beyond the pale of the terse extensional language used by orthodox economic theoreticians in their mathematisation of economic theory.

To conclude this section, it goes without saying that being rigorous implies being logical. However, as indicated above, there is no consensus on how to be logical in the intentional domain of wants, beliefs, desires, etc. Some maintain that extensional logic is adequate while others develop modal logics to rigorously investigate rational decision making in an intentional world. Prima facie, since economic theory is concerned with rational decision making based on beliefs, desires, etc. expressed in natural languages and since the logic of these beliefs is not extensional, the sole use of extensional logic in orthodox mathematical economic theory is too limiting for the construction of a comprehensive, descriptively adequate and rigorous mathematical theory of economic rationality. In the economic domain of intentional action, a more comprehensive logic, which includes both doxastic and tense modal logics, is required.

Debreu and the achievement of generality

In this section we turn to Debreu's second value, namely generality. Our aim is to explain how the term generality is understood by Debreu. Firstly, we show

how generality was achieved in geometry, culminating in topology, a branch of mathematics indispensable to Debreu. We then turn to how mathematicians achieve generality by recourse to variables. The formalist school to which Debreu belongs takes mathematical generality beyond the level of variables to a higher level. This higher level is that of the empty symbol or sign – a move which was rejected by some eminent logicians and mathematicians. Mathematical generality is also achieved by means of the universal quantifier – the technical terms in logic for 'all' or 'none'. Finally mathematicians gain generality by quantifying over actual infinite domains, i.e. they investigate all the elements in actual infinite sets. Debreu operates at this highest level of generality. This gives rise to the methodological question as to whether or not an economic mathematical model which presupposes an actual infinite domain is the most appropriate way to prove the existence of equilibrium, which pertains to a finite world.

We start with a very schematic and incomplete survey of the march towards increased generality achieved in nineteenth-century geometry. We focus on geometry as its achievement of generality furnished Debreu with key mathematical innovations for proving the existence of general equilibrium, namely n-dimensional spaces and topology. Kant's *Critique of Pure Reason*, first published in 1781, was a classic in philosophy of mathematics. In the *Critique*, Kant defended Euclidean geometry on the grounds of its universality or generality, i.e. its applicability to *all* observable phenomena. In this Kantian approach, Euclidean geometry is privileged as the universal geometry true of the observable world, in the sense of that it is both prior to, and true of, all objects given in sensory experience. This philosophical privileging of Euclidean geometry did not hinder mathematicians in their pursuit of generality along different lines. We note three such developments. Firstly, Euclidean geometry was historically confined to three dimensions – the geometry privileged in classical Newtonian mechanics. By severing the link to experimental physics/ mechanics, mathematicians generalised Euclid by considering spaces with more than three dimensions – hence the mathematical study of n-dimensional geometry, where n is any positive integer. Of course we cannot imagine a space with, for instance, a thousand dimensions, but mathematicians can consistently develop its geometry. This generality, which from the point of view of classical physics was of no practical interest, will be exploited by Debreu in representing an economy with vast numbers of actions, goods and services.

Secondly in privileging Euclid as the geometry of the physical world, Kant privileged the Euclidean definition of distance, technically called the Euclidean metric. However, since Euclid first axiomatised geometry, mathematicians over the centuries were intrigued by his parallel postulate, namely, given any point outside a straight line, one and only one line can be drawn through the given point parallel to the given line. Could one develop a consistent geometry without the parallel postulate? A definite answer to this question was developed notably by Lobachevsky and Riemann with the birth of Lobackewskian and Riemannian geometries – thereby generalising in another direction the inherited notion of geometry. These geometries postulated different metrics – definitions of distance – to that of Euclid – thereby generalising the concept of a metric from its traditional Euclidean conception privileged by Kant. Thirdly, if one can have consistent geometries without the Euclidean metric, can one have a consistent geometry where one abstracts from any and every concept of a metric? – a space where relationships hold which are completely independent of, and thus is no way based on, the notion of distance? At the close of the nineteenth and the beginning of the twentieth century, mathematicians, like Poincaré and Brouwer, developed such a geometry, which is today known as topology. Topology is a very general geometry, totally independent of any measure of magnitude. This very general geometry, especially Brouwer's fixed point theorem, is crucial to Debreu's proof of general equilibrium. Thus without this mathematical pursuit of generality, General Equilibrium Theory as developed by Debreu would not be achievable.

According to the formalist school the quest for logico-mathematical generality does not stop there. As we have seen with the geometrical concept of an n-dimensional space, mathematical generality is achieved by use of the variable 'n'. Normally mathematicians do not stop to consider what a variable is. Rather they go ahead and use them. In foundational studies, however, one must be logically clear about variables and their roles. For instance, as Frege points out, the variable 'x' in (i) if x>1 then x>0, is not playing the same role as the numeral '5' plays in if 5>1 then 5>0. Moreover, claims like the variable 'x' refers to an indefinite number or a variable number are utterly misleading. Whatever numbers are, each number is something definite. Rigorously speaking, there is no such thing as an indefinite number or a variable number. The expression 'indefinite number' or 'variable number', like the expression 'square circle', is contradictory.[17] Rather, as Frege argued, the variable 'x' in (i) above is used *to gain generality*. Moreover, and what is crucial for Frege, the level of generality achieved in (i) is not devoid of content or meaning. (i) conveys the meaningful (and indeed true) proposition, namely whatever number is greater than one is a positive number. In this vein, according to Frege, as a discipline becomes more formal by the use of variables, it becomes more general. However, no matter how general it becomes, it always has some content or other no matter how abstract. Thus while logic and mathematics are rendered general by their recourse to variables, they still remain within the boundary of semantics: the symbolic formulae of logic and of mathematics are not contentless. On the one hand logical and mathematical formulae do not have the concrete content or meaning which, for instance, a descriptive sentence in a natural language conveys. On the other hand these formulae are not empty strokes on paper, totally devoid of any sense or meaning. In short the formulae of logic and of mathematics have a distinct, very general, semantical component.

The formalist school rejects this Fregian, semantical philosophy of mathematical variables. The correct level of logico-mathematical generality is at the level of the empty symbol or sign and not at the level of the semantical reading of variables. To attain this level of generality, one has to abstract from the different meanings traditionally associated with variables in mathematical formulae, culminating in symbols or signs without any semantical content. Another way of putting this is as follows. In ordinary language we distinguish between a symbol and what it symbolises. The fundamental subject matter of pure mathematics consists of symbols alone, without any reference to what a symbol is conventionally taken to symbolise. Thus according to the formalist school pure mathematics is a purely syntactical system which is (a) axiomatised and (b) proven to be consistent.[18] In short the fundamental building block of pure mathematics is the empty symbol or sign. Hilbert sums up this highest level of generality achieved in pure mathematics by altering the opening sentence of St. John's Gospel to 'in the beginning was the sign' (Hilbert 1922: 202). In this same formalist idiom, Debreu insists on 'the divorce of form from content' (Debreu 1986: 1265).

One may well wonder how this formalist philosophy of pure mathematics is relevant to economic methodology. As we have insisted on various occasions, theoretical economics is applied, not pure, mathematics. We will discuss this issue in detail in the next chapter when we interrogate Debreu's conception of the axiomatisation of theoretical economics. For the moment we note two points. Firstly, this formalist philosophy of pure mathematics is central to Debreu's conception of applied mathematics. *Applied mathematics is defined in terms of this formalist conception of pure mathematics.* In general, applied mathematics is, by definition, any semantical interpretation of the empty symbolism of pure mathematics. Thus applied mathematics is not necessarily about the real, observable world. Applied mathematics has a much more extensive range: in principle it ranges over any semantical interpretation, from fact to fiction, of the syntactical calculus. As we will see in the next chapter this is crucial to the correct understanding of Debreu's own 'philosophy of economic analysis' (Debreu 1992: 114).

The second point concerns the critical evaluation of Debreu's philosophy of economic analysis. One way of criticising Debreu's philosophy of economics is to undermine the formalist conception of pure mathematics used in the definition of applied mathematics. In this connection eminent logicians, such as Frege, and outstanding mathematicians, such as Poincaré, argue that the formalist conception of pure mathematics is in principle and in fact inoperable. According to Frege 'no one ever really puts this theory (formalism) into practice or indeed could put it into practice, since if he did, it would very quickly become useless' (Frege 1971: 145). Formalism doesn't work 'because formal arithmetic cannot do without the sense which its objects have in nonformal arithmetic' (Frege 1971: 137). Poincaré makes much the same point.

You (the formalist) give a subtle definition of number and then, once the definition has been given, you think no more about it, because in reality it is not your definition that has taught you what a number is, you knew it long before, and when you come to write the word number further on you give it the same meaning as everyone else.

(Poincaré 1956: 154)

In short the formalist philosophy of pure mathematics presupposes the normal sense of the word number in its formalist theory of number. Whatever the value of this objection, Debreu's specific understanding of the mathematical commitment to generality is in need of closer scrutiny, a scrutiny which is found not in the philosophy of science, but rather in the philosophy of mathematics.

The final dimension of generality presupposed by Debreu plays a crucial role in the methodological evaluation of the success or otherwise of Debreu's proof of the existence of equilibrium. This dimension concerns the domain of mathematical quantification. In this connection, philosophers of mathematics distinguish between three distinct domains of universal quantification. The first domain is uncontroversial: it is the domain of the finite. For instance consider the finite set of all prime numbers between 10 and 20. This finite set has the following elements: 11, 13, 17, 19. This set is complete and can be surveyed in its totality. Completeness and surveyability are defining characteristics of a finite set. The second domain of universal quantification is the domain of what is called potential infinity. For instance the sequence of all natural numbers, 1, 2, 3 … 1000,000,001 *and so on* is a potentially infinite sequence. There is no bounded natural number at which this sequence will terminate. Unlike the finite, the process of generating this sequence will never terminate. This is indicated by the phrase 'and so on'. This sequence or set, unlike the finite, is essentially incomplete and the outcome can never be surveyed in its totality. Prior to the revolutionary research by Cantor, quantification in mathematics was believed to be exhausted by the domains of the finite and the potentially infinite. Cantor, however, argued for the extension of the domain of quantification beyond that of potential infinity to what philosophers of mathematics call actual infinity. For instance, the set of real numbers between 2 and 3 including 2 and 3, (this set contains all the rational numbers between 2 and 3 and all non-rational numbers like the cube root of 5) is an actual infinite set. This infinite set is not open-ended, i.e. is not incomplete. Also it appears to be surveyable. As Dummett puts it, in the case of an actual infinite set it is 'as if we could be presented with the entire output of an infinite set' (Dummett 2000: 41). In having recourse to actual infinite sets the defining characteristic of potential infinity, namely incompleteness, is dropped.

The following is a non-rigorous rationale for extending mathematical infinity to include actual infinity. Take the potential infinite sequence of natural numbers and the infinite sequence of rational numbers (fractions). Are there more rational numbers than natural numbers? The answer is no. The rational numbers can be put in one-to-one correspondence with the natural numbers. The set of rational numbers is a countable potential infinite set. Now consider the infinite set of real numbers which includes all the natural numbers, all the rational numbers and all the other numbers, like the cube root of 5 and so on. This infinite set of real numbers cannot be put in one-to-one correspondence with the set of natural numbers. It is, as it were, bigger than the potential infinite set of natural numbers. Thus there is more to mathematical infinity than the domain of potentially infinity. Mathematical infinity must include actual infinity. Indeed by developing what is called power sets, Cantor argued that there is an infinity of levels of infinity.[19]

From the outset this ingenious Cantorian approach to infinity in mathematics proved controversial. For instance Kronecker, a member of the Berlin Academy and Professor of Mathematics at the University of Berlin, vehemently opposed Cantor's recourse to actual infinity. Cantor was accused of illegitimately transferring the characteristics of completeness and surveyability – characteristics of the finite – to mathematical infinity, a transfer which destroys the essence of infinity, namely a structure which is never complete. The formalist school totally rejects this critique of Cantor. Hilbert's claim 'no one shall drive us out of the paradise that Cantor has created for us' (Hilbert 1926: 191) is a cornerstone of formalism.[20]

In particular the real number system is an actual infinite set. This is the concept of the real number system used by Debreu in his *Theory of Value*. Thus the mathematical domain in which Debreu proves the existence of equilibrium is an actual infinite domain. In this connection we introduce a prevailing undercurrent to this and subsequent chapters, which we call the Poincaré malaise. In proving the existence of equilibrium, presumably the theoretical economist is concerned with the possibility of equilibrium existing in some socio-economic organisation which is realisable in some finite time horizon, however large. After all an actual infinity of years or days is way beyond say trillions and trillions of years or days! The Poincaré malaise is the uneasiness in using actual infinity as the domain of proof for any such finitely realisable system. We call this the Poincaré malaise because Poincaré was one of the first to raise questions about approaching the finite in mathematics from the starting point of actual infinity. Those advocating a Cantorian approach to the finite:

> propose to teach mathematics to a pupil who does not yet know *the difference that exists between infinity and the finite*; they do *not* hasten to teach him what this difference consists of; they begin by teaching him all that can be known about infinity without being concerned about this distinction. Then in a *remote* region of the field in which they made him wander, they show him a small corner where the finite numbers are hidden.
>
> (Poincaré 1963: 64, italics ours)

In Debreu's mathematical model of an economy constructed in the domain of Cantorian actual infinity, is the finite world so remote as to render his proof of the existence of equilibrium economically superfluous? To conclude this section, Debreu's commitment to the value of generality is very far from being simple. In this section we have briefly introduced various dimensions of this value and briefly indicated some reservations. In the next section we turn to his notion of simplicity. Like the concept of generality, its use too proves to be rather complex!

Debreu, simplicity and existence proofs

Debreu's *Theory of Value* is celebrated for its rigorous proof of the existence of general equilibrium. In this section we address the concepts of existence and of proof used by Debreu and how his existence proof is related to his value of simplicity. We explain how Debreu's notion of existence does not imply that the concept of equilibrium is actually or approximately true of some actual socio-economic system. Rather Debreu, in line with his commitment to the formalist school, and contrary to some eminent non-formalist logicians, such as Frege, equates existence with freedom from contradiction. Moreover, vis-à-vis his proof of the existence of equilibrium, we introduce the crucial distinction between constructive and non-constructive proofs in mathematics. Debreu's proof of the existence of equilibrium is a non-constructive one. Given his commitment to simplicity, we argue that Debreu would not be concerned about the non-constructive nature of his proof. However, for someone not committed to formalism, the facts that (a) the domain of mathematics used in this proof is, as we saw in the last section, Cantorian actual infinity and (b) the proof is inherently non-constructive, the Poincaré malaise, introduced in the previous section becomes more troubling: the methodological question as to whether or not a non-constructive proof of existence in the domain of Cantorian actual infinity is relevant to the question of existence in a real economic system which is assumed to be a finite, constructable system cannot be easily dismissed.

According to Debreu 'mathematics also dictates the imperative of simplicity. It relentlessly searches for short transparent proofs' (Debreu 1991: 4). This commitment to simplicity in proofs is a key characteristic of the formalist school. As Weyl, for instance, points out 'in Hilbert's approach to mathematics *simplicity* and *rigor* go hand in hand' (Weyl 1944: 616).[21] This is clearly evident in Hilbert's famous address to the Second International Congress of Mathematics in Paris, in 1900, where he maintains that:

> it is an error to believe that rigor in the proof is the enemy of simplicity. On the contrary, we find it confirmed by numerous examples that the rigorous method is at the same time the simpler and more easily comprehended. The very effort of rigor forces us to discover simpler methods of proof.
>
> (Hilbert 1900: 78)

For the formalist school we can say that, ceteris paribus, one chooses the simpler of two or more proofs. We argue that this commitment to simplicity has implications for Debreu's proof of the existence of equilibrium.

However, before addressing the kind of proof used, one must first clarify the concept of existence presupposed in Debreu's proof. According to Frege, Russell and numerous other logicians, the concept of existence is a logical concept – technically called the existential quantifier. This means that logical analysis is required to grasp the correct, rigorous meaning of existence. Logicians, however, do *not start* their logical analysis with the concept of existence. Rather they commence their analysis with elementary, or atomic propositions – the simplest range of propositions. An atomic proposition logically is analysed into a name and a predicate. For example 'Debreu is a famous economist' or 'seven is a prime number' are examples of atomic/elementary propositions. The presence of the names 'Debreu', 'seven' enables us to identify elementary propositions. The logical form of an atomic proposition is 'ax', where 'a-' is a predicate variable and 'x' is a name variable. Complex propositions are derived from elementary propositions. An existential proposition is a specific complex pro-position which is derived from elementary propositions. For instance, 'famous economists exist' or 'prime numbers exist' are complex propositions, derived from elementary propositions in two steps. In the first step the logician drops the name from the elementary proposition, resulting in a predicate. In the above examples '- is a famous economist' or '- is a prime number' are the predicates obtained in this way. These predicates are sometimes symbolised as $\hat{x}ax$, where '$\hat{x}$' is called an abstractor: '$\hat{x}$' indicates that the predicate is obtained by abstracting from the name variable in the elementary propositional form ax.[22] In the second step the logician attaches the existential quantifier, 'E', to the predicate $\hat{x}ax$ to obtain the complex propositional form, E$\hat{x}ax$, i.e. *a* exists. Thus E$\hat{x}ax$ is the logical form of the proposition 'famous economists exist'. The proposition 'prime numbers exist' exhibits this same logical form.

In this logical context, to claim, for instance, famous economists exist one is claiming that the concept 'famous economist' is not empty: some entity falls under the concept 'famous economist'.[23] Similarly to claim prime numbers exist is to claim that some object falls under the concept prime number. This is the logical meaning of the concept of existence. This meaning does not change as one moves from one domain to another. For instance take the existence claims (whether justifiable or not is not the issue) prime numbers exist, electro-magnetic fields exist, viruses exist, social structures exist, equilibrium exists, heaven exists, ghosts exist. The common element is the existence claim, namely something falls under each of these concepts.

According to some logicians, e.g. Frege, this concept of existence is *not* to be confused with the concept of non-contradiction. Certainly if a concept is contradictory, e.g. square circle, one can logically infer that nothing falls under it. For instance, square circles do not exist follows from the truth that the con-cept of square circle is contradictory. However, if a concept is non-contradictory, one cannot imply that something falls under it. Frege illustrates this point by recourse to the concept of God. Suppose theists and atheists agree that the concept of God is not contradictory. The dispute between them is whether or not some being falls under the consistent concept of God, i.e. whether or not the concept of God is empty. Thus logical existence as conveyed by the existential quantifier is not equivalent to freedom from contradiction.

However, in virtue of their commitment to generality and simplicity, the formalist school rejects this Fregian analysis of existence. As we saw in the last section on generality, formalists insist that the meanings of symbols play no role whatsoever in mathematics. Rather they insist that mathematics operates at the more general and simpler level of the empty symbol. Formalists take what Debreu aptly calls 'the divorce of form from content' (Debreu 1959: x) seriously. Instead of a plurality of symbols with distinct, different meanings, the formalist operates with distinct but meaningless symbols. Thus the concept of existence as outlined above, where the meaning of the existential quantifier plays a logical role, has no role to play in the formalist school's approach to pure mathematics.

How then does the formalist use the concept of existence in mathematics? There is one door still open to the formalist: define mathematical existence as freedom from contradiction. For the formalist mathematical existence is equated with freedom from contradiction − a thesis rejected by Frege and other logicians on the grounds that existence is an univocal concept which has a fixed logical meaning in domains ranging from theology to mathematics, which goes beyond claiming a system is consistent. We are not taking sides in the debate between formalists and their opponents. Our thesis is that, however plausible it may seem, the formalist's equation of existence with freedom from contradiction is a contentious one in the philosophy of logic. Be that as it may, by embracing the formalist school's approach to mathematics, Debreu in proving the existence of general equilibrium does not prove that there is an actual economy which is either in or approximates to equilibrium.[24] Neither does it prove that equilibrium correctly describes some existing economy. Rather, at best he has rigorously demonstrated that the concept of equilibrium as defined by the theory is free from contradiction in a Cantorian infinite world.

Having briefly addressed the conception of existence in the formalist school, we now turn to the issue of proof. Most mathematicians have an intuitive understanding of what a correct and an incorrect proof is: they do not concern themselves with the foundational question of what precisely is a proof? As we saw, the formalist school does not rely on intuition. It furnishes a systematic explicit account of proof which we will address in the next chapter. For our present purposes, i.e. the role of simplicity in a rigorous proof, we focus on two kinds of proof, namely constructive proof and non-constructive proof. Firstly, take the notion of a constructive proof. For example, does a solution to the equation $3x^2 + 6x + 1 = 0$ exist? If we claim such a solution exists how do we prove it? We prove it by constructing the real number using the algorithmetic rule:

$$x = \frac{-b \pm \sqrt{b^2 - 4ac}}{2a}$$

for solving the quadratic equation $ax^2 + bx + c = 0$. In general a constructive proof is an effective mechanical procedure which can be carried out in a finite number of steps for finding the required entity. It supplies an algorithm for obtaining the given object.

A non-constructive proof does not have recourse to such algorithms. The following is a template of a non-constructive existence proof:

1   Assume the object, *m*, does not exist.[25]
2   Demonstrate that (1) leads to a contradiction. Hence the assumption that *m* does not exist is contradictory.
3   By the logical principle of the excluded middle, either *m* exists is true or *m* does not exist is true.
4   By step (2) *m* does not exist, cannot be true.
5   Therefore by step (3) m exists is true.

This template of a non-constructive existence proof is called *a reductio ad absurdum* proof. It gives us no information about how to access or obtain, in a finite number of steps, the object proven to exist.

In pure mathematics both constructive and non-constructive methods are used to prove existence. In a constructive existence proof, a finite, effective procedure or algorithm is used to display the entity, i.e. the entity is shown to be accessible in a finite number of explicitly stated steps. In a non-constructive existence proof no information about how to, in a finite number of steps, access the object is given or used in the proof. As is well known, Debreu's proof of the existence of equilibrium, being based on the Brouwer/Kakutani fixed point theorems, is a non-constructive proof.[26] This is not problematical to a formalist. As Weyl for instances emphasises, non-constructive proofs are generally simpler than constructive ones.[27] Given Debreu's commitment to simplicity of proofs, he would see no reason to question the appropriateness of a non-constructive existence proof. However fine this may be in pure mathematics, Debreu's central focus is the applied mathematical discipline of theoretical economics. As we have already seen the Poincaré malaise concerns the issue of the appropriateness of the unquestioning use of Cantorian actual infinity as a means of logically analysing a finite domain. When one adds that the existence proof is non-constructive, this malaise becomes more worrying. Vis-à-vis Debreu's proof the Poincaré malaise raises the following methodological question. Given the domain of proof is Cantorian actual infinity, which includes an infinity of infinities, and given the existence proof is non-constructive and thus cannot be transformed into a process or procedure which can be carried out in a finite number of steps (however large that finite number might be), how can such an entity be given an interpretation in a finite domain? In particular, how is such a proof helpful in solving the two central problems of Debreu's *Theory of Value,* namely '(1) the explanation of the prices of commodities resulting from the interaction of agents of a private ownership economy through markets, (2) the explanation of the role of prices in an optimal state of an economy' (Debreu 1959: vii)?

In this and the previous sections we have attempted to elucidate what Debreu calls 'the local views' (Debreu 1986: 1260) of the mathematisation of economics and on how the final phase of this process of mathematisation imbues theoretical economists with the values of rigour, generality and simplicity. We have briefly reflected on how these values operate according to the form-alist school to which Debreu belongs. In the remaining sections we turn to what he calls 'a global view' (Debreu 1986: 1260) which is also indispensable to his 'philosophy of economic analysis' (Debreu 1992: 114).

Debreu's global view of the mathematisation of economics

According to Debreu the local view of the mathematisation of economics, if taken as a complete account of this process, 'would yield a distorted historical perception' (Debreu 1986: 1260). The contingencies of the local view must be 'complemented by a global view which sees in the development of mathematical economics a powerful, irresistible current of thought' (Debreu 1986: 1260–1261). In this global view 'a perfect fit of mathematical form to economic content is evident' (Debreu 1986: 1262). For instance,

> in a global historical view, the perfect fit between the mathematical concept of a fixed point and the social science concept of an equilibrium stands out. A state of a social system is described by listing an action for each one of its agents. Considering such a system, each agent reacts by selecting the action that is optimal for him given the actions of all others. Listing those reactions yields a new state, and thereby a transformation of the set of states of the social system into itself is defined. A state of the system is an equilibrium if, and only if, it is a fixed point of that transformation.
>
> (Debreu 1986: 1262)

This relationship of perfect fit is between two totally separate and distinct elements namely mathematical form and economic content. Obviously one needs to be absolutely clear on (a) the mathematical form, (b) the economic content and (c) the manner in which this perfect fit is established.

Firstly we address the concept of mathematical form. As we have already seen, mathematical form is given an extremely general and unique characterisation by the formalist school. Pure mathematics is a vast, overarching, contentless, axiomatic structure.[28] This mathematical structure must be used in any piece of applied mathematics. Anyone engaged in applied mathematics has to identify the relevant parts or substructures of this overarching structure of pure mathematics and show how the domain of application fits that given sub-structure.[29] In this vein the parts of this overarching structure of pure mathematics relevant to theoretical economics as an applied mathematical discipline are clearly identified by Debreu in Chapter 1 of his *Theory of Value*.

We now turn to the economic content. In this connection it is crucial to note that Debreu does *not* claim that a perfect fit exists between mathematical form and real economies. Rather he has recourse to the language of the formalist school by claiming the fit is to 'economic content' (Debreu 1986: 1261). Debreu is using the term 'content' as it is explicated by the formalist school. As we have already seen, according to the formalist, the axiomatic symbolisation of pure mathematics is purely syntactical, with no semantical component, and is thus contentless. Content is equated with the extensive domain of semantics, i.e. the domain of meaning. In this formalist explication any semantical component has content. In particular content is not equated with observational or empirical content. Rather, any meaningful discourse, ranging from semantical logic to the humanities, to the empirical sciences, to fiction or any non-contradictory combination of these, has content.

Aside from specifying the outer limits of content in terms of semantics, formalists, qua formalists, have nothing to say about the content of specific domains. The content in a specific domain is determined by the domain in question and its researchers. In this connection Debreu identifies the economic content in Chapters 2 to 5 of his *Theory of Value* where he introduces us to his account of commodities, prices, producers, consumers and the total resources of an economy and so on. This economic content is a sophisticated combination of numerous, explicitly stated assumptions and very general characteristics of an economy derived by a process of empirical abstraction from the observation of economic agents and their actions and reactions.

In connection with what we call 'the empirical process of abstraction', it is crucial to note that Debreu in his *Theory of Value* uses the term 'abstract' in two distinct senses. In this he is following normal practice. As we have already seen when introducing the mathematical concepts and terms of Chapter 1, he emphasises the 'ability to think abstractly' (Debreu 1959: 1). Here abstract means general, as opposed to concrete, such as the capacity to conceptualise without visualising an n-dimensional space. However, in Chapter 3 he uses the verb 'to abstract' in the sense of the empirical process of abstraction. Thus he maintains that the economic concept of a producer is acquired in this fashion.

> In the study of production, when one abstracts *from* legal forms of organization (corporations, sole proprietor shops, partnerships, …) and types of activity (Agriculture, Mining, Construction, Manufacturing, Transportation, Services, …), one *obtains* the concept of a producer, i.e. an economic agent whose role is to choose (and carry out) a production plan.
>
> (Debreu 1959: 37, our italics)

The same process is used to obtain the concept of a consumer. Epistemologically, the empirical process of abstraction is claimed to show how we acquire concepts from observation. This empirical process of abstraction has two defining characteristics: (a) one leaves aside or ignores specific characteristics observed in only some of the objects or range of objects pointed to or presented for observation, and (b) after this abstracting from is completed, *the real common property* of all the objects in the range becomes apparent.

Debreu's central claim is that there is a perfect fit between the mathematics of Chapter 1 and economic content. How is this fit accomplished? It is accomplished in three steps. Firstly, in line with the formalist conception of pure mathematics, all elements of meaning are eliminated from these mathematical concepts, culminating in a specific syntactical sub-structure of the vast purely syntactical structure of the whole axiomatic structure of pure mathematics. This purely syntactical sub-structure is what is mathematically given. In the next step theoretical economists examine the empirical content about producers, consumers and so on, obtained by abstracting from legal forms of corporations and other characteristics, to see whether or not this empirical content has the syntactical structure of the mathematics identified in the first step. They see that the fit is not perfect. In the third step, in order to establish a perfect fit, this empirical content is modified by processes of idealisation and of assumptions. This modification of the empirical content is driven by the mathematics of Chapter 1. This modified content thus has the mathematical form identified in Chapter 1.[30] The outcome is Debreu's much quoted definition of an economy.

> An economy E is defined by: for each $i = 1, \ldots , m$ a non-empty subset X_i of R^l completely preordered by $\precsim_i$; for each $j = 1 , \ldots , n$ a non-empty subset Y_j of R^l; a point ω of R^l. A state of E is an $(m+n)$-tuple of points of R^l.
>
> (Debreu 1959: 75)

As Weintraub and Mirowski point out, at the time of publication 'few would have readily recognized this portrait of an "economy" … While more than one member of the profession might have thought that this species of economist had dropped from Mars, in fact he had migrated from France' (Weintraub and Mirowski 1994: 258).

   To further clarify Debreu's approach, we compare the above definition of an economy to the algebraic definition of a circle, viz. $x^2 + y^2 + 2gx + 2fy + c = 0$. Like Debreu's definition, when this definition of a circle was first introduced few would have recognised this portrait of a circle. However this is an accurate definition of a circle. Debreu, however, does *not* claim that his definition is an accurate representation of a real economy. Rather he is claiming that, when interpreted, it is not devoid of economic content. More precisely it represents the mathematical structure of the economic content of his *Theory of Value*, which is the outcome of the process of empirical abstraction qualified by numerous, explicitly stated, assumptions. As we will see in Chapter Five, for empirically minded economists, like Kaldor, this model, based on Debreu's specific abstractions, idealisations and assumptions, is of no help in their studies of actual economies. Debreu could reply that the empirical study of actual economies was not his problem in his *Theory of Value*. Rather his basic problem was to find a rigorous mathematical proof of Adam Smith's thesis of the hidden hand. The formalist model of applied mathematics is the rigorous method to attaining that end. In this formalist approach to applied mathematics, Debreu is unquestionably justified in insisting on (a) that his idealisations and assumptions still leave his model in the domain of content as defined by formalists and (b) that his process of empirical abstraction legitimates characterising that very abstract content as economic.[31] Given Debreu's model or definition of an economy quoted above the proof of the existence of equilibrium is not very complex. The existence of equilibrium is logically established by applying the

Brouwer/Kakutani fixed point theorem to this definition. We know of no better summary than that given by Debreu himself which we repeat here.

'But in a global historical view, the perfect fit between the mathematical concept of a fixed point and the social science concept of an equilibrium stands out. A state of a social system is described by listing an action for each one of its agents. Considering such a state, each agent reacts by selecting the action that is optimal for him given the action of all others. Listing those reactions yields a new state, and thereby a transformation of the set of states of the social system into itself is defined. A state of the system is in equilibrium if, and only if, it is a fixed point of that transformation. More generally, if the optimal reactions of the agents to a given state are not uniquely determined, one is led to associate a set of new states, instead of a single state, with every state of the system. A point-to-set transformation of the set of states of the social system into itself is thereby defined; and a state of the system is an equilibrium if, and only if, it is a fixed point of that transformation'.

(Debreu 1986: 1262).

This fixed point is demonstrated to exist by Brouwer's fixed point theorem and Kakutanai's generalisation of Brouwer's theorem.[32] Thus general equilibrium is proven to exist in a proof which meets the standards of rigour of the formalist school.

To conclude, in light of the foregoing, Debreu feels justified in claiming that a 'powerful irresistible current of thought' exists in the mathematisation of economics where the perfect fit between mathematical form and economic content is discovered. This powerful current of thought is not evident in 'local views' (Debreu 1986: 1262), limited to significant, historical contingencies. Local views must be complemented with this global view, rooted in the formalist school's understanding of rigour, generality and simplicity.

Debreu's proof of the existence of equilibrium and the Poincaré malaise

In this chapter we have been engaged in a dual process. Firstly, in light of the formalist school's distinction between pure and applied mathematics and its commitments to the values of generality, rigour and simplicity, we have attempted to deepen our understanding of Debreu's philosophy of economic analysis, especially his proof of the existence of equilibrium. Secondly, we used alternative philosophies of mathematics to that of the formalist school to raise some critical questions vis-à-vis Debreu's own philosophy of economic analysis. In this section we sum up these methodological questions under the heading already used, namely the Poincaré malaise. The name, the Poincaré malaise, is chosen because Poincaré's philosophy of pure and applied mathematics inspired some of our formulations of these reservations. The rationale for this summing up is that the themes of this malaise continue to inform the critical elements in subsequent chapters.

There are five distinct themes to the Poincaré malaise. The first concerns the formalist school's conception of pure mathematics. This is relevant to any critical evaluation of Debreu's own philosophy of economic analysis. As we have seen, Debreu's conception of applied mathematics, under which his notion of theoretical economics falls, is defined in terms of the formalist school's characterisation of pure mathematics – a conception not available to Walras. However, Poincaré raised the issue of the adequacy of the formalist school's characterisation of pure mathematics: it is not adequate to pure mathematical practice. If this kind of objection is legitimate,[33] then Debreu's definition of applied mathematics is defective. The second theme is extensionality. The logic presupposed by the mathematics used by Debreu is, as noted by Arrow, an extensional logic. The question arises as to whether or not this kind of mathematics is the appropriate mode for the scientific study of the intentional domain in which economic decision making operates. We used non-extensional, model logic to indicate the limitations of extensional mathematics for a comprehensive analysis of rationality in a non-extensional domain.[34] The third theme is Cantorian, actual infinity. This is the mathematical domain used by Debreu in proving the existence of general equilibrium. Two key objections to Cantorian infinity are raised by Poincaré. Firstly he argues that in order to avoid the paradoxes in the foundations of mathematics, the only infinity available to mathematicians is potential infinity. Secondly, he expresses reservations about any analysis which starts with Cantorian infinity to elucidate the finite. For Poincaré 'infinity is derived from the finite; infinity exists because there is an infinity of possible finite things. For others (Cantorian) infinity exists before the finite; the finite is obtained by cutting out a small piece from infinity' (Poincaré 1963: 66). Prima facie this Cantorian approach to the finite does not appear helpful to a social science like theoretical economics, which, as acknowledged by Debreu, lacks recourse to sophisticated experimentation.

The fourth theme concerns the proof of the existence of equilibrium based on Brouwer's fixed point theorem. Brouwer's fixed point theorem, however, is not logically derived by means of a constructive proof which can be effected in a finite number of steps. If it were there would be no objection to its use in the proof of the existence of equilibrium: its use in the proof would be, in principle, translatable into a finite number of steps. Since the proof of Brouwer's fixed point theorem is a non-constructive one, it cannot be translated into a finite number of steps. Hence its use to prove the existence of the social science concept of equilibrium suggests that the existence established cannot be effected in a finite number of steps. As Poincaré says 'even though the notion of infinity plays a role in the statement of a theorem, there must be no reference to it in the proof; otherwise this proof would be impossible' (Poincaré 1963: 66). For a constructivist like Poincaré, a Debreu-type proof is 'devoid of meaning' (Poincaré 1963: 67).

The final theme concerns Debreu's characterisation of economic content. As we saw in the last section, Debreu's concepts of producers, consumers and commodities are very general. They abstract from kinds of economic activity, legal requirements and so on which actually effect economic decisions. Moreover these abstractions are rendered more remote from economic reality by recourse to idealisations and assumptions. For Debreu the exact formulation of these assumptions is 'an effective safeguard against the ever-present temptation to apply economic theory beyond its domain of validity' (Debreu 1986: 1266). In this he is undoubtedly correct. However, the Poincaré malaise re-echoes the malaise Poincaré raised vis-à-vis Walras, namely some of these assumptions go beyond proper empirico-scientific limits. This raises a crucial methodological question: can one construct an equally powerful, alternative mathematical model of the general features of an economy to that of Debreu? To do so, one requires an alternative mathematics. Brouwer, under the influence of Poincaré, constructed intuitionist mathematics in opposition to Cantorian mathematics. Is this Brouwerian mathematics more appropriate or as appropriate to economic theorising than the Cantorian mathematics exploited by Debreu under the influence of the formalist school? We will address this question in Chapter Seven.

The methodological angst, sourced in the Poincaré malaise, is due to the combined effect of these symptoms. Any one taken on its own may not be sufficient. When taken together, however, the malaise needs closer examination. As we will see in the next chapter, the formalist school's response to this angst is further training in formalism.

Debreu, Walras and the proof of the existence of equilibrium

By way of concluding this chapter we briefly compare and contrast Debreu's *Theory of Value* with Walras' *Elements*. Debreu is very clear that

> contemporary developments in the theory of general equilibrium took Walras' work as their point of departure, but some of Walras' ideas had a long lineage that included Adam Smith's (1776) profound insight. Smith's idea that many agents of an economy, making independent decisions, do not create utter chaos, but actually contribute to producing a social optimum raises a scientific question of central importance.
>
> (Debreu 1984: 275)

This is the question of proving the existence of general equilibrium. Smith's 'profound insight' is frequently characterised by the metaphor of the hidden hand. This metaphor sums up the claim that the actions of vast numbers of producers and of consumers, each acting in self-interest, without any central authority, could culminate in an equilibrium set of prices, i.e. a price system which is socially optimum and hence no further change in prices would be necessary. Prima facie the thesis of the hidden hand is astonishing and requires justification. This justification in the form of a rigorous proof is supplied by Debreu's *Theory of Value*.

Firstly, in any comparison between Walras' *Elements* and Debreu's *Theory of Value*, one is struck by the different intellectual milieus. Walras' *Elements* was published in an intellectual climate which was suspicious of, and at times hostile to, the mathematisation of economics. Debreu's *Theory of Value* was published in a more congenial intellectual climate to the exploitation of mathematics in economic theorising. Because of the suspicious intellectual climate, Walras' *Elements*, while certainly innovative at the level of theory construction, is also rhetorical: it is an original effort to rationally persuade its readership of the scientific value of the exercise. However, no such rhetorical effort is required on the part of Debreu: the assumption is that Walras has won the rhetorical battle.

Also, as noted by Debreu, there is a marked contrast in the mathematics used. Walras exploits differential calculus, which proved so successful in classical mechanics, whereas differential equations play no role in Debreu's *Theory of Value*. Debreu uses topology, including Brouwer's fixed point theorem, set theory, n-dimensional vector space, etc. to prove the existence of equilibrium. Debreu contrasts his proof of the existence of equilibrium with that of Walras as follows:

> The mathematical model of a competitive economy of L. Walras (1874–77) was conceived as an attempt to explain the state of equilibrium reached by a large number of small agents interacting through markets. Walras himself perceived that the theory he proposed would be vacuous without a mathematical argument in support of the existence of at least one equilibrium state. However for more than half a century the equality of the number of equations and of the number of unknown of the Walrasian model remained the only, *unconvincing*, remark made in favour of the existence of a competitive equilibrium ...
>
> (Debreu 1982: 697, italics ours).

The same point is repeated in his Nobel Prize lecture in 1983.

> Walras and his successors for six decades perceived that his theory would be vacuous without an argument in support of the existence of at least one equilibrium point and noted that in his model the number of equations equals the number of unknowns, *an argument that cannot convince a mathematician*. One must, however, immediately add that the mathematical tools that later made the solution of the existence problem possible did not exist when Walras wrote one of the greatest classics, if not the greatest of our science.
>
> (Debreu 1984: 268, italics ours)

The standards of rigor demanded by formalist mathematicians is not met by Walras' assumption that when the number of equations and the number of unknowns are equal, a solution exists. Indeed as Scarf points out,

> although the observation that a system of n equations in n unknowns, generally has a solution is fairly credible when the equations are linear, it is

misleading for nonlinear equations of the type arising in the competitive model. Such a system may easily have no solution at all, or only those which are meaningless from an economic point of view.

(Scarf 1973: 2)

Since the 1930s alternative approaches to this challenge were pursued. According to Debreu a number of these approaches were 'uniformly obtained by application of a fixed-point theorem of the Brouwer type or the Kakutani type ...' (Debreu 1982: 697) and his *Theory of Value* is among these approaches. These tools, as Debreu points out, were not available to Walras. Despite this difference, Debreu emphasises the continuity with Walras. The goals of his research 'were to make the theory rigorous, to generalize it, to simplify it and to extent it in new directions' (Debreu 1984: 267). In this sense the *Theory of Value* successfully applies the formalist school's understanding of the values of rigour, generality and simplicity to the original Walrasian programme, an understanding which was not available to Walras. This is a core achievement of Debreu's *Theory of Value*, which renders it distinct from Walras' *Elements*.

The other claimed core achievement of the *Theory of Value* is that it furnishes economists with '(1) the explanation of the prices of commodities resulting from the interaction of the agents of a private ownership economy through markets, (2) the explanation of the role of prices in an optimal economy' (Debreu 1959: vii). Clearly Debreu's explanation is not the scientific realist kind of explanation proposed by Walras in his *Elements*. As we have already seen, Debreu rejects the analogy to mathematical physics used by Walras. Mathematical economics does not explain in the manner in which mathematical physics explains. Rather the *Theory of Value* explains an equilibrium price system by conclusively proving that an equilibrium price system is rigorously derivable from his definition of economic content in terms of very general characteristics of consumers, producers and goods combined with numerous explicitly stated assumptions. This is a distinctive kind of explanation which is not to be confused with accounts of explanation emanating from the philosophy of science.

To conclude, Walras' *Elements* and Debreu's *Theory of Value* are established classics in the history of economic thought. The *Theory of Value*, however, is not, as such, a pioneering work. As Hahn remarks 'this beautiful and austere book marks a summing up' of research already published (Hahn 1961: 204). This summing up provides 'a definitive statement of the theory of competitive equilibrium' (Hahn 1961: 204). Despite not being a pioneering work, it is an exceptionally original work. Debreu creatively deploys the formalist school's[35] distinction between pure and applied mathematics in conjunction with that school's unique understanding of the mathematical values of rigour, generality and simplicity in his definitive statement of the theory of competitive equilibrium. Moreover, the *Theory of Value* marks a paradigm shift within mathematical economics: the values of pure mathematics replace those of mathematical physics espoused by Walras. By furnishing a definitive, rigorous proof of the existence of equilibrium, Debreu's *Theory of Value* represented the triumph of formalism. Finally what we termed the Poincaré malaise is totally absent: there is no hint of it at all. However, given Debreu's commitment to the formalist's understanding of the values of rigour, generality and simplicity this is not surprising. The angst of the Poincaré malaise is to be treated by further education in the tenets of formalism.

Notes

1　Poincaré was well aware of the novel developments which eventually resulted in quantum mechanics. He prioritised experimental results in arbitrating between methodological clashes between classical rational mechanics and these new challenges. Walras did not address the possible implications of the emerging science of quantum mechanics for his scientific realist reading of classical mechanics.

2　We also reflected upon Poincaré's reservations/objections to Walras' methodological defence of his *Elements*.

3　We have already referred to some of these in previous chapters.

4　Demarcation is, perhaps, too strong a term. Numerous mathematicians at the time addressed problems in topology or set theory on the one hand and problems posed by classical mechanics without explicitly separating these into problems of pure mathematics and problems of applied mathematics. Indeed for some, such as Poincaré, historically and pedagogically, the insistence on a total separation of pure mathematics from applied mathematics is questionable.

5　In the following chapter we spell out this conception of applied mathematics.

6　Debreu (1986) gives a brief socio-empirical analysis of this course.

7　These developments are among the key pieces of mathematics exploited by Debreu in his *Theory of Value*. von Neumann's use of topology, Brouwer's fixed point theorem and von Neumann's lemma of 1937 reformulated as Kakutani's fixed point theorem are also acknowledged by Debreu in his 'local' synopsis. For a formalist analysis of von Neumann's model see Gloria-Palermo (2010).

8　This could suggest that, in Debreu's terminology, theoretical economics has 'completely surrendered to the embrace of mathematics and to its inherent compulsion toward logical rigor' (Debreu 1991: 2). If so, what makes theoretical economics an empirical science as distinct from a piece of pure mathematics? For instance Blaug maintains that 'economists have gradually converted the subject into a sort of social mathematics in which analytical rigor as understood in the maths department is *everything* and empirical relevance (as understood in physics departments) is *nothing*' (Blaug 1998: 13, italics ours). As we will see in a later section, Debreu counteracts this suggestion by recourse to his 'global view' of economic theorising, which must complement the 'local view' for a comprehensive understanding of economic theorising.

9　We suggest that the reader could usefully consult Poincaré's writings for an intriguing defence of intuition in mathematics. In Chapter Seven, we discuss in detail Brouwer's Intuitionism

10　Arrow offers an interesting rebuttal of this counter argument. However, if our suggestion is on the right tracks – i.e. there is more to logic than extensionality – then the very identification of irrationality by orthodox economists is challenged in cases where intentional logics come into play.

11　The interest in modal logic in the twentieth century is frequently traced to C.I. Lewis' research in the first decade of the twentieth century and to his collaboration with Langford which resulted in their famous *Symbolic Logic* of 1932 (Lewis and Langford 1959). Hughes and Cresswell (1996) is considered to be an excellent text and for a brief summary of applications of modal logic Girle (2000) is useful. Later we briefly explain the rationale for modal logics.

12 According to Frege foundational questions 'catch even mathematicians, for that matter, or most of them, unprepared with any satisfactory answer. Yet is it not a scandal that our science should be so unclear about the first and foremost among its objects, and one which is apparently so simple? Small hope, then, that we shall be able to say what number is. If a concept fundamental to a mighty science gives rise to difficulties, then it is surely an imperative task to investigate it more closely until those difficulties are overcome ...' (Frege 1968: II).

13 In the next chapter we will examine more closely how the formalist school interprets this logical innovation.

14 This distinction between 'intension' and 'extension' is also called the distinction between 'sense' and 'reference' or the distinction between 'the connotation' and 'denotation' of a term. The expert in the history of logic will rightly note that these distinctions have been understood in different ways by different logicians. Fortunately these differences do not concern us here.

15 As we will see in Chapter Seven, some mathematicians, such as Brouwer, reject the adequacy of extensional logic to mathematics.

16 A brief historical survey of the relationship between logic and time is given by Prior in an appendix in his *Time and Modality* (Prior 1957).

17 Tarski makes the same point. 'Thus it is said that the symbols "x", "y" ... also denote certain numbers or quantities, not "constant numbers" however (which are denoted by constants like "0", "1," ...) but the so-called "variable numbers" or rather "variable quantities." Statements of this kind have their source in a gross misunderstanding. The "variable number" x could not possibly have any specific property, for instance, it could be neither positive, nor negative, nor equal to zero; or rather the properties of such numbers would change from case to case, that is to say the number would sometimes be positive, sometimes negative and sometimes equal to zero. But entities of such a kind we do not find in our world at all, their existence would contradict the fundamental law of thought' (Tarski 1965: 4).

18 Historians of the philosophy of mathematics will immediately notice that Hilbert and his school did not use the terms semantics and syntax to explain formalism. We introduced these terms as we felt that they are useful to convey the distinctive aspect of the formalist school to an audience not familiar with its fundamental tenets. We are not alone in doing this. Church in his famous *Introduction to Mathematical Logic* does something similar. The interested reader will find that Church's footnotes contain the history, while the text presents the logic to a reader not acquainted with the history.

19 One can define a power set of an infinite set, A, as the infinite set of all subsets of A. It can be shown that the power set of A is 'bigger' than A.

20 Hilbert is quite explicit in making Cantorian actual infinity a cornerstone of pure mathematics 'But this (potential infinity) is not the true infinite. We meet the true infinite when we regard the totality of numbers 1, 2, 3, 4, ... itself as a completed unity or when we regard the points of an interval as a totality of things which exist all at once. This kind of infinity is known as *actual infinity*. ... But it was Cantor who systematically developed the concept of the actual infinite' (Hilbert 1926: 188). As we will see in Chapter Seven, this has Brouwer's Intuitionism as its target.

21 Weyl gives numerous examples of how Hilbert achieved simpler proofs (Weyl 1944: 613). We will see in Chapter Seven that simplicity is also used in opposition to Brouwer's intuitionistic mathematics.

22 This symbolism has two advantages over other symbolisms used. Firstly, it acknowledges the primacy of elementary propositions in that it shows that predeicates are derived from propositions. Secondly we can symbolise complex predicates, e.g. $\hat{x}(ax \rightarrow bx)$ for which no simple term is available in English. Intuitively $\hat{x}(ax \rightarrow bx)$ is the predicate if a then b.

23 Philosophers of logic would point out that this way of explaining the existential quantifier is using Fregian language, which may be too sympathetic to Frege's own analysis. We concede that. However, we know of no better way of explaining the Fregian analysis of existence as conveyed by the existential quantifier of logic.
24 Hahn, for instance, emphasises this (see Boylan and O'Gorman 2012 for further information).
25 We are assuming existence is not freedom from contradiction.
26 These theorems are introduced in Chapter 1 and used in Chapter 5 of the *Theory of Value*.
27 This simplicity was one of the main reasons Weyl abandoned his defence of Brouwerian mathematics of intuitionism which was based solely on constructive methods of proof. It should be noted that Brouwer's fixed point theorem is *not* a theorem in intuitionistic mathematics. We will return to this issue in Chapter Seven.
28 This overarching structure is another way of expressing what Weyl calls 'the methodological unity of mathematics' (Weyl 1944: 617) introduced earlier.
29 As we will see later, some logicians and mathematicians challenge this formalist approach.
30 In the last section we saw how the logic of Debreu's mathematics is an extensional one and now the economic content of the notion of a commodity in Chapter 2 of his *Theory of Value* is adjusted to this extensionality in various ways. One way is by the dating of goods '[Thus] a good at a certain date and the same good at a later date are *different* economic objects and the specification of the date at which it will be available is essential' (Debreu 1959: 29). Similarly 'the price of a commodity is the amount to be paid *now* for the future availability of one unit of that commodity' (Debreu 1959: 28). As we already indicated from the point of view of non-extensional, modal logic these forms of idealisations constitute a cosmic exile point of view. Clearly the various idealisations and assumptions used by Debreu lowers the empirical content of the already low threshold of empirical content based on his various abstractions from types of economic activities and legal impositions on corporations and so on.
31 In Chapter Seven the task of undermining Debreu's formalist's characterisations of applied mathematics is carried out.
32 Kakutani's generalisation is found in Kakutani (1941)
33 One might say that this Poincaré objection to formalism received a rigorous formulation by Gödel in his famous incompleteness theorems.
34 Poincaré does not address the issue of modal logic. However he held that some natural sciences other than physics are 'compelled to have recourse to other modes of generalization' than mathematics (Poincaré 1952: 159). We assume the same would apply to the social sciences.
35 Debreu does not define what he means by the formalist school. One may well wonder to what extent the formalist philosophy of mathematics was structured into a school. In this connection we speculate that Debreu use of the word 'school' may have been borrowed from Weyl. In his obituary, 'David Hilbert and his Mathematical Work', Weyl explains 'I wanted merely to sketch the mathematical side of his (Hilbert's) personality in attempting to explain, however incompletely, the peculiar charm and the enormous influences which he exerted. In appraising the latter one must not overlook the environmental factor. A German university in a small town like Göttingen, especially in the halcyon days before 1914 was a favourable milieu for the development of a scientific school' (Weyl 1944: 616). If our speculation is not correct, at least we can point out that Debreu was not unique in using the term 'school'.

4 The axiomatic method in the foundations of mathematics

Implications for economics

Introduction

A central aim of this work is to enhance our understanding of the mathematisation of economics.[1] To this end we interrogated Walras' *Elements* by recourse to the Walras–Poincaré correspondence and we engaged Debreu's *Theory of Value* in light of his commitment to the formalist school. Both Walras and Debreu share the thesis that theoretical economics is applied mathematics but they do not share the same conception of applied mathematics. Walras' conception of applied mathematics was that which prevailed at the end of the nineteenth century. In that prevailing intellectual climate the axiomatisation of applied mathematical science was not a priority. The theme of the axiomatisation of applied mathematical sciences is a twentieth-century one. This took hold largely among philosophers with an interest in a logical approach to the sciences. Philosophers of science as divergent as Carnap and Popper shared an admiration for the axiomatisation of the applied mathematical sciences. In this twentieth-century intellectual climate, Debreu maintains that his *Theory of Value* is axiomatic.

Prima facie, the task of axiomatising General Equilibrium Theory appears unproblematical: there is one and only one way of axiomatising any domain be it pure or applied, namely à la Euclid. As Blanché, for instance, points out, Euclid's *Elements* 'has long been regarded as a paradigm of deductive theory …' (Blanché 1955: 1). A small number of propositions – the axioms – are stated at the outset. These are the basic principles of the domain. Any new term introduced must be defined by recourse to the primitive notions of the system. Theorems are deductively derived from the axioms or theorems already established. These theorems are proved by recourse to the laws of deductive logic: resource to any other source of demonstration is forbidden. As we have already seen, Debreu's *Theory of Value* is claimed to meet the standards of rigour of the formalist school which 'dictates the axiomatic form …' (Debreu 1959: viii).

However, when one looks at the *Theory of Value*, it does not appear to be presented according to the Euclidean template of an axiomatic system where one would start with the basic principles of the economic domain and then one would use logic to obtain the economic theorems. The axiomatic template of the *Theory of Value* is, prima facie, not that of Euclid. A possible explanation for this is that Debreu's axiomatic references are merely methodological remarks which have no influence on what Debreu actually does in his economic theorising. In Corry's terminology Debreu's reference to axiomatisation is 'the image', not 'the body', of Debreu's economic theorising.[2] According to Corry a central historical task 'is to characterize the images of knowledge of a given period and to explain their interaction with the body of knowledge' (Corry 1989: 418). In Debreu's case when this task is accomplished, the claim is that his references to axiomatisation are merely part of his philosophical image of economic theorising which does not in any way interact with the body of his economic theorising.

We do not agree with this explanation of the failure of Debreu to meet the axiomatic requirements of Euclidean axiomatisation. We argue that the reason why Debreu's *Theory of Value* does not fit the Euclidean template of axiomatisation is that Debreu, as a formalist, uses the Hilbertian, purely formalist conception of axiomatisation and not the Euclidean conception. This Hilbertian, purely formalist conception of axiomatisation demands a different template for the axiomatisation of any applied mathematical domain to that of Euclid. For a pure formalist, there is one and only one way of rigorously axiomatising any scientific theory and that is à la Hilbert and not à la Euclid. Methodologists of economics to the detriment of economic methodology have not addressed this crucial distinction between the old, Euclidean conception of the axiomatisation of any applied mathematical domain and the new Hilbertian purely formalist conception. We contend that Debreu's *Theory of Value* conforms to this purely formalist template of axiomatisation. In Corry's terminology the image, viz. the axiomatisation interacts with the body, viz. the economic theory, but the image is that of the Hilbertian, purely formalist school, and not that of Euclid. Having used the philosophy of mathematics to gain a richer, more sophisticated understanding of Debreu's axiomatisation of General Equilibrium Theory in his *Theory of Value*, we extend our analysis by addressing his thesis that 'mathematical form powerfully contributes to defining a philosophy of economic analysis' (Debreu 1992: 114). An empirical minded economist may well wonder how mathematical form could define an accurate philosophy of economic analysis. We explain how Debreu arrives at this surprising prima facie thesis and conclude that this thesis is a fundamental corner stone of Debreu's own philosophy of economic analysis.

The chapter is structured as follows. We open with a brief account of the development of axiomatic systems from Euclid to Hilbert. We then turn our attention to the manner in which any scientific theory is to be axiomatised. In this connection, we distinguish, à la Bernays (one of Hilbert's gifted colleagues), between the old, Euclidean model of the axiomatisation of a scientific theory and the new, Hilbertian formalist model.[3] In the following section we demonstrate how Debreu's *Theory of Value* applies this Hilbertian formalist model. We then address Debreu's fundamental commitment to the thesis that mathematical form is an indispensable corner stone of the philosophy of economic analysis. We conclude the chapter with a brief analysis of what Debreu sees as the assets of his philosophy of economic analysis.

Rigour and axiomatisation

Over the centuries Euclid's *Elements* has been regarded as the locus classicus of a deductive system. Euclidean geometry is not organised like a good encyclopaedia. Rather, by virtue of its axiomatic method, it is the classical paradigm of an internally organised, rational science. Euclid's *Elements* was recognised as the model of the art of demonstration and indeed for some philosophers, especially Cartesians, it was the model of the art of philosophising. With the evolving concept of mathematical rigour, especially during the nineteenth-century, various efforts were made to reconstruct Euclidean geometry to meet these new standards. These efforts culminated in Hilbert's famous *Grundlagen der Geometrie* of 1899. Running parallel to the project of the rigorous reconstruction of Euclidean geometry, another project, viz. the distillation of the axiomatic method from its geometrical content, was also in operation.

We briefly sum up the project of the distillation of the axiomatic method from its geometrical content in four phases.[4] A key question to keep in mind in each phase is what is an axiom? Keeping a close eye on Euclid's *Elements*, in phase one, axioms were seen as self-evident truths. These self-evident truths were non-demonstrable. One cannot prove everything. Some propositions must be the starting point of any logical proof. These non-demonstrable propositions are the axioms. These axioms in turn are distinct from the postulates. The best known postulate is perhaps Euclid's parallel postulate: from a fixed point outside a straight line, one and only one line can be drawn parallel to the given line. Postulates lack the self-evidence of the axioms but, like axioms, they are not proven within the system. Thus axioms and postulates are the basic, non-demonstrable principles of an axiomatic system. Finally axioms are distinct from definitions. Definitions are used to introduce new terms into an axiomatic system. Just as one cannot prove everything, one cannot define everything. There must be basic, indefinable terms in an axiomatic system. Any new term introduced must be definable in terms of the primitive concepts of the system.

The major event in the evolution of the concept of an axiomatic system in phase two was the construction of non-Euclidean geometries. We note three key characteristics of phase two. Firstly, the notion of self-evidence is dropped. What is self-evident is either too subjective or culturally relative. Whatever axioms are, they are not self-evident. Secondly, as we saw in the last chapter, over the centuries various mathematicians expressed reservations about Euclid's parallel postulate. Eventually Lobachewsky and Riemann developed non-Euclidean geometries. These mathematical developments shifted the focus away from the issue of the truth of an axiom on to the consistency of the system. An axiom is no longer claimed to be a fundamental truth. It is the non-demonstrable starting point in a *hypothetical* system which is consistent. Hence the terms 'axiom' and 'postulate', which were distinct in Euclid's *Elements*, are now interchangeable. Thirdly, the quest for rigour puts the emphasis on reducing the number of axioms by requiring that the axioms be independent of each other. If a set of axioms can be deduced from a smaller set of independent axioms, the initial set is replaced by the smaller set of independent axioms.

In both phases one and two logic is the basic tool used in an axiomatic system. All inferences must conform to the principles of deductive logic. Theorems are defined as the outcomes of the applications of the laws of logic to the axioms or postulates. In classical logical textbooks, three fundamental principles were identified. These were known as 'the laws of thought'.[5] These three principles are the principles of identity, the principle of non-contradiction and the principle of the excluded middle. These principles were formulated in several ways. For instance, the principle of identity states if anything is A it is A; the principle of non-contradiction states that nothing can be both A and not A; and the principle of the excluded middle states: anything must be either A or not A.[6] Moreover, in phases one and two the question of the systematic organisation of logic into an axiomatic system did not arise. The axiomatisation of logic brings us to phase three.

Phase three is characterised by the axiomatisation of arithmetic and of logic. Prima facie the axioms of arithmetic and of logic are distinct from those of geometry. As Frege puts it:

> For purposes of conceptual thought we can always assume the contrary of some or other of the geometrical axioms, without involving ourselves in any self-contradictions when we proceed to our deductions, despite the conflict between our assumptions and our intuition … Can the same be said of the fundamental propositions of the science of number? Here we have only to try denying anyone of them, and complete confusion ensues. Even to think at all seems no longer possible. The basis of arithmetic lies deeper, it seems, than that of any of the empirical sciences and even than that of geometry.
>
> (Frege 1968: 20–21)

Unlike the axioms of geometry, the axioms of arithmetic are true propositions, the contrary of which would make coherent discourse impossible. The same holds for the axioms of logic. The negation of any logical axiom results in incoherence. Moreover, since the axioms of arithmetic are true, the issue of their consistency does not arise. Truth implies consistency, while consistency does not imply truth. Furthermore in phase three, logic itself is subjected to a more rigorous scrutiny than that which prevailed in phases one and two. Historically Frege's *Begriffschrift*, published in 1879, marked this revolutionary, more rigorous approach to logic. In order to clearly identify the elements required for logical validity an ideal language must be created. This ideal language has three indispensable components, namely, the syntactical, the symbolic and the semantical. Firstly, a comprehensive, explicitly stated, precise syntax is specified. This logical syntax corrects the defects in the grammars (syntax) of natural languages.[7] Secondly, a new symbolism, richer than that of traditional logic, is introduced. Thirdly, the meanings of the core logical concepts, such as conjunction,

disjunction, existence, implication and negation – which are represented sym-
bolically in step two – are explicitly specified. With components one and two,
i.e. the formal syntax and symbolism, logicians acquire a formal calculus,
indispensable to the correct enunciation of the law's logic.[8] For the first time in
its history, formal syntax becomes an integral part of logic – hence the name
formal logic. In phase three of the process of axiomatisation, however, this
formal calculus is semantically dominated. The calculus serves the quest for
truth. It is not an end in itself.

   This semantical domination is shown in two ways. Firstly, the formal calculus
is not self-evident: it results from philosophical reflection. Frege sums up this
point as follows.

> It is possible of course to operate with figures mechanically, just as it is
> possible to speak like a parrot: but that hardly deserves the name of
> thought. It only becomes possible at all after the mathematical notation
> has, *as a result of genuine thought*, been so developed that it does the thinking
> for us, so to speak.
>
> (Frege 1968: iv, italics ours)

A powerful syntactical calculus is not God-given. Rather it is the fruit of genuine
thought. Secondly the formal calculus is semantically dominated in its actual
usage. The validity of any inference and thus the identification of mathematical
theorems also depend on the meanings of the core logical concepts. If we do
not know how to properly use concepts like negation, conjunction and
implication, we do not understand what a theorem is. To readjust Frege's
metaphor, formal syntax is comparable to a creeper twining around the tree of
semantics, losing all hold once its semantical support and source of sustenance
are removed.[9] In short, the axiomatisation of mathematics in phase three, unlike
phases one and two, recognises the indispensable role of a formal syntactical
calculus. However, like phases one and two, semantics is also indispensable.
With phase three the book of mathematics, in its most rigorous formulation,
would be completed. This hope, however, was dinted with the discovery of
various paradoxes in the foundations of mathematics. In the face of these
paradoxes some, for example Frege, were despondent. Others adopted the
attitude of Poincaré who compared the discovery of the paradoxes to the discovery of a medical pathology. 'Whatever be the remedy adopted, we can
promise ourselves the joy of the doctor called in to follow a fine pathological
case' (Poincaré 1956: 45).

   Phase four of the axiomatisation of mathematics, what Debreu calls the formalist
school, diagnoses that the semantical dimension of the old axiomatics,[10] – those
of phases one, two and three – is the source of the pathology of the paradoxes. The remedy is the elimination of all traces of meaning in logic and in
mathematics. This ingenious remedy of the formalist school gives us a new
conception of pure mathematics. Pure mathematics is a purely syntactical,
axiomatic system. This axiomatic system has four parts.[11] First, a list of

primitive symbols which have no meaning whatsoever is given. This is followed by a list of syntactical rules which are applied mechanically to the primitive symbols, resulting in the well-formed formulae of the system. These well-formed formulae are also meaningless. Thirdly, a small group of these well-formed formulae are picked out. These are the axioms. Fourthly, syntactical transformation rules are specified. These rules are applied mechanically to the axioms. The outcome of these applications are theorems. These theorems also are devoid of meaning. In this way the formalist school syntactically reconstructs the whole of classical mathematics from elementary arithmetic to Cantorian set theory. The price paid for this reconstruction is both mathematical and logical content. In Debreu's apt phrase, the axiomatic system 'in the strict sense, is logically entirely disconnected from its interpretation' (Debreu 1959: viii).[12]

However, to safeguard this purely syntactical reconstruction of classical mathematics from the difficulty of the paradoxes, what Hilbert calls 'meta-mathematics' is also required (Hilbert 1922: 212).[13] Unlike mathematics, metamathematics is semantical. A central task of metamathematics is to prove, in a finite number of steps, the consistency of this purely syntactical axiomatic system. Thus in metamathematics, the whole of classical mathematics, including Cantorian set-theory, taken as a purely syntactical calculus, is shown to be consistent and thus cannot be paradoxical. The metamathematical challenge is to construct such a proof.[14] To sum up, the project of the distillation of the axiomatic method from its geometrical origins culminated in a major fault-line in twentieth-century philosophy of mathematics. Two radically conflicting conceptions of pure mathematics emerged, namely the semantical and the syntactical. For semanticists pure mathematics has mathematical content. There are pure mathematical truths, such as $2+2=4$. Mathematicians like Brouwer and Poincaré and logicians like Frege were committed to a semanticist view of pure mathematics. Hilbertian formalists pioneered the purely syntactical reading of pure mathematics. For formalists there are no pure mathematical truths. Rather pure mathematics is a purely syntactical, meaningless calculus which is proven in metamathematics to be consistent, complete and decidable.

From the point of view of economic methodology, especially Weintraub's project of exploring 'how economics has been shaped by economists' ideas about the nature and purpose and function and meaning of mathematics' (Weintraub 2002: 2) this fault-line is crucial. More precisely it is crucial for Debreu. Debreu's ideas about the nature, purpose, function and meaning – more precisely the lack of meaning – of mathematics are those of a Hilbertian formalist and not of a semanticist. We contend that this formalist conception of mathematics informs his *Theory of Value* and more generally it is indispensable to his intriguing and sophisticated philosophy of economic analysis. To establish this thesis we must first address another crucial issue, namely the Hilbertian formalist's philosophy of an applied mathematical science. After all theoretical economics is not pure mathematics. Rather it is applied mathematics.[15]

The applied mathematical sciences and axiomatisation

The project of axiomatising the applied mathematical sciences, as already pointed out, is a theme which took hold among philosophers with an interest in a logical, as opposed to a historical, approach to the sciences. One should not assume that this project was received with the same enthusiasm in science departments. Hilary Putnam recalls a conversation he had with Carnap on how Carnap became a philosopher. While studying at the University of Jena, Carnap was fascinated with both formal logic and Einstein's special theory of relativity. Carnap chose the axiomatisation of Einstein's special theory as a topic for his thesis. 'It was because the Physics Department at Jena would not accept this that Carnap became a philosopher he told me' (Putnam 1993: 125). To what extent the physics department at Jena was representative of science departments across the research world of the applied mathematical sciences is a socio-historical question. Anecdotes, like that of Putnam, however, alert one to the possible significance of Corry's distinction between 'the image' and 'the body' of scientific knowledge. If Carnap's experience was typical, then one could say that physics departments, as the custodians of the body of scientific knowledge, were not concerned with its image, namely its axiomatisation.

Popper correctly acknowledges that the founder of the formalist school, Hilbert, as a pioneer in the project of axiomatising the physical sciences. Indeed according to Bernays, Hilbert 'characterizes the axiomatic method as a general procedure for scientific thinking. This procedure can be applied in all areas of knowledge where one has come to the point of setting up a theory …' (Bernays 1922: 193). A little earlier Bernays points out that:

> from the beginning Hilbert envisaged the point of view of the uniformity of the axiomatic method in its application to the most diverse domains, and guided by this viewpoint he tried to bring this method to bear as widely as possible. In particular he succeeded in grounding axiomatically the kinetic theory of gases as well as the elementary theory of radiation in a rigorous way.
>
> (Bernays 1922: 193)[16]

In view of this Hilbertian principle of the uniformity of the axiomatic method, one can say that, for the formalist school, the axiomatic method is the rigorous logical architecture of any scientific theory.

Prima facie the overall scheme of this axiomatic reconstruction of a theory is not complicated. A small number of propositions are used as axioms and the rest of the theory is derived by logico-mathematical deductions from these axioms.[17] The axioms are the core principles of the theoretical domain. In the case of the physical sciences these axioms either originated in experience or are experimentally confirmed. This is a schematic summary of what Bernays calls 'the old axiomatics' (Bernays 1922: 193). This 'old' axiomatic approach to the applied mathematical sciences is, in our terminology, characteristic of the semantical approaches to axiomatics, three phases of which were outlined in the previous section. Bernays contrasts the 'old axiomatics' with what he calls 'Hilbert's axiomatic standpoint' (Bernays 1922: 193). Hilbert's axiomatic standpoint is centrally located in *'the domain of pure formalism'* (Bernays 1922: 196, italics ours). In this purely formalist domain 'Hilbert's view on the nature of mathematics and on the axiomatic method then finds *its actual conclusion'* (Bernays 1922: 196, italics ours). In other words Hilbert's final reflections on the nature of the axiomatic system culminate in the thesis that it is purely syntactical. The old, Euclidean, semantical view of an axiomatic system is replaced by a purely syntactical account. This gives rise to two central questions. How does this purely syntactical conception of an axiomatic system operate in the applied mathematical sciences? Secondly, how does this image interact with the body of knowledge?

The concise answer by the formalist school to the first question is that the applied mathematical sciences are domain-specific interpretations of sections of the axiomatised, syntactical calculus of pure mathematics and logic. This concise answer needs unpacking. Basically it consists of four steps. Firstly applied mathematicians have the complete syntactical axiomatised calculus of the whole edifice of pure mathematics and of logic at their disposal. This syntactical calculus is, as it were, the consistent and complete reservoir of all deductive inferences and theorems. Staying within this axiomatised syntactical domain of the whole corpus of pure mathematics, the applied mathematician, on pragmatic grounds, choses a relevant subdomain which he or she believes could prove useful in the mathematico-logical investigation of the specific scientific domain.[18]

In the next step the applied mathematician moves into the domain of the specific science. Through the lens of the piece of pure mathematics chosen in step one, the applied mathematician focuses on a selection of specific scientific concepts and their interrelationships. These concepts and their interrelationships are the outcome of past scientific achievements. The applied mathematician analyses these scientific concepts and their interrelationships with a view to seeing how well they fit the chosen mathematics of step one. The aim of this analysis is to attain the logico-mathematical structure of the chosen scientific concepts and their interrelationships. If the analysis shows that the fit is not perfect, since the chosen piece of mathematics cannot be changed, the scientific concepts and their interrelationships are adjusted to make the fit perfect. These adjustments are accomplished by processes such as idealisation or the use of assumptions. Alternatively, the applied mathematician, sometimes by a stroke of genius, sees that an alternative piece of syntactical mathematics furnishes the logico-mathematical structure, or at least approximates to this logico-mathematical structure of the chosen scientific domain. Again, if the fit is not perfect, the scientific concepts, and their interrelationships, are altered to make the fit perfect.[19] This opens the way to the third step.

Having identified the logico-mathematical structures of the adjusted theoretico-scientific content, the applied mathematician moves back into the chosen axiomatised syntactical calculus. In other words the applied mathematical scientist behaves like a pure mathematician in deriving theorems in this piece of pure mathematics. These theorems are meaningless concatenations of empty symbols of the chosen calculus of step one. This leads to the final step, namely finding an interpretation for the theorems in the adjusted scientific domain. If the applied mathematician finds an interpretation, the theoretico-scientific content of the domain is thereby extended. At this stage the work of the applied mathematician halts and now the work of experimental scientists commences. They experimentally test these interpretations. Formalists do not maintain that applied mathematicians actually, i.e. psychologically, follow this template. Rather the research of applied mathematicians in any scientific domain, *when rigorously presented*, necessarily exemplifies this template, where the syntactical axiomatic form is utterly divorced from empirical or theoretico-empirical content. In short, in this formalist philosophy of applied mathematics the following four steps are indispensable. (1) the selection of the relevant subdomain of the consistent and complete domain of the axiomatised syntactical calculus of contentless mathematics cum logic; (2) the adjustment of the theoretical content of the scientific domain to fit the mathematico-logical structure of step (i); (3) the identification or formal derivation of syntactical theorems of (i); (4) the interpretation of these theorems in the adjusted theoretico-empirical content of the scientific domain.

The old axiomatics, from Euclid to Frege, being semantical, failed to appreciate the purely syntactical nature of the axiomatic system. For the formalist no axiom has content. Rigorously speaking axioms reside only in pure, i.e. syntactical, mathematics. Rigorously, there are no such things as axioms of physics or of economics: the axioms are not derived from the fundamentals of the scientific domain. In the old Euclidean model of axiomatisation some propositions, seen as fundamental or essential to the real world, and thus semantical, were incorrectly identified as axioms. The demand of both accuracy and rigour require an alternative, non-Euclidean analysis of axiomatisation. This alternative is supplied by Hilbertian formalists.

Having outlined how the formalist school's philosophy of axiomatisation operates in the applied mathematical sciences, we now address the second question, viz. how does this image interact with the body of knowledge? Of course it may interact in various ways. We outline three of these. Firstly, as we have already seen, if the fit between a selected sub-domain of the axiomatised calculus of pure mathematics and the original theoretico-empirical content of the specific scientific domain is not perfect, in order to exploit the selected sub-domain of the mathematical calculus, this original theoretical-empirical content must be altered. The normal routines for effecting this alteration are idealisations or assumptions. The extent of the modifications of the original theoretico-empirical content depends on the nature and extent of the idealisations and assumptions used.

The second way the image interacts with the body of knowledge does not apply to the economic theorising of general equilibrium. This impact hinges on the experimental vindication or otherwise of the final step of the scientific interpretation of a derived theorem. If this interpretation is experimentally vindicated, the empirical content of the axiomatised science is clearly augmented. Thus the weakening of empirical content by the introduction of idealisations or assumptions is to be balanced against this gain in empirical content resulting from the experimental vindication of the interpreted theorem.

Thirdly, if sophisticated experimentation à la advanced physics is not a viable option, one may, as it were, carry out some 'thought experiments' by adjusting either the idealisations or assumptions. For the formalist the chosen piece of pure axiomatised mathematics was the driving force for the modification of the original theoretico-empirical content by recourse to assumptions or idealisations. Now the applied mathematician is proposing to alter some of their assumptions or idealisations. For the formalist, this may entail severing the fit between the chosen piece of pure mathematics and the assumption-laden theoretico-empirical content. In other words the original chosen piece of pure mathematics may fail to accurately model this new theoretico-empirical content. In this scenario either a different piece of pure mathematics must be chosen which fits the new theoretico-empirical content or additional mathematics must be added to the original choice of pure axiomatised mathematics.

In this section we briefly outlined the formalist school's philosophy of axiomatisation and how that philosophy impinges on the process of the mathematisation of a scientific domain. In particular we showed how this formalist model of the mathematisation of the sciences differs from the Euclidean model. In the following section we return to Debreu's *Theory of Value* to show how it fits the formalist school's model of the mathematisation of the sciences. Debreu actually puts this formalist model into practice: he practices what he philosophically preaches.

Debreu's formalist mathematisation of economic theory

For a number of eminent mathematical economists, Debreu's *Theory of Value* provides 'a definitive statement of the theory of competitive equilibrium' (Hahn 1961: 204). However, as we already noted, unlike Walras' *Elements*, it is not a pioneering work. Rather, as Hahn puts it, 'this beautiful and austere book marks a summing up of earlier research', a point explicitly acknowledged by Debreu himself in his preface (Hahn 1961: 204). In this section we argue that Debreu's definitive summing up of the theory of competitive equilibrium is constructed in accordance with the formalist school's model for the mathematisation of a scientific theory which, for reasons of rigour, replaced the older Euclidean model.

As Berneys and other members of the formalist school point out, before the rigorous axiomatisation of a piece of science can be carried out, that scientific piece must have reached a fairly advanced stage of development. This is clearly the case with Debreu's *Theory of Value*. In the previous chapter we, following Debreu, noted some of this research. Debreu's originality lies in his formalist mode of rigorously axiomatising that research. This rigorous formalist axiomatisation is evident in the layout of his *Theory of Value*, i.e. Debreu adheres to the template of the four steps outlined in the previous section. In line with the first step of this formalist template for the most rigorous possible axiomatisation of any piece of an applied mathematical science, Debreu in his opening chapter explicitly identifies the regions of pure axiomatised mathematics which are to be exploited in his monograph. In line with step two, in the opening sections of Chapters 2 to 5 Debreu moves out of this formalist domain of pure mathematics outlined in Chapter 1 into the scientific domain of economics. As we already pointed out much of this research has been carried out elsewhere. Thus he introduces the reader to the economic notions of commodities, prices, consumers, producers and so on. For instance in Chapter 2 'the dual concepts of commodity and price are introduced in this chapter. *The meanings of these terms, somewhat different from current usage will be made precise* in the next sections. Many examples will be given as illustrations' (Debreu 1959: 28, italics ours). Here Debreu is clearly concerned with economic content. Moreover, Debreu is clearly signalling that the conventional meanings of terms like commodity and price are altered. In order to be able to fit this economic content conveyed in current usage to the pure mathematics identified in Chapter 1, the meaning of these terms have to be made precise. In each chapter the specific ways in which economic terms are made precise are specified. In line with the formalist's template for the rigorous mathematisation of any piece of science, this process of precision culminates in a perfect fit between this revised content and the syntactical domain of pure mathematics of chapter one. For instance Chapter 2 concludes with the formulation of all the above concepts (of commodity, price, action of any agent) in the language of the theory:

> The number ι of commodities is a given positive integer. An action a of an agent is a point R^ι, the commodity space. A price system p is a point of R^ι. The value of an action a relative to a price system p is the inner product $p.a$.
>
> (Debreu 1959: 35)

Clearly this formulation contains terms like commodity and price. Debreu insists that the economic meanings of these terms are not those conveyed by normal usage. We might say that these are now technical terms of his theory. These technical economic terms obtain their novel economic content by the various processes of precision-making. *The formalist contention is that even this novel economic content plays no role in Debreu's mathematical deductions.* Logically or rigorously applied mathematical economists ignore even their novel meanings in their *logical* development of their mathematical model. Debreu puts it this way. Immediately after stating the above quoted formulation he remarks 'all that precedes this statement is irrelevant for the logical development of the theory' (Debreu 1959: 35). In other words the logical development of his theory rests solely on the purely syntactical deductive calculus of pure mathematics. Economic content plays no role in this logical exploitation. This point becomes clearly evident in his characterisation of an economy in Chapter 5:

> An economy E is defined by: for each $i = 1, \ldots , m$ a non-empty subset X_i of R^ι completely preordered by $\underset{i}{\precsim}$; for each $j = 1, \ldots , n$ a non-empty subset of Y_j of R^ι; a point ω of R^ι.
>
> A state of E is an $(m+n)$-tuple of points of R^ι.
>
> (Debreu 1959: 75)

Chapters 1 to 5 culminate in this pure mathematical model *which is stripped of all economic content. This model furnishes the theoretical economist with the pure mathematico-logical structure of an idealised economy.* In other words there is a perfect fit between this pure mathematical structure and the interactions of Debreu's idealised and assumption-laden characterisation of agents, commodities, prices, etc. Clearly this pure mathematical model is not the structure of an actual economy.

   This pure mathematical model is embedded in the much larger framework of the consistent and complete axiomatic system of pure mathematics. Thus as a formalist Debreu is now in a position to exploit this pure mathematical model. In line with his formalist philosophy of mathematics, Debreu's third step is to pick out or derive various theorems which are derivable in this piece of pure mathematics. For instance, Brouwer's fixed point theorem is derivable. Once again economic content plays no role whatsoever in this derivation. Rather Brouwer's fixed point theorem is a provable empty formula of pure mathematics which has no content whatsoever – mathematical or economic. Finally, in line with steps of the formalist template for an applied mathematical science, the question arises of whether or not this theorem of contentless mathematics can be given an interpretation in Debreu's idealised economy thereby extending our knowledge of this idealised economy? The answer is yes. As Debreu puts it

> the perfect fit between the mathematical concept of a fixed point and the social science concept of an equilibrium stands out. A state of a social system is described by listing an action for each one of its agents. Considering such a state, each agent reacts by selecting the action that is optimal for him given the actions of all others. Listing those reactions yields a new state, and thereby a transformation of the set of states of the social system into itself is defined. A state of a system is an equilibrium if, and only if, it is a fixed point of that transformation.
>
> (Debreu 1986: 1262)

This is the economic interpretation of Brouwer's fixed point theorem derivable from Debreu's pure mathematical model. In this way Debreu proves that, in the modified theoretical economic content of Chapters 2 to 5 of his *Theory of Value*, the existence of the social science concept of equilibrium is possible, i.e. is not self-contradictory. This is the *rigorous* proof of the existence of equilibrium which, through no fault of his own, eluded Walras.

Unlike the Euclidean model of the axiomatisation of a scientific domain, there is no question of identifying axioms in the economic domain. In a sense one could say that it was the earlier, Euclidean model of axiomatisation which misled Walras in identifying his core propositions as economic axioms, revealing the essential mechanisms of an economy. Debreu, unlike Walras, does not refer to any economic proposition as an axiom. Axioms do not reside in the content of any scientific domain from mathematical physics to mathematical economics. Contrary to the Euclidean models, axioms are empty, syntactical formulae of the pure mathematical calculus.

> An axiomatised theory first selects its primitive concepts and represents each of them by a mathematical object … Next assumptions on the objects representing the primitive concepts are specified, and consequences are mathematically derived from them. The economic interpretation of the theorems so obtained is the last step of the analysis. According to this schema, an axiomatised theory has a mathematical form that is completely separated from its economic content. If one removes the economic interpretation of the primitive concepts, of the assumptions, and of the conclusions of the model, its bare mathematical structure must still stand. This severe test is passed only by a small minority of papers in economic theory …
>
> (Debreu 1986: 65)

Debreu's *Theory of Value* excels in passing this severe test, rarely achieved in economic theorising.

We now turn to the issue raised by Weintraub, namely how does this image of economic theory interact with the body of knowledge? This image concerns the rigorous methodological manner of mathematising economic theory. As such, it appears to be independent of the content of the economic theory. However, on a more detailed examination, this is not the case. This rigorous methodology of the mathematisation of economic theory requires the theoretical economist, by recourse to the various strategies used in Chapters 2 to 5 of the *Theory of Value*, especially its idealisations and assumptions, to alter what Debreu calls 'the current usages' of economic terms (Debreu 1959: 28). By various means, including idealisations and assumptions, economic terms are given more precise meanings and thus their standard meanings are altered. The degree of alteration depends on the details of the specific processes of precision making. This in turn effects the empirical content of the economic theory: ceteris paribus the more unrealistic the assumptions, the less the empirical content.

The theoretical content may also be changed by the economic interpretations of the mathematical theorems. In the experimental mathematical sciences, the scientific interpretations of the mathematical theorems are subjected to detailed experimental scrutiny and, if vindicated, they enrich the empirical content of the scientific theory. However, Debreu is emphatic that this kind of experimental testing is not available to the equilibrium theorist: there is, for instance, no question of experimentally vindicating the postulated existence of general equilibrium. Without this experimental vindication, Debreu's proof of the existence of equilibrium remains at the level of theoretical, as distinct from verified empirical, content. Debreu's proof of the existence of equilibrium means that, subject to the numerous constraints specified in his *Theory of Value*, the social science concept of equilibrium is not contradictory.

Debreu's mathematical model: formalist or semanticist?

In this section we attempt to unpack Debreu's commitment to the thesis that '*mathematical form* powerfully contributes to defining a philosophy of economic analysis whose major tenets include, rigor, generality and simplicity' (Debreu 1992: 114, italics ours). In the previous chapter we introduced the reader to the formalist analysis of the contribution of rigour, generality and simplicity to mathematical form. In this section we reflect on how the formalist's purely syntactical understanding of mathematical form impacts on the interpretation of Debreu's mathematical model. In this connection we introduce some core semanticist objections to Debreu's mathematical model. We then show, given Debreu's commitment to the purely formalist conception of mathematical form, how these semanticist objections would hold no weight for Debreu.

As we saw in the last chapter the concept of mathematical form is contested in the foundations of mathematics: we drew a major fault line between the semanticist and the formalist conceptions of mathematical form. Semanticists commence their analysis of mathematical form with logical form. A basic semanticist commitment is that an inference is logically valid in virtue of its form and not its content. Take for instance the inference if the car is running then there is petrol in the tank and the car is running therefore there is petrol in the tank, and the inference if Peter is drunk then his wife is upset and Peter is drunk therefore his wife is upset. The empirical content of these arguments is different but they share the same logical form: if p then q and p therefore q, where 'p' and 'q' are propositional variables. In this logical form in addition to the variables there are also the logical constants 'if – then –' 'and' 'therefore'. These and other logical constants such as 'or', 'it is not the case that –' are essential to the semanticist analysis of logical inferences. In symbolic logic these constants are replaced by symbols. For instance 'and' is replaced by '&'. However, symbolised, these logical constants have an objective *meaning* which is conveyed by truth-tables. For instance the meaning, i.e. the indispensable semantic component, of p&q is given by Truth-table 4.1, where T is short for true and F is short for false.

Truth-table 4.1

p&q
TTT
TFF
FFT
FFF

The table tells us that if we conjoin two true propositions with 'and' the resultant proposition is true and in all other cases the resultant conjunction proposition is false. That is the objective logical meaning of 'and'/'&'. In this way logical form, a fundamental building block of mathematical form, has an indispensable semantical component. In short, while the distinction between form and empirical content is absolutely necessary, there is no logical form without some logical content.

In addition to logical form mathematical form also contains, among others, number variables such as 'x', 'y' which range over numbers and symbols such as $f(x)$ for mathematical functions. According to semanticists these symbols also have an indispensable semantical component. For instance the symbol $f(x)$ represents functions in general, as opposed to the representation of a specific function such as $3x^2 + 7x - 6$. Mathematically, $f(x)$ is a rule-governed mapping which assigns to each element of a domain a unique element in a range. Something like that is the indispensable semantical component of $f(x)$, i.e. is the objective meaning of the concept of mathematical function. If a student does not grasp that meaning then the student does not comprehend the concept of a mathematical function. In short just as there is no logical form without logical content, there is no mathematical form without some mathematical content. While logico-mathematical thought approaches the pinnacle of abstract thinking, i.e. thought which in no way is influenced by the concrete world, it still contains logico-mathematical content.

The formalist rejects this semanticist conception of mathematical form. According to formalists mathematical form is irrevocably divorced from content. There is an absolute dualism of form and content: mathematical form has no mathematical content. One way of approaching this novel, counter-intuitive theory of mathematical form is to locate it in the context of the formalist's central agenda namely to absolutely and finally prove that the whole edifice of logic cum pure mathematics is consistent, complete and decidable. In this way if a mathematician fails to find a solution to a well-formulated problem, the failure would reflect on the mathematician's ability. To achieve the goal of this rigorous, definitive proof of the consistency, completeness and decidability of the whole edifice of mathematics one must, among other things, replace the old semanticist conception of mathematical form with the formalist's purely syntactical conception. In this fashion the whole edifice of logic cum mathematics is reconstructed as a purely syntactical axiomatic system with no content whatsoever.

Given that pure mathematics is wholly syntactical, Debreu's economic model has no mathematical content whatsoever. This model is embedded in the pure mathematics of Chapter 1 of his *Theory of Value* which, according to Debreu, must in the name of rigour be understood in the formalist way. The semanticist, however, rejects the formalist's claim that Debreu's model has no mathematical content. The reason for this is that, as we have just seen, according to semanticists, while pure mathematics is immunised from the content of specific empirical domains, it still has *mathematical* content. For instance, take again Brouwer's fixed point theorem. Clearly it does not concern the specific empirical content of say, astrophysics or sociology. To that extent the formalist is correct in emphasising mathematical form. However, according to semanticists, formalists go too far in claiming that Brouwer's theorem is a meaningless concatenation of meaningless symbols which is proven by the mechanical, meaningless application of purely syntactical, meaningless rules of inference. Rather Brouwer's fixed point theorem is meaningful: it has mathematical content. The theorem is about elements of sets and their transformations and the existence of a fixed element. Thus for the semanticist, when Brouwer's fixed point theorem is used to establish the existence of general equilibrium in theoretical economics, this mathematical meaning or content *is indispensable* to that economic interpretation. This pure mathematical content is part and parcel of the full theoretico-economic content of Debreu's model. This non-empirical, mathematical content is not, as it were, lost in the process of economic interpretation. For the formalist, however, there is nothing to be lost in the process of economic interpretation for the simple reason that there is no content in pure mathematics: pure mathematics is purely syntactical.[20]

In order to spell out the implications of this fundamental philosophical divide for the evaluation of Debreu's model, we revisit the Poincaré malaise outlined in the last chapter. We focus on three aspects of that malaise. The first aspect is the claim that the formalist school's wholly syntactical characterisation of pure mathematics is inoperable: formalists cannot practice what they preach. To repeat, according to the formalist, Brouwer's fixed point theorem is a meaningless concatenation of meaningless symbols which is mechanically proven by meaningless, purely syntactical rules of inference. There is, moreover, a potentially infinite number of such theorems. All of these theorems have equal standing from a purely mathematical point of view, viz. each is a meaningless concatenation of meaningless symbols which is proven by meaningless purely syntactical rules of inference. Given that theorems are just this and that there is a potential infinite number of such theorems, how does one pick out Brouwer's fixed point theorem from all of these for economic interpretation? From a formalist point of view Brouwer's fixed point theorem contains the empty symbol '∃' (which for semanticists symbolises the existential quantifier, 'there is –'). Moreover, formalists correctly insist that this empty symbol '∃' is systematically replaceable by any other meaningless, but previously unused symbol. Let us thus replace '∃' by '∅' in the formal system. If the empty symbol '∅' were used in place of '∃' in Brouwer's fixed point theorem would anyone pick it out from the other meaningless theorems for an economic interpretation? Its choice for economic interpretation would be miraculous. According to the semanticist the reason why formalists choose Brouwer's fixed point theorem is because they already know the mathematical meaning of the symbol '∃' and the other symbols of the theorem.

Indeed the semanticist could maintain that this is actually what Debreu does in claiming that:

> The perfect fit between a mathematical concept of a fixed point and the social science concept of an equilibrium stands out. A state of a social

system is described by listing an action for each one of its agents. Considering such a state, each agent reacts by selecting the action that is optimal for him given the action of all others. Listing these reactions yields a new state, and thereby a *transformation* of the *set* of states of the social system into itself is defined. A state of a system is in equilibrium if, and only if, it is a *fixed point* of that transformation.

(Debreu 1986: 1262, italics ours)

Clearly Debreu is using the mathematical meanings of the terms 'set', 'transformation' and 'fixed point'. According to the semanticist, to gain his economic interpretation these mathematical meanings must be used.

The formalist disagrees with this semanticist thesis. The actual rigorous proof of the existence of equilibrium is given by Debreu in Chapter 5 of his *Theory of Value*. That proof is carried out in complete accordance with the formalist template for the axiomatisation of any science, without any reference to the mathematical meaning/content of Brouwer's fixed point theorem. The above quote from Debreu is merely an explanatory commentary on that rigorous proof which is aimed at a readership not educated to the highest standards of rigour of the formalist school. For those educated, the above commentary is a dispensable piece of rhetoric which, logically speaking, is superfluous.[21] In a logically rigorous mathematical proof there is only mathematical form: there is no mathematical content/meaning. Hence the sheer austerity of Debreu's *Theory of Value*. This is also evident in the fact that no effort is made to convey the intuitive content of its mathematics. Such intuitive content is a prop for logically feeble minds. Strong, i.e. logical, minds use and only use mathematical form as defined by the formalist school. Logically there is no such thing as content or meaning in pure mathematics. Meaning or content comes with interpretation.[22]

The second concern raised by the Poincaré malaise is that Debreu's proof of the existence of equilibrium is established in the specific mathematical domain of Cantorian set theory and thus in Cantorian actual infinity. Consequently this infinitist mathematical content is integral to Debreu's mathematical model of an economy. According to the semanticist this content is plainly evident in Debreu's recourse to Cantorian set theory in his construction of his model. Debreu is using Cantorian sets, not empty symbols, in his model. Thus equilibrium is shown to exist, i.e. is possible, in the mathematical domain of Cantorian actual infinity. Hence there is no logical guarantee that equilibrium exists in a finite domain – the domain of actual economies. However, according to the formalist, this semanticist claim is not justifiable. Any reference to a Cantorian actual infinite domain is necessarily excluded by the wholly syntactical nature of the mathematics used by Debreu in presenting the mathematical form of his economic model.[23] The symbols in this purely syntactical mathematics do not refer to mathematical entities in any domain either finite or infinite. The pure mathematical symbols do not refer at all or, if one prefers, each mathematical symbol refers to itself and only itself. These pure mathematical symbols are meaningless. Thus the semanticist distinction between a finite set and an infinite set plays no role whatsoever in Debreu's purely syntactical mathematics. The semanticist has got the theory of mathematical form wrong.

The third aspect of the Poincaré malaise is that Debreu's existence proof of equilibrium, based on Brouwer's fixed point theorem, is non-constructive. As we have just seen, according to the semanticist, Debreu establishes the existence of equilibrium in the pure mathematical domain of Cantorian actual infinity. In addition to this the semanticist maintains that this proof is non-constructive. To show how it is non-constructive the semanticist asks the formalist the following question. How many operations would it take *to actually construct* Brouwer's fixed point? The formalist's reply is that *an infinite* number of steps would actually be required. This non-constructivity is integral to the objective mathematical meaning of Brouwer's fixed point theorem. Thus, according to the semanticist it cannot be dropped out of the objective evaluation of Debreu's proof.

The formalist unequivocally rejects this semanticist claim. In this case, i.e. recourse to the non-constructivity of Brouwer's fixed point theorem, the semanticist is fundamentally confused. The semanticist is confusing the distinct discipline of metamathematics, which undoubtedly is semantical, with the discipline of pure mathematics which is a purely syntactical calculus. The distinct semantical discipline of metamathematics is *about* mathematics, and thus has content, whereas the mathematical calculus itself is contentless. As Nagel and Newman put it, metamathematical statements:

> are statements about the signs occurring within a formalized mathematical system (i.e. a calculus) − about the kinds and arrangements of such signs when they are combined to form longer strings of marks called 'formulas', or about relations between formulas that may obtain as a consequence of the rules of manipulation specified for them.
>
> (Nagel and Newman 2005: 21)

For example the statement 'x' is a variable belongs to metamathematics: it says something meaningful about the meaningless symbol 'x'. Thus, for instance, the true metamathematical statement, 'x' is a variable, does not express a mathematical truth for two reasons. Firstly, there are no mathematical truths − mathematics is a purely syntactical calculus − and secondly that true metamathematical statement can not occur in the pure syntactical calculus of pure mathematics: it is not derivable within the syntactical calculus.

In particular the assertion that pure mathematics is consistent is a metamathematical statement about the mathematical calculus. It is not part of the purely syntactical calculus of pure mathematics. Thus the proof of the consistency of mathematics is a metamathematical task. Moreover, according to the formalist, this metamathematical proof must be constructive, i.e. must be capable of being carried out in a finite number of algorithmetic steps. This constructivist constraint on the metamathematical proof of the consistency of mathematics is *not* part of the purely syntactical calculus of mathematics. The meaningful distinction between a constructive and a non-constructive proof is integral to meta-mathematics but is not integral to the mathematical form of the purely syntactical calculus of pure mathematics. The formalist medicine for the Poincaré malaise based on non-constructivity is further education about the formalist's funda-mental distinction between mathematics and metamathematics. In Debreu's model it is the mathematical calculus alone which receives an economic inter-pretation. Metamathematics, by constructive means, guarantees the consistency of that formal calculus and thereby renders it use in economic theorising unquestionable.[24]

In this section we introduced the reader to how the commitment to the formalist philosophy of mathematical form, as distinct from the commitment to a semanticist philosophy of mathematical form, can inform one's methodological defence of neo-Walrasian theorising. As we saw Debreu roots his philosophy of economic analysis in mathematical form. However, he does not inform the reader that his concept of mathematical form is a contentious one in the philosophy of mathematics. Debreu is committed to the formalist philosophy of mathematical form. In that philosophy the Poincaré malaise can be cured by more formalism. On the semanticist side the situation is not that simple. The Poincaré malaise is symptomatic of a more fundamental disease which requires a different kind of intervention to that of formalism. This more fundamental disease and the radical kind of intervention are spelled out in Chapter Seven.

Debreu's formalist philosophy of economic analysis: its assets

According to Debreu his philosophy of economic analysis based on the formalist philosophy of mathematical form has 'many assets' (Debreu 1986: 1268). This philosophy of economic analysis puts the Hilbertian formalist model, rather than the Euclidean model, of axiomatisation centre stage. One obvious asset here is the model's insistence on 'the exact formulation of assumptions' (Debreu 1986: 1266). As already explained these assumptions are indispensable to establishing a perfect fit between the theoretico-economic content obtained from previous research and the pure mathematical form given in Chapter 1 of his *Theory of Value*. Thus the formulation of these assumptions leaves no room for ambiguity. The advantage of this explicit and precise articulation of assumptions is that it is 'an effective safeguard against the ever-present temptation to apply an economic theory beyond its domain of validity' (Debreu 1986: 1266). If an economist fails to recognise the clear boundaries of the valid application of Debreu's neo-Walrasian model, explicitly and distinctively specified in its assumptions, the fault does not lie with the model. Rather it lies with the economist. We will see in the next chapter that Hahn accuses various orthodox economists of succumbing to this temptation. Clearly the blame for not resisting this temptation cannot be placed on Debreu's model.

Another advantage of this formalist mode of economic theorising is the manner in which it enables economists to navigate through the seas of the ideology-ladenness of the social sciences. The issue of whether or not the social sciences could be ideology-free was a central issue in the philosophy of the social sciences in the 1960s and 1970s. According to Debreu his model of economic theorising can bring economic analysis 'closer to its ideology-free ideal' (Debreu 1986: 1266). He uses the two main theorems of welfare economics to illustrate his thesis.

> Foes of state intervention read these two theorems as a mathematical demonstration of the unqualified superiority of market economies, while advocates of state intervention welcome the same theorems because the explicitness of their assumptions emphasizes discrepancies between the theoretic model and the economies they observe.
>
> (Debreu 1986: 1266)

Debreu is suggesting that the ideal of an ideology-free economics is not pie in the sky. The formalist, as distinct from the Euclidean, model of axiomatisation makes a significant contribution to the achievement of this ideal. In the Euclidean model, the axioms are claimed to represent fundamental truths about actual economies, whereas in Debreu's formalist model that is not the case. Debreu's *Theory of Value* is a rigorous, theory-laden and assumption-laden mathematical model which is not claiming to accurately picture a real economy. However, its theorems can be accepted by both sides in the ideological debate on the merits or otherwise of state intervention. The rigorous proofs of its theorems are not up for debate.[25] This presumably makes formalist economic theorising unique among the other social sciences.

In terms of economic method perhaps its advantage of having the capacity to 'give ready answers to new questions when a novel interpretation of primitive concepts is discovered' (Debreu 1984: 275) is most significant. When a new economic question arises it *may* sometimes happen that *the same piece of pure mathematics* can be given a novel interpretation, thereby answering or partially answering this new economic question. Clearly this does not happen on every occasion a new question arises: the development of mathematical economics is not that simple! Rather this possibility could happen and actually has happened. Debreu refers us to Chapter 7 of his *Theory of Value*, titled Uncertainty, for an example. In that chapter, Debreu opens with his own definition of a commodity given in Chapter 2. A commodity is a good or service whose physical properties, delivery date and location are specified. When this definition is mapped into mathematics it culminates in 'the commodity space', i.e. the mathematical vector space R^ℓ (Debreu 1959: 32). Now suppose the following economic question is posed: what happens in an unstable environment? Debreu maintains that the points in the vector space R^ℓ can be given a *new interpretation* which will enable economists to respond to this new question concerning an uncertain environment. The new interpretation is accomplished by changing Debreu's definition of a commodity, given in Chapter 2. 'A contract for the transfer of a commodity now specifies in addition to its physical properties, its location and its date, an event on the occurrences of which the transfer is conditional' (Debreu 1959: 98). By adding that kind of conditional event to the defining characteristics of a commodity, one is taking into account an uncertain environment while simultaneously altering the definition of a commodity given in Chapter 2. What is crucial here, however, is that the points in the vector space R^ℓ can be interpreted as commodities in this new sense. Thus these points are given a novel interpretation. 'In this manner one obtains, *without any change in the form of the model*, a theory of uncertainty …' (Debreu 1984: 275, italics ours). In other words, the same points of the mathematical vector space R^ℓ are given this novel interpretation where uncertainty is accommodated. Moreover, according to Debreu, this theory of uncertainty 'is free from any probability concept and *formally identical with* the theory of certainty in the preceding chapters' (Debreu 1959: 98, italics ours). Thus, according to Debreu, there is, in principle, no difficulty in accommodating uncertainty into his mathematically deterministic model. This is so because the determinism or certainty belongs solely to the form of the model, not to its economic content, whereas the uncertainty relates solely to the economic content. This example clearly illustrates the richness/sophistication of the formalist approach to axiomatisation over the older Euclidean approach.[26]

Debreu's praise of the axiomatisation of economics does not stop here. Axiomatisation also dictates its 'aesthetic code' (Debreu 1992: 114). This aesthetic code relates to Debreu's values of simplicity and generality discussed in the previous chapter. 'Again their aesthetic appeal suffices to make them desirable ends in themselves for the designer of a theory' (Debreu 1984: 275). This may appear to be an exaggeration. For instance in theoretical physics these values are not ends in themselves. Theory in physics is corralled by experimentation. However, economic theory cannot be similarly corralled. Thus generality and simplicity become ends in themselves for the theoretical economist. Moreover, for Debreu, in economic theorising generality and simplicity go far beyond aesthetics. 'Simplicity makes a theory usable by a great number of research workers. Generality makes it applicable to a broad class of problems' (Debreu 1984: 275). As we will see in the next chapter, according to some economists, such as Kaldor, these so-called desirable ends in themselves have not served economic theory well. On the contrary their abandonment is required if economic theory as an empirical science is to flourish.

Debreu's axiomatisation of economics has also the advantages of 'imposing its terse language' (Debreu 1992: 114). This terse language is 'the superbly efficient language of mathematics' (Debreu 1984: 275). This efficient language is the language of the pure formalist which is wholly syntactical.[27] In this sense it is very much what philosophers call an ideal language. This raises the question as to what extent such a language can illuminate actual economic situations. In this connection Debreu remarks that 'the seductiveness' of this language may tempt economists 'to shun economic problems that are not readily amenable to mathematization' (Debreu 1986; 1268). Is there a suggestion here that all economic problems are amenable to mathematisation, while some are more readily amenable than others? Be that as it may, we certainly know that Debreu draws a distinction between the discovery/elaboration phase of theory construction and its rigorous, axiomatic phase. 'Although an axiomatic theory may flaunt the separation of its mathematical form and its economic content in print, their interaction is sometimes close in the discovery and elaboration phases' (Debreu 1986: 1266). In this connection Debreu's example of what he has in mind is, in our opinion, methodologically instructive. An aggregate excess demand function:

> in an ℓ-commodity exchange economy maps a positive price vector into an aggregate excess demand vector, and Walras' Law says that those two vectors are orthogonal in the Euclidean commodity-price space. That function is also homogeneous of degree zero. For a mathematician, these are compelling reasons for normalizing the price vector so that it belongs to the unit sphere. Then aggregate excess demand can be represented by a vector tangent to the sphere at the price vector with which it is associated. In other words, the aggregate excess demand function is a vector field on the positive unit sphere. Hugo Sonnenschein (1973) *conjectured* that any continuous function satisfying Walras' Law is the aggregate excess demand function of a finite exchange economy. A *proof* of that *conjecture* (Debreu 1974) was *suggested by the preceding geometric interpretation* ...
>
> (Debreu 1986: 1266, italics added)

Prima facie, the recognition of the roles of conjecture and, in particular, of mathematical content – in this case the geometric interpretation – in the elaboration phase suggests that Debreu's formalist philosophy of economic analysis is incomplete. At very best it is adequate to the axiomatic phase but it is not adequate to the prior elaboration phase. In the elaboration phase the indispensable role of mathematical content is explicitly acknowledged. This mathematical content is indispensable for the identification and selection of the appropriate theorems to be used in the rigorous proof. However in the axiomatic phase, this mathematical content disappears.[28] In our opinion the sole reason for its disappearance is the commitment to the formalist philosophy of applied mathematics, a commitment not shared by semanticist philosophers of applied mathematics.

Finally, as we noted on various occasions, Debreu's philosophy of economic analysis recognises that his mode of theorising:

> cannot achieve a grand unified explanation of economic phenomena. Instead it adds insights to the perception of areas to which it turns its search. When they are gained by accepting mathematical challenges, those insights are the highest prizes sought by a mathematical economist.
>
> (Debreu 1992: 114)

Thus general equilibrium theory is not a grand unified explanation of economic phenomena. Rather it merely furnishes insights into the perception of some of these phenomena. Assuming that Debreu did not change his mind, these insights include (1) 'the explanation of the prices of commodities resulting from the interaction of the agents of a private ownership economy through markets', (2) 'the explanation of the role of prices in an optimal state of an economy' (Debreu 1959: vii). One might contend that, while not achieving the status of a grand unified theory of economic phenomena, equilibrium theory's claim to explain prices in a private ownership economy through markets, merits more than the status of 'an insight into the perception' of some economic phenomena. Indeed Debreu himself goes further. General equilibrium theory is 'a benchmark', 'a role which prompted extensions to incomplete markets for contingent commodities, externalities, indivisibilities, increasing returns, public goods, temporary equilibrium ...' (Debreu 1986: 1268). Thus methodologically its role as benchmark 'established secure bases from which exploration could start in new directions' (Debreu 1984: 275). Moreover, 'it has freed researchers from the necessity of questioning the work of their predecessors in every detail' (Debreu 1984: 275). These roles as a benchmark leaves general equilibrium theory close to a paradigm in the Kuhnian sociological sense. For Kuhn, paradigm-based science:

> is research firmly based on one or more past scientific achievements, achievements that some particular scientific community acknowledges for a time as supplying the foundation for its further practices. Today such achievements are recounted ... by science text books, elementary and advanced.
>
> (Kuhn 1970: 10)

These achievements:

> shared two essential characteristics. Their achievements were sufficiently unprecedented to attract an enduring group of adherents away from competing modes of scientific activity. Simultaneously, it was sufficiently open-ended to leave all sorts of problems for the redefined group of practitioners to resolve.
>
> (Kuhn 1970: 10)

To conclude, in this and the previous chapter we have attempted to show the subtlety and sophistication of Debreu's own philosophy of economic theorising. We are not claiming that his philosophy of economic theorising was representative of his generation. Certainly, as we will see in the next chapter, it was not shared by Hahn, another outstanding general equilibrium theorist. In our opinion Debreu was par excellence the formalist economic theoretician in the philosophical sense of formalism. Thus he can insist that 'mathematical form powerfully contributes to defining a philosophy of

economic analysis whose major tenets include rigor, generality and simplicity'
(Debreu 1992: 114).

Notes

1 As already indicated, our aim includes that of Weintraub, i.e. 'to study how economics
   has been shaped by economists' ideas about the nature and purpose and function and
   meaning of mathematics' (Weintraub 2002: 2). In this sense our analysis complements
   Weintraub. However, our presentation of Debreu's conception of the nature, purpose,
   function and meaning of mathematics is quite different to Weintraub's analysis of
   Debreu's conception.
2 As indicated, we first came across Corry's terminology in Weintraub's research.
   In our view Corry's account of the dynamic relationship between image and
   content is quite different from Dasgupta's distinction between what economists say
   and what they do. When addressing 'internal' attacks on economics (i.e. attacks by
   economists rather than by methodologists) he locates them in 'a lineage which often
   operates at an Olympian height of generality' and which 'usually works round what
   modern economists *say* in their 'literary moments' rather than what they *do* in their
   technical work' (Dasgupta 2002: 58). In Dasgupta's terminology our thesis is that
   Debreu does in his technical *Theory of Value* what he says he is doing in his 'literary'
   moments.
3 This is one of the many places where our analysis of Debreu's philosophy of economic
   analysis differs from Weintraub's.
4 We introduce these phases for conceptual clarity. We are not suggesting that these
   phases constitute a strict chronological order which is to be found in the history of
   mathematics.
5 These logical principles are not psychological laws. They are laws of thought in the
   sense that anyone wishing to attain truth in their deductive inferences *must* adhere
   to these principles. The fact that some people in their inferences do not actually
   adhere to them is beside the point. Such people would be claimed to be illogical in
   their thinking.
6 The principle of identity can be stated as follows: if any proposition is true it is true.
   The principle of non-contradiction asserts that no proposition can be both true and
   false and the principle of the excluded middle asserts that any proposition must be
   either true or false.
7 For instance, the grammar of a natural language allows for exceptions to its rules of
   syntax. No such exceptions are allowed in an ideal language.
8 The logical laws in phase three, however, are not the laws of thought of phase two.
   Logic in phase three is radically different from logic in phases one and two. Logic
   now includes truth – functional logic and quantification theory.
9 Formal arithmetic 'is comparable to a creeper twining around non-formal arithmetic,
   losing all hold once its support and source of sustenance are removed. Accordingly,
   formal arithmetic presupposes the non-formal one; its pretension of replacing the latter
   herewith falls to the ground' (Frege 1971: 137).
10 The phrase 'old axiomatics' is not our own. This insightful term is found in Bernays
   (1922: 193).
11 As with phase one, two and three our account is very schematic and incomplete.
   We are focusing on themes which prove useful in enriching our understanding of
   Debreu's *Theory of Value*.
12 This is how Bernays makes the same point. 'Just as he (Hilbert) had formally stripped
   the basic relations and axioms of geometry of their intuitive content, he now elim-
   inates the intellectual content of the inferences from the proofs of arithmetic and
   analysis that he makes the object of his investigation. He obtains this by taking the

system of formulas that represent those proofs in the logical calculus, *detached from their contentual-logical interpretations*, as the immediate object of study, and *by replacing the proofs of analysis with a purely formal manipulation that takes place with certain signs according to definite rules'* (Bernays 1922: 196, italics ours).

13 For the formalist school – the school to which Debreu belongs – it is crucial to distinguish between pure mathematics per se and metamathematics. Pure mathematics is a meaningless, wholly syntactical calculus. Metamathematics consists of meaningful statements about the empty signs, formulae and relationships between these formulae of pure mathematics. Thus metamathematics is semantical; its statements have objective meaning or content, whereas mathematics per se is a meaningless purely syntactical calculus. For example the meaningless symbol '*x*' occurs in a mathematical calculus. The statement '*x*' is a variable is not part of mathematics. The central task of the formalist school was to provide a metamathematical proof of the consistency, completeness and decidability of the pure calculus of classical mathematics. Thus for the formalist school there is a three-fold division (a) pure mathematics – a purely syntactical calculus (b) metamathematics (c) the application of pure mathematics to the sciences, i.e. applied mathematics. For semanticists, the formalist characterization of metamathematics is wrong. For instance Gödel was a semanticist and for him metamathematics 'is a science describing objective mathematical states of affairs' (Gödel, quoted in Wang 1974: 10).

14 For an account of how Hilbert proposed to do this see Potter 2002, Chapter 9. The joy of this ingenious remedy for the pathology of the paradoxes was short-lived. Church, Gödel and Turing undermined the Hilbert project. See chapter seven of this work.

15 We are using the term 'applied mathematics' in the broad sense of any discipline where pure mathematics is used. Mathematical physics was a paradigm of applied mathematics. We do not mean by applied mathematics the technological exploitation of mathematics. Neither do we means its industrial application.

16 For a recent scholarly analysis of this work see Corry (2004).

17 This of course is a very broad-brush portrait of the axiomatisation of a scientific theory. For instance, it does not address how theoretical, as distinct from observational, terms are to be introduced. Nonetheless this broad-brush portrait is accurate for our purposes here.

18 Logically, pure mathematics is a consistent, complete and decidable axiomatic system. Thus the choice of a subdomain within this system is a pragmatic issue: the boundaries are arbitrary.

19 This, it could be argued, lies behind the exploitation of more advanced mathematics in neo-Walrasian theory.

20 As we will see in the next section the formalist distinguishes sharply between the elaboration phase of a discipline and its rigorous logical reconstruction. Logically the semanticist interpretation of pure mathematics is redundant. However, the semanticist interpretation may play a psychological role in the elaboration phase but this possible psychological role is, rigorously speaking, redundant.

21 See Note 20.

22 In so far as a practising mathematician is a semanticist one could say that from the point of view of formalism such a mathematician is doing applied, not pure, mathematics. Pure mathematics is a formal calculus which the semanticist mathematician interprets. Consequently the semanticist pure mathematician is, rigorously speaking, an applied mathematician.

23 One could also say that the formalist use of Cantorian actual infinity in pure mathematics is purely instrumental. Its role in the pure calculus is to facilitate the construction of simple proofs. These are echoes of Debreu's value of simplicity lurking here.

24 As we will see in Chapter Seven, Gödel undermined this guarantee.

25 We will see in Chapter Seven, how intuitionist mathematics, founded by Brouwer, challenges these very proofs!
26 Our appreciation of the subtlety of this aspect of Debreu's formalist account of axiomatisation does not imply that we concur with this analysis of uncertainty. The reader will find alternative views of uncertainty in Chapter Six.
27 Also as pointed out by Arrow and discussed in the previous chapter this terse language presupposes that the logic of economic decision-making is extensional.
28 The semanticist could argue that this is just conceding the actual inoperability of formalism.

5 Hahn and Kaldor on the neo-Walrasian formalisation of economics

Introduction

By focusing on Walras's and Debreu's philosophies of economic analysis we have responded to Weintraub's challenge to reflect on 'how economics has been shaped by economists' ideas about the nature and purpose and function and meaning of mathematics' (Weintraub 2002: 2). In connection with Debreu we saw how he imposed the Hilbertian formalist philosophy of applied mathematics on to the historical developments of the neo-Walrasian programme accomplished in journals from the 1930s to the 1950s. The result of this imposition is an austere, rigorous 'definitive statement of the theory of competitive equilibrium' (Hahn 1961: 204). Debreu's *Theory of Value* is not a definitive analysis of the actual methods used by individual economists who pioneered neo-Walrasian theorising: it has nothing to say about how these economists actually theorised. Rather this *Theory of Value* is a rigorous definitive axiomatic representation of the outcome of their research, namely competitive general equilibrium theory.

In this chapter we focus on the reception of Debreu's formalisation. Some economists saw it as a monumental achievement, others were utterly hostile to it. Those who saw it as a major achievement did not form a homogeneous group.[1] Among these neo-classical economists we distinguish a majority opinion from a minority opinion. A majority of neo-classical economists read Debreu's contribution as being indispensable to their *scientific* investigations of actual economies. For instance, writing in the 1970s Kaldor maintains that neo-classical economists hold that Debreu's contribution 'is the one and only starting point' (Kaldor 1972: 1238) for their scientific theorising. In a similar vein, and writing much later, Hahn points out that various neo-classical economists – particularly American – read it as making an indispensable contribution to their *scientific descriptions* of actual economies. The mention of Hahn brings us to a minority view. According to Hahn, those neo-classical economists who read general equilibrium theory as an empirical science are utterly mistaken. Whatever Debreu has accomplished and that is outstanding – it does not establish that some real economy will be or tends towards an equilibrium state.[2] Indeed general equilibrium theory, contrary to numerous American economists, is not a *scientific* theory at all. Rather Debreu's *Theory of Value* makes a major contribution to an objective, clearly articulated *grammar of argumentation* which enables applied economists to critically and objectively interrogate economic policy. Practically speaking 'it is a line of first defence against madmen and witches' (Hahn 1985: 4). Theoretically, it furnishes economists with an objective instrument in their efforts at understanding 'the messy reality' (Hahn 1996: 193) of actual economies.

In particular, in this chapter we compare and contrast Hahn's own philosophy of the formalisation of economics with that of Debreu. In this connection we show how Hahn is in line with the Hilbertian formalists in maintaining that Debreu's existence proof merely establishes the logical possibility of equilibrium and nothing more. However, in developing his own unique philosophy of the formalisation of economics as a grammar of argumentation, Hahn does *not* espouse Debreu's Hilbertian formalist template for the axiomatisation of economics. Rather he has recourse to what we called the Euclidean Template. Given his grammar of argumentation, Hahn then undermines various erroneous scientific interpretations of general equilibrium theory on the part of various neo-classical economists.

It would be utterly misleading to give the impression that the general equilibrium formalisation of economics was not radically questioned by reputable economists. Because of the unambiguity of his challenge and, in particular, because of his objections to its formalisation we focus on Kaldor's rejection of the neo-Walrasian programme. Kaldor, like Hahn, is fully aware that Debreu's *Theory of Value* is 'an elegant, exact and logically precise' account of general equilibrium (Kaldor 1972: 1237). Unlike Hahn, Kaldor emphasises Debreu's formalist approach to economic theorising. This formalist approach, according to Kaldor, is its Achilles' heel. In place of Debreu's formalist template for economic theorising Kaldor proposes an empirical template. According to Kaldor scientific theorists begin their theory construction with a summary of the known observational facts of the domain under investigation. In the case of economics, since the required summary is frequently presented in statistical fashion, economic theorists start with a stylised view of its facts. These stylised facts are statistical generalisations about observed empirical regularities. The culmination of this empirical approach is 'a body of theorems based on assumptions that are empirically derived (from observations) and which embody hypotheses that are capable of verification both in regard to assumptions and predictions' (Kaldor 1972: 1238). In light of this empirical view of economic theorising and Debreu's formalist approach to economic theory it is not surprising that Kaldor concludes that 'without a major act of demolition – without destroying the basic conceptual framework – it is impossible to make any real progress' (Kaldor 1972: 1240).

The role of economic theory

One way of approaching the contribution of Debreu's *Theory of Value* is to locate it in the broad context of the general perception of economics and in the specific context of its perception by orthodox, neo-classical economists. Vis-à-vis the broad context of the 1950s we have recourse to Friedman (1953) in his influential methodological paper, 'The Methodology of Positive Economics'. Indeed one may feel that Friedman's summary has a lot going for it today. According to Friedman the subject matter of economics is regarded by most 'as vitally important' but also that 'it is the source of continuous and extensive controversy' (Friedman 1953: 3–4). These controversial differences are evident in debates about economic policy, such as the minimum wage, where 'a welter of arguments for and against' (Friedman 1953: 5) is evident. In these policy disputes 'self-proclaimed "experts"' (Friedman 1953: 4) voice their conflicting opinions. In addition to Friedman's self-proclaimed experts one could add that reputable economic advisors also contribute to these conflicting opinions. This situation in economics is in marked contrast to 'the prestige and acceptance' of the views of physicists, which as Friedman correctly points out derives 'from the evidence of their works, the success of their predictions and the dramatic achievements from applying their results' (Friedman 1953: 4).

To extricate the discipline of economics from this world of divergent opinion, Friedman argued for the clear-cut distinction between 'normative economics' – the domain of policy decision-making – and 'positive economics' which is totally independent of normative judgements. Positive economics, being a scientific discipline on par with physics, is to serve as the objective basis for consensus in policy issues. According to Wade Hands, Friedman's piece is 'clearly the best-known work in twentieth-century economic methodology' (Hands 2001: 53) and according to Hausman even almost fifty years after its publication it remains 'the only essay on methodology that a large number, perhaps a majority of economists, have ever read' (Hausman 1992: 162). Hahn would not object to these assessments of Friedman's influence: Friedman's methodological piece informed the context into which Debreu's *Theory of Value* was integrated. Thus numerous economists, especially American, read Debreu as making a major contribution to economics understood as a science on par with physics. In a similar vein according to Kaldor by the 1970s Debreu's general equilibrium theory was the prevailing *scientific* theory of value among neo-classical economists. Neo-classical economists held 'a deep underlying belief' that general equilibrium theory 'is the one and only starting point for any logically consistent explanation of the behaviour of decentralized economic systems' (Kaldor 1972: 1238).

This methodological approach to general equilibrium theory is vehemently opposed by Hahn: general equilibrium theory is *not* a scientific theory in the sense in which physics is a scientific theory.[3] According to Hahn the methodological claim that theoretical economics is a science 'is not only premature and not very honest but also, perhaps worse, pretentious' (Hahn 1993b: 163). By insisting that economics is a science, 'the subject gets a bad name' (Hahn 1993a: 91). One cannot imagine theoretical physicists insisting to their students that 'everything I will teach you is in a sense false but useful' (Hahn 1996: 191). Neither would theoretical physicists claim that Hahn's thesis that economic theory 'is at best a powerful aid to thought about the world, *not because it provides a very satisfactory description*, but because it provides clear limits to understanding' (Hahn 1993b: 164) conveys the contribution of theoretical physics to our knowledge and technological control of the physical world. Hahn amasses a diverse body of evidence in favour of his unconventional thesis that theoretical economics is not a scientific theory. Firstly, relative to theoretical physics theoretical economics' predictive record is very poor. For instance it is no match for quantum physics in the accuracy of its predictions. Moreover, he concurs with Debreu that economic theory cannot claim to be substantiated or confirmed by experimental testing à la physics. Like Debreu, mathematical economics is not, in this regard, akin to mathematical physics. Thirdly, unlike physics 'economics has no laws' (Hahn 1996: 192). Indeed Hahn loses his patience with economists who insist on the iron laws of economics. These so-called iron laws 'are not laws which hold in all societies and at all times' (Hahn 1993a: 91). In Hahn's opinion this 'babble' (Hahn 1993a: 95) about economic laws is rooted in the erroneous belief that economics is a science. When economists claim to be scientists 'they sooner or later babble about "the laws of economics" ... The subject gets a bad name' (Hahn 1993a: 95).

Hahn, in his forceful opposition to the conventional assumption that theoretical economics is a science, may sound like a fundamentalist hermeneutical philosopher who relishes in pointing out the impossibility of any scientific study of human interactions. This of course is not the case. Hahn is, at it were, a whistle blower who, because of his deep-seated commitment to general equilibrium theory and because of the damage caused by its presentation as a science, feels he has no option but to undermine this harmful methodology of economics. In this connection he singles out Friedman's catastrophic methodological defence of economic theory. Friedman's prescriptive methodology 'may be fine for Quantum theory (predictions confirmed to a higher order of decimals) but only *dangerous sloppiness* and *blinkered arguing* can result from its use in economics' (Hahn 1996: 185, italics ours). Rather than being a science, general equilibrium theory is an objective grammar of argumentation which is very useful in policy matters as 'a line of first defence against madmen and witches' (Hahn 1985: 4). In short, in order to extricate economics from the world of opinion there is no need, à la Friedman, to exaggerate the undoubted success of economic theory by misrepresenting it as a science on par with physics. Rather the success of economic theory lies in it being an objective, rigorous grammar of argumentation which enables economists to gain an objective footing in their studies of our complex, dynamic world. This objective footing, however, is not in the business of predicting, á la physics, the course of any economy. Rather economic theory protects us from self-proclaimed experts who possess all the answers to contemporary economic challenges. This is its practical usefulness. Its theoretical usefulness is that it contributes to the objective, understanding of our economic world, by furnishing economists with a rigorous grammar of argumentation.

Hahn's grammar of argumentation: the first step

In his Jevon's Memorial Fund Lecture, delivered at University College London in November 1984, which he titled 'In Praise of Economic Theory', Hahn remarks that 'In Praise of Theorizing in Economics' would have been a more appropriate title. This shift in proposed title from economic theory to economic theorising marks Hahn's shift in emphasis to the grammar of argumentation which he sees as informing the on-going, dynamic process of general equilibrium theorising. Hahn is undoubtedly correct in insisting that general equilibrium theorists 'are not slouches' (Hahn 1996: 187). They have forged and continue to forge innovations at the frontiers of their research. To gain an accurate appreciation of neo-Walrasian general equilibrium theory, economists and methodologists need to focus on this dynamic activity of theorising at the frontiers of research. When one examines this activity one sees that it is informed by a grammar of argumentation which gives economists an objective footing in their attempts to come to grips with 'the messy reality' (Hahn 1996: 193) of actual economies.

This grammar of argumentation renders theoretical economics unique. One such unique characteristic is its solid starting point. The solidity of this starting point in this grammar of argumentation is guaranteed by Debreu's rigorous proof of the existence of equilibrium. As Hahn puts it 'if we did not have Arrow-Debreu theory, it would be priority number one to construct it. For, while it does not describe the world, it is a solid starting point for the quest for understanding it' (Hahn 1985: 14). This solid starting point 'is precise, complete and unambiguous' (Hahn 1973: 3). Arrow and Debreu 'wrote down precisely and beyond the power of misunderstanding by a normal person, what state of an economy was to be designated as an equilibrium' (Hahn 1985: 12). This clear, unambiguous definition of equilibrium is required for at least two reasons. Firstly, while the term equilibrium is extensively used in various applied contexts such as popular analyses of economic situations or speeches by ministers for finance, these meanings do not suffice for mathematical economics, where clearly defined terms are the norm. Thus Debreu clearly defines for all to see what he meant by the term equilibrium. As we have already seen, this unambiguous meaning of the term equilibrium is achieved by various idealisations and assumptions which are explicitly stated and not tacitly assumed.

The second reason for such a clear, unambiguous characterisation of equilibrium is that, since Adam Smith, economists have been divided on his thesis of the Invisible Hand. For many the Invisible Hand thesis is an astounding claim. How can millions of agents each solely concerned with his or her own individual interests and acting only on the sparse information of prices attain any coherent economic arrangement? Without a clear, unambiguous definition of such an equilibrium arrangement and a rigorous proof of its possibility, the debate on the Hidden Hand is condemned to remain in the subjective domain of opinion. The genius of Arrow-Debreu is that they 'provided the first essential step in any discussion of the Invisible Hand ...' (Hahn 1985: 13). This essential first step included, as we have already indicated in the previous paragraph, a clear unambiguous definition of an equilibrium state. This essential first step culminates in Debreu's rigorous proof that such an equilibrium state is logically possible. In other words, by recourse to very sophisticated mathematics, Debreu conclusively proves that the concept of an equilibrium state, as defined by the idealisations and assumptions of his *Theory of Value*, is free from contradiction.

Contrary to what some neo-classical economists assume, Hahn points out that Debreu's monumental achievement does *not* prove that this logically consistent concept actually or even approximately applies to or describes an actual economy. As Hahn puts it 'There is nothing here (Debreu's proof) to tell us that any given economy will be in that state or that it tends to that state' (Hahn 1985: 12). Anyone who understands the various idealisations and assumptions readily sees that Debreu's *Theory of Value* is not describing an actual economy. In particular this solid starting point, contrary to the misleading image created by Friedman's methodology, is not a body of knowledge which has been experimentally tested and vindicated by successful predictions. Rather the monumental achievement of Debreu lies in spelling out in no uncertain terms the idealisations and assumptions under which an equilibrium state is shown to be logically possible. This remarkable achievement is the solid starting point for the neo-Walrasian grammar of argumentation which will enrich our objective understanding of the messy reality of actual economies.

Axioms, assumptions and the grammar of argumentation

Hahn is well aware that some eminent economists – he explicitly names Kaldor and Kornai – are hostile to the axiomatisation of economics. Contrary to this hostility Hahn maintains that 'any coherent general propositions are decomposable into this form …' (Hahn 1985: 5). Taken literally, Hahn is not claiming that economic theorising is or should be carried out as an axiomatic-logico deductive system. Rather he is claiming that given any piece of economic theorising one can analyse or decompose it by recourse to the axiomatic template. The basic advantage of such a decomposition is that economists become very clear on both the axioms, and assumptions used in any piece of economic theorising. In other words axioms and assumptions pervade economic theorising and by recourse to the axiomatic template economists make their axioms and assumptions clear and explicit. Our thesis is that Hahn, in analysing a piece of economic theorising into axioms and assumptions, is using the Euclidean, as distinct from Debreu's Hilbertian formalist, template of axiomatisation. This, we contend, is substantiated by the manner in which Hahn draws the distinction between axioms and assumptions. As we saw in Chapter Four, the distinction between axioms as fundamental truths and assumptions which lack that fundamental basis plays no role in the formalist axiomatisation of economics exploited by Debreu. For Hahn, however, this distinction between axioms and assumptions is indispensable to Hahn's own analysis of the grammar of argumentation of economic theorising.

Few would challenge Hahn's claim that 'the best known and most important axiom is, of course, that of the rational agent …' (Hahn 1985: 5). He insists that this axiom is not a Friedmanite, implausible, 'as if' hypothesis which neo-classical economists plucked out of thin air with no basis in the real economic world. On the contrary, the rational agent axiom is 'a claim about this world so widely agreed as to make further argument unnecessary' (Hahn 1985: 5). This is clearly correct within neo-classical economics: the consensus among neo-classical economists is that this axiom is, in Hahn terminology, 'an abstract unifying principle' of their theorising. The same consensus, however, does not prevail among so-called heterodox economists. Be that as it may, Hahn makes an additional claim, namely 'in the first instance the axiom says that economic agents are persons' (Hahn 1985: 6). This additional claim is crucial for Hahn. We all recognise that the proposition economic consumers and producers are human beings is self-evidently true. Hahn maintains that this fundamental, self-evident truth is an indispensable component of the rational agent axiom. If that is the case then it necessarily follows that the grammar of argumentation based on the rational agent axiom has a genuine foothold in the real economic world. By virtue of this self-evident truth, the outcome of the grammar of argumentation of neo-Walrasian theorising is not pure fiction. This self-evident truth is the umbilical cord connecting theoretical economics to the real economic world.

However, if one consults either textbooks or research papers where the rational agent axiom is used, one certainly will not find it expressed as rational agents are persons. It goes without saying that Hahn is very well aware of this. As he points out, the term rational is vigorously debated in philosophy and elsewhere. To avoid these debates, mathematical economists are very precise in their use of the term rational. In economics the rational agent axiom means the following. 'The rational agent knows what he wants and from the among the alternatives available to him chooses what he wants' where 'knowing what he wants' means that the agent 'has a proper preference ordering over a relevant domain' (Hahn 1985: 5). Hahn's claim is that this precise axiom contains the self-evident truth that economic agents are persons. In this connection Hahn contrasts persons with other animals on the one hand, and with beings with no preferences at all on the other. While a person and an animal reveal their preferences in their respective behaviours, a person, unlike other animals, has opinions and beliefs about the elements in his domain of choice which he articulates in language. Indeed, a person, unlike other animals, gives reasons for his preferences. On the other hand, a being with no preferences – which of course should not be confused with a being which is indifferent between the elements of its choice set – is not a person at all. Thus the neo-classical rational agent is in the first instance a person, not an animal nor a being with no preferences at all. As we already indicated, a basic reason for Hahn's insistence on this point is to counteract those who dismiss neo-Walrasian theorising on the grounds that it is not in touch with economic reality.

Of course Hahn readily admits that there is more to the rational agent axiom than what is conveyed by the self-evident truth that economic agents are persons. The self-evident truth that economic agents are persons is transformed into the rational agent axiom by a process of idealisation and strengthening.

Indeed, as Hahn points out, the rational agent axiom is 'idealized and strengthened by theorists *beyond the point at which it commands universal consent*' (Hahn 1985: 7). In other words whereas the claim that economic agents are persons rightly commands universal consent, the rational agent axiom does not command the same universal consent. For instance in addition to the self-evident truth that economic agents are persons the rational agent axiom contains the idealisation that the agent's preferences are transitive. This idealisation may be questioned. Indeed an integral part of Hahn's grammar of argumentation is the rigorous mathematical interrogation of such idealisations. This interrogation is evident, for instance, in some of Sonnenshein's research. There are, however, limits beyond which this interrogation can go. In this case the limits are set by the fundamental truth that economic agents must be capable of giving reasons for their actions. For instance, if the proposed specific kind of intransitivity, which of course must be clearly articulated in mathematical terms, made it impossible for economic agents to give coherent reasons for their actions, then that kind of intransitivity would have to be rejected.

At the level of economic axioms an indispensable dimension of Hahn's grammar of argumentation may be summed up as follows. The theoretical economist starts with fundamental or agreed features of the economic world. These basic or self-evident truths are then sharpened by the process of idealisation. This process culminates in rigorously formulated economic axioms which serve as unifying principles in economists' endeavours at understanding the events of the economic world. At some subsequent state economists may have sound reasons to interrogate a particular idealisation used to sharpen a fundamental or consensus truth. There are, however, limits to this process of interrogation of idealisations, namely any alternative rigorously constructed idealisation must not contradict the pre-theoretical, fundamental or self-evident truths of economics.

Hahn, moreover, is emphatic that one should distinguish between economic axioms and assumptions. Axioms are inextricably linked to fundamental truths whereas assumptions are not. However, like axioms, assumptions are not capriciously imposed. There has to be some good reason for imposing assumptions. For Hahn these reasons range from cutting down the domain of choice, to requirements of tractability and simplicity to what he calls 'a casual empiricism' (Hahn 1985: 6). Hahn furnishes a number of examples of his distinction between axioms and assumptions. For instance 'agents have preferences and try to satisfy them' is a axiom, whereas 'universal perfect competition must count as an assumption' (Hahn 1985: 10). His explicit reason for locating universal perfect competition as an assumption is that 'neither introspection nor observation make it self-evident up to an acceptable margin of error' (Hahn 1985: 10–11). Universal perfect competition is too far removed from basic truths and hence cannot be deemed to be an axiom. Take another example. Managers have preferences is an axiom, while it is assumed that these preferences are linear in expected profit.

While recourse to simplifying assumptions is indispensable to Hahn's grammar of argumentation, he advises 'circumspection in praising simplicity in economic theorizing' (Hahn 1994: 250). In this connection he concludes that various neo-classical economists have not exercised due care. These economists end up proposing 'silly models' (Hahn 1994: 251). Hahn lays the blame for this at Friedman's door. Under Friedman's influence – who insists that theoretical economics is an empirical science which should be evaluated *solely* on its predictive merits, without any consideration being given to the realism of its assumptions – these economists engage in 'blinkered' theorising. For instance vis-à-vis his own research on the Solow growth model with many capital goods in which the steady state turned out to be a saddle point with the consequence that numerous equilibrium points are possible, 'the Chicago economists' responded by simplifying even more than what Solow had done by using 'the silly assumption' that 'the economy followed an equilibrium path over infinite time' (Hahn 1994: 251). In principle Hahn's circumspection vis-à-vis simplicity goes quite far: 'if at a certain stage of knowledge nothing can be said without drastic simplifying falsification, then perhaps we should keep quiet' (Hahn 1994: 251).

In practice, however, Hahn admits that he himself has not adhered to his own reservations about simplicity in his economic theorising. Despite maintaining that 'the perfect competition simplification has had rather disastrous effects on macro-economics' (Hahn 1994: 252) he concedes that a good deal of his own research is based on that simplification. One is thus left with the issue of what would be contained in the outcome of neo-classical theorising if theoretical economists practised what Hahn preached about the limited use of simplicity. Be that as it may, Hahn agrees that 'the basic assumptions of much of our theory are often of low descriptive merit' (Hahn 1993b: 163). Given this, another indispensable dimension of Hahn's grammar of argumentation is the project of increasing the descriptive merit of these assumptions. For instance he readily admits that increasing returns constitute a telling objection to the simplification of perfect competition. His grammar of argumentation requires the rigorous mathematical explication of increasing returns and thereby the reshaping of the original Debreu theory. Indeed he maintains that the integration of increasing returns into his grammar of argumentation means that Adam Smith's invisible hand 'is likely to be unsure in its operations and occasionally downright arthritic' (Hahn 1982a: 129). The crucial point is that this is not a matter of opinion. It is the outcome of a rigorous grammar of argumentation. Overall the outcome is that the Debreu conception of an equilibrium is replaced by 'a more feet on the ground Keynesian notion' (Hahn 1973: 16).

Hahn is well aware that he is portrayed as 'a dyed-in-the-wood neo-classical who considered Arrow-Debreu adequate for all economics' (Hahn 1984: 18). Obviously Hahn rejects this portrayal. An important reason for this rejection lies in his view that neo-Walrasian theorising is an objective grammar of argumentation which starts with Arrow-Debreu but does not end there. Indeed Hahn confesses to be 'completely agnostic' (Hahn 1984: 18) on the final truths of economics. However, what he is not agnostic about is the grammar of argumentation: unambiguous results in economic theorising can only be achieved by this grammar of argumentation. In Hahn's view this grammar of argumentation is grounded in 'three commitments' (Hahn 1984: 2), namely rationality, equilibrium and methodological individualism. As the focus of this work is on the role of mathematics in economic theorising, we have excluded Hahn's commitment to methodological individualism. In the last two sections we introduced a brief synopsis of Hahn's, possibly unique, conception of the formalisation of economics as a grammar of argumentation, grounded in his commitments. According to Hahn, this grammar of argumentation questions almost everything in the Debreu original formulation. However, among the items which cannot be questioned is the rigorous proof of the existence of equilibrium furnished by Debreu.[4]

Kaldor on Debreu's achievement and legacy

Like Hahn, Kaldor notes that the term 'equilibrium' is used in all kinds of economic contexts. His disenchantment is with the specific notion of equilibrium originally formulated by Walras and rigorously developed by the mathematical economists of his own generation 'of whom perhaps the French economist, Gerard Debreu, is now regarded as the most prominent exponent' (Kaldor 1972: 1237). This research informs 'the prevailing theory, as taught in regular textbooks in most of the universities of the Western World' (Kaldor 1975: 347). This prevailing theory's 'declared objective is to explain how economic processes work in a decentralized market economy' (Kaldor 1975: 347).

Kaldor draws out attention to the original aspiration of the neo-Walrasian programme, namely to establish the existence of an equilibrium set of prices that is unique, stable and satisfies the conditions of Pareto optimality. Uniqueness would establish that there is one and only one such equilibrium and stability would demonstrate that this equilibrium set of prices would maintain itself in the face of chance disturbances. Existence, uniqueness, stability and Pareto optimality constituted, in the language of Ingrao and Israel, 'the invariant paradigmatic nucleus' of the neo-classical interpretation of Adam Smith's hidden hand (Ingrao and Israel 1990: 3). Debreu's *Theory of Value* was seen as the first major step in the justification of this invariant nucleus. This invariant paradigmatic nucleus, however, quickly disintegrated when it was established that uniqueness and stability proofs eluded these mathematical economists. It is not unreasonable to assume that Kaldor would agree with Kirman that 'without stability and uniqueness the intrinsic interest of economic analysis based on general equilibrium is extremely limited' (Kirman 2006: 257). This is presumably part of the reason for Kaldor's call for 'a major act of demolition' (Kaldor 1972: 1240). These significant failures, however, did not bring about the demise of the neo-Walrasian programme. Neither did it adversely impact on its influence. On the contrary, Kaldor believes that 'the great majority of academic economists take for granted that the economy always approaches, or is near to a state of "equilibrium"' (Kaldor 1972: 1239), with the consequence that this near equilibrium state is a major causal factor in the real economic world. Allowing for some rhetorical flourish, it is clear that Hahn would concur with this view. Moreover, like Hahn, Kaldor is very clear that this erroneous belief has not been established by pure mathematical economists. In this connection he acknowledges that Debreu describes his *Theory of Value* as the explanation of prices of commodities in a private sector economy. Kaldor, however, draws our attention to Debreu's formalism and correctly concludes that, given this form-alism, Debreu is not claiming that his *Theory of Value* explains, in either the ordinary or scientific sense of the term 'explanation', these prices. Rather, as Kaldor maintains, Debreu's theory:

> is not put forward as an explanation of how actual prices of commodities are determined in particular economies or in the world economy as a whole. By the term 'explanation' Debreu means a set of theorems that are *logically* deducible from precisely formulated assumptions; and the purpose of the exercise is to find the minimum 'basic assumptions' necessary for establishing the existence of an 'equilibrium' set of prices (and output/ input matrixes) that is (a) unique, (b) stable, (c) satisfies the conditions of Pareto optimality.
>
> (Kaldor 1972: 1238)

In short, for Kaldor Debreu's conception of explanation should not be confused with the scientific notion of explanation.

In this connection Kaldor contrasts the situation in theoretical physics with that of theoretical economics. Contemporary theoretical physics is such that its basic axioms are not derivable by the scientific process of induction. However, these non-inductive, first principles of theoretical physics come before the bar of experience. As noted by Friedman, this is done by the empirical interrogation of their consequences. This contrasts with the situation in general equilibrium theory. Here the

> observations which contradict the basic hypotheses of prevailing theory are generally ignored: the "theorist" and the 'empiricist' operate in two isolated compartments and the challenge of anomalous observations is ignored by the theorist as something that could be taken into account at the stage of 'second approximation' without affecting the basic hypotheses.
>
> (Kaldor 1972: 1239)

Unlike Hahn, Kaldor does not attempt to draw a fundamental methodological distinction between economic axioms and economic assumptions. His focus is on the basic hypotheses of general equilibrium theory which he characterises as assumptions. While not attempting to fully enumerate these, he gives the reader a flavour of what he has in mind. These include perfect knowledge of all relevant prices on the part of economic agents; perfect foresight in the sense that individual agents' future experiences will confirm, and not disappoint, their expectations on which they based their past decisions; perfect competition such that each agent can sell or buy anything in unlimited amounts without affecting market prices with the consequence that prices are the only type of information required for individual decisions. Kaldor's key methodological point is that such like assumptions are not chosen on the basis of direct observation. On the contrary some are unverifiable while others are directly contradicted by observation. These arbitrary basic assumptions are necessitated by the demands of logical consistency.

In view of their low descriptive value, why, in Kaldor's view, is Debreu's *Theory of Value* so central to neo-classical economics? Kaldor maintains that neo-classical economists have 'the deep underlying belief ... that general equilibrium theory is the one and only starting point for any logically consistent explanation of the behaviour of decentralized economic systems' (Kaldor 1972: 1239). In the face of the arbitrariness of its assumptions, this deep underlying belief 'sustained' (Kaldor 1972: 1239) general equilibrium theory. If we unpack this, we see that, in Kaldor's opinion, neo-classical economists have, in Hahn's phrase, two commitments, namely the commitment to decentralised economic systems and the commitment to Debreu's *Theory of Value* as the one and only starting point for the explanation of the behaviour of these systems. Whether or not it is the one and only starting point, Hahn agrees that it supplies a solid starting point. Starting with the indubitable proof of the existence of equilibrium as characterised by Debreu, the neo-Walrasian programme entails the application of Hahn's grammar of argumentation, which includes the relaxing of the unreal assumptions. According to Kaldor 'the process of removing the "scaffolding," as the saying goes – in other words of *relaxing* the unreal basic assumptions – has not yet started' (Kaldor 1972: 1239). According to Hahn, Kaldor is just plainly wrong on this point. Hahn focuses on neo-Walrasian research which aims at a notion of equilibrium that is 'sequential in an essential way' which requires 'that information processes and costs, transactions and transaction costs and also expectations and uncertainty be explicitly included in the equilibrium notion. That is what the Arrow-Debreu construction does not do' (Hahn 1973: 16).

Kaldor, however, is not denying that such research has taken place. On the contrary he is assuming that research. Unlike Hahn, he sees neo-classical economists as introducing yet more unrealistic assumptions in that research. In this connection he draws our attention to what Hahn calls 'silly' models above. For instance, he points out that theoretical models which attempt 'to construct an equilibrium path through time with all prices for all periods fully determined at the start under the assumption that everyone foresees future prices to eternity correctly' (Kaldor 1972: 1239) is more unrealistic than the original Walrasian theory. In short, according to Kaldor, the neo-Walrasian theorist has 'successfully (though perhaps inadvertently) demonstrated that the main implications of this theory cannot possibly hold in reality, but has not yet managed to pass his message down the line to the textbook writer and to the classroom' (Kaldor 1972: 1240). In this sense the process of relaxing the assumption has utterly failed. The efforts at relaxing the assumptions have ended in a 'cul-de-sac': it made the theory a less usable tool than it was thought to have been in its early and crude stage before the full implications of general equilibrium had been so thoroughly explored.

(Kaldor 1975: 347)

In short his 'basic objection' to general equilibrium theory 'is that it starts from the wrong kind of abstraction, and therefore gives a misleading "paradigm" … of the world as it is: it gives a misleading impression of the nature and the manner of operation of economic forces' (Kaldor 1975: 347).

This is not the place to analyse in detail the intricacies of the Hahn–Kaldor altercation.[5] Our focus is on the formalisation of economics and responses to that formalisation. Within neo-classical economics we considered the response which saw the formalisation of the neo-Walrasian programme as resulting in a science, like theoretical physics, and the response of those like Hahn who utterly oppose that interpretation. We then took Kaldor as an exponent of those calling for its completion demolition. From our point of view what is interesting is the consensus among neo-classical economists that the formalisation of economics, exemplified in Debreu's *Theory of Value*, is a solid starting point in their theorising, be it called scientific or grammatical, about decentralised economies. By recourse to developments in the philosophy of mathematics we will show how this consensus can be challenged. Debreu's existence proof itself – the solid starting point of neo-Walrasian theorising – will be shown not to be as solid as originally thought. This only remaining component of the original nucleus of existence, uniqueness, stability and Pareto optimality will be logically undermined. Its Achilles' heel will be shown to lie in the mathematics presupposed by Debreu!

Notes

1 For a detailed discussion of these see Boylan and O'Gorman (2012).
2 Thus Hahn is located in the Euclidean tradition of axiomatisation where the distinction between axioms and assumptions are crucial. See the previous chapter for details of this.
3 See Boylan and O'Gorman (2012) for a more detailed exposition and critique of Hahn's philosophy of economics.
4 We will see in Chapter Seven how this proof may be challenged.
5 We have already addressed that challenge in Boylan and O'Gorman (2012).

6 Rationality and conventions in economics and in mathematics

Introduction

As we have seen in the previous chapter the commitments to rationality and to equilibrium are fundamental to the neoclassical formalisation of economics. In this chapter our aim is to explore how a specific development in the philosophy of pure mathematics at the turn of the twentieth century impinges on various analyses of economic rationality.[1] In Chapter Two we interrogated Walras' exploitation of calculus in his analysis and methodological defence of economic rationality. Without getting involved in the intriguing details of well-developed economic theories of the rational agent including their respective intriguing historical origins, for the purposes of this chapter we sum up as follows: the original Walrasian analysis of the rational agent evolved into that of the self-interested agent who makes his/her choices on the grounds of maximum expected utility.[2] The two core mathematical pillars here are the deductive system of pure mathematics and probability theory. Deductive mathematics, especially calculus, is used in the modelling of maximisation, whereas probability theory is exploited in the analysis of expectations and risk.[3]

The central theme of this chapter is set by Keynes' *General Theory*, notably Chapter 12, where he has recourse to convention in his analysis of investment. Keynes maintains that investors' expectations about the future cannot be adequately understood in terms of the resources of probability theory. The probability calculus enables economists to investigate situations of risk, but investment concerns the radical uncertainty of the economic future. Faced with radical uncertainty the investor has recourse to convention. Since a radical uncertain future cannot be adequately analysed in terms of probability theory, a Keynesian recourse to convention prima facie places it beyond the pale of rationality as represented in neoclassical economics. Thus, as Lawson correctly points out, 'the question of whether, and if so how, rational conduct is possible in situations characterized by significant uncertainty is central to economic analysis' (Lawson 1993: 174). This chapter proposes to respond to Lawson's question by recourse to the philosophy of mathematics.

In this connection we distinguish between the general issue of the rationality of recourse to convention per se in economic decision making from the specific issue of the specific rationale offered for recourse to a specific convention in a specific economic context.[4] Vis-à-vis the issue of the rationality of recourse to convention per se, we follow Keynes' suggestion that economists should look to other domains where conventions are used.[5] The two principal philosophical figures who addressed conventions in the social domain are David Hume and, two centuries later, David Lewis. Both have cast their respective shadows over the issue of the rationality of recourse to convention. For those influenced by Hume's sceptical philosophy, the issue of the rationality of conventions falls into much the same considerations as recourse to induction in the sciences: it is ultimately down to habit. In our view Lewis, by recourse to game theory, which of course was not available to Hume, gives an ingenious solution to the issue of the rationality of recourse to convention by showing how one can reconcile recourse to convention with the neoclassical concept of rationality. In this chapter we introduce the reader to the divergent philosophical contexts of Humean and Lewisian analyses of convention and argue that these analyses do not fully illuminate Keynesian and post-Keynesian recourse to convention. Keynes, like Hume, in recourse to convention is concerned with the spectre of social instability. However, we argue that the Keynesian and post-Keynesian recourse to convention is not only concerned with the establishment and maintenance of social stability; it is also concerned with the proper way to respond to what we call ontological-epistemic indeterminacy. Ontologically the future economic order is open-ended in that some parts of it are not determined by the existing economic order. Epistemologically, our present knowledge does not determine some future rational decisions and probability theory is also ineffective. Rather the rational response is recourse to convention. Given this ontological-epistemic indeterminacy we contend that Lewis' reconciliation of convention with the neoclassical conception of rationality is of no help to post-Keynesians: it fails to address this basic ontological-epistemic indeterminacy.

In order to address Lawson's fundamental challenge, viz. the question of whether or not rational conduct is possible in the face of this radical uncertainty now understood as ontological-epistemic indeterminacy, we follow Keynes' suggestion by looking for some other domain where ontological-epistemic indeterminacy prevails and where recourse to convention is proposed as the rational solution. Our contention is that recourse to convention as the rational response to ontological-epistemic indeterminacy arises in the philosophy of pure mathematics where clearly the issue of social stability does not arise. To anyone not familiar with the history of the philosophy of pure mathematics this claim may seem surprising. What has convention to do with pure mathematics? The answer would appear to be nothing: pure mathematics is a deductive, axiomatic system in which convention plays no substantive role.[6] At the turn of the twentieth century this not uncommon philosophical portrait of pure mathematics was challenged by Poincaré.[7] Poincaré is famous for his thesis of geometrical conventionalism in the philosophy of pure mathematics.[8] As the very name of his thesis suggests, convention is indispensable to pure geometry:

mathematicians cannot furnish a complete account of pure geometry without recourse to convention. Moreover the grounds for the recourse to convention is ontological-epistemic indeterminacy. Mathematical rationality, the fine details of which are evident in the various practices of its different research domains, is not adequately conveyed by the simplified image of pure mathematics as an axiomatised deductive system. Recourse to convention in the face of ontological-epistemic indeterminacy is another indispensable dimension of mathematical rationality. In short, just as recourse to convention in the face of ontological-epistemic indeterminacy extends the received notion of mathematical rationality, recourse to convention in post-Keynesian economics, also in the face of ontological-epistemic indeterminacy, similarly extends the received notion of economic rationality.

Hume, convention and the foundations of justice

Under the influence of recent research by economists such as Robert Sugden and H. Peyton Young, there has been a growing interest among economic methodologists in the role of conventions in economic life. This interest has also been added to by the contributions of the 'école des conventions' in France, which Latsis interprets as a new heterodox movement within economics which aims 'to bring economics closer to other social science disciplines such as law and sociology solving a range of problems in neoclassical economics by dropping implicit assumptions and introducing a different style of analysis' (Latsis 2006: 255). Totally independent of the 'école des conventions', Young maintains that 'conventions regulate much of economic and social life ... Conventions with direct economic implications include species of money and credit, industrial and technological standards, accounting rules and forms of economic contract' (Young 1996: 105). For Sugden the market 'may ultimately be a form of spontaneous order', the analysis of which requires recourse to conventions (Sugden 1989: 86).

In much of the methodological literature on conventions, Hume's *A Treatise of Human Nature*, first published in 1739 and Lewis' *Conventions*, first published in 1969, are frequently cited as key contributions to the philosophical analysis of convention.[9] Young is surely correct in maintaining that 'the key role of convention in defining and maintaining property rights was first articulated by Hume' (Young 1998: 822). According to Vanderschraaf 'Hume is rightly credited with giving a brilliant, and perhaps the best, account of justice as convention' (Vanderschraaf 1998: 215).[10] On its publication, however, Hume's *Treatise* was not well received. In Hume's view its hostile reception was largely due to a misunderstanding of his views. Thus in 1740 he published an anonymous pamphlet *An Abstract of a Book Lately Published. Entitled A Treatise of Human Nature, &c Wherein The Chief Argument of that Book is further Illustrated and Explained*. That pamphlet fell into oblivion until a copy of it was discovered by Keynes in the 1930s. Keynes and Sraffa published it under the title *An Abstract of a Treatise of Human Nature, 1740: A Pamphlet hitherto unknown by David Hume*.

This pamphlet focused on Hume's theory of knowledge which divides the domain of objective knowledge into a priori truths of reason which convey no information about the world and matters of fact which, grounded in experience, are the sole source of objective knowledge about the world. In light of this theory of knowledge Hume analyses the received notion of causality. Hume identifies three elements: (1) the cause is temporally prior to the effect; (2) cause and effect are spatially contiguous; (3) the effect is said to be necessarily related to the cause. Hume correctly argues that (3) is incompatible with his theory of knowledge: the notion of a necessary connection between events in nature does not stand up to a Humean epistemological scrutiny. What is epistemological justifiable is a constant observed regularity between the events which are illegitimately claimed to be necessarily related. Hume sums up his celebrated analysis of causal reasoning in the sciences as follows: 'all our reasoning concerning causes and effects are derived from nothing but custom ...' (Hume 1985: 234). This is a source of what various commentators call Hume's scepticism.

In ordinary usage, the terms 'custom' and 'convention' are closely related: both mean a social regularity in a population. However, in Book I of his *Treatise*, where Hume develops his theory of knowledge, he never uses the term 'convention' as a stylistic alternative to the term 'custom'. One may speculate that among the reasons for Hume not using the term 'convention' in Book I is that, in addition to conveying a social regularity, the term 'convention' also connotes the availability of an alternative option. For instance one community may adopt the convention of driving on the left-hand side of the road where another community could adopt the alternative convention of driving on the other side. However, given Hume's theory of knowledge, in the case of humanity's attempts to obtain objective information about the world, there is no such conventional choice available: there is no viable alternative to observation and inductive causal reasoning as explicated by Hume.

Book II of *A Treatise*, entitled 'Of the Passions', continues Hume's 'attempt to introduce the experimental Method of Reasoning into Moral Subjects' (Hume 1985: 323). In Book II Hume develops a scientific portrait of a human being which rejects traditional metaphysical pictures such as those of the Socratic-Platonic and Cartesian traditions where a human being is a thinking being, modelled on mathematical reasoning. In opposition to such metaphysical portraits, Hume's scientific portrait is grounded in observation and inductive reasoning. Hume's inductive portrait is of a complex being whose actions are dominated by an intricate interplay of appetites, emotions, passions and sentiments. He opens Book II with a survey of the passions which he divides into direct and indirect. The direct passions include desire, aversion, grief, joy, hope, fear, despair and security. These arise immediately from pain or pleasure. The indirect passions include pride, humility, ambition, vanity, love, hatred, envy, pity, malice, generosity. These also arise from pleasure and pain but in conjunction with other qualities. For instance, beautiful clothes may produce the direct passion of desire. This same quality which produces the direct passion of desire is a necessary condition for the indirect passion of being proud of these beautiful clothes, but that is not sufficient. For the indirect passion of pride to arise the beautiful clothes must also be in some way related to the person who is proud of them (e.g. he/she designed them, or own them, or manufactured them, etc.). Additional pleasure is added by this relationship and this pleasure is conjoined to the original desire giving it additional force.

These passions in turn vary along the spectrum from calm to violent. Moreover each individual has a natural instinct of sympathy. Hume, while attempting to be faithful to his theory of knowledge introduced in Book I (entitled 'Of The Understanding'), gives the reader a sophisticated account of the interplay between these various passions and instinct and how they are related to pleasure and pain. To illustrate this sophistication, a few words on Hume's analysis of the abstract idea of pleasure may be useful. Again his analysis is governed by his theory of knowledge. Hume subscribes to Berkeley's epistemological account of abstract or general ideas. In this account 'all general ideas are nothing but particular ones, annexed to a certain term, which gives them a more extensive signification and makes them recall upon occasion other individuals which are similar to them' (Hume 1985: 64). In particular this thesis holds for the ideas of grief, hope, etc. under the rubric of the direct passions and for the ideas of pride, humility, etc. summed up under the rubric of indirect passions and for the idea of pleasure to which all of these are inextricably linked. Vis-à-vis the idea of pleasure '

> 'ts evident under the term *pleasure*, we comprehend sensations, which are very different from each other, and which have only such a distant resemblance, as is requisite to make them be express'd by the same abstract term. A good composition of music and a bottle of good wine equally produce pleasure; and what is more, their goodness is determin'd merely by the pleasure. But shall we say on that account, the wine is harmonious, or the music is of a good flavour?
>
> (Hume 1985: 523)

Individual pleasures from this infinite array of distinct pleasures motivate individual actions. This scientific portrait of a human being, combined with his theory of knowledge, constitutes the philosophical framework for Hume's reflections in Book III of his *Treatise*, entitled 'Of Morals'. This is where Hume addresses what he calls 'the foundation of justice' where he has recourse to convention (Hume 1985: 534).

By the foundations of morality Hume means philosophical foundations, i.e. foundations compatible with the conclusions of Books I and II.[11] Hume's analysis begins with what he calls 'common experience' (Hume 1985: 507). This common experience shows that morals influence human actions and affections. Hume's foundational question is: on what grounds do humans distinguish between vice and virtue, i.e. 'pronounce an action blameworthy or praiseworthy?' (Hume 1985: 508). In this connection he opposes various traditions in Western philosophy which locate the foundations of morality in reason. 'The rules of morality, (therefore) are not conclusions of our reason' (Hume 1985: 509).[12] As established in Book I, reason is confined to the domain of relationships between ideas and thus cannot explain how morality influences actual actions. On the other hand morality does not consist in '*any matter of fact*' (Hume 1985: 520): moral actions have not distinct empirical moral qualities inherent in them which make them moral. According to Hume an action has both an external and an internal dimension. Moreover the external performance of an action has no moral merit. The moral merit resides in the internal dimension.

> If any action be either virtuous or vicious 'tis only as a sign of some quality of character ... We are never to consider any single action in our enquiries concerning the origins of morals; but only the quality or character from which the action proceeded. These alone are *durable* enough to affect our sentiments concerning the person. Actions are indeed better indications of character than words ...
>
> (Hume 1985: 626)

In particular any quality of character which causes love or pride is virtuous and any quality of character which causes hatred or humility is vicious. In short, 'to have the sense of virtue is nothing but to feel a satisfaction of a particular kind from the contemplation of a character. That very *feeling* constitutes our praise or admiration' (Hume 1985: 523). Moreover 'tis only when a character is considered in general, *without reference to our particular interest*, that it causes such a feeling or sentiment as denominates it morally good or evil' (Hume 1985: 524, italics ours).[13] In short, 'the approbation of moral qualities ... proceeds entirely from a moral taste, and from certain sentiments of pleasure or disgust, which arise upon the contemplation and view of particular qualities or characters' (Hume 1985: 632).

This intricate constellation of considerations ranging from an empiricist theory of knowledge, through the differentiation between direct and indirect passions to the analysis of morality in terms of moral taste and the pleasures of the indirect passions constitutes the context for Hume's analysis of justice in terms of convention. Hume's foundations of justice hinges on the case he makes for the thesis that some *principles* of morality are not natural. Fundamentally morality is grounded in a moral sense inextricably linked to feelings and sentiment. However, according to Hume, we cannot remain at this fundamental level. If we did, our morality would consist of an astronomical number of specific precepts for an astronomical number of specific individual actions and it would be impossible to teach such a morality to our children. Hume maintains that

> such a method of proceeding is not conformable to the usual maxims, by which nature is conducted, where a few principles produce all the variety we observe in the universe, and everything is carry'd on in the easiest and most simple manner. 'Tis necessary, therefore to abridge these primary

impulses, and find some more general principles, upon which all our notions of morals are founded.

(Hume 1985: 525)

Thus our limited number of moral principles are human-made abridgements of the vast number of more fundamental moral sentiments governing particular actions.[14] Hume follows on by immediately asking whether or not these moral principles are natural. In this connection he makes three points. Firstly, if natural is contrasted with the miraculous, then clearly moral principles are natural. Secondly, if natural is contrasted with the unusual and rare, then moral principles are also natural. Thirdly, however, if natural is opposed to artificial then the principles of morality are artificial. After this very long and complex journey Hume finally arrives at his foundations of justice.

Justice, for Hume, operates in a unique moral space. He brings this out by contrasting the good that results from some other moral virtues to the good that derives from justice. For instance, a particular act of generosity is beneficial to the person who is deserving of the generosity shown. This, however, is not always the case with a particular act of justice: a judge may take from a poor man to give to a rich individual or may order the return of a weapon to a vicious person. Such judgements are delivered because justice is *not arbitrary*, i.e. is not capricious. Thus while such an individual judgement is not beneficial to the poor man in question nor to the potential victim of the vicious person, the system of justice as a whole is advantageous to society. This system is not natural.[15] Rather it is a human artifice, which when established 'is *naturally* attended with a strong sentiment of morals ...' (Hume 1985: 630).

To identify this specific artifice Hume commences with the thesis that, among all the animals, nature has been most cruel to humans. On the one hand nature has left us with numberless wants and necessities and on the other was miserly in furnishing us with the means of relieving these necessities. The artifice of society enabled man to overcome this cruel situation. In particular in society one can augment one's very limited physical powers and also, by the division of labour, we increase our abilities. Moreover, in society, by mutual help, we are less exposed to accidents or torture, etc. Thus society becomes advantageous by 'this additional *force, ability* and *security*' (Hume 1985: 537). However, according to Hume, men 'in their wild uncultivated state' could not possibly know or be aware of these advantages (Hume 1985: 537). So how did society originate? Hume's answer is that the natural appetite between the sexes and their concern for their offspring is 'the first and original principle of human society' (Hume 1985: 538). In this vein Hume is opposed to the view of man as a self-interested agent: the emphasis on our selfishness has, in his view 'been carried too far' (Hume 1985: 538). Rather for Hume the source of the problem is precisely the generosity and affections among extended families. These, given the scarce resources of nature, give rise to conflict between these groupings.

There are three 'different species of goods, which we are possess'd of; the internal satisfaction of our minds, the external advantages of our body, and the enjoyment of such possessions as we have acquir'd by our industry and good fortune' (Hume 1985: 539). Given their scarcity and instability of their possession, the third category, i.e. external goods, are most at risk: they are most exposed to the violence of others and may be easily transferred. 'In *uncultivated nature*' no remedy for this is available (Hume 1985: 539). On the other hand in 'the *golden age*' of the poets where avarice, selfishness, cruelty, etc. does not exist and where nature is lavish with its gifts, the institution of justice would not be required (Hume 1985: 545). Rather as humans 'acquire a new affection to company and conversation'; and with 'their early education in society', they observe

> that the principal disturbances in society arises from these goods ... (T)hey must seek for a remedy by putting these goods, as far as possible, on the same footing with the fix'd and constant advantages of mind and body. This can be done after no manner, than by a convention entered into by all the members of the society to bestow stability on the possession of those external goods, and leave everyone in the peaceable enjoyment of what he may acquire by his fortune and industry.
>
> (Hume 1985: 541)

This remedy is not derived from nature; rather it is an *artifice*. Without this convention, society would be inherently unstable.

Hume emphasises the thesis that this convention cannot be analysed in terms of promises. In general promising presupposes conventions. To illustrate how conventions are not promises Hume gives a number of examples of conventions which in his view are in no way related to promises. 'Two men who pull the oars of a boat do it by agreement or convention, tho' they have never given promises to each other' (Hume 1985: 542). His second example is language.[16] He points out that both in the case of justice and of language, the convention 'arises gradually and acquires force by a slow progression and by our repeated experience of the inconveniences of transgressing it' (Hume 1985: 542). Moreover in the cases of both justice and language 'the sense of interest has become common to all our fellows and gives us a confidence of the future regularity of their conduct: And 'tis only on the expectation of this, that our moderation and abstinence are founded' (Hume 1985: 542). His third example is the conventional use of gold and silver as the common measure of exchange.[17]

Hume sums up as follows:

> And thus justice establishes itself by a kind of convention or agreement; that is by a sense of interest, suppos'd to be common to all, and where every single act is perform'd in expectation that others are to perform the like. Without such a convention, no one wou'd ever have dream'd, that there was such a virtue as justice or have been induc'd to conform his actions to it. Taking any single act, my justice may be pernicious in every respect, and 'tis only upon the supposition, that others are to imitate my example, that I can be induc'd to embrace that virtue, since nothing but

this combination can render justice advantageous, or afford me any motives to confirm myself to its rules.

(Hume 1985: 549)

In this fashion Hume contextualises his conventional foundations of justice in the details of his epistemology and of his scientific picture of humans as complex passionate and moral animals. This of course does not preclude either economic methodologists or philosophers from having recourse to Hume as a *precursor* in their game theoretic analysis of convention. Our point is that Hume's own complex philosophy is not that of a strict game theorist.

Lewis, convention and neo–classical rationality

The philosophical climate of Lewis' *Convention*, first published in 1969, is very different to the philosophical climate of Hume's *Treatise*, first published in 1739. An integral dimension of the philosophical climate prevailing in the twentieth century is the extensive expansion of the influence of logic into philosophy: an influential trend in American-British twentieth-century philosophy proposes the adoption of a logical, rather than a psychological, approach to philosophical problems. As we have already seen, at the turn of the twentieth century, at the hands of Frege in Germany and Russell in Britain, traditional logic was utterly transformed. Logical tools, undreamt of at the time of Hume, were for the first time available to philosophers. This approach gave rise to an abstract logico-philosophical view of language. However, under the influence of the later Wittgenstein and numerous others an alternative approach to language emerged which put the focus on natural languages. These two trends in the philosophy of language constitutes the philosophical context of Lewis' *Convention*.

In his 'Languages and Language', Lewis clearly articulates his central problematic. On the one hand we have the contemporary logico-philosophical view of language where a language

> is a function, set of ordered pair of strings and meanings. The entities in the domain of the function are certain finite sequences of types of vocal sounds or types of inscribable marks ... The entities in the range of the function are meanings.
>
> (Lewis 1983: 163)[18]

On the other hand, there is the socio-historical view of languages. In this view a language is

> a social phenomenon which is part of the history of human beings; a sphere of human action, wherein people utter strings of vocal sounds or inscribe strings of marks, and wherein people respond by thought or action to the sounds or marks which they observe has been produced.
>
> (Lewis 1983: 164)

Lewis' central problematic is the connection between these two views.

> We know what to *call* this connection we are after: we can say that a given
> language $\mathcal{L}$ is *used by*, or is a (or the) language *of*, a given population P.
> We know also that this connection holds by virtue of the conventions of
> language prevailing in P. Under suitably different conventions, a different
> language would be used by P. There is some sort of convention whereby
> P used $\mathcal{L}$- but what is it? ... My proposal is that the convention whereby a
> population P uses a language $\mathcal{L}$ is a convention of *truthfulness* and *trust* in
> $\mathcal{L}$. To be truthful in $\mathcal{L}$ is to act in a certain way: to try never to utter any
> sentence of $\mathcal{L}$ that are not true in $\mathcal{L}$ ... To be trusting in $\mathcal{L}$ is to form
> beliefs in a certain way: to impute truthfulness in $\mathcal{L}$ to others and thus to
> tend to respond to another's utterance of any sentence of $\mathcal{L}$ by coming to
> believe that the uttered sentence is true in $\mathcal{L}$.
>
> (Lewis 1983: 166–167)

Clearly Lewis is not concerned with issues in economic methodology.
His central problematic is in the philosophy of language. To substantiate his
ingenious thesis, Lewis needs a clear, precise definition of convention. This
definition was worked out in his *Convention* and modified in his 'Languages and
Language'. In his *Convention* Lewis has recourse to game theory, especially
games of pure co-ordination, to arrive at his definition of a convention. One
keynote of conventionality is a certain indifference, where the appropriate sense
of indifference is explicated via the existence of multiple-equilibria solutions in
games of pure co-ordination. At an equilibrium it is possible that some or all of
the agents would have been better off if some or all had acted differently.
'What is not possible is that anyone of the agents would have been better off if
he alone acted differently and all the rest acted as they did' (Lewis 2002: 8).[19]
The fact that in general there is not a unique equilibrium solution means that
rationally more than one solution is available and thus in principle a genuine
choice is available. The emergence of the predominance of one choice over
others culminates in conventional behaviour.

However there is much more to Lewis's definition of convention than the
above sense of indifference. Lewis specifies six conditions which are both
necessary and sufficient conditions of a convention. A regularity R in action or
in action and belief in a population P is a convention if and only if

1 Everyone conforms to R.
2 Everyone believes that others conform to R.
3 The belief that others conform to R gives everyone a good and decisive
  reason to conform to R himself ...
4 There is a general preference for general conformity to R rather than
  slightly-less-than-general conformity ... This condition serves to distinguish cases of convention, in which there is a predominant coincidence of
  interest, from cases of deadlocked conflict ...

5   R is not the only possible regularity meeting the last two conditions. There is at least one alternative R' such that the belief that the others conformed to R' would give everyone a good and decisive practical or epistemic reason to R' likewise ... Thus the alternative R' could have perpetuated itself as a convention instead of R; this condition provides for the characteristic arbitrariness of conventions.

6   Finally the various factors listed in conditions (1) to (5) are matters of *common* (or *mutual*) *knowledge*: they are known to everyone, it is known to everyone that they are known to everyone, and so on ...

(Lewis 1983: 165)

Much has been written on the extent to which this rigorous definition of a convention by Lewis is or is not independent of co-ordination game theory. Lewis himself remarks that game theory is merely dispensable scaffolding.[20] Without getting involved in this intriguing controversy, we concur with Pettit that 'Lewis's (1969) work on convention is often taken as a first rate example of how economic explanation can do well in making sense of a phenomenon outside the traditional economic domain of the market' (Pettit 2002: 239). According to Pettit's 'gloss' (Pettit 2002: 240) Lewis is neither explaining the emergence nor the continuance of conventions. Rather he is explaining their resilience 'under various shocks and disturbances' (Pettit 2002: 238).[21] To legitimatise this gloss Pettit draws our attention to Lewis's response to the counter claim that we actually produce and respond to utterances by habit and not as a result of any sort of strategic reasoning or deliberation which is presupposed in game theory.

> An action may be rational and *may be explained by the agent's beliefs and desires*, even though that action was done by habit, and the agents gave no thought to the beliefs and desires which were his reason for acting. A habit may be under the agent's rational control in this sense: if the habit ever ceased to serve the agent's desires according to his beliefs, it would at once be overridden and corrected by conscious reasoning. Action done by a habit of this sort is both habitual and rational.
>
> (Lewis 1983: 181)[22]

Our concern in this chapter is not with the possible extensions of economic explanation into other domains of the social sciences. Our primary concern is with the mathematical theorising of economic rationality. Among our central questions is the issue of the implications of Lewis's analysis of convention for the rationality of the post-Keynesian account of recourse to conventions in the face of radical uncertainty. Our thesis is that, if Lewis's analysis/definition of convention is comprehensive and correct, Keynesian radical uncertainty is no threat to orthodox economic rationality. Indeed one can go much further and agree with Pettit that Lewis 'reconciles' (Pettit 2002: 241) recourse to conventions in coordination situations with the strategic reasoning of orthodox economics as explicated in game theory.[23] In game theory strategic reasoning culminates in multiple-equilibria solutions: no single unique solution is guaranteed. However, by various means, including Schelling's salience, one of these equilibria solutions gains conventional precedence in a population P. In such a conventional equilibrium situation, there is no gain to be attained by the unilateral deviation on the part of an individual in P. Now suppose this convention comes under severe threat from external shocks, such that the convention is no longer seen to serve the interests of the members of P. In these circumstances the previous established conventional equilibrium will give way and be replaced by another equilibrium solution which in turn becomes a different convention. In this sense, convention, for a time, guarantees the persistence of one particular rational solution and whenever that convention is undermined by external shocks, strategic thinking leads to other multiple-equilibria solutions and again by convention one of these becomes established in that community. In this way convention and orthodox rationality are reconciled.[24] Thus Lawson's problem posed in the introduction of this chapter, viz. whether, and if so how, rational conduct is possible in situations characterised by radical uncertainty (Lawson 1993: 174) is resolved in favour of orthodox economic reasoning. In short if co-ordination in the social domain is the one and only key determining factor in post-Keynesian analysis and if Lewis's analysis of co-ordination in terms of convention is correct, then post-Keynesian rationality is utterly compatible with the orthodox theory of rationality.

In the following sections we take up the Davidsonian theme of the ontological foundations of post-Keynesian radical uncertainty by showing how this theme is connected to conventions where (a) the concept of convention, unlike Lewis, has no connection whatsoever to game theory and (b) conventional choice is fundamentally rational, but not in the sense of rationality in mathematicised orthodox economics. We contend that a primary source of conventional decision-making in post-Keynesian economics arises from ontological-epistemic indeterminacy. Moreover this ontological-epistemic indeterminacy is not unique to the economic world. This ontological-epistemic indeterminacy also holds in the domain of pure geometry, where considerations of social instability à la Hume and considerations of social co-ordination à la Lewis are ipso facto excluded. In pure geometry ontological-epistemic indeterminacy alone necessitate recourse to convention. Thus contrary to what is tacitly assumed, conventional choice is indispensable to mathematical rationality. In this fashion the rationality of recourse to convention per se in situations of ontological-epistemic indeterminacy is guaranteed without recourse to either Humean inductive considerations on the one hand or to orthodox economic rationality à la Lewis on the other.

Keynes and post-Keynesians on uncertainty and conventions

As already indicated, conventions and conventional behaviour made their appearance initially in Chapter 5 but more extensively in Chapter 12 of Keynes's *General Theory*. Here Keynes analysed investors' long-term expectations of

prospective yields in situations where they are unable to compute definite probabilities of the outcomes of their investment decisions arising from the prevailing
uncertainty. Keynes's considered answer to this situation was that:

> In practice we have tacitly agreed, as a rule, to fall back on what is, in truth, a
> *convention*. The essence of this convention – though it does not, of course,
> work out quite so simply – lies in assuming that the existing state of affairs
> will continue indefinitely, except in so far as we have specific reasons to
> expect a change. This does not mean that we really believe that the existing
> state of affairs will continue indefinitely.
>
> (Keynes 1936: 152, emphasis in original)

In *The General Theory*, uncertainty, or what post-Keynesians would later call
radical uncertainty, was the centre of Keynes's analysis of long-run expectations
and the estimates of prospective yields from long-run investments. In a telling
passage Keynes wrote:

> The outstanding fact is the extreme precariousness of the basis of knowl-
> edge on which our estimates of prospective yield have to be made. Our
> knowledge of the factors which will govern the yield of an investment
> some years hence is usually slight and often negligible. If we speak frankly,
> we have to admit that our basis of knowledge for estimating the yield ten
> years hence of a railway, a copper mine, a textile factory, the goodwill of a
> patent medicine, an Atlantic liner, a building in the City of London
> amounts to little or sometimes to nothing; or even five years hence.
>
> (Keynes 1936: 149–150)

In the following year, 1937, Keynes returned to the topic of uncertainty in his
Quarterly Journal of Economics (QJE) article. Here Keynes clearly identified the
mainstream position with respect to uncertainty with the capacity of mathematically calculable probabilities to describe current and future events within a
standard and unified framework, namely, the calculus of probability. As he
argued in the 1937 article: the calculus of probability, though mention of it was
kept in the background, was supposed to be capable of reducing uncertainty to
the same calculable status as that of certainty itself (Keynes 1937: 112–113).
However, this was not a position that Keynes could subscribe to, arising from his
belief that in many instances our expectations about the future could not be
accommodated within the framework of the calculus of probability. Consequently for Keynes, with respect to these matters, 'there is no scientific basis
upon which to form any calculable probability whatever. We simply do not
know' (Keynes 1937: 114). While the relative merits of this position remain
contentious for many, there is no ambiguity about the fact that a clear distinction
between risk as calculable probability and radical uncertainty was defended by
Keynes, as it had been earlier by Frank Knight (1921) in his celebrated *Risk,
Uncertainty and Profits*. This distinction has become central to post-Keynesianism.

In the face of this analysis, Keynes, in the 1937 article, poses the question, 'How do we manage in such circumstances [of radical uncertainty] to behave in a manner which saves our faces as rational, economic men?' In response to his own question he provided what he described as 'a variety of techniques', comprised of the following three:

1   We assume that the present is a much more serviceable guide to the future than a candid examination of past experience would show it to have been hitherto. In other words we largely ignore the prospect of future changes about the actual character of which we know nothing.
2   We assume that the *existing* state of opinion as expressed in prices and the character of existing output is based on a *correct* summing up of future prospects, so that we can accept it as such unless and until something new and relevant comes into the picture.
3   Knowing that our own individual judgment is worthless, we endeavour to fall back on the judgment of the rest of the world which is perhaps better informed. That is, we endeavour to confirm with the behaviour of the majority on average. The psychology of a society of individuals each of whom is endeavouring to copy the others leads to what we may strictly term a *conventional* judgment.

(Keynes 1937: 214, emphasis in original)

The above quotations from both *The General Theory* and in particular the 1937 *Quarterly Journal of Economics* article represent the most extensive account of convention provided by Keynes in what is termed his mature economic writings, with the *QJE* article addressing the specific circumstances of highly volatile financial markets. What unfolded in the wake of Keynes's contributions was an increasing focus on the implications of uncertainty for both economic theory and policy issues. Two early contributors who identified uncertainty as fundamental to economics were George Shackle and Paul Davidson.

While Shackle's unique and highly individualistic contributions never forged any alliance with the emerging post-Keynesian school, the writing of Paul Davidson over the last forty years established him as a most prolific and pivotal figure in the analysis of uncertainty. After Sydney Weintraub's death, Davidson emerged as the intellectual leader of American post-Keynesianism and has been a major influence on international post-Keynesianism (Davidson 1972, 1982–1983, 1988, 1991, 2003). Central to his analysis of uncertainty is his rejection of the ergodic hypothesis, which for Davidson postulates:

In an ergodic environment, knowledge about the future involves the projection of calculated averages based on the past and/or current cross section and/or time-series data to forthcoming events. *The future is merely the statistical reflection of the past.* Economic activities are timeless and commutable.

(Davidson 1994: 90, emphasis in original)

If, however, as Davidson contends, some economic process are *not* ergodic,

> then conditional expectations based on past distribution functions can persistently differ from the probabilities that will be generated as the future unfolds and becomes historical fact. If people believe that the economic environment is uncertain (non-ergodic) then it is perfectly sensible for them to disregard past and present market signals. The future is not statistically calculable from past data and therefore is uncertain.
>
> (Davidson 1994: 90)

Davidson is also at pains to establish a methodological basis for post-Keynesianism by grounding his analysis in the reality of historical time, uncertainty, expectations, and political and economic institutions, all of which for Davidson 'represent fundamental characteristics of the world we inhabit – *the real world*' (1981: 171, emphasis in original). Davidson is here establishing an ontological foundation for post-Keynesian radical uncertainty. Economic agents for Davidson are not able to predict the future arising from either Shackle's lack of imaginative abilities or Herbert Simon's limited cognitive or information-processing capacities on the part of economic agents, and the ontological indeterminism of the future. Predicting the future is not due merely to epistemic limitations, it also arises from the in-built non-ergodic characteristics of the real economy: 'For Keynes and the post-Keynesians, long-run uncertainty is associated with a non-ergodic and transmutable reality concept' (Davidson 1996: 492).

Davidson went on to enshrine non-ergodicity, along with the nonneutrality of money and the absence of gross substitutability between money and other goods, as the three foundational characteristics of post-Keynesian economics that differentiates it from mainstream neoclassical economics.[25] In the following section we consider Davidson's ontological separation of the non-ergodic from the ergodic in the context of the philosophy of mathematics.

Ontological-epistemic indeterminacy, conventions and the philosophy of mathematics

In Chapter Two we contrasted Walras's scientific realist reading of the principles of mechanics (which we saw is a methodological cornerstone of his philosophy of mathematical economics) with Poincaré's conventionalist reading of these same principles. The grounds for Poincaré's conventionalist reading of the principles of mechanics lies in their origins in observed regularities which are open to further empirical investigation. The principles of mechanics are creative conventional constructs from these observed regularities which (a) given their small number, serve the relatively stable, systematisation of the ever increasing vast flux of factual knowledge and (b) simultaneously enhance the inherited scientific conceptual-linguistic framework used for the accurate articulation of scientific facts and regularities. If we compare Lewis's definition of a convention with

Poincaré's conventionalist reading of the principles of mechanics, we are struck by the contrast between Lewis's focus on behavioural regularities in communities and Poincaré's focus on *the correct epistemic analysis* of a small group of scientific sentences which are claimed to be the fundamental principles of the discipline of mechanics. Poincaré is not concerned with regularities in patterns of behaviour of the members of the community of mathematical physicists. Rather he is addressing the epistemic role of the principles of mechanics within the extensive corpus of objective knowledge conveyed in the mathematical physics. For instance, Poincaré is claiming that, contrary to Walras, the principles of mechanics cannot serve in any scientific causal explanation precisely because, *as conventions,* they do not convey any information about the world. Poincaré's point is that within mathematical physics, as well as scientific facts, regularities based on observation and experimentation and extensive applied mathematical reasoning, conventions, i.e. sentences which are neither true nor false and result from a genuine choice and are not capricious, i.e. arbitrary, also play an indispensable role. This indispensable role of conventions in mathematical physics was largely ignored by the scientific community and philosophers of science prior to Poincaré. As Carnap, one of the most outstanding philosophers of science of the twentieth century, remarks, 'Poincaré can be called a conventionalist only if all that is meant is that he was a philosopher *who emphasized more than previous philosophers the great role of convention*' (Carnap 1966: 59, italics ours).[26] Thus the laurels for highlighting the indispensable role of conventions in our mathematico-scientific knowledge undoubtedly goes to Poincaré: this constitutes a part of his major contribution to philosophy of applied mathematics. By focusing on this role, Poincaré expands our inherited conception of scientific rationality.

In addition to the indispensable role of conventions in mathematical physics, Poincaré also draws our attention to the indispensable role of convention in pure geometry. Here we focus on Poincaré's case for the existence/indispensable role of conventions in pure geometry because (a) in this instance, unlike mathematical physics, ontological-epistemic indeterminacy is clearly isolated as the sole grounds for the pure geometer's recourse to convention and (b) we want to argue that the same kind of ontological-epistemic indeterminacy is an integral component of the post-Keynesian non-ergodic world. In other words given Davidson's division of the post-Keynesian world into the ergodic and non-ergodic, we focus on this non-ergodicity. The non-ergodicity of the future economic world includes ontological-epistemic indeterminacy and that indeterminacy rationally necessitates recourse to convention. However, unlike the case of pure geometry, other constraints also impinge of the specific chosen convention: these constraints include social stability and coordination. Thus while social stability and coordination are more than demanding constraints on any post-Keynesian decision about future investment, a fundamental source of recourse to convention in post-Keynesian rational decision-making also lies in the ontological-epistemic indeterminacy of the long-run future of the economic world.

By the concluding decades of the nineteenth century the subject matter of geometry was dramatically enhanced since its origins in Euclid. For instance, by recourse to Cartesian co-ordinates, geometry was opened up to algebraic representation and analysis. This in turn led to the study of spaces of more than two or three dimensions – n-dimensional space. While it is extremely difficult, if not impossible, to imagine a space of four dimensions, the conceptualisation of such a space is clearly articulated in n-dimensional geometry. Moreover, the challenge to Euclid's parallel postulate, namely through a point outside a straight line, one and only one line can be drawn parallel to the given line, resulted in the birth and development of non-Euclidean geometries. Also interest in projective geometry grew at a phenomenal pace in the nineteenth-century. This geometry is not primarily concerned with issues of distance. Rather it studies the projections of figures in a plane from a fixed point outside the given plane by projecting rays on to another plane. Finally the geometry of topology emerged: this geometry studied the properties of continuous manifolds, without any reference to straightness, angle or distance. Philosophically many of these developments were seen as mere logical curiosities.[27] With the success of Newtonian mechanics, the Newtonian picture of space dominated much of science.[28] In Newtonian mechanics physical space is a kind of container (like a bucket) which extends in three dimensions to infinity and physical bodies are placed in this container. Thus the container space is independent of the material bodies contained in it. Moreover, this container space has an intrinsic metric: its geometry is Euclidean. Later Kant and numerous post-Kantians privileged Euclidean geometry by arguing that it is synthetic a priori. As such there is no way of challenging its truth. This is a very brief summary of the mathematico-philosophical context of Poincaré's reflections on space and geometry.

Poincaré was not a professional philosopher. Rather he was an exceptionally talented mathematician who, as it were, shared his philosophical reflections on his research with the informed public of his time. Included in his various contributions to mathematics, one finds his pioneering research into the relatively new geometrical discipline of topology.[29] In topology space is as it were stripped down to its bare bones: fundamentally from the mathematical point of view of topology space is a continuous manifold. Given the post-Kantian climate at the time it was assumed that such a space would have an intrinsic metric which is Euclidean. The creativity of Poincaré was to challenge that assumption. Poincaré showed that this assumption is incorrect: topological space has not an intrinsic metric. On the contrary it is metrically amorphous. Ontologically, topological space is metrically indeterminate.[30] There is nothing in the nature of a continuous manifold which privileges say, a Euclidean metric over, say, a Riemannian metric or vice versa. More precisely there is nothing in the nature of topological space which privileges any metrical geometry whatsoever. When it comes to the ascertainment of distance, both the nature of a continuous manifold and mathematicians' complete knowledge of such a continuous manifold are no guide whatsoever in how to progress. The only rational recourse is convention.[31] A choice of metric must be made: this is the only route into considerations of distance. Without a conventional choice, there is no metrical future for mathematicians. In this way Poincaré places convention alongside traditional axiomatisation at the core of geometrical and therefore mathematical rationality.

We now turn to post-Keynesian conventions and, to use Pettit's term, our 'gloss' on post-Keynesian radical uncertainty is as follows. We concur with Davidson that post-Keynesian radical uncertainty has an ontological dimension. The long-term future of an economy is ontologically indeterminate. Economies exist in a socio-historical time framework and history teaches us that the long-term future is ontologically indeterminate.[32] This is not just an epistemic indeterminacy. The long-run economic future is also ontologically indeterminate. Some may very well wish that the economic future will be the statistical reflection of the past while others may not. The point is that (a) neither the short-term nor the long-term future exist; (b) the long-term future of an economy is not historically determined; and (c) major, non-routine, economic or economico-political or political decisions or events can have major unintentional and unforeseeable consequences. In the face of this kind of ontological-epistemic indeterminacy, as shown by Poincaré any rational response must necessarily involve recourse to some convention or other.

Vis-à-vis Lawson's 'central question of economic analysis' viz. 'whether and if so how, rational conduct is possible in situations characterized by radical uncertainty' (Lawson 1993: 174) our answer is that rational conduct is possible. As to how this is possible is established by recourse to Poincaré: convention in the face of radical uncertainty understood as ontological-epistemic indeterminacy is not unique to economics; it also, as shown by Poincaré, occurs in the domain of pure mathematics. Poincaré has demonstrated that mathematical rationality, which is a paradigm of rationality, includes recourse to convention. Thus we concur with O'Donnell that in post-Keynesian economics conventions 'are defined as practical measures for resolving undeterminate decision problems' (O'Donnell 2003: 99). For us the source of these undeterminate decision problems lies in the ontological-epistemic indeterminacy of the long-run future. Economists, like pure geometers, face undeterminate decision problems and, like pure geometers, recourse to convention is an indispensable component of any proposed solution. Moreover O'Donnell is correct in emphasising the practicality of the conventional measures in post-Keynesian economics. In the case of pure geometry these practical concerns do not arise. Thus, for instance, the practical concerns of socio-economic stability and of co-ordination do not arise in the case of pure geometry.[33] Clearly these practical concerns also operate as major constraints on any conventional choice made by post-Keynesians in the face of the ontological-epistemic indeterminacy of the long-run future.

Conclusion

In this chapter, by recourse to Hume, Lewis and Poincaré, we identified three distinct and intriguing ways in which recourse to convention emerged in the philosophical literature. Hume in his quest for the foundation of justice highlights the issue of social instability and the recourse to the conventions of justice to gain stability. Lewis is primarily concerned with language and has recourse to co-ordination game theory to elucidate the conventional nature of language. Poincaré is primarily concerned with a totally different domain, namely the relationship between the geometry of topology and metrical geometry and the indispensable role of convention in that relationship. To date the post-Keynesian debate on conventions has focused on Hume and Lewis. With the exception of Boylan and O'Gorman (2013), Poincaré has not been addressed in the post-Keynesian debate on the issue of the rationality of conventions. This is regrettable. Poincaré – recognised as the father of conventionalism – in his reflections on the indispensable role of convention in pure geometry highlighted the ontological-epistemic, metrical indeterminacy of topological space. The rational response in pure mathematics to this ontological-epistemic indeterminacy is recourse to convention. Thus mathematical rationality, contrary to popular opinion, contains an indispensable conventional component. We contend that an identical ontological-epistemic indeterminacy holds in the non-ergodic dimension of the economic world. Given that convention in the face of ontological-epistemic indeterminacy is rational in pure mathematics – the paradigm of a rational discipline – recourse to convention in the face of ontological-epistemic indeterminacy in post-Keynes economics is equally rational. There is more to economic rationality than what falls within orthodox formalisations of rationality.

Notes

1 In the following chapter we address the issue of the mathematical modelling of equilibrium in the neo-Walrasian programme.
2 This view, it could be argued, is complemented by or incorporated into game theory. Game theory focuses on interactive situations in which the outcomes are determined by deliberating agents and where the concept of a Nash equilibrium is taken as 'the embodiment of the idea that economic agents are rational: that they simultaneously act to maximize their utility' (Aumann 1985: 43). As Skyrms puts it 'a simultaneous choice of acts by all players is called a *Nash equilibrium* if no player can improve his or her payoff by a unilateral defection to a different act. In other words, at a Nash equilibrium, *each player maximizes his or her utility conditional on the other player's act*' (Skyrms 1990. 13).
3 More advanced deductive pure mathematics is required to prove the existence of a Nash equilibrium in finite n-person zero sum games with mixed strategies. As Skyrms points out, Nash used Brouwer's fixed point theorem to prove the existence of equilibrium. We will see in the next chapter why one may have legitimate reservations about recourse to Brouwer's fixed point theorem in theoretical economics!
4 The specific rationale for a specific convention may prima facie be plausible. However, recourse to the theory of rationality could undermine this prima facie case. Hence our concern with the rationality of recourse to convention per se.
5 Keynes in a letter to Townsend in 1938 draws our attention to the role of conventions in other non-economic domains. The relevant passage from this letter is quoted in Lawson (1993).
6 In an axiomatic system, nominal definitions which are conventions are extensively used. These conventions, however, can in principle be eliminated. See Boylan and O'Gorman (2013) for more details.

7 We will see in the next chapter that Brouwer also challenges this axiomatic portrait. Brouwer's challenge is more radical than that of Poincaré.

8 Much of the secondary literature focuses on Poincaré's conventional of applied geometry. See O'Gorman (1977).

9 Lewis' *Convention* is frequently presented as a neo-Humean analysis.

10 Vanderschraaf argues that Hume's account of convention 'can plausibly be interpreted as an informal game theory which predates the first formal theory of games presented by von Neumann and Morgenstern (1944) by more than two centuries' (Vanderschraaf 1998: 216).

11 'I am not, however, without hope, that the present system of philosophy will acquire new force as it advances; and that our reasonings concerning morals will corroborate whatever has been said concerning the *understanding* and the *passions*. Morality is a subject that interests us above all others ...' (Hume 1985: 507).

12 Reason plays a merely instrumental role in morality. It may be used to discover that a passion is based on a false judgement, e.g. when the object of one's fear is shown by reason to be non-existent. It may also be used to show that a chosen means is not adequate to the task at hand. However, reason is not the philosophical foundation of morality.

13 Hume admires the moral qualities on an enemy, even though the enemy has not Hume's interests at heart.

14 This thesis does not receive an extended elaboration by Hume.

15 Justice, for Hume is not grounded in a universal sentiment of concern for the whole of humanity. While sympathy is universal, there is no universal sense of public interest.

16 In Hume's epistemology language is conventional. Knowledge begins with sensory perceptions. From these, images are derived and ideas are but faint images. Then each individual idea is annexed to a linguistic term. Thus a Frenchman uses a French term whereas an Englishman uses an English term. In this way French and English are conventional regularities.

17 Vanderschraaf (1998) gives an excellent game-theoretic analyses of Hume's examples. However, as is evident in our very brief synopsis of Hume's reflections, morality is a key interest of Hume. Indeed 'it is a subject which interests us above all others ...' (Hume 1985: 507). For various reasons we are not convinced that Hume anticipated the strategic notion of a Nash equilibrium in this analysis. If morality were taken out of Hume's deliberations – which would be like Hamlet without the Prince – then of course one would be free to give his examples a strategic game-theoretic analysis. For Hume, much of practical rationality is morality-laden whereas the strategic rationality of game-theory in orthodox economics is explicitly morality-neutral.

18 The meaning of a sentence is in turn another function from possible worlds to truth-values.

19 Lewis does not use the expression Nash equilibrium. In line with various commentators we are assuming that Lewis's notion is the same as a Nash equilibrium. However, one should recall that Nash's focus is on non-cooperative games, while, given his interest in language, Lewis's focus is primarily on games of coordination.

20 For various views on this see Topoi (2008).

21 Pettit's gloss is at variance with other interpretations of Lewis. For instance according to Skyrms Lewis is responding to Quine's challenge, in Quine's famous 1936 piece 'Truth by Convention'. In that piece Quine raised the issue of how convention without communication is possible? This question 'has two parts: (1) How can convention without communication be sustained? And (2) How can convention without communication be generated? Lewis gave the answer to the first question in terms of equilibrium (or stable equilibrium) and common knowledge. His discussion of the second question – following Schelling (1960) – is framed in terms of salience ...' (Skyrms 1990: 54). In our gloss Lewis is responding to all of these issues but that

the issues of continuance and of resilience are much more important to him than the issue of origins.

22 For instance one might use Lewis's thesis to analyse the demise of the Irish language. After the external shock of colonisation the population of Ireland over a period of time, on the grounds of conscious strategic thinking, abandoned its conventional Irish language and embraced the conventional language of its English colonial power. We doubt that historians of the colonisation of Ireland would concur with this analysis. However, Lewisians might reply that this account is *the logic* of the situation which should inform any historical account.

23 We hope that this is not 'a gloss' on Pettit's own 'gloss'!, i.e. that it accurately represents a significant aspect of Pettit's thesis.

24 A number of epistemological issues arise here.

    (1)   Can or should the concept of convention be defined in terms of necessary and sufficient conditions?

    (2)   Is Lewis's definition merely persuasive: is he merely prescribing how we should use the term convention?

    (3)   If the concept of convention can be defined in terms of necessary and sufficient conditions has Lewis correctly identified these? After all he changed his own mind on these. Thus much debate has occurred around, for instance, his condition of common knowledge.

    (4)   What presuppositions underlie his recourse to game theory? See Skyrms (1990) for some of these.

25 See Boylan and O'Gorman (2013) for a very brief summary of other developments.

26 Carnap's intention is to undermine the view that Poincaré was a radical conventionalist who held that even the laws of science are conventions. 'Poincaré also has been accused of conventionalism in this radical sense but that, I think, is a misunderstanding of his writings. He has indeed often stressed the important role conventions play in science, but he was also well aware of the empirical components that come into play. He knew that … we have to accommodate our system to the facts of nature as we find them …' (Carnap 1966: 59).

27 A notable exception was the young Bertrand Russell. In his early writings he read projective geometry as synthetic a priori.

28 The famous exception here of course is Leibniz.

29 See Stirwell (1996).

30 Grünbaum's (1964) was the first to fully appreciate the ontological dimension of Poincaré's geometrical conventionalism.

31 Because Newtonian space is mathematically a continuous manifold and because of the dualism of space and matter in Newtonian mechanics, Poincaré also argued for the conventionalism of applied geometry (see O'Gorman 1977). In Einstein's general theory of relativity this dualism no longer holds. Poincaré had died before the publication of Einstein's general theory. However much has been written on Poincaré's anticipation, as it were, of Einstein's special theory (see Miller 1996).

32 Poincaré was among the first to identify a conventional dimension in the mathematisation of time in mechanics (see Poincaré 1958: Chapter 2). The issue of the simultaneity of events separated by astronomical distances requires recourse to convention. The issue of simultaneity is not relevant here.

33 As we pointed out in Boylan and O'Gorman (2013), we disagree with O'Donnell in identifying this rationality as weak. In our analysis recourse to convention is strongly rational. The reason for this is that the same kind of recourse to convention also occurs in pure mathematics which is the par excellence rational discipline.

7 The emergence of constructive and computable mathematics

New directions for the formalisation of economics?

Introduction

In Chapters Three and Four we engaged Debreu's conception of economic theorising, or, in his own words, his 'philosophy of economic analysis' (Debreu 1992: 114). As already outlined, his conception of theoretical economics is rooted in Hilbert's formalist philosophy of mathematics, both pure and applied. In Chapter Five we considered the reception of the neo-Walrasian programme within economics, taking Hahn as a representative of those fully committed to that programme and Kaldor as a representative of its critics. In this connection we highlighted the commitments to both rationality and to equilibrium in the orthodox mathematisation of economics. In Chapter Six we used specific developments in the philosophy of geometry to buttress the challenge posed to the orthodox mathematical modelling of rationality by the post-Keynesian emphasis on the role of conventions in economic decision-making. In this chapter we return to the general philosophy of mathematics by bringing two well-known critiques of the Hilbert formalist philosophy of mathematics to bear on the orthodox commitments to both rationality and equilibrium. These critiques we argue furnish methodologists with a range of insights and themes into both the analysis and the critical evaluation of these orthodox commitments. Moreover, these critiques suggest an alternative way of formalising economic theory.

The first critique of the Hilbertian formalist programme – which we call the external critique – is associated with Brouwer and culminated in a new mathematics, called constructive or intuitionistic.[1] In this connection it is crucial to note that constructive/intuitionistic mathematics is not a new chapter which can be simply added on to the existing corpus of classical mathematics. Rather it is a different mathematics grounded in a different logic! Intuitionistic mathematics rejects the logic which underpins classical mathematics and replaces it with a different logic, called intuitionistic logic. The emergence of constructive/ intuitionistic mathematics raises a fundamental issue for the project of the mathematisation of economics – an issue which has not received due recognition in the methodology of economics dominated by the philosophy of science. For numerous economists the project of the mathematisation of economics is unproblematical: basically economists are using mathematics as a logical tool for the rigorous analysis of economic issues. However, in light of the emergence of intuitionistic mathematics, the issue is not that simple. Theoretical economists are, prima facie, faced with a genuine choice between constructive/intuitionistic mathematics and classical mathematics in their formalisation of economics. *There is more than just one way to formalise economics.* This choice in turn raises a fundamental methodological question: which mathematics – intuitionistic or classical – is more appropriate to the specific discipline of economics? Alternatively what are the respective advantages and disadvantages of classical and of intuitionistic mathematics for the formalisation of economics? In this chapter we address this fundamental issue.

The second critique of the Hilbert programme, which we call the internal critique, is associated with Gödel, Church and Turing. This culminated in the construction of the first electronic, store-programmed digital computer in 1948. Fundamental to this revolutionary engineering success is what we call computable mathematics. Computable mathematics, like constructive/intuitionistic mathematics, emphasises algorithmetic mathematical procedures but, unlike constructive/intuitionistic mathematics, uses classical, rather than intuitionistic, logic. Thus one could say that computable mathematics, unlike intuitionistic mathematics, is a specialised branch which limits itself to algorithmetic procedures within the broader corpus of classical mathematics. Perhaps the most amazing result in the development of computable mathematics is the proof of the existence of undecidable propositions within classical mathematics by Church and Turing in the 1930s. Contrary to what is sometimes tacitly assumed, post Church-Gödel-Turing, classical mathematics divides into algorithmetically decidable and algorithmetically undecidable theorems. This division raises another central question for the project of the mathematisation of economics, viz. does recourse to an algorithmetically undecidable theorem in economic modelling effect the explanatory value of such a model? In this connection we present a methodological case for the thesis that Debreu's general equilibrium explanation of prices is rendered economically vacuous by its recourse to algorithmetically undecidable theorems.

Finally, in light of the poor prognosis for the neo-Walrasian programme, we address the following question. If theoretical economists were to confine their mathematical modelling to the resources of computable economics what positive contributions could they make to the scientific understanding of the economic world? If the economic exploitation of computable mathematics could deliver a range of positive results, then perhaps it could, in Mirowski's words, 'serve as a new template for an entirely new approach to the formalization of economic life' (Mirowski 2012: 180). Whether or not that is likely to happen depends on numerous contingencies, ranging from economic theoreticians' willingness to devote time to mastering the resources of computable mathematics to the power of influential institutions, for whatever reasons, committed to the status quo.[2] These contingencies aside, our concern is with, in Debreu's terminology, the extent to which 'the fit' (Debreu 1986: 1262) between economic content and computable mathematics can be demonstrated to be better than the fit held to be established between the full resources of classical mathematics and economic content in orthodox theorising. Clearly this issue cannot be resolved by economic methodology: its resolution depends on the fruits or otherwise of economic theorising confined to the resources of computable mathematics. In our opinion, however, economic methodology has a significant contribution to make to this issue, especially when economic methodology is expanded to include the philosophy of mathematics. In light of the philosophy of mathematics we argue that a prima facie methodological case can be made for limiting mathematical resources to computable mathematics in economic theorising. In light of this prima facie case sufficient time should be given to the exploration of this potential alternative approach to the formalisation of economics.

Strict intuitionism and the neo-Walrasian programme

Intuitionistic mathematics is associated with the Dutch mathematician, L.E.J. Brouwer.[3] In the early decades of the twentieth century, Brouwer explicitly developed intuitionistic mathematics in opposition to Hilbert's formalism. Indeed the Brouwer–Hilbert controversy in the foundations of mathematics is very well known, probably for the wrong reasons. Van Stigt sums up this infamous controversy as follows.

> The Brouwer–Hilbert controversy grew increasingly bitter and turned into a personal feud. The last episode was the 'Annalenstreit' or, to use Einstein's words, 'the frog-and-mouse battle.' It followed the unjustified and illegal dismissal of Brouwer from the editorial board of the *Mathematische Annalen* by Hilbert in 1928 and led to the disbanding of the old *Annalen* company and the emergence of a new *Annalen* under Hilbert's sole command without the support of its former chief editors, Einstein and Carathéodory.
> (van Stigt 1998: 3)

Early in his mathematical career Brouwer had accomplished outstanding research in the domain of topology. This research was within the parameters of classical mathematics and included his famous fixed point theorem, exploited by Debreu. Brouwer's research was acknowledged throughout Europe, including Hilbert and his school. Thus Brouwer's credentials as an outstanding mathematician were universally acknowledged. However, even when engaged in his PhD research in Amsterdam, Brouwer was utterly dissatisfied with contemporary approaches to the foundations of mathematics from Russell to Hilbert. According to various scholars Brouwer's intuitionistic mathematics 'can only be fully understood in the context of his particular philosophy of mathematics' (van Stigt 1998: 4).

As van Stigt sums up,

> Brouwer's main concern was the nature of mathematics as pure 'languageless' thought-construction. He set himself the task of bringing the

mathematical world around to his view, convincing them of the need for reform, and had started the programme of reconstructing mathematics on an Intuitionist basis.

(van Stigt 1998: 2)

Brouwerian scholars contextualise Brouwer's intuitionistic mathematics in his unique romantic pessimistic and radical individualistic view of life.[4] In addition to his own unique philosophy of life, scholars also identify the influences of Descartes, Kant, Poincaré and others. With his Cartesian emphasis on individual consciousness, according to Brouwer, the mind has a direct, languageless, Kantian-type intuition of time.[5] This primordial intuition is pure time awareness, without any external influence. In this subjectivist philosophical context mathematics is a free creation of the mind which is developed from this single, a priori, primordial intuition of time, totally independent of external experience. In other words the time-bound individual mind creatively constructs mathematics subject to the constraint of this primordial intuition. Thus, as Heyting puts it, 'a mathematical construction ought to be so immediate to the mind and its results so clear that it needs no foundation whatsoever' (Heyting 1956: 6). For the Brouwerian intuitionist, the pure intuition of time is bedrock and hence does not require any further legitimation. This pure intuition of time as continuing on *ad infinitum* is the foundational source of the universe of discourse of pure mathematics. This mathematical universe of discourse is thus a potentially infinite sequence, i.e. a domain which is never complete. Thus for intuitionistic mathematicians mathematics, *ab initio*, concerns the potentially infinite: this open-ended potentially infinite domain is immediately grasped by the individual mind in its pure intuition of time. Hence mathematics is totally independent of all discourse about, or our conception of, the physical world.

Instead of engaging the various, but significant nuances and historical evolution of Brouwer's Intuitionism, for the purposes of deepening our understanding of the methodological issues involved in the mathematisation of economics, we distinguish between strict and pragmatic intuitionism. Strict intuitionism has a negative and a positive dimension. Negatively the strict intuitionist holds that classical mathematics, including its logic, 'is incoherent and illegitimate, that classical mathematics, while containing, in distorted form, much of value, is, nevertheless, as it stands unintelligible' (Dummett 2000: 250). The positive thesis is that 'the intuitionist way of construing mathematical notions and logical operations is a coherent and legitimate one, that intuitionist mathematics forms an intelligible body of theory' (Dummett 2000: 250).

In other words strict intuitionism maintains that our inherited, classical mathematics – defended by Hilbert – is fundamentally flawed and thereby must be radically overhauled. When this is done, there is one and only one way of doing mathematics, viz. the intuitionistic way. We will be addressing pragmatic intuitionism in a later section. For the present purposes, we note one major difference between strict and pragmatic intuitionism. According to pragmatic intuitionism, classical mathematics, contrary to strict intuitionism, is not fundamentally flawed. Classical and intuitionistic mathematics peacefully co-exist: each has an authentic, but distinct, mathematical domain.

Our contention is that the neo-Walrasian programme is flawed beyond redemption within strict intuitionism. In Chapter Five we saw how Kaldor advocated the total demolition of the neo-Walrasian programme. We content that within strict intuitionism the neo-Walrasian programme is undermined at its mathematical core. In the remainder of this section we outline the grounds for this radical claim. These grounds concern (i) the universe of discourse of mathematics, (ii) logic, (iii) the concept of mathematical existence and (iv) legitimate mathematical techniques and theorems.

As we saw in Chapter Three classical mathematics insists that Cantorian set theory with its unequivocal commitment to, what philosophers call, actual, as opposed to potential, infinity is indispensable to mathematics. Consequently the universe of discourse of classical mathematics is much more extensive than the potentially infinite domain of discourse of strict intuitionistic mathematics. The actual infinite domain of discourse of classical mathematics contains a complete infinity of infinities of elements. According to the strict intuitionist such a conception of the universe of discourse of mathematics is illegitimate and illusory because it is incompatible with the fundamental basis of all of mathematics, viz. the pure, primordial, mental intuition of time. This illegitimacy is exposed by the paradoxes in the foundations of mathematics: the source of these paradoxes is the misconceived notion of a complete, actual infinite domain of discourse.[6] By acknowledging that potential infinity is the only legitimate conception of mathematical infinity, the paradoxes are avoided. For the strict intuitionist, Debreu, in using classical mathematics in his economic theorising, is *ipso facto* operating within this illegitimate domain of discourse of actual infinity.

In conjunction with this crucial, ontological fault-line between strict intuitionists and classical mathematicians concerning the universe of discourse of mathematics another equally crucial fault-line emerges. This fault-line concerns logic.[7] Prior to the development of intuitionistic mathematics it was tacitly assumed that classical logic, which originated in Aristotelian logic and which was rigorously reconstructed by Frege and Russell, was the indispensable core of all legitimate deductive inferences, including those of mathematics. This assumption was challenged by strict intuitionism. Classical logic must be rejected: it is not adequate to the potential infinite domain of discourse of mathematics. Strict intuitionists maintain that classical logic was devised for finite domains of discourse and that classical mathematicians unhesitatingly, but illegitimately, transferred it to the potential infinite domain of discourse of mathematics.

The famous Aristotelian principle of the excluded middle became a focal point of this fundamental conflict between intuitionistic and classical mathematicians. This principle states that for any object x, x is b or x is not b, where b is a well-defined property of objects. Alternatively any proposition must be either true or false. The principle clearly holds for any finite class: one can in principle identify each member of the finite class and check whether or not the property b holds. For the strict intuitionist, this principle is not transferrable to the potential infinite domain of discourse of mathematics. Take, for instance, Troelstra's and van Dalen's example 'there are infinitely many twin primes (twin primes are two consecutive prime numbers which differ by two, e.g. 3 and 5 are twin primes but 7 and 11 are not)' (Troelstra and van Dalen 1988: 6). This proposition is currently undecidable. To date mathematicians have not created a systematic method to prove this proposition and neither have they created a systematic method to prove its negation. The classical mathematician, committed to the principle of the excluded middle, maintains that, despite its current undecidability, the proposition 'there is an infinite number of twin primes' is in reality either true or false. The strict intuitionist responds that it is possible that mathematicians may never create a systematic method which will either prove or disprove that there are an infinite number of twin primes. Again for the classical mathematician that response is also beside the point: there either is or is not, in reality, an infinite number of twin primes. Both the classical and the strict intuitionistic mathematician agree that (a) the only way of knowing whether or not there is an infinite number of twin primes is to prove it and (b) it is logically possible that mathematics will never resolve this issue one way or the other. The classical mathematician does not find the combination of (a) and (b) perturbing: the fundamental commitment is that in reality there either is or is not an infinite number of twin primes. The strict intuitionistic mathematician is genuinely perturbed with this commitment on the part of classical mathematicians. If that classical commitment is true and (a) and (b) are true, what does that combination assume? Given (a), it assumes that a proof exists in some realm or other which transcends the realm of humanly constructable mathematical proofs! In other words the classical mathematician is assuming beings with mathematical abilities which transcend our own human deductive abilities. The moral is clear: abandon the cornerstone of traditional logic, viz. the principle of the excluded middle. A logic without the principle of the excluded middle is required. This logic, called intuitionistic logic, was rigorously formalised by Brouwer's outstanding pupil, Heyting.[8] Intuitionistic logic is the only authentic logic. Classical logic is fundamentally flawed.

This novel logic of strict intuitionism undermines the neo-Walrasian programme at its logical core. A basic thesis of the neo-Walrasian programme is that Debreu has unquestionably proved *the logical possibility* of general equilibrium. As we have just seen, according to strict intuitionism, classical logic must be rejected and replaced by intuitionistic logic. Contrary to Debreu's tacit assumption, classical logic *is not the criterion of logical possibility*. Rather the criterion of logical possibility is furnished by intuitionistic logic. By tacitly assuming, with the formalists, that classical logic is the one true logic and failing to recognise that the one true logic is that of intuitionism, Debreu fails to prove the logical possibility of general equilibrium. In this fashion the neo-Walrasian programme crumbles at its logical core: its so-called proof of the possibility of general equilibrium is grounded in a spurious logic. As we noted in Chapter Five a number of economists and methodologists reject the neo-Walrasian programme on the grounds that, while Debreu has rigorously proved the logical possibility of general equilibrium, his proof shows that the economic conditions of this logical possibility are so unrealistic as to render it valueless to the economic analysis of real world economies.[9] The objection above on the grounds of strict intuitionism is much more radical in that it challenges the tacit assumption of these methodologists, viz. Debreu has rigorously established the logical possibility of general equilibrium. According to strict intuitionism he has done no such thing. Debreu's so-called proof is illogical. He failed to recognise that intuitionistic logic is the one and only logic available to human beings.

We now turn to the third theme where classical mathematics as understood by formalists is mistaken, namely mathematical existence. As already emphasised for the strict intuitionist, mathematical existence is mind dependent. Moreover, the intuitionist mind is fundamentally creative: based on the primordial intuition of time, it constructs its mathematical entities. Thus mathematical existence means constructability in a finite number of algorithmetic steps. Debreu, as a committed member of the Hilbertian formalist school, is utterly confused on this matter: he fails to recognise that the concept of mathematical existence is completely distinct from the concept of formal consistency. To prove that a mathematical entity exists, one must show that it is in principle algorithmetically constructable. However, by equating mathematical existence with formal consistency, Debreu's so-called proof of the existence of general equilibrium does no such thing.[10]

Fourthly, the rejection of classical logic and its replacement by intuitionistic logic entails that some of the proof-techniques and various theorems cherished by classical mathematicians are spurious. Weyl, a member of the Hilbert formalist school who for a period was more than impressed by Brouwer's intuitionistic programme, sums up as follows:[11]

> Mathematics with Brouwer gains its highest intuitive clarity. He succeeds in developing the beginnings of analysis in a natural manner, all the time preserving the contact with Intuition much more closely than had been done before. It cannot be denied, however, that in advancing to higher and more general theories the inapplicability of the simple laws of classical logic eventually results in an almost unbearable awkwardness. And the mathematician watches with pain the larger part of his towering edifice, which he believed to be built on concrete blocks dissolve into mist before his eyes.
>
> (Weyl 1949: 54)

In this fashion Weyl identifies two major objections to strict intuitionism. Firstly, by rejecting classical logic, the proof techniques of intuitionist mathematics become unbearably cumbersome. We saw in Chapter Three how Debreu picks up this theme by insisting on the simplicity of mathematical proofs. The strict intuitionist response is that this lack of simplicity is not too dear a price to pay for limiting mathematical proofs to constructive ones, especially since such a limitation avoids the paradoxes in the foundations of mathematics. Vis-à-vis the second objection, viz. the destruction of a large part of the edifice of classical mathematics, the strict intuitionist concurs with Heyting's response.

> As to the mutilation of mathematics of which you accuse me, it must be taken as an inevitable consequence of our standpoint. It can also be seen as the excision of noxious ornaments, beautiful in form but hollow in substance.
>
> (Heyting 1956: 11)

Among the theorems which are noxious ornaments is Brouwer's fixed point theorem, a mathematical cornerstone of Debreu's equilibrium theorising.

To sum up, the strict intuitionist maintains that classical mathematics misidentifies the domain of discourse of mathematics, uses a pseudo-logic, misconstrues mathematical existence and is mistaken in its identification of genuine mathematical theorems. The neo-Walrasian programme collapses on each of these basic themes. (1) It is mistaken in its assumption that the mathematical domain of discourse is Cantor's actual infinity. (2) It fails to recognise that classical logic is not the genuine logic of mathematics. (3) It is incorrect in its formalist commitment to the identification of mathematical existence with formal consistency. (4) The Brouwerian-type fixed point theorems of classical mathematics are not genuine mathematical theorems at all. In Heyting's colourful language Debreu's equilibrium theorising is a 'noxious ornament, beautiful in form but hollow in substance', The strict intuitionist, in the spirit of Kaldor, demolishes the neo-Walrasian programme at its logico-mathematical core.

The Bourbaki critique of Brouwerian intuitionism

The good news for the neo-Walrasian programme is that Brouwer's attempted revolution failed: the vast majority of mathematicians continued their researches within the framework of classical mathematics. In this connection we briefly dwell on Bourbaki's account of this failure.[12] We focus on Bourbaki because of the manner in which he identifies the Achilles' heel in Brouwerian intuitionism. Also historians of economic thought have argued that Bourbaki was a major influence on Debreu's formalist conception of mathematics.[13] Bourbaki concurs with Weyl that the majority of mathematicians value the simplicity of the proof procedures of classical mathematics over the more cumbersome procedures of intuitionistic mathematics and that they are more than reluctant to sacrifice the large portion of classical mathematics demanded by strict intuitionism. According to Bourbaki there is a very good reason for this reluctance, namely Brouwer's flawed philosophical psychology.

Bourbaki, while in no way attempting to summarise 'a doctrine as complex as intuitionism,' maintains that 'it consists as much of psychology as mathematics' (Bourbaki 1994: 37). This claim is in keeping with the conventional interpretation of Brouwer's intuitionism: his mathematical programme is grounded in, and driven by, a specific philosophical psychology.[14] Indeed Bourbaki identifies 'some of the most striking aspects' of this philosophical psychology

(Bourbaki 1994: 37). The first of these is the Brouwerian thesis that mathematics is 'the "exact" part of our thought, based on the first intuition of the sequence of natural numbers' (Bourbaki 1994: 37). This reading of Brouwer is not controversial and for some it may not be that striking. For others, what makes it striking is the fact that for Brouwer this is 'only "exact" in the thought of mathematicians, and it is a chimera to hope to develop an instrument of communication between them which is not subject to all the imperfections and ambiguities of language' (Bourbaki 1994: 37). In other words Brouwer's philosophical psychology includes four theses.

1 Mathematical thought is a private mental activity.
2 This mental activity is totally independent of any language, either natural or formal.
3 All languages are, relative to pure mathematical thought, defective.
4 When mathematical thoughts are expressed in a language, either natural or formal, they are contaminated by the inherent defects of this linguistic process.

The consequences of this philosophical psychology are equally clear: (a) Mathematicians, no matter how gifted, can never accurately convey their mathematical thoughts through language. (b) All mathematical communication conducted in either a natural or a formal language is inherently defective. (c) All the mathematical symbols and terms developed over the centuries in the various branches of mathematics fail to perfectly convey the pure mathematical thoughts underlying these symbols and terms.

Another striking aspect of Brouwer's philosophical psychology is its negative attitude towards logic. 'Intuitionist mathematics attaches hardly more importance to logic than to language' (Bourbaki 1994: 37). This is Bourbaki's way of stating the Brouwerian conviction that formal logic is not productive in mathematics. As the Brouwerian scholar van Stigt puts it, even while approving of, his loyal student, Heyting's explorations into intuitionistic logic, Brouwer remained true to his conviction that engagement in logic 'is an interesting but irrelevant and sterile exercise' (van Stigt 1998: 276).[15] To mathematicians who hold that logic is absolutely indispensable to mathematical thought and that, through the combination of natural and formal languages, mathematicians successfully communicate their thoughts, Brouwer's philosophical psychology is far from appealing. It certainly is not a sufficient reason to reject a large portion of classical mathematics. Hence, not surprisingly, Bourbaki sums up as follows.

> The intuitionist school, of which the memory is no doubt destined to remain only as a historical curiosity, would at least have been of service by having forced its adversaries, that is to say definitely the immense majority of mathematicians, to make their position precise …
>
> (Bourbaki 1994: 38)

In this connection Bourbaki acknowledges that intuitionism forced its adversaries, especially the Hilbert formalists, to make more precise their metamathematical notion of a finite procedure. His point is that, these contributions to adversaries aside, intuitionistic mathematics remains a historical curiosity. In short according to Bourbaki, Brouwer's philosophical psychology, on which intuitionistic mathematics is based, is its Achilles' heel.

If intuitionistic mathematics is not to remain a passing curiosity in the history of mathematics, intuitionists may be well advised to sever its links to Brouwer's philosophical psychology.[16] This it has done in two ways. One route is to retain strict intuitionism but on the basis of an alternative philosophy to that of Brouwer's philosophical psychology. The other route is that of pragmatic intuitionism which abandons all links to philosophy and develops intuitionistic mathematics as a legitimate mathematical domain alongside the equally legitimate domain of classical mathematics.[17]

Dummett's philosophical reconstruction of strict intuitionism

A different philosophical route to strict intuitionism to that of Brouwer was pioneered in a highly original way by the distinguished Oxford philosopher Sir Michael Dummett in the latter decades of the twentieth century.[18] Dummett's fundamental thesis is that

> intuitionistic mathematics is pointless without the philosophical motivation underlying it ... intuitionism will never succeed in its struggle against rival, and more widely accepted, forms of mathematics unless it can win the philosophical battle. If it ever loses that battle, the practice of intuitionistic mathematics itself ... will become a waste of time.
>
> (Dummett 2000: ix)

The philosophical battleground is the philosophy of language, not Brouwer's very questionable philosophical psychology. In the philosophy of language the focus is on the meaning or the objective, intersubjective understanding of mathematical statements.

> For Brouwer mathematics is a mental activity that can only be imperfectly communicated in language. I on the other hand have stressed what I take to be the perfect communicability of mathematics ... as such mathematical language plays a central role in it.
>
> (Dummett 1994a: 305)

In Dummett's philosophy of language, there is no question of denying the reality of mental activities. Rather language is a vehicle of thought but 'it could not serve as a vehicle of thought unless it were first an instrument of communication' (Dummett 1994b: 262). From the point of view of a faithful follower of Brouwer, Dummett is 'a heretic who feels no urge to recant' (Dummett 1994a: 305).

In short for Dummett, mathematical thought, contrary to some other strict Brouwerians, is clearly articulated and communicated by a public language and, contrary to Hilbertian formalists, what is communicated by mathematical language has content, i.e. objective meaning grasped by the mathematical community. In this intersubjective linguistic context, strict intuitionism still retains a positive and a negative thesis. Positively, 'intuitionists succeed in conferring a coherent meaning on the expressions used in intuitionistic mathematics, and, in particular, on the logical constants' (Dummett 2000: 251). (The logical constants are the terms, 'and,' 'or,', 'not,' 'if-then-', which are constantly used in our deductive/ logical inferences). According to the negative thesis 'classical mathematicians *fail* to confer an intelligible meaning on the logical constants, and on mathematical expressions in general, as they use them' (Dummett 2000: 251). Again, contrary to strictly faithful followers of Brouwer, Dummett's way of stating strict intuitionism puts the philosophical spotlight onto logic and on how meaning is conferred on its logical terms. In short, Dummett, like Bourbaki, recognises defects in Brouwer's philosophical psychology but, unlike Bourbaki, defends strict intuitionism on different philosophical grounds. Clearly if Dummett's defence of strict intuitionism stands up to critical scrutiny, the neo-Walrasian programme is once again shown to be contaminated at its logico-mathematical core.

As we have just seen Dummett, unlike Brouwer, puts the philosophical spotlight on language and, in particular, its deductive inferences. Prior to Brouwer, it was accepted without question that the logic of any deductive inference is classical logic. Classical logic, which originated with Aristotle and was rigorously represented by the logical works of Frege and Russell at the turn of the twentieth century, is the one true logic governing all deductive inferences in both natural languages and the specialised language of mathematics. Classical mathematics – the mathematical tool of the neo-Walrasian programme – stands or falls with classical logic. As already discussed in Chapter Three, Kenneth Arrow correctly identified extensionality as a key characteristic of classical logic and pointed to psychological research which shows that the doctrine of extensionality is not adhered to in various choice situations. Dummett goes much further than Arrow. He puts the philosophical spotlight on the fundamental presupposition of the doctrine of extensionality and argues that this fundamental presupposition does not stand up to critical scrutiny. In other words, extensional logic, the logical cornerstone of classical mathematics, does not stand up to critical scrutiny. It must be rejected and replaced by intuitionistic logic – the one true, non-extensional logic of deductive discourse, mathematical and non-mathematical.

In the following we focus on one strand in Dummett's many-layered philosophical argument for this radical conclusion. This strand is his use of mathematical undecidable propositions. Our reason for choosing this, rather than other strands, is that mathematical undecidables also play a central role in the negative assessment of the explanatory success of the neo-Walrasian programme by some theoretical economists.[19] As we will see later, these theoretical economists demonstrate that the neo-Walrasian explanation of value (modelled on

Debreu's *Theory of Value*) uses mathematically undecidable propositions and argue that, given these undecidables, neo-Walrasian theorising has no explanatory value. At the moment, however, our concern is with Dummett's recourse to mathematical undecidables to buttress his claim that classical logic and *ipso facto* classical mathematics (exploited in neo-Walrasian theorising) is fundamentally flawed.

This fundamental flaw lies in what Arrow identified as the doctrine of extensionality, which constitutes the logical basis of classical mathematics. As pointed out in Chapter Three the doctrine of extensionality, when applied to propositions, as distinct from terms within propositions, is based on what philosophers of language call the thesis of bivalence.[20] The thesis of bivalence states that every proposition has a determinate truth-value – it is either true or false – irrespective of our ability to decide which truth-value actually holds. Prima facie, the thesis of bivalence appears plausible. Take, for instance, the proposition 'Napoleon blinked at 11.31 a.m. on July 10th, 1810', That proposition is historically undecidable – we assume there is no evidence one way or the other. Nonetheless, despite this absence of historical evidence, it is in fact either true or false that Napoleon blinked at that time on that date. Based on this kind and other kinds of examples, logicians tacitly assumed the thesis of bivalence in developing classical extensional logic.

According to one strand of Dummett's philosophical argument which we simplify here, the thesis of bivalence, and thus classical logic, is undermined by mathematical undecidable propositions. We distinguish between three kinds of mathematical undecidables. Firstly, some mathematical propositions, such as the proposition there is an infinite number of twin primes, used in the previous section, is currently undecidable. Despite its current undecidability, according to the thesis of bivalence, that proposition has a determinate truth-value: in reality it is actually either true or false. Let us assume that such current undecidables do not undermine the thesis of bivalence. The second kind of undecidables we call hypothetical Gödelian undecidables. Despite the lack of consensus on its full philosophical implications, Gödel's second incompleteness theorem proves

(i)   If T is consistent then U,

Where U is a very complex sentence of T which is undecidable by T and where T is an axiomatisation of standard arithmetic.[21] The mathematical sentence, U, is undecidable. However, it is hypothetical, as it is the consequent of the antecedent, 'T is consistent,' in (i). According to some philosophers, the hypothetical Gödelian undecidable sentence U is not sufficient to undermine bivalence. Let us also assume that these philosophers are correct. A Dummettian intuitionist, *by recourse to philosophical argument*, transforms the hypothetical Gödelian undecidable sentence, U, into a categorical undecidable. Unlike a current undecidable sentence which may at some future date be shown to be decidable, this future possibility of decidability is ruled out in the case of a categorical undecidable.

We focus on three layers to the transformation of the hypothetical Gödelian undecidable sentence U into the categorical undecidable U. The logical layer is the logical principle, *modus ponens* i.e. if p then q and p therefore q, which intuitionist logicians share with classical logicians.[22] The principle *modus ponens* is applied to (i) above: if one can show that the antecedent 'T is consistent' of (i) above is true then by *modus ponens* its consequent, U, is shown to be categorically undecidable. The second layer is a philosophical, not a mathematico-logical, argument to establish that the antecedent of (i), viz. T is consistent, stands up to critical scrutiny and thus is philosophically 'sound' (Dummett 1994b: 331). A central component in this philosophical argument is our shared social arithmetical practices: the number system is indispensable to vast ranges of social interactions based on counting and numerical ordering. These social practices would be meaningless without the natural number system.[23] The third layer is to argue that, since the antecedent of (i) is shown to be philosophically sound it follows that it is philosophically correct to claim that the antecedent of (i), viz. T is consistent, is true. Given this, by *modus ponens* the hypothetical Gödelian undecidable U is categorically undecidable.[24]

The thesis of bivalence in the face of categorical undecidables is, to say the least, paradoxical. On the one hand, we have the categorical undecidability of the Gödelian sentence, U. On the other hand, by the thesis of bivalence, U has in reality a determinate truth value: it is in reality either true or false. There are two ways of resolving this paradox. One is to become a strict intuitionist, i.e. to reject classical logic which is grounded in the thesis of bivalence and replace it with intuitionistic logic and intuitionistic mathematics. The other way of resolving the paradox is to retain the thesis of bivalence in the face of categorical undecidables. According to Dummettian intuitionists this second option of retaining the thesis of bivalence carries a price which they are not willing to pay, namely a resolute commitment to categorical undecidables having determinate truth-values which are forever outside the pale of linguistically bound, mathematical reasoning. In other words it requires postulating beings with logico-mathematical abilities which transcend what is possible for coherent, finitely-bound, linguistic mathematicians. As Dummett states: 'those many people who favour classical over intuitionistic logic are therefore guilty of the presumption of reasoning as if they were God' (Dummett 2008: 109).

To sum up, strict Dummettian intuitionists replace classical mathematics, which is logically flawed, with intuitionist mathematics. Like strict Brouwerian intuitionists, Dummettian intuitionism implies that the neo-Walrasian programme collapses on the four central themes outlined earlier. Firstly, the neo-Walrasian programme misidentifies the domain of discourse of mathematics. Secondly, it incorrectly assumes that classical logic stands up to critical scrutiny. Thirdly, it utterly misconstrues the correct analysis of mathematical existence. Finally, its Brouwerian-type fixed point theorems, central to its proof of existence of equilibrium, are not genuine theorems at all. At its logico-mathematical core, the neo-Walrasian programme, to use Dummett's phrase, 'is incoherent and illegitimate' (Dummett 2000: 250).

Pragmatic intuitionism and economic theorising

In the introduction to this chapter we said that, prima facie, theoretical economists have a genuine choice between constructive and classical mathematics in their programme of the mathematisation of economics. Clearly that is not correct for either a Brouwerian or Dummettian strict intuitionist. For the strict intuitionist – Brouwerian or Dummettian – there is one and only one way of mathematising any theory, including economic theory, namely by recourse to intuitionistic mathematics. The choice we referred to in the introduction applies to pragmatic intuitionism. The pragmatic intuitionist ignores the philosophical grounds for intuitionistic mathematics and focuses on doing intuitionistic mathematics. According to pragmatic intuitionists, classical and intuitionistic mathematics peacefully co-exist. There is no question of, as it were, the colonial expansion of one into the other. Both have distinct, authentic domains. What we call pragmatic intuitionism is summed up by Troelstra and van Dalen in their preface to their *Constructivism in Mathematics* as follows. 'The ending "-ism" has ideological overtones: "constructive mathematics is the (only) right mathematics;" we hasten, however, to declare that we do not subscribe to this ideology ...' (Troelstra and van Dalen 1988: vii). Thus theoretical economists have a genuine choice between the resources of classical mathematics and those of intuitionistic mathematics in their formalisation of economic theory. The methodological issue is the question of the relative merits of the fit between economic content and classical mathematics exploited in the neo-Walrasian programme and the fit between economics and intuitionistic mathematics. By focusing on pragmatic intuitionism we identify two themes in which the fit between economics and intuitionistic mathematics is, ceteris paribus, better than the fit exploited in the neo-Walrasian programme.

The first theme concerns the universe of discourse of intuitionistic mathematics. This domain of discourse is a very general abstract open-ended system, constructed by the human mind. In this connection it is useful to quote Poincaré – the precursor of intuitionistic mathematics. Mathematics 'reflecting upon itself is reflecting upon the human mind which has created it, ... of all its (the mind's) creations, mathematics is the one for which it (the mind) has borrowed least from outside' (Poincaré 1956: 36). In many of its constructions, e.g. a model of an aeroplane, the mind is obliged to exploit the specific empirical characteristics believed to be relevant to the proposed construction. However, the mind in intuitionistic mathematics leaves aside these specific empirical constraints and investigates the logico-mathematical structure of any constructable system – the logic being intuitionistic, not classical. The domain of discourse of intuitionistic mathematics is centrally concerned with what is in principle constructable, where the 'in principle' qualification means subject to the constraints of intuitionistic, not classical, logic. Classical mathematics does not investigate the logico-mathematical structures of an, in principle, constructable system. Its domain of discourse is different to intuitionistic mathematics – the constraints of constructability-in-principle are not relevant to its logico-mathematical investigations. Economies, however, are not natural givens. Economies are very specific, complex, constructed systems. Given that it is a constructed system, an economy, if it can be studied mathematically, the resources of intuitionistic mathematics which are tailored made for what is in principle constructable are a better fit than those of classical mathematics which are not tailored for what is in principle constructable. Orthodox theoretical economists, given their recourse to the full resources of classical mathematics, have no guarantee that their explanations are applicable to what is in principle constructable, whereas by recourse to the resources of intuitionistic mathematics economists are guaranteed that their explanations are applicable to what is in principle constructable. In particular, neo-Walrasian explanations, by recourse to Brouwerian fixed point theorems of classical mathematics, are not shown to be realisable in a logically possible constructable world, never mind our social world of finite historical time.

In the previous theme, we commenced with an in-principle constructable system. In the following theme, we start with the rigorous formalisation of intuitionistic logic by Heyting. Given this starting point, the problematic or challenge is to specify a domain of application or interpretation of this intuitionistic logic. In this second theme we focus on Kolmogorov's 'On the Interpretation of Intuitionistic Logic,' first published in 1932. This short paper is divided into two sections. The first section is directed at those who 'do not accept intuitionistic epistemological assumptions,' while in the second section 'intuitionistic logic is critically investigated while accepting the general intuitionistic assumptions' (Kolmogorov 1998: 328). In line with what we named pragmatic intuitionism, Kolmogorov recognises that both classical and intuitionistic logic have distinct domains of discourse. According to Kolmogorov, classical logic (which he terms theoretical logic) 'systematizes the proof schemata of theoretical truths' (Kolmogorov 1998: 328). He does not elaborate on this characteristic. His primary concern is not with classical logic. Nonetheless, contrary to strict intuitionism, there is no question of claiming that classical logic is fundamentally flawed. Rather Kolmogorov's concern is with Heyting's rigorous formalisation of intuitionistic logic. The challenge is to find a domain of application, different to the domain of application of classical logic, for Heyting's formalisation of intuitionistic logic or, in logical terms, to identify an interpretation of Heyting's formal system. Kolmogorov establishes that Heyting's formalisation of intuitionistic logic systematises a different domain to that of classical logic: it systematises *'the schemata of solutions to problems'* (Kolmogorov 1998: 328). In other words the domain of discourse of classical logic is the domain of theoretical truths and its aim is to systematise the proof schemata of that domain. The domain of discourse of intuitionistic logic is not that of classical logic: its domain is solutions to problems, and its aim is to systematise the schemata of solutions to problems.

Kolmogorov is drawing the mathematical community's attention away from the calculus of classical logic which up to that time dominated mathematical thinking onto what he calls the 'new calculus of problems' (Kolmogorov 1998:

328). This new calculus, like the calculus of classical logic, is well worth developing. 'The proper goal of the calculus of problems consists in giving a method for the solution of problems ... by means of the mechanical application of some simple computational rules' (Kolmogorov 1998: 330). Thus the focus shifts to the computational solutions to problems. Kolmogorov states his central conclusion as follows. 'The following remarkable fact holds: The calculus of problems is formally identical with Brouwerian intuitionistic logic, which has recently been formalised by Mr. Heyting' (Kolmogorov 1998: 328). Thus the framework for the systematic study of constructive solutions to problems is not given by classical logic: rather the correct framework is intuitionistic logic.

Kolmogorov does not define what a problem is; neither does he define the concept of a solution to a problem. Rather he furnishes the reader with examples of problems and their solutions. In this way he hopes to avoid current philosophies of solutions to problems by focusing on what is accepted as problems and solutions in 'concrete areas of mathematics' (Kolmogorov 1998: 329). Clearly Kolmogorov is referring to solutions to mathematical problems. Thus the question arises: how is this related to economic theorising? Economic problems are empirical, not purely mathematical. However, by the process of mathematisation, these economic problems are represented in mathematical terms and then pure mathematics is exploited to solve these problems. Once a solution is found, the economic theoretician finds an economic interpretation for this solution. For instance, take the theoretical problem of whether or not a general equilibrium is possible in some socio-economic arrangement. This problem is represented in mathematical terms and the resources of classical mathematics are used to solve this problem. This solution to the mathematical problem is then given an economic interpretation. A Kolmogorov type objection to this neo-Walrasian approach lies in the method used to solve the mathematical problem. The objection applies to the internal mathematical step of finding a solution to the mathematical problem; it is not concerned with the final step, i.e. to find an economic interpretation to the mathematical solution. *Neo-Walrasians tacitly assume that classical logic, which underpins classical mathematics, is the correct logic of solutions to problems. This assumption is not correct.* The correct logic is intuitionistic, not classical. When intuitionistic logic and mathematics is used, the Debreu neo-Walrasian solution is seen for what it is: it is no solution at all. In short, in so far as economic theory has recourse to mathematics in solving its economic problems, its logic and mathematics must be intuitionistic.

To conclude this section, the external critique of Hilbertian formalism initiated by Brouwer culminated in either strict or pragmatic intuitionism. In strict intuitionism, either Brouwerian or Dummettian, the prognosis for the neo-Walrasian programme is more than bleak: theoretical economists in mathematising their discipline have no choice. The only option open is intuitionistic logic and mathematics. The situation is different for the pragmatic intuitionist. In principle theoretical economists have a genuine choice between classical and intuitionistic mathematics in their programme of mathematisation of economics. By focusing on the fact that an economy is a constructed system and that much of economic theorising is problem solving we outlined how pragmatic intuitionists could argue that the fit between economic theory and intuitionistic mathematics is better than the fit exploited in the neo-Walrasian programme.

The internal critique of formalism and economic theorising

In the previous sections we engaged the mathematisation of economics, especially the neo-Walrasian programme, from the point of view of intuitionistic mathematics introduced by Brouwer. As already pointed out, Hilbertian formalism was a central target of Brouwerian intuitionism. Since Brouwerian intuitionistic mathematics starts with a different vision of mathematics to that of Hilbert, we called the intuitionistic critique of Hilbertian formalism external. In this section we turn to what we called the internal critique of formalism. Among the key logico-mathematical figures in this section are Church, Gödel and Turing. We call this critique of formalism internal for two reasons. Firstly, unlike intuitionism, it does not have recourse to intuitionistic logic; rather it undermines the Hilbertian formalist programme on classical logical grounds. Secondly, this critique, as it were, forensically interrogates the key concepts of consistency, completeness and decidability of the Hilbert programme, culminating in surprising mathematical results. The novel logico-mathematical techniques underpinning these amazing results gave rise to our computer age. These innovative, logico-mathematical techniques also deliver novel alternative ways of mathematically modelling an economy to those exploited in the neo-Walrasian programme.

We divide the internal critique of formalism into two sections. In the following section we introduce the surprising results of Gödel's theorems and explore their implications for the mathematisation of economics. Our conclusion is that while these theorems have adverse implications for Debreu's own formalist philosophy of economic theorising, as such they do not adversely undermine his mathematical representation of an economy. We then return to the issue of undecidables, discussed in our reflections on the impact of intuitionist mathematics on the mathematisation of economics. According to Hilbertian formalism there are no undecidables in mathematics. On the contrary, there is a systematic method for deciding whether or not any mathematical statement is provable. The surprising result that no such systematic method or algorithm exists was established in 1936 by both Church and Turing. This proof of the existence of undecidables in classical mathematics was seismic in the foundations of mathematics. Post Church-Turing one could say that a new, non-formalist image of classical mathematics emerges. Instead of the formalist image of a consistent, complete and decidable meaningless calculus, the new image is that of a semantical system of algorithmetical decidable and algorithmetically undecidable theorems. This gives rise to the methodological issue of how the use of undecidable theorems effect economic modelling. In this connection we argue that the use of undecidable theorems in the neo-Walrasian mathematical model of a private ownership economy renders its explanation of prices economically vacuous.

Gödel's theorems and Debreu's philosophy of economic theorising

A central aim of the Hilbert formalist programme was to establish the consistency, completeness and decidability of the whole edifice of pure, i.e. classical mathematics. Brouwerian considerations aside, the Hilbert school had no reason to be pessimistic about the successful completion of this challenging programme. The first suggestion that all was not well was articulated by Gödel on 7 September 1930 at a conference in Köningsberg. As Dawson remarks, at that time Gödel was virtually unknown outside of Vienna. Indeed at the conference he read a paper summing up the results of his dissertation completed the previous year in which he established 'a result of prime importance for the advancement of Hilbert's programme: the completeness of first order logic' (Dawson 1988: 76). The following day, however, in the course of a discussion on the foundations of mathematics, Gödel made some remarks to the effect that number theory was incomplete! His remarks were largely ignored, with the notable exception of von Neumann. '(A)fter the session he drew Gödel aside and pressed him for details' (Dawson 1988: 77). The rigorous formulation of Gödel's incompleteness remarks was subsequently published in his famous 'On Formally Undecidable Propositions of *Principia Mathematica* and Related Systems I' in January 1931. This paper contains his two incompleteness theorems. The first incompleteness theorem 'shows that any properly axiomatized and consistent theory of basic arithmetic must *remain* incomplete, whatever our efforts to complete it by throwing further axioms into the mix' (Smith 2007: 5). Roughly interpreted, the second incompleteness theory says 'there is no axiomatizable theory of arithmetic which can prove its own consistency' (Epstein and Carnielli 2000: 172).

Von Neumann in March 1951, on the occasion of the award of the Einstein medal to Gödel, said 'Kurt Gödel's achievement in modern logic is singular and monumental – indeed it is more than a monument, it is a landmark which will remain visible far in space and time' (*New York Times*, 15 March: 31, quoted in Kleene 1988: 60). However, as Dawson reminds us, 'we must also recognize the hazard in assessing the cogency of Gödel's arguments from our own perspective' (Dawson 1988: 75). In his brief analysis Dawson's aim is to show that, despite Gödel's own belief that his results were promptly accepted at that time, 'there were doubters and critics as well as defenders and rival claimants to priority' (Dawson 1988: 76). Without getting into such details, it is clear that Gödel's theorems pose a serious challenge to the Hilbert programme: Hilbert's aim of establishing by formal means the consistency and completeness of mathematics is not achievable.

Our concern here, however, is with the philosophy of economics/economic methodology, especially the mathematisation of economic theory. In this connection we make two suggestions. Firstly, Gödel's theorems impact in an adverse way on Debreu's commitment to Hilbertian formalism in his own philosophy of economic theorising. Clearly anyone building a comprehensive case against Debreu's formalist philosophy of economic theorising will, among other themes, have recourse to the negative impact of Gödel's theorems for any such formalism. Secondly, however, Gödel's theorems do not directly impact on Debreu's mathematical representation of the action of an economic agent as a vector in a real vector space, exploited in his *Theory of Value*. Gödel's theorems, unlike strict intuitionism, do not challenge classical mathematics at its logical core. Thus the neo-Walrasian mathematical representation of the actions of an economic agent in terms of real vectors and its recourse to Brouwer's fixed point theorem are not immediately challenged by Gödel's theorems. One might say Gödel's theorems impact on the image of the mathematisation of economics developed by Debreu but they do not as such negatively impact on its substance, in the sense that Debreu's neo-Walrasian mathematical representation of an economy is not directly challenged by Gödel's theorems.

Turing, algorithms and the mathematisation of economics

Kleene draws our attention to another significant aspect of Gödel's theorems, namely 'how seminal his ideas and results have been' (Kleene 1988: 60). One such seminal idea is the reference to undecidable propositions in Gödel's famous paper. This is a reference to the other key aim of the Hilbert programme, namely to resolve the decision problem – the *Entscheidungsproblem*. The decision problem was emphasised by Hilbert as early as 1900 in his famous Paris address. In that address Hilbert maintained that 'in mathematics there is no *ignorabimus*' (Hilbert 1902: 445). As Copeland puts it,

> Hilbert's requirement that the system expressing the whole content of mathematics be *decidable* amounts to this: there must be a systematic method for telling, of each mathematical statement, whether or not the statement is provable in the system. If the system is to banish ignorance totally from mathematics it must be decidable.
>
> (Copeland 2004: 47)

Church gives the following definition of the decision problem.

> By the Entscheidungsproblem of a system of logic is here understood the problem to find an effective method by which, given any expression Q in the notation of the system, it can be determined whether or not Q is provable in the system.
>
> (Church 1936b: 41)

To answer the decision problem one must have a precise definition or articulation of the interchangeable terms, systematic method/effective mechanical procedure/ algorithm. Prior to Hilbert emphasising the significance and centrality of the decision problem, mathematicians did not attempt to precisely define the notion of an algorithm. Normal usage of the term sufficed. In its normal usage an effective mechanical procedure or algorithm was explained by examples and an adjoining commentary. An algorithm, based on these examples, is said to be a set of step-by-step instructions, with each step clearly specified in every detail, thereby ruling out any recourse to imagination, intuition or insight. The steps were thus executed mechanically and the number of steps taken must be finite. Today we would say that an algorithm is any procedure which can be carried out by a modern computer. However, in the 1930s there were no computers: the question 'what precisely is an algorithm?' had to be resolved before one could begin to construct a universal stored-programme computer.

The young British mathematician Alan Mathison Turing resolved this challenge in 1936 in his famous paper 'On Computable Numbers with an application to the Entscheidungsproblem'. In that paper he furnished mathematicians with a precise characterisation of a systematic procedure by outlining an abstract template for a computing machine called the Universal Turing machine. Church sums up Turing's achievement as follows. 'The notion of an effective computation, or algorithm is one for which it would be possible to build a computing machine. This idea is developed into a rigorous definition by A.M. Turing ...' (Church 1956: 52). In a note added in 1963 to his famous 1931 paper Gödel sums up as follows.

> In consequence of later advances, in particular of the fact that due to A.M. Turing's work, a precise and unquestionably adequate definition of the general notion of formal system can now be given ... it can be proved rigorously that *every* consistent formal system that contains a certain amount of finitary number theory there exist undecidable arithmetic propositions and that, moreover the consistency of any such system cannot be proved in the system.
>
> (Gödel 1988: 40–41)

In his paper Turing furnished the mathematical community with a novel and accurate analysis of the received notion of algorithmetic reasoning used by mathematicians. He established that our contemporary notion of an algorithm as a process which could be carried out by a computing machine is correct. Thus his paper is the source of our contemporary notion of an algorithm. Indeed his paper was used by electronic engineers in Manchester. Their work culminated in the construction of the world's first electronic stored-programme digital computer in 1948. Secondly, as Gödel points out, Turing's paper eliminated any reservations one might have had about the existence of undecidables in mathematics. Thus Turing's paper sounded the final death knell of the original Hilbert formalist programme by establishing the existence of undecidables in mathematics.

Vis-à-vis the challenge of mathematising economics, unfortunately this death knell was not heard by Debreu. As we saw in the last section, Gödel's incompleteness theorems undermined Debreu's own formalist philosophy of economic theorising. Turing's results go much further: in our post-Turing mathematical world the economic substance of Debreu's theorising is, it could be argued, also undermined. An economy is a specific, constructed finite system. Because of the finite nature of economies, a minimum condition on the proof of the existence of an economic equilibrium is that it is in principle realisable in a finite number of steps. If an equilibrium is not realisable in a finite number of steps, however large, it lies outside the domain of the finite. Debreu's proof of the existence of equilibrium fails to meet this minimum requirement, precisely because it is grounded in algorithmetically undecidable propositions. For instance, as Velupillai has demonstrated, 'a Walrasian equilibrium vector price is undecidable' (Velupillai 2002: 318) and 'the Walrasian excess demand function is undecidable, i.e. it cannot be determined algorithmetically' (Velupillai 2006: 363).[25] *Prima facie* any entity which is claimed to exist on grounds which include an undecidable mathematical proposition, lies outside the domain of the finite. In this connection it is crucial to note the following difference between theoretical physics and neo-Walrasian theorising. Advanced theoretical physics has at its disposal a vast and sophisticated range of experimental techniques which, at times, enable it to establish the actual existence of some of its theoretically postulated entities. In the absence of such experimental verification, theoretical physics suspends judgment on claims of actual existence. As emphasised by Debreu and Hahn, however, neo-Walrasian economics lacks recourse to that kind of experimental verification of its existence claims. Given that this kind of sophisticated experimental verification is not to be expected and that its proof of the existence of equilibrium hinges on undecidable propositions, neo-Walrasian economists have no justification for either claiming or assuming their equilibrium could exist within any finite economic domain. In short their non-algorithmetic proof of the existence of equilibrium renders their notion of equilibrium economically vacuous.

According to Debreu, his *Theory of Value* furnishes economists with a rigorous model which is 'the explanation of the prices of commodities resulting from the interaction of the agents of a private ownership economy through markets' (Debreu 1959: vii) – an explanation which was pioneered by Walras and Pareto. The thesis here is that the recourse to undecidables in this model undermines its explanatory capacity. Undoubtedly as a piece of pure classical mathematics, Debreu's *Theory of Value* attains the highest standards of rigour as characterised by Hilbertian formalists. However, the combination of two crucial characteristics of classical mathematics undermines the economic interpretation of Debreu's mathematics and thus its explanation of prices. Firstly, the universe of discourse of classical mathematics is Cantorian actual infinity which transcends the limitations of any finite domain. Indeed it transcends the potentially infinite domain of the natural numbers. Secondly, classical mathematics has recourse to *non-algorithmetic* methods of proof. This recourse is clearly illustrated by Poincaré. He takes Zermelo's theorem which proves 'that space is capable of being transformed into a well-ordered set' (Poincaré 1963: 67). Poincaré asks the classical mathematician to actually carry out the transformation but is told that it would take too long. To this Poincaré responds, 'then at least show us that someone with enough time and patience could execute the transformation'

(Poincaré 1963: 67). The classical mathematician responds, 'No, we cannot because the number of operations to be performed is infinite, it is even greater than aleph zero' (Poincaré 1963: 67). Poincaré's concern was with pure mathematics. Our concern is with the application of this pure mathematics which contains undecidable propositions to the interaction of finitely bound agents in finitely bound markets. These economic agents process their information via language and this processing takes time. Thus this processing must be capable of being carried out in a finite number of steps. In particular, price signals must be capable of being processed in a finite number of steps. However, as the Poincaré example above indicates, the use of undecidable propositions in Debreu's *Theory of Value* means that its price signals cannot be processed in a finite number of steps.

Neo-Walrasians forget that the price of the application of a piece of pure classical mathematics to the interaction of agents of a private ownership economy is eternal vigilance. Economic agents process all their information, including price signals, within the constraints of time. However, pure classical mathematicians, unlike Poincaré, have no reservations about abstracting from the limitations of time in their efforts at achieving consistency. The upshot of this is that classical mathematics divides into theorems which are algorithmetically decidable and those which are not algorithmetically decidable. In their application of classical mathematics to the interaction of economic agents, the neo-Walrasians fail to pay attention to this crucial distinction. In their model of a private ownership economy they use undecidable theorems in their explanation of prices which means that its price signals cannot be processed in any finite time horizon.

To sum up, the proof of the existence of undecidables in classical mathematics in the 1930s was seismic within the foundations of mathematics. We contend that it is also seismic for the programme of the mathematisation of economics. Prior to the amazing results of Gödel and Turing, the Hilbertian formalists were not alone in assuming that there is no ignorabimus in classical mathematics. Numerous philosophers of mathematics and practising mathematicians with no affiliation to Hilbertian formalism shared that commitment. Given that commitment to the decidability of classical mathematics, the use of the full resources of classical mathematics in an applied domain was not problematical. In that vein numerous theoretical economists saw no reason why they should not exploit the full resources of classical mathematics in their economic theorising. Indeed various, post-World War Two, pioneering theoretical economists explicitly advocated this exploitation. Gödel's and Turing's research, however, shattered the assumption that there is no ignorabimus in classical mathematics. Turing proved that undecidables exist within classical mathematics. This truth has fundamental implications for the mathematisation of economics. The use of undecidable propositions in economic modelling presupposes one has abstracted from any and every consideration of the linguistic-boundedness of economic information which is processed in a finite number of steps, however large. Thus any explanation of prices grounded in a mathematical model of an economy which exploits undecidables is economically vacuous: its mathematical representation of price signals is such that they cannot be processed in a finite number of steps.

Thus far we have kept three strands in the methodological critique of General Equilibrium Theory quite separate, namely (1) the critique inspired by strict intuitionism (Brouwerian or Dummettian), (2) the critique inspired by pragmatic intuitionism, and (3) the critique inspired by the Turing proof of the existence of undecidables. The critique inspired by strict intuitionism is, perhaps, the most radical. General Equilibrium Theory is fundamentally illogical. The only logic available to both the pure and applied mathematician is intuitionistic logic. Classical logic is fundamentally flawed. In contrast to strict intuitionists, pragmatic intuitionists are not just tolerant: they are pluralists. Classical mathematics, rooted in classical logic, is legitimate. Equally intuitionistic mathematics, rooted in intuitionistic logic, is legitimate. Classical mathematics pertains to a Cantorian infinite universe of discourse whereas intuitionistic logic, being the logic of problem-solving, pertains to a potentially infinite domain of discourse. Thus existence proofs using classical mathematics fails to guarantee existence in either a potentially infinite domain or a finite domain. However, recourse to intuitionistic mathematics, with its methods of proof confined to constructive ones, necessarily limits its application to what is in principle constructable and is thus more appropriate than classical mathematics to economic theorising. The third critique, inspired by Turing's proof of the existence of undecidables in classical mathematics, is distinct from these other two critiques. Turing's conclusion is, as already noted, based on classical, not intuitionistic, logic. Post-Turing classical mathematics divides into algorithmetically decidable and algorithmetically undecidable theorems. The third critique of General Equilibrium Theory – which is not an experimental science – maintains that its mathematical model of an economy uses algorithmetically undecidables and thus fails to have explanatory value.

An algorithmetic revolution in economic theorising?

In the previous section we followed Gödel in giving the laurels to Turing. It could be argued that Alanzo Church at Princeton equally deserves these laurels. In the early 1930s Church was exploring logical systems by recourse to a specific formal procedure, called the lambda calculus. Roughly speaking, a function of positive integers is lambda definable if the values of the function can be calculated by a process of repeated iteration. In the autumn of 1931, when von Neumann addressed the mathematics colloquium, Church became aware of Gödel's theorems. According to Kleene 'Church's immediate reaction was that his formal system … is sufficiently different from the systems Gödel dealt with that Gödel's second theorem might not apply to it' (Kleene 1981: 52). The significance of von Neumann's address, however, was that Church and his students engaged Gödel's original paper. Thus in 1934 when Gödel delivered a series of lectures on his incompleteness theorems, his audience was more than attentive and very well informed.

From the point of view of economic methodology what is significant for us is that in those lectures Gödel advanced ideas of Herbrand about the most general form of recursiveness resulting in what is known as Herbrand-Gödel general recursiveness. For our methodological purposes it suffices to say that Herbrand-Gödel general recursiveness is a generalisation of the elementary inductive-recursive definitions of addition and multiplication. Thus we have two distinct concepts, namely lambda definability and recursion. In 1936 Church published two famous papers, viz. 'An unsolvable problem of elementary number theory' and 'A note on the Entscheidungsproblem', The results of these papers became known as the Church Thesis. The Church Thesis has three dimensions. Firstly, like Turing, Church formalises the received, pre-theoretical notion of an algorithm. However, unlike Turing, he formalises it in terms of his lambda calculus. In other words the lambda calculus is also a rigorous technical replacement of the received pre-theoretical notion of an algorithm. Thus an effective calculable function is lambda definable. Secondly, Herbrand-Gödel recursiveness and lambda definability are equivalent. In other words when we analyse the received notion of an effective procedure/algorithm in terms of lambda definability or in terms of Herbrand-Gödel recursiveness we obtain the same class of functions. The lambda procedure can be translated in Herbrand-Gödel recursiveness in such a way that the two formalisations have the same outputs for the same inputs. Thirdly, like Turing, there are undecidables in mathematics. When Church's results are combined with those of Turing we have the famous Church-Turing thesis. In simple terms the Church-Turing thesis states that the various rigorously formalised systems, such as a Turing machine, the lambda calculus and recursion theory, proposed as a rigorous explication or formulation of the inherited, informal concept of an effective mechanical procedure or algorithm, are equivalent. Thus, for instance, every Turing computable function is recursive and every recursive function is Turing computable.[26]

Vis-à-vis the philosophy of economic theorising, the Church-Turing thesis has nothing new to add to the negative assessment of general equilibrium outlined in the previous section. Mathematics post the Church-Turing thesis enables methodologists to highlight the role of undecidables in general equilibrium theorising. Rather the additional significance of the Church-Turing thesis lies in its expansion of the conceptual resources beyond those of a universal Turing machine which theoretical economists could exploit in addressing various challenges which are bound to arise in the course of the algorithmetic mathematisation of economics. At the pragmatic level, the Church-Turing thesis identifies a rich reservoir of algorithmetic concepts which may be exploited in specific problem situations by the theoretical economist. Despite the fact that ultimately one is operating with the same set of functions, pragmatically in a specific problem situation one may find the concepts used in a Turing machine very cumbersome, whereas the resources of recursion theory may be more easily adapted to the problem or vice versa. We call this range of algorithmetic mathematics computable mathematics.

Computable mathematics, under the rubric of the Church-Turing thesis, by its very nature avoids the undecidable theorems of classical mathematics and is thus in principle applicable to any finite open-ended constructable system. Our question is whether or not computable mathematics has the potential to enrich our understanding of real economies? Prima facie one may claim that the prospects are good and indeed are fairly well advanced, as is evident in computable general equilibrium theory pioneered by Scarf in the 1970s. In the preface to his *Computation of Economic Equilibria*, Scarf opens with the following:

> One of the major triumphs of mathematical economics during the past quarter of a century has been the proof of the existence of a solution for the neoclassical model of economic equilibrium. This demonstration has provided one of the rare instances in which abstract mathematical techniques are indispensable in order to solve a problem of central importance to economic theory.
>
> (Scarf 1973: ix)

This major triumph was accomplished by among others Gerard Debreu, Scarf's 'good friend and valued advisor' (Scarf 1973: x). Thus according to Scarf the triumph of the proof of the existence of general equilibrium by recourse to fixed point theorems is central to his programme of the computation of economic equilibria. In this vein he points out that 'the central problem of this monograph is the description of an efficient computational procedure for the approximation of a fixed point of a continuous mapping' (Scarf 1973: 12). Thus Scarf's programme is an original synthesis of General Equilibrium Theory à la Debreu and the resources of computable mathematics.

A Scarf-type computable general equilibrium theory is *not* what we have in mind in referring to the possibility of a computable revolution in economics. The computable revolution we wish to address is a more radical programme, where the economic theoretician is, without exception, confined to the resources of computable mathematics – a programme advocated over a number of decades by Velupillai. In the opening page of the Festschrift in honour of Professor Kumaraswamy Vela Velupillai, edited by Zambelli, it is claimed that Velupillai 'is the founder of computable economics, a growing field of research where important results stemming from classical recursion theory and constructive mathematics are applied to economic theory. The aim and hope is to provide new tools for economic modelling' (Zambelli 2010: I). According to Velupillai, while Scarf must be given due recognition among the pioneers or precursors of computable economics, Scarf's approach is basically:

> schizophrenic: proof of existence in one domain; implementation of an algorithm to find the provable existent entity in quite a different domain. As a result, the algorithm cannot, in general, locate the fixed point even approximately. This is so because the algorithm cannot, in any effective constructive sense, be given meaningful information about the characteristic of the entity, it is supposed to locate.
>
> (Velupillai 2002: 316)

In Kaldor's metaphor, once the scaffolding of algorithmetic procedures used for the purposes of approximation are removed, one is left with the non-computable classical mathematics of Debreu exemplified by Brouwer's fixed point theorem, which cannot be coherently interpreted in the real historical time of economic systems. Instead of the dualism of non-computable existence proofs combined with computable procedures for estimating approximations, in the computable revolution proposed by Velupillai theoretical economists confine their mathematical resources to computable mathematics under the rubric of the Church-Turing thesis. As Zambelli puts it 'any reasoning in terms of economic theory is meaningful only if one can produce an effective algorithm for the solution of a problem' (Zambelli 2010: 34).[27] In this radical programme computable economics 'is about basing economic formalisms on recursion-theoretical fundamentals. This means we will have to view economic entities, economic actions and economic institutions as computable objects or algorithms' (Velupillai 2000: 2). For instance just as Debreu describes the action of an economic agent by a vector in the commodity space R_l where the commodity space has the mathematical structure of a real vector space, in Velupillai's computable economics one can describe the action of an economic agent as if it 'were a Turing machine; in this case the commodity space would have an appropriate recursive structure ...' (Velupillai 2000: 3).

For readers not familiar with the details of recursion theory or a universal Turing machine, a useful way of approaching Velupillai's computable economics is to start with another major precursor, namely Herbert Simon. Simon's bounded rationality critique of the orthodox model of economic rationality is well known. In this connection Velupillai is surely correct in claiming that 'Simon's research programme pointed the way towards computable economics in a precise sense' (Velupillai 2000: 25). Indeed in correspondence with Velupillai in relation to his *Computable Economics* Simon points out:

> There are many levels of complexity in problems, and corresponding boundaries between them. Turing computability is an outer boundary and as you show, any theory that requires more power than that surely is irrelevant to any useful definition of human rationality.
>
> (Simon 2010: 409)

Clearly, in Simon's opinion, Velupillai succeeds in undermining the orthodox mathematical model of rationality by proving that it is located outside the outer boundary of human rationality – no mean achievement. Moreover one could argue that Velupillai's computable economics goes further. Velupillai takes Simon's fertile, related concepts of rationality and satisficing and re-interprets these within the sophisticated mathematical architecture of computable mathematics. In this fashion he completely undermines the orthodox assumption that Simon's bounded rationality approach is no match for the mathematical sophistication and elaboration of the orthodox model of rationality. He does this by placing economic agents and institutions in a decision theoretic context.

He then shows how to reformalise economic agents and institutions so understood in algorithmetic terms, thereby embedding the insightful concepts of bounded rationality and satisficing behaviour in the sophisticated mathematical architecture of computable mathematics. In this way his programme undermines 'the conventional misconception that a bounded rational agent is simply orthodox's omnipotent substantively rational agent cognitively constrained in various *ad hoc* ways; and that satisficing is simply a "second best" optimization outcome' (Velupillai 2005b: 173). Rather the bounded rational agent is a Turing machine. In this model, unlike the orthodox optimising model, the theoretical economist faces up to incompleteness and undecidability.

It is not our intention to outline Velupillai's defence of his programme of computable economics. Velupillai's defence constitutes an original, detailed, highly sophisticated and nuanced philosophy (methodology) of economic theorising. Rather we refer to his research programme in the spirit of constructivism: it concretely demonstrates that a prima facie case actually exists for the radical programme of a comprehensive algorithmetic mathematisation of economic theorising. This research programme offers the promise of providing new and innovative theoretical foundations for a digital economy. This, in our opinion, includes the possibility of modelling an economy, conceived as vast dynamical system of interacting markets capable of self-reproduction and evolution in terms of Turing-machine, cellular automata pioneered by von-Neumann, e.g. Mirowski's markomata.[28] It also opens up the possibility of the economic exploration by computer simulation. Of course whether or not this novel research agenda of computable economics will succeed depends on whether or not it actually delivers on its initial promise. As one moves from thin to thick descriptions of economic agents and markets whether or not algorithmetic models will deliver fresh insights for both economists and economic policy decision makers is an issue to be settled by future economic research. However, the value of openness in the search for truth which has inspired the scientific mind over the ages points to the need for more detailed research in this potentially challenging research programme of algorithmetic economics.

Notes

1 As noted by Troelstra and van Dalen, there are 'considerable differences in outlook' between various representatives of constructivism (Troelstra and van Dalen 1988: 1). In their opening introductory chapter they give a very brief account of some similarities and differences. In this work we do not dwell on these differences. Rather, like Troelstra and van Dalen, we focus on a number of constructivist trends. The selected trends are significant for economic methodology. Of course the theoretical economist who wishes to exploit constructive mathematics will have to pay more attention to these differences among constructivists.
2 One recalls the resistance to the seventeenth century scientific revolution by various institutions, academic and otherwise.
3 The curious reader could do worse than consult van Dalen's (2005) excellent, two volume biography of Brouwer, *Mystic, Geometer and Intuitionist*.

4 As for instance van Stigt points out, in his *Life, Art and Mysticism* Brouwer 'rails against industrial pollution and man's domination of nature through his intellect and against established social structures and promotes a return to "Nature" and to mystic and solitary contemplation' (van Stigt 1998: 5).

5 Brouwer focuses on the Kantian intuition of time and ignores the Kantian intuition of space. This could be due to the influence of Poincaré on Brouwer. Poincaré's philosophy of geometry undermined Kant's intuitive approach to geometry.

6 More precisely, as we will see later, classical logic combined with Cantorian set theory is the source of the paradoxes.

7 In this presentation of strict intuitionism, we, à la Heyting, emphasize intuitionistic logic. As van Stigt points out, Brouwer, while approving of Heyting's contribution to logic, 'remained true to his conviction than engagement in logic is an interesting but irrelevant and sterile exercise' (van Stigt 1998: 276). Brouwer, in line with J.S. Mill, holds that deductive logic merely makes explicit what is implicit in the premises and thus cannot advance mathematical knowledge. Moreover Brouwer was suspicious of all languages, natural and artificial and contemporary logic requires an artificial, ideal language. These two factors help explain Brouwer's negative attitude to logic which may seem surprising to the contemporary reader.

8 Principles or rules of inference other than the principle of the excluded middle are rejected by intuitionists. Troelstra and van Dalen (1988: 12) give a brief list of classical logical principles rejected by intuitionists.

9 For instance, Debreu points out that in the case of perfect competition, integration theory was invented to 'solve the problem of aggregating negligible quantities so as to obtain a nonnegligible sum ... That application requires the set of agents to be large – larger than the set of integers' (Debreu 1991: 3). To a large number of pragmatic economists this sounds like science fiction: it throws no light on a real economy.

10 In this and previous chapters we focused on the formalist's conception of mathematical existence in terms of freedom from inconsistency. This is not the only philosophy of mathematical existence presupposed in classical mathematics. Frege, for instance, gives us a realist (Platonic) philosophy of mathematical existence, where mathematical entities subsist in a Platonic world independent of the physical world on the one hand and the mind on the other. Both the formalist and realist notions of mathematical existence are rejected by intuitionists.

11 In his 1921 article, 'On the New Foundational Crisis in Mathematics,' Weyl, one of Hilbert's most outstanding pupils, claimed '... and Brouwer – that is the revolution' (Weyl 1998: 99). Weyl's conversion to intuitionism sounded the alarm bells for Hilbert. From 1925, according to Mancosu, Weyl 'attempts to take a middle stand between Hilbert and Brouwer' (Mancosu 1998: 80).

12 Under the influence of Hilbert's formalism, a group of French mathematicians, writing under the pseudonym, Nicholas Bourbaki, beginning in the 1930s, attempted in their *Élements de Mathématique* to give an authoritative summing up of existing mathematical knowledge in the most rigorous way possible. This work was influential both inside and outside France. Vilks (1995) gives an interesting summary of the Bourbaki project's influence on the mathematization of theoretical economics.

13 See, for instance, Weintraub and Mirowski (1994) and Weintraub (2002).

14 The Brouwerian scholar van Stigt (1998) also emphasizes this point.

15 As we already noted that J.S. Mill, for instance maintained that deductive logic does not lead to new knowledge. Thus there is more to creative mathematics than logic. If Brouwer had followed Poincaré on his intriguing analysis of the indispensable roles of both logic and intuition in mathematics, Brouwer would not have given hostage to fortune in remarking that logic is an irrelevant and sterile exercise. To distinguish Poincaré's approach to foundational questions from his own, Brouwer places Poincaré into 'old intuitionism' (Brouwer 1998: 55). For an interesting account of some of the differences between Poincaré and Brouwer see Heinzmann

and Nabonnard (2008). Certainly the present authors believe that the passing remark by Troelstra and van Dalen, i.e. 'one should not, however, expect too much consistency in Poincaré's philosophical writings' (Troelstra and van Dalen 1988: 19), does not do justice to Poincaré's sophisticated analysis of the indispensable role of both logic and of intuition in mathematics. If one were looking for a one sentence summary of Poincaré's view of the indispensable role of intuition in mathematics, the following would not be too misleading: intuition is to discernment and judgment in mathematics what wisdom is to discernment and judgment in practical reasoning.

16 Some intuitionistic mathematicians would not agree with this assessment. They link Brouwerian philosophical psychology to Husserl's phenomenological psychology.

17 We will examine the implications of pragmatic intuitionism for the mathematization of economics in the section after the next.

18 Since the late 1950s Dummett has exerted a dominant influence on British philosophy. Frege, Wittgenstein and Brouwerian intuitionism are the principal influences on Dummett's research. We suggest McGuinness and Oliveri (1994) *The Philosophy of Michael Dummett* as a must for an exploration of its intriguing challenges. Dummett's Intellectual Autobiography is contained in Auxier and Hahn (2007) *The Philosophy of Michael Dummett*.

19 In later sections we will meet, for instance, Velupillai's critique of the neo-Walrasian programme.

20 One could say that the doctrine of bivalence is just another way of expressing the classical logical principle of the excluded middle. This would hold for pre-twentieth-century logicians who maintained that the principle of the excluded middle is among the fundamental principles of all thought. However, in the twentieth century axiomatisation of classical logic, the principle of the excluded middle does not appear among the axioms. Rather it is a theorem. However, this axiomatised logic is grounded on the doctrine of bivalence, i.e. every proposition has a determinate truth-value, irrespective of whether or not we know which one actually applies.

21 The curious reader should consult Wright (1994) and Dummett (1963 1994a,1994b) for more information on the range of issues at play have.

22 More precisely, intuitionistic and classical logicians agree on the outcomes of numerous applications of the *modus ponens* rule of inference. However, since they differ in their respective understandings of logical implication, they do not agree on the meaning of the *modus ponens* rule of inference.

23 For some philosophical traditions the philosophical challenge to establish that the antecedent, T is consistent, of (i) is true is not very difficult. For instance in the Kantian philosophical tradition the axioms of elementary arithmetic are synthetic a priori truths. Since truths implies consistency then the antecedent, T is consistent, is true. Neither is this challenge problematical for a strict Brouwerian intuitionist. Neither of these methods is open to strict Dummettian intuitionists. Rather in line with Frege, they argue that the number system is endemic to our thoughts about the world. The denial of the natural number system would render coherent thought impossible. This is a philosophical thesis.

24 This is a very adumbrated presentation of the strict Dummettian argument. See note 21.

25 Zambelli lists some of Velupillai's results as follows:

- 'there is no effective [universal] procedure to generate preference orderings' (Velupillai 2000: 38). The generation of preference ordering is undecidable or 'rational choice, understood as maximizing choice, is undecidable' (Velupillai 2008c: 8)
- The Walrasian excess demand '$X(p\star)$ is undecidable, i.e., it cannot be determined algorithmetically' (Velupillai 2006b: 363). Alternatively the existence of a 'Walrasian equilibrium price vector is undecidable' (Velupillai 2002: 318)
- 'Uzawa equivalence theorem is neither constructive nor computable' (Velupillai 2005: 862)

- 'The Recursive Competitive Equilibrium of New Classical Macroeconomics, Recursive Macroeconomic Theory, is uncomputable' (Velupillai 2008b: 10)
- 'Scarf's Computable General Equilibrium is neither computable nor constructive' (Velupillai 2006b)
- 'neither the first nor the second welfare theorems are computationally feasible in the precise sense of computability theory and constructive analysis' (Velupillai 2007b: 27–28)
- 'Nash equilibria of finite games are constructively indeterminate' (Velupillai 2008b: 21), (Zambelli 2010: 37–38).

26 It should be noted that the Church-Turing thesis is neither a mathematical definition nor a mathematical theorem. This is so, because mathematics establishes relationships between and only between rigorously formulated concepts, whereas the Church-Turing thesis is primarily concerned with the inherited, but not rigorously formulated concept of an effective mechanical procedure. It is summing up a most amazing fact, viz. all of the above attempts at rigorously formalizing the informal or inherited notion of a computable function yield exactly the same class of functions (See Boylan and O'Gorman (2010) for more details).

27 Here we are emphasizing the computable aspect of Velupillai's research programme. Velupillai himself invokes both computable and Brouwerian constructivist mathematics. According to Zambelli 'among the purists in *classical recursion* theory and the purists in *constructive mathematics* there would be disagreement with this (Velupillai's) somewhat unorthodox view' (Zambelli 2010: 34). It is beyond the scope of this work to critically engage the full implications of Velupillai's research programme, especially the manner in which he exploits both Brouwerian constructivism and computable mathematics in his theorising. In this connection one should recall that Velupillai is above all a mathematical theoretical economist whose interest is the scientific study of real economies. Since economies are finite systems and since Brouwerian constructivists insist that the principle of the excluded middle holds for finite systems, but not for potentially infinite ones, we feel that there is nothing paradoxical in the manner in which Velupillai synergizes both Brouwerian intuitionistic mathematics and computable mathematics. While at the level of pure mathematics the Church-Turing thesis does not hold in Brouwerian intuitionistic/constructivist mathematics, as Dummett points out, 'it is indeed true that Church's Thesis is, when expressed in a suitable form, demonstrably consistent with most intuitionistic formal systems …' (Dummett 2000: 186). In our view one could argue that the logic used in all discourse is intuitionistic but in economics this logic is applied to a finite domain where the principle of the excluded middle is a law-like empirical truth. There is no logical paradox in that viewpoint.

28 The economic methodologist interested in this aspect of what we call computable economics should read Zambelli's (2007) critique of Mirowski's thesis and Rosser Jr's (2010) attempted reconciliation. In our opinion in any new research programme it is too much to expect complete consensus on all matters on the part of those advocating the new research programme. Thus in this work we do not engage the differences between Mirowski and Velupillai. Rather we emphasize their similarities.

8   Economics, mathematics and science

Philosophical reflections

Introduction

In the previous chapters we considered a variety of chords linking issues in economic methodology to issues in the philosophy of mathematics. In this chapter we attempt to weave these chords together. In this attempt we pose the general question: what is the contribution of the philosophy of mathematics to the philosophy of economics/economic methodology? What value is added to the philosophy of economics by making the philosophy of mathematics an indispensable branch? We are shifting the focus from the very specific issues discussed in the previous chapters to a more macroscopic viewpoint.

In praise of the philosophy of mathematics

The philosophy of mathematics makes an invaluable contribution to the critical reading of pioneering works in the formalisation of economics, such as Walras's *Elements* or Debreu's *Theory of Value*. We are fully aware that this practice is obsolete in undergraduate courses and indeed that some eminent economists see no economic value in it. Rather this practice is more central to both the history of economic thought and to the philosophy of economics. The philosophy of mathematics enriches any objective hermeneutical analysis of such texts, in the contemporary sense of hermeneutics. An integral part of such hermeneutical studies is the contextualisation of such canonical texts in their own socio-historical contexts which, given the texts in question, includes the philosophy of mathematics. In this connection we explored the philosophico–mathematical context of the end of the nineteenth and the beginning of the twentieth centuries by using Poincaré's philosophy of applied mathematics to unearth some of the distinguishing characteristics of Walras's own scientific realist defence of theoretical economics as an applied mathematical science on par with the applied mathematical science of mechanics. As already noted, the choice of Poincaré's philosophy of mathematics was motivated by two facts. Firstly Poincaré was then recognised as a towering, and for some, the towering, figure in mathematics across Europe. Secondly Walras wrote to Poincaré for support for the project of the formalisation of economics in what Walras perceived as a hostile environment. By the 1950s when Debreu came to write his *Theory of Value* this hostility had largely disappeared. Moreover, under the shadow of Hilbert's formalist school, the conceptions of pure and of applied mathematics were dramatically altered from the Walras-Poincaré period. Debreu locates his *Theory of Value* in this new Hilbertian mathematico-philosophical climate. The uniqueness and sophistication of Debreu's mathematico-economic commitments are explored by recourse to the Hilbertian formalist school's understanding of the role of mathematics in the applied mathematical sciences.

In addition to enhancing our understanding of the unique philosophies of economic theory of Walras and Debreu, the philosophy of mathematics throws new light on some other developments in twentieth-century economics. In particular we focused on post-Keynesian economics and its emphasis on the role of conventions in economic decision-making in the face of radical uncertainty. In line with Keynes's advice to engage other domains where recourse to conventions occurs, various scholars have focused on either David Hume's or David Lewis's intriguing reflections on conventions. This debate on the rationality of conventions in post-Keynesian economics is enhanced and extended by reflecting on another major contributor to the philosophy of conventions, namely Poincaré. By the turn of the twentieth century Poincaré, in his philosophy of mathematics, had pioneered his famous thesis of geometrical conventionalism, a thesis which incidentally was critically engaged by Bertrand Russell. By focusing on mathematical research at the frontiers of pure geometry, Poincaré showed how the received axiomatic image of mathematical rationality is fundamentally incomplete. Mathematical explorations at the frontiers of geometrical research show that in order to develop any metrical geometry, i.e. a geometry which engages distance, the pure mathematician must have recourse to convention. Thus any complete portrait of mathematical rationality must include recourse to convention. By bringing this amazing result to bear on Davidson's emphasis on the non-ergodic dimension of the economic world, we show how economic decision-making in the face of radical uncertainty is rational in a way which does not reduce its rationality to the orthodox characterisation of rationality.

More generally, recourse to the philosophy of mathematics alerts us to the disputed nature of various logico-mathematical concepts used in economic theorising. For instance, logico-mathematical geniuses of the calibre of Brouwer, Frege and Hilbert fail to agree on how the logical concept of existence is to be understood and used. Thus where Debreu claims to prove the existence of equilibrium we saw that he understood existence as defined by Hilbert, namely freedom from contradiction. This notion of existence was challenged by both Frege and Brouwer: there is more to the logical concept of existence than freedom from contradiction. Pragmatic minded economists, some perhaps under the influence of Hahn who advised young economists to ignore methodology, might want to claim that the disputed nature of much of the philosophy of mathematics is all the more reason for ignoring it. One would, as it were, be immersed in dispute after dispute, like the above. Certainly philosophers of mathematics wash their dirty linen in public, a practice which is perhaps less common in economics. That of course is not to say that total consensus reigns among orthodox economists: as we saw in Chapter Five, Hahn, for instance, castigated some of his American colleagues. Disputes like the above in the philosophy of mathematics, however, reflect fundamental differences between the very best logico-mathematical minds. The fact that brilliant logico-mathematical minds, such as Brouwer, Frege, Hilbert and Russell, to mention but a few, fail to agree on fundamentals cannot be easily dismissed. In particular pretending to have mathematical certainty in one's economic theorising, where such a certainty is not available, rationally leaves a lot to be desired. The integration of the philosophy of mathematics into economic methodology plays a key role here in that it makes explicit what is implicit in the mathematical choices of economic theoreticians and thereby enriches our appreciation of those choices.

Philosophy of mathematics: a new formalisation of economic theorising?

In addition to making a unique and indispensable contribution to the methodological analysis of the complex process of the formalisation of economics, particular developments in the philosophy of mathematics offer philosophers of economics a range of critical tools for their task of the objective evaluation of the orthodox formalisation of economics. In this connection we focused on three major developments in the philosophy of mathematics, viz. the emergence of the twentieth-century modal logic, Brouwerian intuitionism and the Church-Turing thesis. The development of modal logic buttresses Arrow's reservation vis-à-vis the adequacy of classical mathematics in the orthodox modelling of economic decision-making. Arrow correctly draws our attention to the fact that classical mathematics is grounded in classical logic which is extensional. Research in empirical psychology, however, shows that decision-making is intentional. Arrow's reservation raises the critical methodological issue of the empirical adequacy of the representation of economic decision-making in its recourse to extensional classical mathematics. We considered two responses in the philosophy of mathematics available to economic methodologists. The first response is to argue that extensional logic is the one and only true logic. Hence any decision-making which does not conform to extensional logic is illogical and therefore irrational. We draw the reader's attention to the lack of consensus on this philosophical thesis of the reduction of the whole of logic to classical extensional logic. Some who disagree with this reductionist thesis have developed modal logic to rigorously analyse the domain of the intentional. For these there is no objection to the rigorous analysis/formalisation of economic decision-making in terms of non-extensional modal logic. In short the results of empirical psychology combined with the development of modal logic suggest an alternative path to the formalisation of economic decision-making. Classical mathematics may be used in some economic modelling but not in the rigorous formalisation of economic decision- making: here the economic theoretician would have recourse to the rigorous resources of modal logic.

The critique of the orthodox formalisation of economics sourced in the development of intuitionism is much more radical. As we saw, strict intuitionism, either in its original Brouwerian interpretation or in its philosophical reformulation by Dummett, challenges the logico-mathematical core of classical mathematics. Much of classical mathematics has to be abandoned and replaced by intuitionistic mathematics. Consequently the orthodox formalisation of economics is based on a mathematics which does not stand up to critical scrutiny and thus must be abandoned. Of course, given the project of the formalisation of economics, recourse to classical mathematics was, prior to intuitionism, obviously unchallenged: classical mathematics was the only rigorous mathematics available. For the strict intuitionist, however, intuitionistic-constructive mathematics, rather than classical mathematics, is the one and only rigorous mathematics to be used in any mathematical modelling. Thus for the strict intuitionist there is no objection in principle to the formalisation of economics: rather the fundamental error of the orthodox formalisation lies in its exploitation of the pseudo-theorems of classical mathematics. Pragmatically we recognise that the chances of a strict intuitionistic revolution in the formalisation of economics taking place are not good. In addition to the subtleties of a defensible strict intuitionistic philosophy of mathematics, the lack of familiarity of intuitionistic logic on which intuitionistic mathematics is based constitutes a major practical obstacle. Our brief, however, was not to address pragmatic obstacles. Rather our brief was to explore the methodological impact of developments in the philosophy of mathematics on the formalisation of economics. If strict intuitionism stands up to critical scrutiny, the orthodox formalisation of economics is utterly undermined at its mathematical core.

Strict intuitionism was not the only response to the original Brouwerian failed revolution in mathematics. As we saw others opted for, what we called, pragmatic intuitionism. In pragmatic intuitionism classical and intuitionistic mathematics peacefully co-exist. Both are distinct, legitimate mathematical endeavours: classical mathematics is concerned with an actual infinite domain which uses classical logic and both constructive and non-constructive methods of proof, whereas intuitionistic mathematics is concerned with a potential infinite domain which uses intuitionistic logic and only constructive methods of proof. Given pragmatic intuitionism, another fundamental methodological question arises, viz. which mathematics, classical or intuitionistic, is best suited to theoretical economics? In particular what precisely is the methodological case for limiting theoretical economists to restrictive intuitionistic mathematics in their theorising when theoretical physicists are not similarly constrained? After all both theoretical economists and theoretical physicists study highly complex, dynamical systems: hence both should be open to investigation by the same set of mathematical tools, i.e. the tools of classical mathematics used in theoretical physics.

As acknowledged by Debreu, Hahn and others the analogy to theoretical physics is not the most apt. Firstly, relative to the predictive success of theoretical physics, theoretical economics fares rather badly. Secondly, unlike theoretical physics, theoretical economics lacks the sophisticated experimental resources which are a distinguishing characteristic of advanced physics. For instance, when mathematical physics postulates the existence of some theoretical entity, experimental physics extend the boundaries of what is experimentally detectable with a view to, as it were, tracking down the postulated theoretical entity. In the absence of experimental success in tracking down the postulated entity, empirical minded physicists suspend judgement on the existence claim. Given that the situation in theoretical economics is not like that in theoretical physics, what precisely is the situation in theoretical economics? According to formalists like Debreu the situation is as follows. Given the absence of these sophisticated experimental techniques, the theoretical economist uses various theorems of advanced classical mathematics and, by recourse to a range of assumptions, gives these theorems economic interpretations. In this manner, for instance, the possibility of general equilibrium is rigorously established. Much of the methodological opposition to this form of theorising focuses on the economic unrealisticness of the assumptions used. The philosophy of mathematics, as one would expect, does not address these assumptions per se. Rather pragmatic intuitionism *opens up a different front in the attack on this orthodox formalisation of economics.* It undermines the orthodox use of sophisticated, non-constructive theorems of advanced mathematics (such as Brouwer's fixed point theorem) in its efforts at rigorously proving economic possibilities (such as general equilibrium). Like strict intuitionism, pragmatic intuitionism demonstrates that any such possibility cannot, by virtue of the non-constructive theorems used, be established in any finite system and thus cannot be given an economic interpretation.

For pragmatic intuitionists there is no objection in principle to mathematical modelling using the full resources of classical mathematics. Let us thus consider an economic model which proves the existence of some possible economic arrangement, based solely on a piece of non-constructive, classical mathematics. A core step in this economic model is the pure mathematical proof of the existence of an element in the piece of non-constructive classical mathematics exploited in the economic model. The first point to note is that, by virtue of the classical mathematics used, this mathematical element is an element of an actual infinite class of an infinity of classes. This is so because the mathematical domain of classical mathematics is an infinity of infinite classes. Secondly, given the mathematical proof is non-constructive, there is no mathematical way of establishing that such a mathematical entity is in principle accessible to any finite combination of finite systematic processes. Thus there is no mathematical way of demonstrating that the element belongs to some finite subset of the infinity of infinite sets in which it is proven to exist. Given that any economy is necessarily finite and also given the absence of possible experimental vindication of existence claims in theoretical economics, is there any economic point to this kind of mathematical modelling in theoretical economics? Thirdly, the non-constructive mathematics used in this kind of economic modelling necessarily abstracts from any reference to any time frame: any possibility established by a piece of non-constructive classical mathematics has no measurable time frame built into it. As already noted by virtue of the meaning of non-constructive, the established possibility is in principle inaccessible to any finite combination of systematic rule governed procedures. But the implementation of any systematic rule-governed procedure takes time, however short. Thus by virtue of being non-constructive, the logical possibility established has no time constraints imposed on it.

Contrast this with an economic model which proves the existence of some economic possibility using only the resources of intuitionistic mathematics. Since its domain of discourse is potential infinity and since its methods of proof of existence are necessarily constructive, any mathematical entity proven to exist is in principle accessible in a finite number of systematic steps. Thus the mathematical entity is *conclusively established* as being in a finite subset of the potential infinite domain of intuitionistic mathematics. Moreover possibilities established by intuitionistic mathematics have, by the very definition of con-structable, a time tag built into them: each finite step takes time to implement. In view of its origins in the intuition of time, it is not surprising that some sequential time frame or other is built into the established possibilities of intuitionistic mathematics.

The difference between economic modelling based solely on the resources of intuitionistic mathematics as opposed to the full resources of classical mathematics is clearly illustrated in the mathematical modelling of economic decision-making. Any theorem of classical mathematics which is based on a non-constructive proof cannot model the inherent temporality of economic decision-making. Any piece of classical mathematics which has any non-constructive dimension to its proof used to model economic decision-making is in principle inaccessible to any finite combination of rule-governed processes. This necessarily follows from the non-constructive element in the piece of mathematics used to model economic decision-making. By contrast, any outcome of a piece of intuitio-nistic mathematics which may be a candidate for the modelling of economic decision-making is in principle accessible to some finite combination of rigorous rule-governed steps. Since the implementation of a finite rule-governed step takes time, a time tag is necessarily built into a model based on intuitionistic mathematics whereas this time tag is explicitly excluded by any classical math-ematical model which has a non-constructive dimension to its mathematical proof. In short, the resources of intuitionistic mathematics can capture the temporal nature of economic decision making, whereas those of non-constructive classical mathematics cannot capture this temporal dimension.

To sum up, intuitionistic philosophy of mathematics plays a negative and a positive role in the methodological debate focused on the formalisation of economics. Negatively it exposes the illegitimacy of the orthodox attempt to give some transfinite and transtemporal possibilities of classical mathematics, finite and temporal economic interpretations. It thereby exposes the economic vacuousness at the mathematical core of the neo-Walrasian programme – the paradigm of the formalisation of economics for some orthodox economists.

Positively it offers theoretical economists new mathematical resources, viz. the resources of intuitionist mathematics, in their efforts at mathematically modelling economic decision-making and economies. This intuitionistic mathematics necessarily eschews the transfinite and transtemporal possibilities at the core of classical mathematics.

The third major event in the philosophy of mathematics exploited in previous chapters is the Church-Turing thesis which, as we saw in Chapter Seven, arose in the wake of Gödel's incompleteness theorems. Simply put Gödel showed that a strict proof of the consistency of advanced axiomatised mathematics, in Tarski's phrase, 'meets with great difficulties of a fundamental nature' (Tarski 1965: 137). Moreover the situation vis-à-vis completeness is worse: it is possible to set up mathematical problems that can neither be positively nor negatively decided within pure axiomatised mathematics. As Tarski pointed out these results are not premised on the assumption of some current imperfection or other in our axiomatic system which future mathematicians could eliminate. Rather '*never* will it be possible to build up a consitent and complete deductive theory containing as its theorems all true sentences of arithmetic or advanced geometry' (Tarski 1965: 137, italics ours). Without getting involved in the intriguing historical details, we can sum up by saying that 'these exceedingly important achievements' (Tarski 1965: 138) were accomplished over a short period in the 1930s by Gödel, Church and Turing.

As we pointed out in Chapter Seven, these achievements in the foundations of mathematics gave birth to our computer/digital age. From the point of view of the formalisation of economics, these achievements put the spotlight on to what we called computable mathematics. This is a specialised branch of classical mathematics which is limited to algorithmetic methods. Computable mathematics is not to be confused with intuitionistic mathematics: computable mathematics is based on classical logic whereas intuitionistic mathematics is based on intuitionistic logic. Both, however, focus on finite, systematic, rule-governed procedures. The Church-Turing thesis, as it were, collects ranges of specialised computable mathematics under one umbrella, thereby opening up an extensive reservoir of algorithmetic mathematics to the economic theoretician. In particular, given the Church-Turing thesis, the following methodological question vis-à-vis the formalisation of economics arises: given the uniqueness of economic theorising should economic theoreticians confine their mathematical modelling to the resources of computable mathematics? This methodological question is far from simple: there are at least three layers to it. Firstly, what are the advantages of computable mathematical modelling for economists over modelling using the full resources of classical mathematics? Secondly, what are the advantages of computable mathematical modelling over modelling confined to intuitionistic mathematics? Thirdly could a case be made for a judicious combination of computable and intuitionistic mathematics in economic modelling? Vis-à-vis the first layer, i.e. the advantages of computable mathematical modelling over modelling using the full resources of classical mathematics, the answer is that these advantages are the same as those outlined above for economic modelling based on intuitionistic mathematics as understood in pragmatic intuitionism. This overlap of common advantages is not surprising: both pragmatic intuitionistic mathematicians and computable mathematicians share a commitment to finite, rule-governed, systematic, mechanical procedures. The difference between them lies in their logical commitments. Thus the methodological issue in layer two, viz. the advantages of intuitionistic over computable modelling, will centrally include an analysis of which logic, classical extensional logic or intuitionistic non-extensional logic, is most appropriate to actual economic reasoning. To fully address this issue one would require a volume on the philosophy of logic. However, as we have already seen, Arrow points to empirical evidence which suggests that natural language based decision-making is not extensional. In addition we suggested that the resources of modal logic could prove fruitful. However, given that computable mathematics is based on classical extensional logic and that economic decision-making is conducted in natural languages which are not extensional, prima facie either intuitionistic or modal logic or a combination of both is better suited to the analysis of economic decision-making rather than classical extensional logic. The third layer, viz. whether a judicious combination of computable and of intuitionistic mathematics could be used in economic theorising is an intriguing one, which we have not addressed. Given Solow's dictum 'problems must dictate methods, not vice versa' (Solow 1954: 374) the judicious choice from either may prove fruitful. For instance, adherence to the canons of logic is an indispensable ingredient of all rationality, including economic rationality. Thus theoretical economists would exploit intuitionistic mathematics in their modelling of rational economic decision-making. On the other hand, since all economies are finite and, as we saw in Chapter Three, classical logic was devised for finite systems, theoretical economists could use computable mathematics in their modelling of economies.

Clearly these speculations are controversial and require further scrutiny. However what is not controversial is that the philosophy of mathematics brings the age of innocence in the orthodox formalisation of economics to a close: it challenges the orthodox assumption that the recourse to the full range of classical mathematics in economic modelling is unproblematical. In particular the philosophy of mathematics exposes how the exploitation of the full resources of classical mathematics in the neo-Walrasian programme – the paradigm of formalisation in orthodox economics – is fundamentally flawed. In this vein the philosophy of mathematics plays a key role in identifying an insurmountable paradox in the use of the full resources of classical mathematics in modelling real economies. This paradox is rooted in two fundamental truths, one mathematical and the other economic. The mathematical truth is that the domain of classical mathematics is transfinite: it is an infinity of infinite sets which abstracts from any possible time constraint. Moreover, given that various mathematical theorems exploited in these economic models are based on non-constructive proofs, *there is no mathematical constructable route within these transfinite models to any finite sub domain*. The economic truth is that, whatever an economy is, it is a finite temporal system. Numerous orthodox economic models, however, by virtue of the classical mathematics they exploit are rooted in this transfinite mathematical domain. Furthermore, since orthodox economic theorising lacks the sophisticated experimental techniques characteristic of theoretical physics, *there is also no empirical route from its transfinite models to any finite region.* In short there is no route, neither mathematical nor empirical, connecting various elegant and sophisticated models of advanced orthodox theorising based on non-constructive proofs to any finite, temporal region. Ironically this inability to offer any insight into any finite temporal system is rooted in the mathematics celebrated by these orthodox economic theoreticians.

Despite the fact that events in the philosophy of mathematics put the final nails in the coffin of orthodox economic modelling as exemplified in the neo-Walrasian programme, the programme of formalisation of economics per se remains healthy. Its health lies in the wealth of constructive proofs in both intuitionistic and computable mathematics: the constructive nature of their proofs guarantee that their theorems are in principle applicable to finite, temporal systems. Thus intuitionistic and computable mathematics open up rich reservoirs of novel mathematical results for economic modelling. Whether or not such an alternative programme or programmes for the formalisation of economics will succeed is, as we have repeated time and time again, a matter for detailed economic research in an economic climate which aspires to empirical adequacy. In short, the philosophy of mathematics makes an indispensable contribution to both the analysis of the manner in which theoretical economics was formalised and to the critical evaluation of that process, while simultaneously opening up alternative ways of mathematically modelling actual economies in a more realistic way.

Appendix
Philosophy of mathematics: a brief introduction[1]

In this brief appendix we introduce readers to three principal movements in the philosophy of mathematics which emerged at the close of the nineteenth century and the opening decades of the twentieth century. These were logicism, pioneered by Frege and Russell, formalism, pioneered by Hilbert and his school at Göttingen, and intuitionism, pioneered by Brouwer and Heyting. Needless to say we are not engaged in the exegesis of the writings of these pioneers. Neither are we engaged in presenting in a rigorous way the various arguments for or against specific theses adopted within these intriguing philosophies. We used footnotes in the text to suggest where one may begin to gain further information on these issues. Rather our intention is to give the reader some feel for what motivated these distinct approaches. These three movements address a constellation of fundamental questions such as 'what is mathematics?', 'what is logic?', 'what is the relationship between mathematics and logic?', 'are there mathematical truths?', 'what is an axiomatic system?', 'what is a mathematical proof?' We hope that this appendix enables readers to appreciate the genius, ingenuity and creativity of the challenging answers to questions like these proposed in logicism, formalism and intuitionism. In our research, Hilbertian formalism and Brouwerian intuitionism play more direct and extensive roles in the philosophy of economics than does logicism. In this appendix logicism is introduced as an indispensable component required for a comprehensive appreciation of both Hilbertian formalism and Brouwerian intuitionism.

Logicism[2]

Since Pythagoras, mathematics has either played a key role or posed serious challenges in some of the major developments in the history of Western philosophy. Mathematics, for instance, inspired rationalism and posed a serious challenge to empiricism. The Kantian synthesis of rationalism and of empiricism cast a long shadow over nineteenth-century philosophical reflections on mathematics. The truths of arithmetic, such as seven is equal to the positive square root of forty-nine, and the truths of Euclidean geometry were, à la Kant, deemed to be synthetic a priori truths. Negatively, these were not analytic truths, i.e. could not be derived by a priori logical principles from the meanings of their constituent terms. Neither were they synthetic a posteriori truths, i.e. not the outcome of contingent empirical experiences. Rather they are synthetic a priori truths, i.e. like logical truths, they are prior to experience and, like empirical truths, they are informative. Of course naming these synthetic a priori is no solution. Kant constructed an intriguing philosophical explanation of their status as synthetic a priori. By the end of the nineteenth century with developments in empirical psychology, logic and mathematics this Kantian philosophy was critically interrogated.

In mathematics developments in Cantorian set theory and in the construction of the rational and real number system from the natural number system, for instance, became differentiated from developments in geometry, such as the growth of projective geometry and the construction of non-Euclidean geometries. Thus the foundations of mathematics initially focused on arithmetic with Frege's 1884 *Foundations of Arithmetic* now acknowledged as a classic. In this work, Frege introduces the famous thesis of logicism, i.e. the truths of arithmetic, contrary to Kant, are logical truths. Kantians overestimate the extent to which arithmetic is akin to geometry. In geometry one can deny a fundamental proposition without falling into incoherence. However, confusion is the outcome of the denial of a fundamental proposition of arithmetic: we cannot seriously maintain that seven plus three is not equal to ten. The link between arithmetic and logic, contrary to Kantians, is much closer than the link between geometry and logic.

Frege introduces his distinction between sense and reference, what is commonly called the distinction between intension and extension, to show how some mathematical propositions expressing logical identities are informative. If we say $4=4$ we are expressing an obviously true identity. This identity, however, is *not* informative. Take $(10-6)=\sqrt[4]{16}$. Both $(10-6)$ and $\sqrt[4]{16}$ refer to the same number, 4. The sense, however, of $(10-6)$ is different to the sense of $\sqrt[4]{16}$. To grasp the sense of $(10-6)$, one has to know how to subtract whereas to grasp the sense of $\sqrt[4]{16}$, one has to know how to calculate square roots. Because the intension/sense is different but the extension/reference is the same, the proposition $(10-6)=\sqrt[4]{16}$ is informative. Moreover since $(10-6)=\sqrt[4]{16}$ is not a meaningless formula, pure mathematics for Frege, unlike the formalists, is located in the semantics side of the divide between semantics and syntax.

Logicism is not simply a basic philosophical commitment. On the contrary it is a philosophical programme: one has to do the hard technical work of actually reducing arithmetical truths to logical truths. In particular to accomplish this programme it is necessary to accurately specify the domain of logic. Since Aristotle logic is characterised as the science of valid reasoning. It is a prescriptive discipline, not to be confused with cognitive psychology. Cognitive psychology tells us how people actually think; logic studies how we *must* think if we are to attain truth. Moreover, logic is the most universal of all scientific disciplines. For instance, nuclear physics and biology have their own distinctive empirical laws. However, reasoning in both must be governed by the more general laws of logic: otherwise their conclusions would be invalid. There is not a distinct logic for nuclear physics and a different logic for biology.

Reasoning, in whatever the discipline, must adhere to the principles of logic, otherwise the reasoning is invalid. Finally logic is not a collection of ad hoc rules. It is a science and as such it requires systematisation. This Aristotelian challenge of the rigorous systematisation of logic was finally accomplished by Frege and Russell.

This systematisation requires the construction of an ideal language. A fundamental philosophical premise informing this ideal language is that the primary unit of communication is the proposition, i.e. a sentence which is either true or false. The basic propositions of this ideal language are called atomic propositions. These are identified by the presence of names, e.g. Walras promoted mathematical economics is an atomic proposition. Atomic propositions consist of names and predicates. Next the logical constants or truth-functional operators are introduced. These logical constants are 'it is not the case that – ' '- and – ' ' – or – ', 'if – then – '. By means of explicitly stated rules for the application of these logical constants to atomic propositions, complex propositions, such as if England leaves the EU then Ireland will follow, are derivable. Finally, again by recourse to explicitly stated rules of syntax the manner of obtaining quantified propositions, such as some economic advisors are wise or all economists are proficient at mathematics, is clearly specified. Thus this ideal language contains a potential infinite range of complex propositions syntactically derivable from atomic propositions.

The next step is to construct an appropriate symbolism for this ideal language, i.e. a symbolism which is adequate to its sophisticated architecture rather schematically outlined in the previous paragraph. Thus propositional variables, name variables, predicate variables, symbols for the logical constants, symbols for the universal and existential quantifiers are clearly specified. For instance one is *logically confused* if one does not distinguish between a name variable and a predicate variable. Since names play a different logico-semantical role to predicates, name variables are distinct from predicate variables. With this ideal language and its symbolism Frege is in a position to systematically organise the whole edifice of logic. From the point of view of the mathematisation of economics what is crucial to note is that this logical system is extensional. As we already pointed out the fundamental philosophical premise of this logic is that every proposition is either true or false. For instance Clint Eastwood blinked at 10.30 a.m. on 3 November 2010 is either true or false. We have no idea which truth value actually holds but we do know that proposition is either true or false. This *philosophical* thesis of bivalence is at the root of the extensionality of this logical system.

In connection with logic the final theme is the recognition that logic includes Cantorian set theory. This inclusion becomes evident when one reflects on the Fregian sense/reference or intension/extension distinction. Take the predicate the prime numbers between 10 and 20. Its extension is *the set* of numbers, 11, 13, 17 and 19. Sets are the extensions of predicates and contemporary set theory was expertly developed by Cantor. In short, as logicists, Frege and Russell hoped to define numbers in terms of sets and thereby reduce mathematics to logic. In June 1902 Frege's logicist dream was shown to be that. He received a letter from Russell pointing out a paradox in set theory. Consider the predicate '... is a predicate which cannot be predicated of itself'. Call this predicate m. Can m be predicated of itself? Whichever answer we give we are snookered. Frege was devastated by Russell's letter. In 1903 he writes 'Hardly anything more unfortunate can befall a scientific writer than to have one of the foundations of his edifice shaken after the work is finished' (as quoted in Kenny 1995: 174). This and other paradoxes were seismic for the foundations of arithmetic. The burning question is how is one to respond to these paradoxes? The Hilbertian formalists save classical mathematics, including Cantorian set theory, by dropping the logicist's preoccupation with meaning and truth and simultaneously reconceptualising the whole of pure mathematics as a purely syntactical system which can be demonstrated to be consistent, complete and decidable. The Intuitionists diagnose Cantorian set theory, combined with the erroneous extensional logic of Frege and Russell, as the source of the paradoxes. We need an alternative logic and thus a different mathematics to classical mathematics. This new mathematics is called constructive or intuitionistic mathematics.

Formalism[3]

The aim of this brief section is to give the reader some small appreciation of the promise of Hilbertian formalism. As we have just seen, the paradoxes rocked the logicist programme. How can we retain the whole edifice of pure mathematics, including Cantorian set theory, in the face of these paradoxes? Hilbert's response is to propose a novel alternative foundational programme to logicism which would be capable of removing the threat of any paradox. This foundational programme is formalism. This programme proposes moving the foundational spotlight from the logicist's preoccupation with mathematical truths and from its efforts of colonising arithmetic within logic. Instead, the foundational spotlight is shifted onto the whole edifice of both logic and of pure mathematics as a formal axiomatic system. In so doing both logic and pure mathematics are taken as equal partners. Arithmetic, Cantorian set theory and the Frege-Russell extensional logic – the foundational base of the whole of pure mathematics – has to be reconstructed as a formal axiomatic system. This is an indispensable component of the Hilbertian formalist programme. The second component, which is metamathematical, is to conclusively prove that this formal axiomatic system is consistent. Thus the logicist concern with the truths of arithmetic is replaced by the formalist's metamathematical concern for the proof of the consistency of this formal axiomatic system. The accomplishment of this formalist programme would in principle protect mathematics from the threat of paradox.

To accomplish this programme one has to abandon Frege's philosophy of an ideal language – the philosophical lens through which Frege viewed mathematics. Where Frege sees meaningful mathematical truths, Hilbert sees meaningless mathematical formulae. For instance take the formula (pvq). A logician interprets that formula as the logical form of a disjunctive proposition, where 'p' and 'q' are propositional variables and 'v' is the symbol for 'or'. Set theorists, however, interpret the formula (pvq) differently: they interpret it as the union of two sets. For Hilbert pure mathematics has nothing to do with these different interpretations or indeed any other interpretation of the formula (pvq). In short the fundamental constituents of the axiomatised reconstruction of our historically developed pure mathematics are empty symbols. As Hilbert remarked, 'in the beginning there was the sign' (Hilbert 1922: 202). Thus the first task in the axiomatisation of mathematics is a comprehensive list of its symbols. These symbols in pure mathematics have no interpretation. The next step is to state precisely the rules of syntax. These rules specify how to construct the well-formed formulae from the list of symbols. These rules specify the legitimate concatenation of symbols. From these a small subset are identified as axioms. Finally a set of transformation rules are specified. These license various operations on the axioms and also on other well-formed formulae obtained by the previous applications of these transformation rules. These well-formed formulae are theorems. Any well-formed formula which is either an axiom or a theorem is called a thesis of the system. Thus pure mathematics is a purely formal, syntactical axiomatic system with no interpretation at all. In other words it is ultimately a purely syntactical axiomatic calculus, without any reference to the Fregian notion of sense. The next challenge is to define the concept of consistency in syntactical terms, i.e. without any reference to any interpretation. Given this definition the next step is to rigorously establish that this axiomatised syntactical system is consistent.

The Hilbert formalist programme, however, is more ambitious. Its aim is to establish the consistency, completeness and decidability of this purely formal, i.e. syntactical, axiomatic system. Intuitively completeness means that all the mathematical theorems which have been and may be correctly derived in human history are derivable as theses of the formal axiomatised system. Clearly this way of looking at completeness is not acceptable to the Hilbertian formalist: it is a semantical view. Rather a purely syntactical definition of completeness is required. Syntactically we might say that an axiomatic system is complete if it cannot have any more theses than it has without falling into inconsistency, where, as we have seen, inconsistency has been defined syntactically. Decidability means that there must be a systematic method for ascertaining for each well-formed formula of the system whether or not it is provable within the system. A decidable system completely banishes ignorance from mathematics. The accomplishment of this Hilbertian programme would supply mathematics with unassailable foundations. However, just as the paradoxes undermined the logicist programme, Gödel, Church and Turing, as we saw in the text, undermined the Hilbertian programme. The paradoxes remain as a skeleton in the closet of pure mathematics.

Intuitionism[4]

From its initial introduction by Brouwer, intuitionists oppose both logicism and formalism. Despite major differences between logicists and formalists, they share an unequivocal commitment to Cantorian set theory and to classical logic. According to intuitionism, both Cantorian set theory and classical logic are misguided. When these are abandoned and when mathematicians use and only use constructive proofs, intuitionistic mathematics, which is paradox-free, will replace classical mathematics.

Intuitionists start their philosophical reflections on mathematics with the sequence of natural numbers, 1, 2, 3, 4 … n, n+1 …, while logicists start with classical logic including Cantorian set theory and formalists start with an uninterpreted, purely formal, axiomatic system. This sequence of natural numbers is infinite, i.e. not finite. A finite set, e.g. the set of prime numbers between 18 and 46, is a *definite totality*. The infinite set of natural numbers is not a definite totality: it continues on *ad infinitum*. According to intuitionists this is the defining characteristic of mathematical infinity, which is called potential infinity. In Cantorian set theory this defining characteristic of mathematical infinity is rejected: an infinite set is a definite totality with an infinite number of elements. This Cantorian redefinition of mathematical infinity is called actual infinity. Intuitionists reject this Cantorian redefinition of mathematical infinity. This Cantorian definition transfers the defining characteristics of a finite set, viz. a definite totality, to its definition of mathematical infinity, with the inevitable outcome of the paradoxes in the foundations of mathematics. Paradox-free mathematical infinity is potential infinity. This leaves the intuitionist with a major challenge, namely to derive the real number system from its base in the natural number system without recourse to Cantorian set theory. This technical challenge is met head on by intuitionists.

The Achilles' heel of classical mathematics also includes classical logic. Formalists, intuitionists and logicists all agree that logic is the prescriptive science of valid reasoning which must be used in correct reasoning across all domains. Formalists and logicists differ from intuitionists in their specification of the system of logic. Formalists and logicists maintain that the formulation of logic accomplished by Frege and Russell is the correct system. Intuitionists reject this claim: the correct system is intuitionistic logic. Intuitionists legitimate their choice of logic on various grounds. As we saw, the Frege-Russell logic is based on the *philosophical* principle of bivalence, viz. every proposition is either true or false. According to intuitionists this principle holds for numerous propositions, but it is *not* a universal truth. For instance, in mathematics there are well-constructed questions which have no answers one way or the other. In other words there are undecidable propositions in mathematics. This truth was, as it were, vindicated by the ingenious work of Gödel, Church and Turing in the 1930s. Perhaps the most famous of such undecidable propositions is the so-called halting theorem: the halting problem cannot be solved by a computing machine. Insisting that it either can or cannot be solved is required by the philosophical principle of bivalence. But the halting theorem proves otherwise. For intuitionists the moral is clear: the principle of bivalence must be dropped and thereby classical logic.

Intimately related to the *philosophical* principle of bivalence is the *logical* principle of the excluded middle (p or not p), i.e. for every proposition either it or its negation is true. The principle of the excluded middle is a *necessary* truth in classical logic. For instance the proposition Peter is a central banker or Peter is not a central banker, though not informative, is necessarily true. According to intuitionists the principle of the excluded middle is not a necessary truth. Rather it is a meta-empirical truth which holds in any finite system. Since a finite system is in principle surveyable one can in principle ascertain whether any proposition is either true or false. But a potentially infinite domain – the domain of mathematics – is not similarly surveyable: the principle of the excluded middle does *not necessarily* apply in that domain. What actually holds for the finite does not necessarily hold for potential infinity. But a central task of logic is to identify what is necessarily the case in both finite and potential infinite domains. In short the classical logical principle of the excluded middle is based on the confusion of a meta-empirical law of finite systems with a universal necessary truth. The philosophical principle of bivalence on which classical logic rests and some of its logical laws, such as the excluded middle, must be rejected and replaced by intuitionistic logic, as the sole source of necessary truths. Mathematics, like any other coherent discipline, must be logical but its logic is intuitionistic not classical.

We now turn to the kinds of mathematical proofs to be used in establishing mathematical theorems. Logicists see no difficulty with recourse to both constructive and non-constructive proofs. Intuitionists, however, limit mathematical proofs to constructive ones. Formalists, as we saw, hold that pure mathematics is a purely syntactical calculus and as such its proofs can be either constructive or non-constructive. However, the aim of formalism is to prove the consistency, completeness and decidability of that formal calculus and the only methods of proof acceptable in this metamathematical task are constructive ones. In the following we give some examples of constructive and non-constructive proofs.

A constructive existence proof, for instance, provides an effective means of finding the entity. A means of picking out an object is effective when it is governed by explicitly stated, unambiguous rules which are mechanically applied in a finite number of steps. For example if one were asked to prove Euclid's parallel postulate one may do it as follows, Given a line ℓ and a point P outside ℓ, construct the perpendicular from P to ℓ meeting ℓ at the point R, giving the line PR. Next construct another line m perpendicular to the line PR. Since both m and ℓ are perpendicular to PR they are parallel. Alternatively one is asked to prove that there exists within the real number system a solution to the equation $5x^2 + 7x + 9 = 0$. The actual solutions to this equation are specified by the systematic application of the algorithm $x = \frac{-b \pm \sqrt{b^2 - 4ac}}{2a}$ for the general equation $ax^2 + bx + c = 0$ to $5x^2 + 7x + 9 = 0$. Perhaps the most trivial constructive proof is a proof by counter example. For instance the claim all prime numbers are odd is proven false by the specification of a counter example, viz. the number 2.

An example of a non-constructive existence proof in classical mathematics is the use of *the reductio ad absurdum* method of proof. Schematically the task is to prove m exists. The first step in *the reductio ad absurdum* method is to assume m does not exist. Next, in a finite number of steps prove that the assumption m does not exist necessarily implies a contradiction (an absurdity) and therefore is false. The next step applies the principle of the excluded middle, giving either m exists or m does not exist. Since m does not exist is false, m exists is true. In this case the method is carried out in a finite number of steps, but it does *not* provide an effective method of *finding* m. Another way a proof may be non-constructive is by recourse to a theorem with explicit reference to Cantorian actual infinity as one of its steps. According to classical mathematicians such a proof is effective, i.e. is carried out in a finite number of steps. According to intuitionists the use of any theorem making explicit reference to Cantorian actual infinity as a step in a subsequent proof renders that subsequent proof ineffective. This become evident when one examines the reference to Cantorian actual infinity to see whether or not it can be translated into a finite number of effective steps. The explicit, indispensable reference to Cantorian actual infinity means that the theorem cannot be effectively translated into a finite number of steps. Thus any subsequent proof based on a theorem with explicit reference to Cantorian actual infinity renders the number of effective steps of the subsequent proof infinite.

One could claim that intuitionism is a philosophy of mathematics which shifts the philosophical spotlight away from logical or formalist reconstructions of mathematics on to the constructive activities of mathematicians in doing mathematics. When due care is taken in carrying out its proofs, i.e. limiting proofs to constructive ones, there is no question of paradoxes emerging. The price to be paid for this gain is the rejection of Cantorian set theory and other sections of classical mathematics. Also, while its proof procedures will be constructive, its proofs will at times be much more complex than those of classical mathematics. In short intuitionism is simultaneously both conservative and revolutionary. It is conservative in limiting mathematical proofs to constructive ones. It is revolutionary in its rejection of classical logic, the logical cornerstone of classical mathematics. Classical logic is replaced by intuitionistic logic with its novel patterns of inference exploited in intuitionistic mathematics.

The following questions and very brief answers may help economic methodologists unfamiliar with these three movements to navigate their way through the unchartered seas of logicism, formalism and intuitionism:

1   Is the system of logic rigorously formulated by Frege and Russell the correct logic? Logicists and formalists answer yes, intuitionists answer no (the correct system is intuitionistic logic rigorously formalised by Heyting).
2   Is, for instance, the principle of excluded middle a logical law? Logicists and formalists answer yes, intuitionists answer no.
3   Is logic extensional? Logicists and formalists answer yes, intuitionists answer no.
4   Has pure mathematics an indispensable semantical component? Formalists answer no (it is purely syntactical), logicists and intuitionists answer yes (but do not agree on what that component is).

5   Are there mathematical truths? Formalists answer no (pure mathematics is a consistent syntactical system), logicists and intuitionists answer yes (but do not agree on what these truths are).

6   Is, for instance, Brouwer's fixed point theorem a genuine theorem? Logicists and formalists answer yes. Intuitionists answer no (it is not provable in intuitionistic mathematics).

7   Is the definition of mathematical infinity given in Cantorian set theory correct? Logicists and formalists answer yes, intuitionists answer no.

8   What are the legitimate methods of proofs in pure mathematics? Logicists and formalists answer both constructive and non-constructive methods (for formalists in the specific meta-mathematical task of proving the consistency of mathematics only constructive methods are legitimate). Intuitionists limit mathematical methods of proof to constructive ones. Non-constructive methods do not prove anything.

9   Are there well-formed questions in mathematics which cannot be answered one way or the other? (Are there undecidables in mathematics?). Formalists and logicists answer no, intuitionists answer yes.

Needless to say, these answers need nuancing and detailed elaboration: here they signal the genius of those involved in pioneering these distinct philosophies of mathematics and the complexity of that terrain.

Notes

1   The three major systems of ideas that have framed much of the discussion in the philosophy of mathematics since their emergence in the late nineteenth and the first half of the twentieth century, namely Logicism, Formalism and Intuitionism, are the subject matter of this brief Appendix. These different approaches to the philosophy of mathematics, along with their development and extensions, have given rise to a vast literature on the subject area of philosophy of mathematics. A number of source books and anthologies containing many of the original contributions to the field are available. They include van Heijenoort (1967), Benacerraf and Putnam (1983), and Mancosu (1998). For readers who wish to familiarise themselves with the overall field of the philosophy of mathematics, a number of more recent accessible accounts that include recent developments and new topics of concern to philosophies of mathematics are available. They include Bostock (2009), Brown (2008), Colyvan (2012) and Linnebo (2017).

2   For useful overview of the logicist and non-logicist programmes, see Boolos (1998), Heck (1999) and MacBride (2003).

3   For further reading on formalism see von Neumann (1983) and Weir (2010).

4   On intuitionism by its founder, see Brouwer (1983) and Heyting (1983), and on intuitionist logic see Priest (2008).

Bibliography

Agnar, S. (2011) *Economics Evolving*, Princeton: Princeton University Press.

Allais, M. (1943) *A la Recherche d'une Discipline Économique: L'Economic Pure*, Paris: Ateliers Industria.

Amati, F. and Aspromourgos, T. (1985) 'Petty contra Hobbes: a previously untranslated manuscript', *Journal of the History of Ideas*, 46(1): 127 132.

Anderson, G., Goff, B. and Tollison, R. (1986) 'The rise and (recent) decline of mathematical economics', *Bulletin of the History of Economic Society*, 8: 44–47.

Andrews, D.R. (1999) 'Continuity and change in Keynes's thought: the importance of Hune', *The European Journal of the History of Economic Thought*, 6: 1–21.

Arena, R. (2000) 'J.B. Say and the French Liberal School of the nineteenth century: outside the canon', in F.L. Forget and S. Peart (eds), *Reflections on the Classical Cannon in Economics: Essays in Honour of Samuel Hollander*, London: Routledge.

Arrow, K.J. (1951) 'An extension of the basic theorems of classical welfare economics', in J. Neyman (ed.) *Proceedings of the Second Symposium on Mathematical Statistics and Probability*, Berkeley: University of California Press: 507–532.

Arrow, K.J. (1982) 'Risk perception in psychology and economics', *Economic Inquiry*, 20: 1–9.

Arrow, K.J. and Hahn, F.H. (1971) *General Competitive Analysis*, San Francisco: Holden Day.

Arrow, K.J. and Intriligator, M.D. (eds) (1982) *Handbook of Economic Methodology*, Vol. II, Amsterdam: North-Holland Publishing Company.

Arthur, B.W. (1994) *Increasing Returns and Path Dependence in the Economy*, Michigan: The University of Michigan Press.

Aspromourgos, T. (1986) 'Political economy and the social division of labour: the economics of Sir William Petty', *Scottish Journal of Political Economy*, 33(1): 28–45.

Aspromourgos, T. (1988) 'The life of William Petty in relation to his economics: a tercentenary interpretation', *History of Political Economy*, 20(3): 337–356.

Aspromourgos, T. (1996) *On the Origins of Classical Economics: Distribution and Value from William Petty to Adam Smith*, London: Routledge.

Aspromourgos, T. (1998) 'Petty, William', in H.D. Kurz and N. Salvadori (eds) *The Elgar Companion to Classical Economics L-Z*, Cheltenham, UK: Edward Elgar: 195–198.

Aspromourgos, T. (1999) 'An early attempt at some mathematical economics: William Petty's 1687 algebra letter, together with a previously undisclosed fragment', *Journal of the History of Economic Thought*, 21(4): 399–411.

Aspromourgos, T. (2000) 'New light on the economics of William Petty (1623–1687): some findings from previously undisclosed manuscripts', *Contributions to Political Economy*, 19: 53–70.

Aspromourgos, T. (2001a) 'The mind of the economist: an overview of the "Petty Papers" archive', *History of Economic Ideas*, IX(1): 39–101.

Aspromourgos, T. (2001b) 'Political economy, political arithmetic and political medicine in the thought of William Petty', in P.D. Groenewegen (ed.) *Physicians and Political Economy: Six Studies in the Work of Doctor Economists*, London: Routledge.

Aspromourgos, T. (2005) 'The invention of the concept of social surplus: Petty in the Hartilib Circle', *European Journal of the History of Economic Thought*, 12(1): 1–24.

Aumann, R.J. (1985) 'What is game theory trying to accomplish?' in K.Y. Arrow and S. Honkapohja (eds) *Frontiers of Economics*, Oxford: Basic Blackwell: 28–76.

Auxier, R.E. and Hahn, L.E. (eds) (2007) *The Philosophy of Michael Dummett*, The Library of Living Philosophers Vol. 31, La Salle, Illinois: Open Court.

Bacon, F. (1963) *The Works of Francis Bacon*, Edited by J. Speeding, R.L. Ellis and D.D. Health. Fourteen Volumes. Stuttgart-Bad Cannstutt: Friedrich Frommann Verlag_-Günter Holzborg.

Backhouse, R.E. (1998) 'The transformation of US economics, 1920–1960, viewed through a survey of journal articles', in M.S. Morgand and M.H. Rutherford (eds) *The Transformation of American Economics: From Interwar Pluralism to Postwar Neoclassicism, Annual Supplement to Volume 30 of History of Political Economy*, Durham, N.C.: Duke University Press: 85–107.

Baker, K. (1975) *Condorcet: From Natural Philosophy to Social Mathematics*, Chicago: University of Chicago Press.

Barnard, T.C. (2000) *Cromwellian Ireland: English Government and Reform in Ireland 1649–1660*, Oxford: Oxford University Press.

Baumol, W.J. and Goldfeld, S.M. (eds) (1968) *Precursors in Mathematical Economics: An Anthology*, London: London School of Economics and Political Science. Reprints of Scarce Works on Political Economy No. 19.

Benacerraf, P. and Putnam, H. (eds) (1983) *Philosophy of Mathematics Selected Reading*, 2nd edn, Cambridge: Cambridge University Press.

Bennett, K. (ed.) (2015) *John Aubrey, Brief Lives with an Apparatus for the Lives of our English Mathematical Writers*. 2 volumes, Oxford: Oxford University Press.

Bernays, P. (1922) 'Hilbert's Significance for the Philosophy of Mathematics', trans. P. Mancosu and published in P. Mancosu (1998), *From Brouwer to Hilbert: The Debate on the Foundations of Mathematics in the 1920s*, Oxford: Oxford University Press.

Blanché, R. (1955) *Axiomatics*, London: Routledge & Kegan Paul Ltd.

Blaug, M. (1998) 'Disturbing Currents in Modern Economics', *Challenge*, 41(3): 11–34.

Blaug, M. (1999) 'The formalist revolution or what happened to orthodox economics after World War II?', in R.F. Backhouse and J. Creedy (eds) *From Classical Economics to the Theory of the Firm: Essays in Honour of D.P. O'Brien*, Cheltenham, UK: Edward Elgar.

Boolos, G. (1998) 'Gottlob Frege and the foundations of arithmetic', in G. Boolos, *Logic, Logic and Logic*, Cambridge, MA: Harvard University Press.

Bostock, D. (2009) *Philosophy of Mathematics: An Introduction*, Malden, MA: Wiley-Blackwell.

Bourbaki, N. (1968) *Elements of Mathematics, Theory of Sets*, Reading: Addison-Wesley.

Bourbaki, N. (1994) *Elements of the History of Mathematics* (trans. J. Meldrum), Berlin: Springer-Verlag.

Bowen, H.R. (1953) 'Graduate education in economics', *American Economic Review Supplement, Graduate Education in Economics*, 43(4) Part 2, Supplement, ii–xv + 1–223.

Boylan, T.A. and O'Gorman, P.F. (1995) *Beyond Rhetoric and Realism in Economics: Towards a Reformulation of Economic Methodology*, London: Routledge.

Boylan, T.A. and O'Gorman, P.F. (2007) 'Axiomatization and formalism in economics', *Journal of Economic Surveys*, 21: 426–446 (reprinted in D.A.R. George (ed.) (2008) *Issues in Heterodox Economics*, Oxford: Blackwell Publishing).

Boylan, T.A. and O'Gorman, P.F. (2009a) 'Holistic defences of rational choice theory: a critique of Davidson and Pettit', in T.A. Boylan and R. Gekker (eds) *Economics, Rational Choice and Normative Philosophy*, London: Routledge.

Boylan, T.A. and O'Gorman, P.F. (2009b) 'Kaldor and Debreu: the critique of general equilibrium reconsidered', *Review of Political Economy*, 21: 447–461.

Boylan, T.A. and O'Gorman, P.F. (2010) 'Resisting the sirens of realism in economic methodology: a Socratic Odyssey', in S. Zambelli (ed.) *Computable, Constructive and Behavioural Economic Dynamics: Essays in honour of Kumaraswamy (Vela) Velupillai*, London: Routledge.

Boylan, T.A. and O'Gorman, P.F. (2012) *Hahn and Economic Methodology*, London: Routledge.

Boylan, T.A. and O'Gorman, P.F. (2013) 'Post-Keynesian economics, rationality, and conventions', in G.F.C. Harcourt and P. Kriesler (eds) *The Oxford Handbook of Post-Keynesian Economics, Vol. 2: Critiques and Methodology*, Oxford: Oxford University Press.

Brewer, A. (1987) 'Turgot: founder of classical economics', *Economica*, 54: 417–428.

Brewer, A. (1992) *Richard Cantillon: Pioneer of Economic Theory*, London: Routledge.

Bridel, P. and Mornati, F. (2009) 'De l'équilibre général comme "Branche de la Métaphysique" ou de l'opinion de Pareto sur le projet Walrasien', *Revue Economique*, 60(4): 869–890.

Bridel, P. (2011) *General Equilibrium Analysis: A Century after Walras*, London: Routledge.

Brouwer, L.E.J. (1983) 'Intuitionism and formalism', in P. Benacerraf and H. Putnam (eds) *Philosophy of Mathematics Selected Reading*, 2nd edn, Cambridge: Cambridge University Press.

Brouwer, L.E.J. (1988) 'The structure of the continuum', in P. Mancosu (ed.) *From Brouwer to Hilbert: The Debate on the Foundations of Mathematics of Mathematics in the 1920s*, Oxford: Oxford University Press.

Brown, J.R. (2008) *Philosophy of Mathematics: A Contemporary Introduction to the World of Proofs and Pictures*, 2nd edn, Abingdon, Oxon: Routledge.

Brown, R. (1984) *The Nature of Social Laws*, Cambridge: Cambridge University Press.

Carnap, R. (1966) *An Introduction to the Philosophy of Science*, New York: Basic Books Inc.

Cassirer, E. (1951) *The Philosophy of the Enlightenment*, trans. F.C.A. Koelln and J.P. Pettegrove, Princeton: Princeton University Press.

Church, A. (1936a) 'An unsolvable problem of elementary number theory', *American Journal of Mathematics*, 58: 345–363.

Church, A. (1936b) 'A note on the Entscheidungsproblem', *Journal of Symbolic Logic*, 1 (1): 40–41 and 1(3): 101–102.

Church, A. (1956) *Introduction to Mathematical Logic*, Volume 1, Princeton: Princeton University Press.

Clower, R.W. (1995) 'Axiomatics and economics', *Southern Economic Journal*, 62(2): 307–319.

Cohen, B.I. (1994) 'Newton and the social sciences, with special reference to economics, or, the case of the missing paradigm', in P. Mirowski (ed.) *Natural Images in Economics: Markets Read in Tooth and Claw*, Cambridge: Cambridge University Press.

Colander, D.C. (2005) 'The making of an economist redux', *Journal of Economic Perspectives*, 19: 175–198.

Colander, D., Follmer, H., Hans, A., Goldberg, M., Juselius, K., Kirman, A., Lux, T. and Sloth, B. (2008) 'The financial crisis and the systematic failure of academic economics', *Kiel Working Paper*, 1489: 1–17. Reprinted in G.M. Hodgon (ed.) (2012) *Mathematics and Modern Economics*, Cheltenham, UK: Edward Elgar: 529–545.

Collins-Roberts French Dictionary (2006) 8th edn, Glasgow: Harper Collins.

Colyvan, M. (2012) *An Introduction to the Philosophy of Mathematics*, Cambridge: Cambridge University Press.

Copeland, J. (ed.) (2004) *The Essential Turing: The Ideas that Gave Birth to the Computer Age*, Oxford: Clarendon Press.

Corry, L. (1989) 'Linearity and reflexivity in the growth of mathematical knowledge', *Science in Context*, 3(2): 409–440.

Corry, L. (2004) *David Hilbert and the Axiomatization of Physics. From Grundlagen der Geometrie to Gruablagen der Physik*, Dordrecht: Kluwer Academic Publishers.

Courtault, J.M., Kabunov, Y., Bru, B., Crépel, P., Lebon, I. and Le Marchand, A. (2000) 'Louis Bachelier on the centenary of Théorie de la Spéculation', *Mathematical Finance*, 10(3): 339–353.

Crillo, R. (1978) *The Economics of Vilfredo Pareto*, Abingdon, Oxon: Frank Cass.

Cunningham Wood, J. and McLure, M. (1999) (eds), *Vilfredo Pateto: Critical Assessments of Leading Economists*, Volume 1, London: Routledge.

Dasgupta, P. (2002) 'Modern economics and its critics', in U. Mäki (ed.) *Fact and Fiction in Economics*, Cambridge: Cambridge University Press.

Davidson, P. (1972) 'Money and the real world', *Economic Journal*, 82(325): 101–115.

Davidson, P. (1981) 'Post-Keynesian economics', in D. Bell and I. Kristol (eds) *The Crisis in Economic Theory*, New York: Basic Books.

Davidson, P. (1982–1983) 'Expectations: a fallacious foundation for studying crucial decision-making processes', *Journal of Post-Keynesian Economics*, 5(2): 182–197.

Davidson, P. (1988) 'A technical definition of uncertainty and the long run non-neutrality of money', *Cambridge Journal of Economics*, 12(3): 329–337.

Davidson, P. (1991) 'Is probability theory relevant for uncertainty? A post-Keynesian perspective', *Journal of Economic Perspectives*, (5)1: 129–143.

Davidson, P. (1994) *Post-Keynesian Macroeconomic Theory*, Aldershot: Edward Elgar.

Davidson, P. (1996) 'Reality and economic theory', *Journal of Post Keynesian Economics*, 18(4): 479–508. Davidson, P. (2003) 'The terminology of uncertainty in economics and the philosophy of an active role for government policies', in J. Runde and S. Mizuhara (eds) *The Philosophy of Keynes's Economics Probability, Uncertainty and Convention*, London: Routledge.

Dawson, J.W.Jr. (1984) 'Discussion on the foundation of mathematics', *History and Philosophy of Logic*, 5: 111–129.

Dawson, J.W.Jr. (1988) 'The reception of Gödel's incompleteness theorems' in S.G. Shanker (ed.) *Gödel's Theorem in Focus*, London: Routledge.

Debreu, G. (1959) *Theory of Value: An Axiomatic Analysis of Economic Equilibrium*, New York: John Wiley.

Debreu, G. (1982) 'Existence of competitive equilibrium', in K.J. Arrow and M.D. Intriligator (eds) *Handbook of Economic Methodology*, Vol. 2, Amsterdam: North Holland Publishing Company.

Debreu, G. (1984) 'Economic theory in the mathematical mode', *The American Economic Review*, 74(3): 267–278.

Debreu, G. (1986) 'Theoretic models: mathematical form and economic content', *Econometrica*, 54(6): 1259–1270.

Debreu, G. (1991) 'The mathematization of economic theory', *The American Economic Review*, 81: 1–7.

Debreu, G. (1992) 'Random walk and life philosophy', in M. Szenberg, *Eminent Economists: Their Life Philosophies*, Cambridge: Cambridge University Press.

Debreu, G. (2008) 'Mathematical economics', in *The New Palgrave Dictionary of Economics*, 2nd edn, Vol. 5, S.N. Durlauf and L.E. Blume (eds), Basingstoke: Palgrave Macmillan: 454–460.

Dennehy, C.A. (ed.) (2008) *Restoration Ireland: Always Settling and Never Settled*, Aldershot: Ashgate.

Dobbs, B.J.T. and Jacob, M. (1995) *Newton and the Culture of Newtonianism*, Atlantic Highlands, NJ: Humanities Press.

Dow, S.F. (2002) *Economic Methodology: An Inquiry*, Oxford: Oxford University Press.

Dummett, M. (1963) 'The philosophical significance of Gödel's theorem', *Ratio*, 5: 140–155.

Dummett, M. (1994a) 'Reply to Oliveri', in B. McGuinness and G. Oliveri (eds), *The Philosophy of Michael Dummett*, Dordrecht: Kluwer Academic Publishers.

Dummett, M. (1994b) 'Reply to Wright', in B. McGuinness and G. Oliveri (eds), *The Philosophy of Michael Dummett*, Dordrecht: Kluwer Academic Publishers.

Dummett, M. (2000) *Elements of Intuitionism*, 2nd edn, Oxford: Clarendon Press.

Dummett, M. (2008) *Thought and Reality*, Oxford: Clarendon Press.

Düppe, T. and Weintraub, E.R. (2014) *Finding Equilibrium: Arrow, Debreu, McKenzie and the Problem of Scientific Credit*, Princeton, NJ: Princeton University Press.

Dupré, L. (2004) *The Enlightenment and the Intellectual Foundations of Modern Culture*, New Haven: Yale University Press.

Durlauf, S.N. and Blume, L.E. (2008) *The New Palgrave Dictionary of Economics*, 2nd edn, Basingstoke: Palgrave Macmillan.

Eatwell, T., Milgate, M. and Newman, P. (1989) (eds) *The New Palgrave: General Equilibrium*, London: Macmillan Press.

Ekelund, R.B. and Hébert, R.F. (2000) *Secret Origins of Modern Microeconomics: Dupuit and the Engineers*, Chicago: University of Chicago Press.

Ekelund, R.B. and Hébert, R.F. (2014) *A History of Economic Method*, 6th edn, Long Grove, IL: Waveland Press.

Eltis, W. (1975a) 'Francois Quesnay: a reinterpretation 1: the Tableau Économique', *Oxford Economic Papers*, 27: 167–200.

Eltis, W. (1975b) 'Francois Quesnay: a reinterpretation 2: the theory of economic growth', *Oxford Economic Papers*, 27: 327–351.

Epstein, R.L. and Carnielli, W.A. (2000) *Computability and Computable Functions, Logic and the Foundations of Mathematics*, 2nd edn, London: Wadsworth Thomson Learning.

Faccarello, G. (ed.) (1998) *Studies in the History of French Political Economy: From Bodin to Walras*, London: Routledge.

Fanning, B. (2015) *Histories of the Irish Future*, London: Bloombury Academic.

Ferrone, V. (2015) *The Enlightenment: History of an Idea*, New Jersey: Princeton University Press.

Fitzmaurice, E. (1895) *The Life of Sir William Petty, 1623–1687*, London: John Murray.

Fleetwood, S. (ed.) (1999) *Critical Realism in Economics: Development and Debate*, London: Routledge.

Forget, E.L. (1999) *The Social Economics of Jean-Baptiste Say: Markets and Virtue*, London: Routledge.

Fox, A. (2009) 'Sir Willliam Petty, Ireland and the making of a political economist, 1653–1687', *The Economic History Review*, 62(2): 388–404.

Frege, G. (1968) *The Foundations of Arithmetic, Die Grundlagen Der Arithmetic*, German text with English translation by J.L. Austin, Oxford: Basic Blackwell.

Frege, G. (1971) *On the Foundations of Geometry and Formal Theories of Arithmetic*, trans. E.H.W. Kluge, New Haven: Yale University Press.

Friedman, M. (1953) 'The methodology of positive economics', in M. Friedman (ed.) *Essays in Positive Economics*, Chicago: Chicago University Press.

Fullbrook, E. (2009) (ed.) *Ontology and Economics: Tony Lawson and his Critics*, Abingdon, Oxon: Routledge.

Girle, R. (2000) *Model Logics and Philosophy*, Teddington: Acumen Publishing Limited.

Gloria-Palermo, S. (2010) 'Introducing formalism in economics: the Growth Model of John von Neumann', *Panoeconomicus*, 2: 153–172.

Gödel, K. (1988) 'On formally undecidable propositions of *Principia Mathematica* and related systems I (1931)' in G.S. Shanker (ed.) *Gödel's Theorem in Focus*, London: Routledge.

Graunt, J. (1662) *Natural and Political Observations, Mentioned in a following index, and made upon the Bills of Mortality*, London: James Martyn, James Allestry, and Thomas Dicas.

Gray, J. (2012) *Henri Poincaré: A Scientific Biography*, Princeton: Princeton University Press.

Greffe, J-L, Heinzmann, G. and Lorenz, K. (eds) (1996) *Henri Poincaré: Science et Philosophie*, Paris: Albert Blanchard.

Groenewegen, P. (1977) *The Economics of A.R.J. Turgot*, Hague: Martinus Nijhoft.

Groenewegen, P. (2002) *Eighteenth-Century Economics: Turgot, Beccaria and Smith and their Contemporaries*, London: Routledge.

Grubel, H. and Boland, L. (1986) 'On the efficient use of mathematics in economics', *Kyklos*, 39: 419–442.

Grünbaum, A. (1964) *Philosophical Problems of Space and Time*, London: Routledge and Kegan Paul Ltd.

Guerlac, H. (1981) *Newton on the Continent*, Ithaca, NY: Cornell University Press.

Hahn, F.H. (1961) 'Review of G. Debreu's Theory of Value: An Axiomatic Analysis of Economic Equilibrium', *Journal of Political Economy*, 62(2): 204–205.

Hahn, F.H. (1973) *On the Notion of Equilibrium in Economics*, Cambridge: Cambridge University Press.

Hahn, F.H. (1982) 'Reflections on the invisible hand', *Lloyds Bank Review*, April, 1–21. Reprinted in F. Hahn (1984) *Equilibrium and Macroeconomics*, Oxford: Basil Blackwell.

Hahn, F.H. (1984) *Equilibrium and Macroeconomics*, Oxford: Basil Blackwell.

Hahn, F.H. (1985) *In Praise of Economic Theory*, London: University College London.

Hahn, F.H. (1993a) 'Predicting the economy', in L. Howe and A. Wain (eds) *Predicting the Future*, Cambridge: Cambridge University Press.

Hahn, F.H. (1993b) 'Frank Hahn: autobiographical notes', in M. Szenberg (ed.) *Eminent Economists: Their Life Philosophies*, Cambridge: Cambridge University Press.

Hahn, F.H. (1994) 'An intellectual retrospect', *Bance Nationale Del Lavoro Quarterly Reviewx*, 190: 245–258.

Hahn, F.H. (1996) 'Rerun cognoscere causas', *Economics and Philosophy*, 12: 183–195.

Hands, D. Wade (2001) *Reflections without Rules: Economic Methodology and Contemporary Science Theory*, Cambridge: Cambridge University Press.

Hausman, D.M. (1992) *The Inexact and Separate Science of Economics*, Cambridge: Cambridge University Press.

Heck, R. (1999) 'Frege's theorem: an introduction', *Harvard Review of Philosophy* 7(1): 56–73.

Heinzmann, G. and Nabonnad, P. (2008) 'Poincaré: intuitionism, intuition and convention', in M. Van Atten, P. Boldini, M. Bordeau and G. Heinzmann (eds) *One Hundred Years of Intuitionism (1907–2007)*, Berlin: Springer Science and Business Media.

Hendricks, V.F., Pedersen, S.A. and Jørgensen, K.F. (2000) *Proof Theory: History and Philosophical Significance*, Dordrecht: Kluwer Academic Publishers.

Hesse, M. (1966) *Models and Analogies in Science*, Notre Dame: University of Notre Dame Press.

Heyting, A. (1956) *Intuitionism: An Introduction*, Amsterdam: North-Holland.

Heyting, A. (1983) 'The intuitionist foundation of mathematics', in P. Benacerraf and H. Putnam (eds) *Philosophy of Mathematics Selected Reading*, 2nd edn, Cambridge: Cambridge University Press.

Hicks, J.R. (1939) *Value and Capital*, Oxford: Clarendon Press.

Hicks, J.R. (1979) *Causality in Economics*, Oxford: Basil Blackwell.

Hilbert, D. (1900) 'The future of mathematics', in C. Reid (1986) *Hilbert Courant*, New York: Springer Verlag.

Hilbert, D. (1902) 'Mathematical problems: lecture delivered before the International Congress of Mathematicians at Paris in 1900', *Bulletin of the American Mathematical Society*, 8: 437–479.

Hilbert, D. (1922) 'The new groundings of mathematics', in P. Mancosu (1998) *From Brouwer to Hilbert: The Debate on the Foundations of Mathematics in the 1920s*, Oxford: Oxford University Press.

Hilbert, D. (1926) 'On the infinite', trans. E. Putnam and G.J. Massey, in P. Benacerraf and H. Putnam (eds) *Philosphy of Mathematics: Selected Readings*, 2nd edn, Cambridge: Cambridge University Press.

Hochstrasser, T.J. (2006) 'Physiocracy and the politics of *laissez-faire*', in M. Goldie and R. Wokler (eds) *The Cambridge History of Eighteenth-Century Political Thought*, Cambridge: Cambridge University Press.

Hodgson, G.M. (ed.) (2012) *Mathematics and Modern Economics*, Cheltenham: Edward Elgar Publishing Company.

Hodgson, G.M. (2013) 'On the complexity of economic reality and the history of the use of Mathematics in Economics', *Filosofia du la Economía*, 1(1): 24–45.

Hollander, S. (2005) *Jean-Baptiste Say and the Classical Canon in Economics: The British Connection to French Classicism*, London: Routledge.

Hoppit, J. (1996) 'Political arithmetic in eighteenth-century England', *Economic History Review*, XLIX: 516–540.

Hughes, G.E. and Cresswell, M.J. (1996) *A New Introduction to Model Logic*, London: Routledge.

Hull, C.H. (ed.) (1899) *The Economic Writings of Sir William Petty*, 2 vols, Cambridge: Cambridge University Press.

Hull, C.H. (1900) 'Petty's place in the history of economic theory', *The Quarterly Journal of Economics*, 14(3): 307–340.

Hume, D. (1985 [1739]) *A Treatise of Human Nature*, Harmondsworth: Penguin Books Ltd.

Hutchison, T. (1988) *Before Adam Smith: The Emergence of Political Economy, 1662–1776*, Oxford: Basil Blackwell.

Ingrao, B. and Israel, G. (1990) *The Invisible Hand: Economic Equilibrium in the History of Science*, Cambridge, MA: The MIT Press.

Israel, J. (2001) *Radical Enlightenment: Philosophy and the Making of Modernity 1650–1750*, Oxford: Oxford University Press.

Israel, J. (2006) *Enlightenment Contested: Philosophy, Modernity and the Emancipation of Man, 1670–1752*, Oxford: Oxford University Press.

Israel, J. (2010) *A Revolution of the Mind: Radical Enlightenment and the Intellectual Origins of Modern Democracy*, New Jersey: Princeton University Press.

Israel, J. (2011) *Democratic Enlightenment: Philosophy, Revolution and Human Rights, 1750–1790*, Oxford: Oxford University Press.

Jaffé, W. (1960) 'A.M. Isnard progenitor of the walrasian general equilibrium model', *History of Political Economy*, 1: 19–43.

Jaffé, W. (1965) *Correspondence of Léon Walras and Related Papers*, 3 vols, Amsterdam: North Holland Publishing.

Jaffé, W. (1977a) 'A centenarian on a bicentenarian: Leon Walras's eléments on Adam Smith's Wealth of Nations', *The Canadian Journal of Economics/Revue canadienne d'Economique*, 10(1): 19–33.

Jaffé, W. (1977b) 'The Walras-Poincaré correspondence on the cardinal measurability of utility', *The Canadian Journal of Economics/Revue canadienne d'Economique*, 10(2): 300–307.

Jaffé, W. (1983) *William Jaffé's Essays on Walras*, ed. D.A. Walker, Cambridge: Cambridge University Press.

Jolink, A. (1996) *The Evolutionist Economics of Léon Walras*, London: Routledge.

Jolink, A. and Van Daal, A. (1989) 'Leon Walras's mathematical economics and the mechanical analogies', *HES Bulletin* 11(1): 25–32.

Jordan, T.E. (2007) *Sir William Petty, 1623–1687: The Genius Entrepreneur of Seventeenth-Century Ireland*, Lampeter: Edwin Mellon Press.

Kakutani, S. (1941) 'A generalization of Brouwer's fixed point theorem', *Duke Mathematical Journal*, 8: 457–459.

Kaldor, N. (1972) 'The irrelevance of equilibrium economics', *Economic Journal*, 82(4): 1237–1255.

Kaldor, N. (1975) 'What is wrong with economic theory?', *Quarterly Journal of Economics*, 89: 347–357.

Kates, S. (ed.) (2003) *Two Hundred Years of Say's Law*, Cheltenham: Edward Elgar.

Kenny, A. (2000) *Frege: An Introduction to the Founder of Modern Analytic Philosophy*, Oxford: Blackwell Publishers Ltd.

Keynes, G. (1972) *A Bibliography of Sir William Petty, F.R.S. and of observations on the Bills of Mortality by John Graunt, F.R.S.*, Oxford: Clarendon Press.

Keynes, J.M. (1936) *The General Theory of Employment, Interest and Money*, London: Macmillan. Reprinted in D. Moggridge (ed.) (1973) *Collected Writings of John Maynard Keynes*, Vol. 7, London: Macmillan for the Royal Economic Society.

Keynes, J.M. (1937) 'The general theory of employment', *Quarterly Journal of Economics*, 51(2): 209–223. Reprinted in D. Moggridge (ed.) (1973) *Collected Writings of John Maynard Keynes*, Vol. 14, London: Macmillan for the Royal Economic Society.

Kirman, A. (1998) *Elements of General Equilibrium Analysis*, Oxford: Blackwell Publishers.

Kirman, A. (2006) 'Demand theory and general equilibrium: from explanation to introspection, a journey down the wrong road', in P. Mirowski and D. Wade Hands (eds) *Agreement on Demand: Consumer Theory in the Twentieth-Century (Annual Supplement to Volume 38, History of Political Economy)*, Durham, NC: Duke University Press.

Kleene, S.C. (1936) 'Lambda definability and recursiveness', *Duke Mathematical Journal*, 2: 340–353.

Kleene, S.C. (1981) 'Origins of recursive function theory', *Annuals of the History of Computing*, 3(1): 52–67.

Kleene, S.C. (1988) 'The work of Kurt Gödel', in S.G. Sharker (ed.) *Gödel's Theorem in Focus*, London: Routledge.

Knight, F.H. (1921) *Risk, Uncertainty and Profit*, Boston: Houghton Mifflin.

Kolmogorov, A. (1998) 'On the interpretation of intuitionistic logic', in P. Mancosu *From Hilbert to Brouwer*, Oxford: Oxford University Press.

Kuczynski, M. and Meek, R. (eds) (1972) *Quesnay's Tableau Économique*, London: Macmillan.

Kuhn, T.S. (1970) *The Structure of Scientific Revolutions*, 2nd edn, Chicago: Chicago University Press.

Lansdowne, Marquis of (ed.) (H.W.E. Petty-Fitzmaurice) (1927) *The Petty Papers: Some Unpublished Writings of Sir William Petty*, 2 vols, London: Constable & Co.

Larson, B.D. (1989) 'A reappraisal of Canard's theory of price determination', in D.A. Walker (ed.) *Perspectives on the History of Economic Thought: Volume 1: Classical and Neoclassical Economic Thought*, Aldershot: Edward Elgar: 38–66.

Latsis, J. (2006) 'Convention and intersubjectivity: new developments in French economics', *Journal for the Theory of Social Behaviour*, 36: 255–277.

Lawson, T. (1993) 'Keynes and conventions', *Review of Social Economy*, 51(2): 174–200.

Lawson, T. (1997) *Economics and Reality*, London: Routledge.

Lawson, T. (2003a) *Reorienting Economics*, London: Routledge.

Lawson, T. (2003b) 'Keynes's realist orientation', in J. Runde and S. Mizuhara (eds) *The Philosophy of Keynes's Economics: Probability, Uncertainty and Convention*, London: Routledge.

Lawson, T. (2015) *Essays on the Nature and State of Modern Economics*, Abingdon, Oxon: Routledge.

Leontief, W. (1941) *The Structure of the American Economy, 1919–1929*, Cambridge MA: Harvard University Press.

Letwin, W. (1963) *The Origins of Scientific Economics: English Economic Thought 1660–1776*, London: Methuen.

Lewis, C.I. and Langford, C.H. (1959) *Symbolic Logic*, New York: Dover Publications Inc.

Lewis, D. (1983) 'Languages and language', in D. Lewis *Philosophical Papers*, Vol. 1, Oxford: Oxford University Press.

Lewis, D. (2002) *Convention*, Oxford: Blackwell.

Lindenfeld, D.F. (1997) *The Practical Imagination: The German Sciences of State in the Nineteenth Century*, Chicago: University of Chicago Press.

Linnebo, Ø. (2017) *Philosophy of Mathematics*, Princeton, NJ: Princeton University Press.

MacBride, F. (2003) 'Speaking with shadows: a study of neo-logicism', *British Journal for the Philosophy of Science*, 54: 103–163.

McCloskey, D.N. (1994) *Knowledge and Persuasion in Economics*, Cambridge: Cambridge University Press.

McCormick, T. (2008) '"A Proportionate Mixture": Sir William Petty, political economy, and the transmutation of the Irish', in C. Dennehy (ed.) *Restoration Ireland: Analysis Settling and Never Settled*, Aldershot: Ashgate.

McCormick, T. (2009) *William Petty and the Ambition of Political Arithmetic*, Oxford: Oxford University Press.

McGuinness, B. and Oliveri, G. (eds) (1994) *The Philosophy of Michael Dummett*, Dordrecht: Kluwer Academic Publishers.

McLure, M. (2001) *Pareto, Economics and Sociology: The Mechanical Analogy*, Abington, Oxon: Routledge.

Malcolm, N. and Stedall, J. (2005) *John Pell (1611–1685) and his Correspondence with Sir Charles Cavendish: The Mental World of an Early Modern Mathematician*, Oxford: Oxford University Press.

Mancosu, P. (1998) *From Brouwer to Hilbert: The Debate on the Foundations of Mathematics in the 1920s*, Oxford: Oxford University Press.

Martinich, A.P. (2005) *Hobbes*, Abingdon, Oxon: Routledge.

Mas-Collel, A. (1985) *The Theory of General Economic Equilibrium: A Differentiable Approach*, Cambridge: Cambridge University Press.

Meek, R.L. (1962) *The Economics of Physiocracy: Essays and Translations*, London: George Allen and Unwin.

Meek, R.L. (1973) *Turgot on Progress, Sociology and Economics*, translated, edited and with an introduction by R.L. Meek, Cambridge: Cambridge University Press.

Miller, A. (1996) 'Why did Poincaré not formulate special relativity in 1905', in J. Greffan, G. Heinzmann and K. Lorenz (eds) *Henri Poincaré Science et Philosphie*, Paris: Albert Blanchard.

Mirowski, P. (1989) *More Heat than Light: Economics as Social Physics, Physics as Nature's Economics*, Cambridge: Cambridge University Press.

Mirowski, P. (1991) 'The when, the how and the why of mathematical expression in the history of economic analysis', *Journal of Economic Perspectives*, 5: 145–157.

Mirowski, P. (2002) *Machine Dreams: Economics Becomes a Cyborg Science*, Cambridge: Cambridge University Press.

Mirowski, P. (2007) 'Markets come to bits: evolution, computation and markomata in economic science', *Journal of Economic Behaviour and Organization*, 66: 209–242. Special Issue on 'Markets as Evolving Algorithms'.

Mirowski, P. (2012) 'The unreasonable efficacy of mathematics in modern economics', in U. Mäki (ed.) *Handbook of the Philosophy of Science, Vol. 13: Philosophy of Economics*, Amsterdam: Elsevier.

Mirowski, P. and Cook, P. (1990) 'Walras' "Economics and Mechanics" translation, commentary and context', in W. Samuels (ed.) *Economics and Rhetoric*, Norwell: Kluwer.

Mongin, P. (2003) 'L'axiomatisation et les theories économiques', *Revue Economique*, 54(1): 99–138.

Moravia, S. (1974) *Il Pensiero degli Ideologues: Scienza e Filosofia in Francia (1785–1815)*, Firenze: La Nuova Italia.

Morishima, M. (1977) *Walras's Economics: A Pure Theory of Capital and Money*, Cambridge: Cambridge University Press.

Murphy, A.E. (1986) *Richard Cantillon: Entrepreneur and Economist*, Oxford: Clarendon Press.

Murphy, A.E. (2009) 'Sir William Petty: national income accounting', in A.E. Murphy, *The Genesis of Macroeconomics: New Ideas from Sir William Petty to Henry Thornton*, Oxford: Oxford University Press.

Nagel, E. and Newman, J.R. (2005) *Gödel's Proof*, London: Routledge.

O'Donnell, R. (2003) 'The thick and the thin of controversy', in J. Runde and S. Mizuhara (eds) *The Philosophy of Keynes's Economics, Probability, Uncertainty and Convention*, London: Routledge.

O'Gorman, P.F. (1977) 'Poincaré's conventionalism of applied geometry', *Studies in History and Philosophy of Science*, 8(4): 303–339.

Pagden, A. (2013) *The Enlightenment and Why It Still Matters*, Oxford: Oxford University Press.

Palmer, R.R. (1976) 'Turgot: paragon of the continental enlightenment', *Journal of Law and Economics*, 19: 607–619.

Palmer, R.R. (1977) *J.B. Say: An Economist in Troubled Times*, Princeton NJ: Princeton University Press.

Pasinetti, L.L. (1974) *Growth and Income Distribution: Essays in Economic Theory*, Cambridge: Cambridge University Press.

Petri, F. and Hahn, F. (2003) *General Equilibrium: Problems and Prospects*, London: Routledge.

Pettit, P. (2002) *Rules, Reasons and Norms*, Oxford: Clarendon Press.

Petty, W. (1648) *The advice of W.P. to Mr. Samuel Hartlib, For the advancement of some particular parts of learning*. Reprinted in *The Harleian Miscellany* (1810), 6: 141–158.

Petty, W. (1662) *A Treatise of Taxes and Contributions*. Reprinted in C.H. Hull (ed.) (1899) *The Economic Writings of Sir William Petty*, 2 vols, Cambridge: Cambridge University Press, vol. 1: 1–97.

Petty, W. (1683) *Another Essays in Political Arithmetic, Concerning the Growth of the City of London*, London: Mark Pardoe.

Petty, W. (1686) *An Essay Concerning the Multiplication of Mankind*, London: Mark Pardoe.

Petty, W. (1690) *Political Arithmetic*, London: Robert Clavel and Henry Mortlock. Reprinted in C.H. Hull (ed.) (1899) *The Economic Writings of Sir William Petty*, 2 vols, Cambridge: Cambridge University Press, vol. 1: 233–313.

Petty, W. (1691a) *The Political Anatomy of Ireland*, London: D. Brown and W. Rogers. Reprinted in C.H. Hull (ed.) (1899) *The Economic Writings of Sir William Petty*, 2 vols, Cambridge: Cambridge University Press, vol. 1: 121–231.

Petty, W. (1691b) *Verbum Sapienti*. Published originally as an appendix to Petty (1691a) and reprinted in C.H. Hull (ed.) (1899) *The Economic Writings of Sir William Petty*, 2 vols, Cambridge: Cambridge University Press, vol. 1: 99–120.

Petty, W. (1695) *Sir William Petty's Quantulumcunque concerning Money, 1682*, London: [n.s.]. Reprinted in C.H. Hull (ed.) (1899) *The Economic Writings of Sir William Petty*, 2 vols, Cambridge: Cambridge University Press, vol. 2: 437–448.

Petty, W. (1769) *Tracts Chiefly Relating to Ireland*, Dublin: Boulter Grierson.

Poincaré, H., Darboux, G. and Appell, P. (1908) 'Examen critique des divers système ou études graphologiques auxquels a donné lieu le bordereau', in Tome 3 of *Affaire Dreyfus. La révision du procès de Renne. Enquête de la Chambre Criminelle de la Cour de Cassation, 5 mars – 10 novembre 1904*, Paris: Ligue Francaise des Droit de L'homme et du Citoyen.

Poincaré, H. (1952) *Science and Hypothesis*, New York: Dover.

Poincaré, H. (1956) *Science and Method*, trans. F. Maitland, New York: Dover.

Poincaré, H. (1958) *The Value of Science*, trans. G.B. Halsted, New York: Dover.

Poincaré, H. (1963) *Mathematics and Science: Last Essays*, trans. J.W. Bolduc, New York: Dover.

Poincaré, H. (2002) *Scientific Oppertunism: An Anthology*, compiled by L. Rougier and edited by L. Rollet, Basel: Birkhauser Verlag.

Poovey, M. (1998) *A History of the Modern Fact*, Chicago: University of Chicago Press.

Porter, T.M. (2001) 'Economics and the history of measurement', in J.L. Klein and M.S. Morgan (eds) *The Age of Economic Measurement*, Durham and London: Duke University Press.

Potter, M. (2002) *Reason's Nearest Kin: Philosophies of Arithmetic from Kant to Carnap*, Oxford: Oxford University Press.

Potts, J. (2000) *The New Evolutionary Microeconomics: Complexity, Competence and Adaptive Behaviour*, Cheltenham UK: Edward Elgar.

Pribam, K. (1983) *A History of Economic Reasoning*, Baltimore: John Hopkins Press.

Priest, G. (2008) *An Introduction to Non-Classical Logic: From If to Is*, 2nd edn, Cambridge: Cambridge University Press.

Prior, A.N. (1957) *Time and Modality*, Oxford: The Clarendon Press.

Putnam, H. (1972) *Philosophy of Logic*, London: George Allen & Unwin Ltd.

Putnam, H. (1991) *Representation and Reality*, Cambridge, MA: MIT Press.

Putnam, H. (1993) *Reason, Truth and History*, Cambridge: Cambridge University Press.

Putnam, H. and Walsh, V. (eds) (2012) *The End of Value-Free Economics*, London: Routledge.

Quine, W.V.O. (1953) *From a Logical Point of View*, New York: Harper & Row Publishers.

Quine, W.V.O. (1998) 'Truth by convention', in P. Benacerraf and H. Putnam (eds) *Philosophy of Mathematics*, 2nd edn, Cambridge: Cambridge University Press.

Rattansi, P.M. (1982) 'Voltaire and the Enlightenment image of Newton', in H. Lloyd-Jones, V. Pearl and B. Worden (eds), *History and Imagination: Essays in Honour of H.R. Trevor-Roper*, New York: Holmes and Meier.

Resnik, M.D. (1974) 'The Frege-Hilbert controversy', *Philosophy and Phenomenological Research*, 34(3): 386–403.

Robbins, L. (1998) *A History of Economic Thought: The LSE Lectures*, in S.G. Medema and W.J. Samuels (eds), Princeton: Princeton University Press.

Rollet, L. (1997) 'Autour de l'affaire Dreyfus Henri Poincaré et l'action politique', *Revue Historique* (extract), 298(I): 49–101.

Roncaglia, A. (1985) *Petty: The Origins of Political Economy*, Cardiff: University of Cardiff Press.

Roncaglia, A. (2005) *The Wealth of Ideas: A History of Economic Thought*, Cambridge: Cambridge University Press.

Rosser, Barkley J.Jr. (2010) 'Constructivist logic and emergent evolution in economic complexity', in S. Zambelli (ed.) *Computable, Constructive and Behavioural Economic Dynamics*, London: Routledge.

Rothschild, E. (2001) *Economic Sentiments: Adam Smith, Condorcet and the Enlightenment*, Cambridge, MA: Harvard University Press.

Rothschild, E. (2011) 'Political economy', in G. Stedman Jones and G. Claeys (eds) *The Cambridge History of Nineteenth-Century Political Thought*, Cambridge: Cambridge University Press.

Say, J.B. (1971 [1826]) 'Discours Préliminaire', in *Traité d'Economie Politique*, 5th edn, with a preface by G. Tapinos, Paris: Calmann-Levy.

Samuelson, P.A. (1947) *Foundations of Economic Analysis*, Cambridge, MA: Harvard University Press.

Samuelson, P.A. (1952) 'Economic theory and mathematics – an appraisal', *American Economic Review*, 42(2): Papers and Proceedings of the Sixty-Fourth Annual Meeting of the American Economic Association (May): 56–66.

Scarf, H. with the collaboration of Terje Hansen (1973) *The Computation of Economic Equilibria*, New Haven: Yale University Press.

Schelling, T. (1960) *The Strategy of Conflict*, London: Oxford University Press.

Schmid, A.M. (1978) *Une Philosophie de Savant Henri Poincaré et le logique mathématique*, Paris: Francois Muspero.

Schumpeter, J.A. (1954) *History of Economic Analysis*, London: George Allen & Unwin.

Screpanti, E. and Zamagni, S. (1995) *An Outline of the History of Economic Thought*, Oxford: Clarendon Press.

Shackle, G.L.S. (1955) *Uncertainty in Economics and Other Reflections*, Cambridge: Cambridge University Press.

Shackle, G.L.S. (1972) *Epistemics and Economics*, Cambridge: Cambridge University Press.

Shanker, S.G. (ed.) (1988) *Gödel's Theorem in Focus*, London: Routledge.

Shank, J.B. (2008) *The Newton Wars and the Beginning of the French Enlightenment*, Chicago: Chicago University Press.

Simon, H. (2010) 'Letter to Kumaraswamy Vela Velupillai, 25 May 2000'. Reprinted in K. Vela Velupillai *Computable Foundations for Economics*, London: Routledge, 409–410.

Skinner, Q. (1966) 'Thomas Hobbes and his disciplines in France and England *Comparative Studies in Society and History*, 8(2): 153–167.

Skyrms, B. (1990) *The Dynamics of Rational Deliberation*, Cambridge, MA: Harvard University Press.

Small, A. (2001 [1909]) *The Cameralists: The Pioneers of German Social Policy*, Kitchener, Ontario: Batoche Book.

Smith, A. (1976 [1776]) *An Inquiry into the Nature and Causes of the Wealth of Nations*, eds R. Campbell, A.S. Skinner and W.B. Jodd, Oxford: Clarendon Press.

Smith, P. (2007) *An Introduction to Gödel's Theorems*, Cambridge: Cambridge University Press.

Solow, R. (1954) 'The survival of mathematical economics', *Review of Economics and Statistics*, 36(4): 372–374.

Sonnenschein, H. (1973) 'Do Walras' identity and continuity characterize the class of community excess demand functions', *Journal of Economic Theory*, 6(4): 345–354

Stark, W. (1944) *The History of Economics in its Relation to Social Development*, London: George Unwin.

Steiner, P. (1998) 'Jean-Baptiste Say: the entrepreneur, the free trade doctrine and the theory of income distribution', in G. Faccarello (ed.) *Studies in the History of French Political Economy: From Bodin to Walras*, London: Routledge.

Stewart, L. (1992) *The Rise of Public Science: Rhetoric, Technology, and Natural Philosophy in Newtonian Britain*, Cambridge: Cambridge University Press.

Stigler, G. (1965) *Essays in the History of Economics*, Chicago: University of Chicago Press.

Stigler, G.T., Stigler, S.M. and Friedland, C. (1995) 'The journals of economics', *Journal of Political Economy*, 105: 331–359.

Stirwell, J. (1996) 'Poincaré, geometry and topology,' in J. Greffe, G. Heinzmann and K. Lorenz (eds) *Henri Poincaré: Science et Philosophie*, Berlin: Akademie Verlag and Paris: Albert Blanchard.

Strauss, E. (1954) *Sir William Petty: Portrait of a Genius*, London: The Bodley Head.

Sugden, R. (1989) 'Spontaneous order', *Journal of Economic Perspectives*, 3(4): 85–98.

Suppe, F. (ed.) (1979) *The Structure of Scientific Theories*, Urbana: University of Illinois Press.

Sutherland, I. (1963) 'John Graunt, a tercentenary tribute', *Journal of the Royal Statistical Society*, A 126: 537–556.

Taggu, M.S. (2001) 'Bachelier and his times: a conversation with Bernard Bru', *Finance and Stochastics*, 119: 1–45.

Tarascio, V. (1968) *Pareto's Methodological Approach to Economics: A Study in the History of Scientific Aspects of Economic Thought*, Chapel Hill: University of North Carolina Press.

Tarski, A. (1965) *Introduction to Logic and to the Methodology of Deductive Science*, New York: Galaxy Book.

Theocharis, R.D. (1983) *Early Developments in Mathematical Economics*, 2nd edn, London: Macmillan.

Topoi (2008) 'An international review of philosophy', *Special Issue on Conventions: An Interdisciplinary Study*, 27(1–2): 1–164.

Touffut, J.P. (2007) *Augustin Cournot: Modelling Economics*, Cheltenham: Edward Elgar.

Tribe, K. (2003) 'Continental political economy from the Physiocrats to the Marginal Revolution', in T.M. Porter and D. Ross (eds) *The Cambridge History of Science, Vol. 7, The Modern Social Sciences*, Cambridge: Cambridge University Press.

Troelstra, A.S. and van Dalen, D. (1988) *Constructivism in Mathematics: An Introduction*, Vol. 1, Amsterdam: North Holland.

Turing, A. (2004) 'On computable numbers, with an application to the Entscheidungs problem', in J. Copeland (ed.) *The Essential Turing*, Oxford: Clarendon Press.

Turk, M.H. (2006) 'The fault line of axiomatization: Walras' linkage of physics with economics', *The European Journal of the History of Economic Thought*, 13(2): 195–212.

Turk, M.H. (2012) 'The mathematical turn in economics: Walras, the French mathematicians, and the road not taken', *Journal of the History of Economic Thought*, 134(2): 149–167.

Ullmer, J.H. (2004) 'The macroeconomic thought of Sir William Petty', *Journal of the History of Economic Thought*, 26(3): 401–413.

Ullmer, J.H. (2011) 'The scientific method of Sir William Petty', *Erasmus Journal for Philosophy and Economics*, 4(2): 1–19.

Vaggi, G. (1987) *The Economics of Quesnay*, Basingstoke: Macmillan.

Vanderschraaf, P. (1998) 'The informal game theory in Hume's account of convention', *Economics and Philosophy*, 14: 215–247.

Van Atten, M., Boldini, P., Bordeau, M. and Heinzmann, G. (eds) (2008) *One Hundred Years of Intuitionism (1907–2007)*, Berlin: Springer Science and Business Media.

Van Daal, J. and Jolink, A. (1993) *The Equilibrium Economics of Leon Walras*, London: Routledge.

Van Dalen, D. (1999) *Mystic, Geometer and Intuitionist. The Life of L.E.J. Brouwer, Volume 1, The Dawning Revolution*, Oxford: Clarendon Press.

Van Dalen, D. (2005) *Mystic, Geometer, and Intuitionist. The Life of L.E.J. Brouwer, Volume 2, Hope and Dissolution*, Oxford: Clarendon Press.

Van der Berg, R. (2005) *At the Origins of Mathematical Economics: The Economics of A.N. Isnard (1748–1803)*, London: Routledge.

Van Heijenoort, J. (1967) *From Frege to Gödel. A Source Book in Mathematical Logic, 1879–1931*, Cambridge, MA: Harvard University Press.

Van Stigt, W.P. (1990) *Brouwer's Intuitionism*, Amsterdam: North Holland.

Van Stigt, W.P. (1998) 'Brouwer's intuitionist programme', in P. Mancosu, *From Hilbert to Brouwer. The Debate in the Foundations of Mathematics in the 1920s*, Oxford: Oxford University Press.

Velupillai, K. Vela (2000) *Computable Economics*, Oxford: Oxford University Press.

Velupillai, K. Vela (2002) 'Efficiency and constructivity in economic theory', *Journal of Economic Behaviour and Organization*, 49: 307–325.

Velupillai, K. Vela (2005a) 'The unreasonable ineffectiveness of mathematics in economics', *Cambridge Journal of Economics*, 29: 848–872.

Velupillai, K. Vela (2005b) *Computability, Complexity and Constructivity in Economic Analysis*, Oxford: Blackwell Publishing.

Velupillai, K. Vela (2006) 'Algorithmic foundations of computable general equilibrium theory', *Applied Mathematics and Computation*, 179: 360–369.

Velupillai, K. Vela (2010) *Computable Foundations for Economics*, Abingdon, Oxon: Routledge.

Vilks, A. (1992) 'A set of axioms for neoclassical economics and the methodological status of the equilibrium concept', *Economic and Philosophy*, 8: 51–82.

Vilks, A. (1995) 'On mathematics and mathematical economics', *Greek Economic Review*, 17(2): 177–204.

Von Neumann, J. (1928) 'Zur theorie der Geselschaftsspiele', *Mathematizche Annalen*, 100: 295–320.

Von Neumann, J. (1947) 'The mathematician', in *The Works of the Mind* ed. R.B. Heywood, Chicago: University of Chicago Press.

Von Neumann, J. (1983) 'The formalist foundations of mathematics', in P. Benacerraf and H. Putnam (eds) (1993) *Philosophy of Mathematics Selected Reading*, 2nd edn, Cambridge: Cambridge University Press.

Von Neumann, J. and Morgenstern, O. (1944) *Theory of Games and Economic Behaviour*, Princeton: Princeton University Press.

Wakefield, A. (2009) *The Disordered Police State: German Cameralism as Science and Practice*, Chicago: University of Chicago Press.

Wald, A. (1935) 'Über die eindeutige positive Losbarkeit der neuen Produktionsgleichungen (Mitteilung I)', in K. Menger (ed.) *Ergebnisse eines Mathematischen Kolloquiums, 1933–1934*, Leipzig and Vienna: Franz Deutiche. Reprinted as 'On the unique non-negative solvability of the new production equations, Part I', in W.J. Baumol and S.M. Goldfeld (eds) (1968) *Precursors in Mathematical Economics: An Anthology*, London: London School of Economics and Political Science. Reprints of Scarce Works on Political Economy No. 19: 281–288.

Wald, A. (1936a) 'Über die produktionsgleichungen der ökonomischen wertlehre (Mitteilung II)', in K. Menger (ed.) *Ergebnisse eines Mathemaatischen Kolloquiums, 1934–1935*, Leipzig and Vienna: Franz Deutiche. Reprinted as 'On the production equations of economic value theory II', in W. Baumol (translator), in W.J. Baumol and S.M. Goldfeld (eds) (1968) *Precursors in Mathematical Economics: An Anthology*, London: London School of Economics and Political Science. Reprints of Scarce Works on Political Economy No. 19: 289–293.

Wald, A. (1936b) 'Über einige gleichunssysteme der mathematischen ökonomie', *Zeitschrift für Nationalökonomie* 7: 637–670. Reprinted as 'On some systems of equations in mathematical economics', *Econometrica* 19(1951): 368–403.

Walker, D.A. (1996) *Walras's Market Models*, Cambridge: Cambridge University Press.

Walker, D.A. (2006) *Walrasian Economics*, Cambridge: Cambridge University Press.

Walras, L. (1874) 'Principe d'une théorie mathématique de l'échange', in *Compterendu des Séances et Travaux de l'Académie des Sciences Morales et Politique, séances du 16 et 25 Août 1873*, January 1874, 97–120. Reprinted in *Journal des Economistes*, 34(100): 5–21.

Walras, L. (1909) 'Economique et mechanique', *Bulletin de la Société vaudoise des Sciences Naturelles*, 45(66): 313–327.

Walras, L. (2003) *Elements of Pure Economics Or the Theory of Social Wealth*, trans. W. Jaffé, London: Routledge.

Wang, H. (1974) *From Mathematics to Philosophy*, London: Routledge and Kegan Paul.

Weintraub, R. (1983) 'On the existence of a competitive equilibrium: 1930–1954', *Journal of Economic Literature*, 21: 1–39.

Weintraub, R. (1985) *General Equilibrium Analysis: Studies in Appraisal*, Cambridge: Cambridge University Press.

Weintraub, R. (2002) *How Economics Became a Mathematical Science*, Durham NC: Duke University Press.

Weintraub, R. (2006) 'A review essay on Leo Corry's David Hilbert and the Axiomatizatoin of Physics (1898–1918)', *Research in the History of Economic Thought and Methodology*, 24-A: 181–185.

Weintraub, E.R. and Mirowski, P. (1994) 'The pure and the applied: Bourbakism comes to mathematical economics', *Science in Context*, 7(2): 245–272.

Weir, A. (2010) *Truth through Proof: A Formalist Foundation for Mathematics*, Oxford: Oxford University Press.

Weiss, B. (2002) *Michael Dummett*, Chesham: Acumen.

Weyl, H. (1944) 'David Hilbert and this mathematical work', *Bulletin of the American Mathematical Society*, 50: 612–654.

Weyl, H. (1949) *Philosophy of Mathematics and Natural Science*, Princeton: Princeton University Press.

Weyl, H. (1998) 'On the new foundational crisis in mathematics', trans. B. Muller from the 1921 original, in P. Mancosu (ed.) *From Brouwer to Hilbert. The Debate on the Foundations of Mathematics in the 1920s*, Oxford: Oxford University Press.

Whatmore, R. (2000) *Republicanism and the French Revolution: An Intellectual History of Jean-Baptiste Say's Political Economy*, Oxford: Oxford University Press.

Wright, C. (1994) 'About "The philosophical significance of Gödel's theorem": some issues', in B. McGuinness and G. Oliveri (eds) *The Philosophy of Michael Dummett*, Dordrecht: Kluwer Academic Publishers.

Young, H.P. (1996) 'The economics of convention', *The Journal of Economic Perspectives* 10(2): 105–122.

Young, H.P. (1998) 'Social norms and economic welfare', *European Economic Review*, 42: 821–830.

Zambelli, S. (2007) 'Comments on Philip Mirowski's article "Markets come to bits: evolution, computation and markomata in economic science"', *Journal of Economic Behaviour and Organization*, 63: 354–358.

Zambelli, S. (ed.) (2010) *Computable Constructive and Behavioural Economic Dynamics. Essays in honour of Kumaraswamy (Vela) Velupillai*, London: Routledge.

Index

Achenwall, Gottfried 43–4n5
Agnar, S. 45n20
'Algorithme of Algebra' (Petty, W.) 22
algorithms, economic theorising and:
    Brouwer, L.E.J. 190; Church, Alonzo
    187–9; Debreu, Gerard 189, 190;
    Gödel, Kurt 187–8; Herbrand,
    Jacques 188; Kaldor, Nicholas 190;
    Kleene, S.C. 187; Mirowski, Philip
    191; Simon, Herbert 190–91; Turing,
    Alan Mathison 187, 188–9, 190, 191;
    Velulillai Vela, Kumaraswamy 189–91;
    von Neumann, John 187, 191;
    Zambelli, Stefano 189, 190
algorithms, mathematisation of economics
    and: Hilbert, David 183, 185, 186;
    Turing, Alan Mathison 183–7
Allais, Maurice 41
Amati, F. and Aspromourgos, T. 19
Anderson, G., Goff, B. and Tollison, R. 12
Arena, R. 35, 45n23
argumentation, grammar of 135–6
Aristotle 81, 82, 169; mathematics,
    philosophy of 205–6
Arithmetic, Foundations of (Frege, G.) 205
Arrow, Kenneth J. 80–81, 98, 102n10,
    130; constructive and computable
    mathematics, emergence of 175, 176;
    neo-Walrasian formalisation of
    economics 135, 139, 142; philosophical
    reflections 197, 202
Arthur, Brian 70
Aspromourgos, T. 19, 20, 22, 44n13
Aubrey, John 44n9
Aumann, R.J. 162n2
Auxier, R.E. and Hahn, L.E. 193n18
axiomatic method, economics and
    105–28; applied mathematical sciences,
    axiomatisation and 111–14; commodity

and price, concepts of 115; Debreu,
Gerard 105–6, 109–10; distillation of
axiomatic method 107–8; economic
analysis, assets of Debreu's formalist
philosophy of 123–8; economic
domain, axioms in 117; economic
theory, Debreu's formalist
mathematisation of 114–18; *Élements
d'economie politique pure* (Walras, L.)
105, 114; Euclidean axiomatisation
105–6, 107–8, 112–14, 117, 123–4,
126; formalist philosophy of applied
mathematics, indispensable steps in
113; General Equilibrium Theory,
axiomatisation of 105–6; Hahn, F.H.
114, 123, 127; Hilbert, David 106,
107, 110, 111–12, 113, 123, 129n14;
Hilbertian principle of uniformity
of axiomatic method 111–12;
ideology-free economics, Debreu's
ideal of 124; image of economic
theory, body of knowledge and
117–18; logic, basic tool of any
axiomatic system 108; logico-
mathematical structures 112–13;
mathematical form, semanticist
conception of 119; mathematical
model of Debreu, formalist or
semanticist? 118–23; metamathematics,
Hilbert's notion of 110; pathology of
the paradoxes in, formalist remedy for
109–10; Poincaré, Henri 109, 110,
120, 121, 122, 123; Poincaré malaise,
concerns raised by 120–22; pure
formalism, domain of 112; pure
mathematics, mathematical content and
119–20; rigour, axiomatisation and
107–10; semantical domination,
semanticism and 108–9, 110, 112, 113,

geometry 204; Euclid's parallel postulate 210; excluded middle, principle of 93, 108, 128n6, 169–70, 192n8, 193n20, 194n27, 209–10, 211; finite systems, meta-empirical law of 210; formal axiomatic system, development of 207–8; formalism 204, 207–8, 211–12, 212n1; formalism and intuitionism, conflict between 2–3; formulae, symbols and 208; Frege, Gottlob 204, 205, 206–7, 208, 209, 211; geometry 205; Gödel, Kurt 208, 209; Heyting, Arend 204, 211, 212n4; Hilbert, David 204, 207–8; ideal language, construction of 206; infinity, actual or potential 209–10, 211; intuitionism 2, 3, 204, 208–12, 211–12, 212n1; Kant, Immanuel 204–5; Kenny, Anthony 207; logic, reasoning and 205–6, 209; logic, set theory and 206–7; logicism 204–7, 207–8, 211–12, 212n1; logico-mathematical analysis 3; logico-philosophical analysis 2, 8, 75, 152; logico-semantics 206; mathematical infinity 209; mathematical proofs 210–11; natural number system 205; natural numbers 209; a posteriori truth 205; a priori truth 204–5; pure mathematics 207–8; rational number system 205; rationalism 204; rationality, mathematical modelling of 4–5; real number system 205; reasoning, logic and 205–6, 209; reductio ad absurdum method 210; Russell, Bertrand 204, 206–8, 209, 211; sense and reference, distinction between 205; set theory 205, 206, 207–8, 209; set theory, logic and 206–7; symbolism, construction of 206; theorems 208; totality 209; Turing, Alan Mathison 208, 209; Walras, Leon 206
Mathematics and Modern Economics (Hodgson, G.) 9
Maxwell, James Clerk 71n8
Meek, R.L. 45n21–2
Menger, K. 49
Mill, John Stuart 192–3n15, 192n7
Miller, A. 164n31
Mirowski, P. Cook, P. 46, 47, 58, 60, 62
Mirowski, Philip 6, 12, 42, 72n23, 166, 194n28; algorithms, economic theorising and 191
modus ponens rule of inference 193n22

Montesquieu 24, 27–8, 32
Introduction to Moral Philosophy (Smith, A.) 24–5
moral sciences, Walrasian programme in context of 47–9
morality, Hume's philosophical foundations of 148–50
Moravia, S. 33
Morgenstern, Oskar 41, 77
Morishima, M. 45n27
An Essay Concerning the Multiplication of Mankind (Petty, W.) 19
Murphy, A.E. 16, 45n16

Nagel, E. Newman, J.R. 122
Napoleonic political order 31, 32
Nash equilibrium 162n2–3, 163n19
Natural and Political Observations mentioned in a following Index, and made upon the Bills of Mortality (Graunt, J.) 19
The Nature of Social Laws (Brown, R.) 11
neo-Walrasian formalisation of economics 131–43; Arrow, Kenneth J. 135, 139, 142; axioms, assumptions and grammar of argumentation 136–40; Brouwer, L. E.J. 110, 116, 119–20, 121, 122, 130n25; Cantor, Georg 110, 121, 122, 129n23; Debreu, Gerard 131–2, 133, 134, 135–6, 139; Debreu's formalisation, economists' reception of 131–2; economic policy, debates about 133; economic theorising, simplification of assumptions in 138–9; economic theory, role of 132–4; equilibrium, near equilibrium state as causal factor in real world 140–41; explanation, Kaldor on Debreu's conception of 141; Frege, Gottlob 108–9, 110, 113, 128n9; general equilibrium theory, methodological approach to 133–4; general equilibrium theory, neo-classical economics and 142; Hahn, F.H. 131–2, 133–4, 136–40, 141, 142, 143; Hahn's grammar of argumentation 135–6; Hilbert, David 131, 132, 136; Invisible Hand thesis, Smith and 135–6; Kaldor, Nicholas 131, 132, 133, 136; Kaldor on Debreu's achievement and legacy 140–43; neo-classical economics, scientific theory of value in 133; normative economics, distinction between positive economics and 133; rational agent axiom 137–8; theoretical

For Product Safety Concerns and Information please contact our EU
representative GPSR@taylorandfrancis.com
Taylor & Francis Verlag GmbH, Kaufingerstraße 24, 80331 München, Germany